CW00820226

FOOD SECURITY AND GLOBAL ECONOMY

FOOD SECURITY AND GLOBAL ECONOMY

Edited by

Dr. Avanish K. Tiwari

and

Jeevan Nair

Food Security and Global Economy

First Indian Edition: 2009

ISBN 978-81-8274-359-5

© Reserved

All rights reserved. No part of this publication may be reproduced, stored in a retrieval system, or transmitted, in any form or by any means, electronic, mechanical, photocopying, recording, or otherwise, without first obtaining written permission of the copyright owner.

Published in India by

PENTAGON PRESS
206, Peacock Lane, Shahpur Jat, New Delhi-110049
Phones: 011-64706243, 26491568
Telefax: 011-26490600
email: rajan@pentagon-press.com
website: www.pentagon-press.com

Printed at New Elegant Printers, New Delhi

Preface

'The number of people without enough food to eat on a regular basis remains stubbornly high, at over 800 million, and is not falling significantly. Over 60% of the world's undernourished people live in Asia, and a quarter in Africa. The proportion of people who are hungry, however, is greater in Africa (33%) than Asia (16%). The latest FAO figures indicate that there are 22 countries, 16 of which are in Africa, in which the undernourishment prevalence rate is over 35%.'

The State of Food Insecurity in the World 2003

TODAY, in 2008, the situation is no longer the same: it has deteriorated dramatically. The latest UN update of the *World Economic Situation* states that the total number of food insecure people was probably closer to three billion or about half the population of the world.

Food security is inexorably linked to the eradication of hunger and poverty. Hunger, and the malnourishment that accompanies it, prevents poor people from emerging from poverty because it diminishes their ability to learn, work, and care for themselves and their family members. Food insecurity is said to exist when people are undernourished as a result of the physical unavailability of food, their lack of social or economic access to adequate food, and/or inadequate food utilization. Conversely, food-insecure people are those individuals whose food intake falls below their minimum calorie (energy) requirements, as well as those who exhibit physical symptoms caused by energy and nutrient deficiencies resulting from an inadequate or unbalanced diet or from the body's inability to use food effectively because of infection or disease.

There are strong, direct relationships between agricultural productivity, hunger, and poverty. Three-quarters of the world's poor live in rural areas and make their living from agriculture. Hunger and child malnutrition are greater in these areas than in urban areas, although the percentage of urban poor is now also increasing. Moreover, the higher the proportion of the rural population that obtains its income solely from subsistence farming (without the benefit of pro-poor technologies and access to markets), the higher the incidence of malnutrition. Therefore, improvements in agricultural productivity aimed at small-scale farmers will benefit the rural poor first.

Increased agricultural productivity enables farmers to grow more food, which translates into better diets and, under market conditions that offer a level playing field, into higher farm incomes. With more money, farmers are more likely to diversify their production and grow higher-value crops, benefiting not only themselves but the economy as a whole the following:

> On the flip side the use of agricultural produce as a biofuel has opened up a new debate on its impact on food availability and affordability.

The terms 'agricultural prices' and 'food security' have become synonymous, so much so that they are often used interchangeably, depending on which term better covers the topic discussed. The practice is also followed in this book.

The spectre of food insecurity has taken on an extremely grim visage in 2007-08. According to UN reports, commodity prices surged in 2007 and the first quarter of 2008. Agricultural commodities and food items were the most affected. During this period the price of rice went up by a massive 215 per cent (up to April, 2008) while wheat price surged by 83 per cent.

Analysts and food experts have suggested a number of measures to ensure the food security of the growing number of the poor. Essentially, they all come down to meeting the objectives of improving availability, accessibility and affordability food, the three basic measures that need attention in this regard. As will be seen, it is not going to be at all an easy task, given that the professional consensus is that the global economy is presently caught in a downward spiral.

This could have both positive and negative impact on food security. It could increase affordability as prices tend to reduce during an economic slowdown but, at the same time, the negative aspect is that such a slowdown may also affect availability. Economists have their task cut out as they endeavour to find a path to food security through this minefield.

This book does not claim to present any unique solutions to the problem. What it does (and what was long required) is to bring together, as succinctly as possible, the genesis of the causes that led to the present alarming food insecurity fears, what are the possible short- and long-term solutions and how long before results can be expected. Since some forecasts see food insecurity lasting till the 2050s, this is no mean task. The options are many, complexly interconnected and impossible to map on a linear continuum making it easy to grasp. The problem has many dimensions and will affect not only the present generation but also those in the future. At the best, there is the possibility of a happier life where the benefits of development are inclusive of all categories of people. At the worst, rebellion, violence and bloodshed—in a word, chaos. Any solution that comes up is likely to lie within these two extremes.

This book is an attempt to bring into focus various issues that inadvertently affect food security. Oil prices, climate change, use of agricultural products as biofuel, trade and agricultural policies of the governments of major developed and developing nations are some of these issues. The purpose of this book, therefore, is to put together the available data on food security, discuss its implications for good or bad and review the solutions that have been projected by professionals and institutions. In short, to promote thought on a subject that has already started affecting the common man and can only grow worse before it gets better. This book should therefore cause people to think.

New Delhi, India
August, 2008

Avanish K. Tiwari
Jeevan Nair

Contents

APPENDICES:

CHAPTER 1

THE CONCEPT OF GLOBAL FOOD SECURITY

OVER the years, there has been mounting concern over the state of the world's food stocks. The first remedial step promoted by scientists and administrators was the need for a programme that would ensure the sustainability of agriculture, that is, that output would increase so as to adequately meet the growing demand in a sustained manner.

This concept became very popular, commendable work was done in the laboratories and in the field and there was much optimism that agriculture was on the right path. Today, as food insecurity has become a global concern, it is still considered to be the best form of attack. In fact, it has been claimed that if sustainable development measures (largely agriculture) had been followed with the same vigour as was evident when first taken up, and modified to meet new perils to people's sustenance, most of the food problems facing the global community today would not have arisen; at the least, it was felt, their present tragic consequences would have been considerably reduced.

At that time, food prices remained constant, or rose only slightly, food was abundantly available and there were no major dark clouds on the agricultural horizon. It says much for the situation that in America, one of the largest grain producers in the world, the government was paying farmers *not* to plant grain: not only because the granaries were overflowing but also because export realisation was going down.

Then came globalisation of the economy which was based on the doctrine of *laissez faire* or the market as the ultimate decider on prices and, consequently, of national growth strategies, especially among the upcoming countries. The scientific breakthrough which brought about the use of hybrids and disease-resistant plants had already pushed up agricultural production dramatically. The 'Green Revolution' was considered the last word in agricultural productivity. Naturally, therefore, globalisation was concentrated on industry and service sectors.

The poorer countries were now almost self-sufficient in food and could concentrate on developing their industrial and, later, their service industries. Countries like Brazil, Russia, India and China (the BRIC countries) became models of development. Growth rates surged spectacularly, stock markets were on a seemingly never-ending northern path, and the standards of living of the middle classes of developing countries rose to heights that stunned the world. More so, because the gains were based on solid industrial growth which led to a huge outlay in infrastructure activities (another engine of growth); this was more pronounced in the countries where there was a greater amount of centralised governance (Russia and China) than federalism and democracy (India).

Also, education of the youth came centre-stage, especially in high population countries, as the growth of industry and services was being hampered for want of managers and skilled workers. This was a major factor in rural youth spurning the age-old practice of agriculture and hastening towards the glistening riches of urban life. Asian countries like China and India, with their huge populations, became the preferred sources of skills and intellectual talent to the rest of the world.

Another factor was that the developing countries 'opened up' to globalisation as they gained confidence and felt more sure of their future. This led to a merging of cultures worldwide, which further aggravated the skewing of the urban-rural (industry-agriculture) divide and also had a dramatic impact on the lifestyles of a middle-class which, heretofore, was more noted for its conservative attitude than for risk-taking behaviour. Fortunes were made overnight on the stock markets, salaries quadrupled over a period of 15 years and 'a house, a car and a good life' became the new *mantra* of urban youth.

In this they were supported not only by their parents and peer competition but also by the growth of educational and vocational infrastructure in the various countries which rose swiftly to meet the rapidly rising demand. Industrialised Western nations began to poach on the talent of Asian countries or alternatively outsourced almost everything from telephone sales to doing tax work for American and European corporations and high-worth individuals. This spurred the growth of the 'affluent society' in the developing world which, of course, did not include the poorer sections of society.

The above is a very brief and general (and rather ragged) attempt at picturing the world economic situation in which, as we will see, lay the seeds of the food security crisis; a subject that is, today, on everybody's lips. The food security crisis appeared as a dark cloud on the horizon a few years into the second millennium.

Actually, it was a paradox. Food production was still adequate at an estimated 2,700 calories per person per day for every man, woman and child in the world. Yet, millions are suffering from malnutrition in the more populous newly developed countries and from lifestyle diseases due to over-consumption in the more prosperous countries. There was no shortage of food, as such; what was lacking was equal accessibility and affordability brought about by dramatically skewed consumption patterns. It is no longer a question of just ensuring that good, healthy food is accessible to all persons; global food security now has encompassed the important issues of health, social justice and the environment.

The sharp increase in food prices over the first decade of the new millennium has raised serious concerns about the food and the nutritional development of poor people in developing countries, about inflation, and in some countries, about civil unrest. Real prices are still below their mid-1970s peak, but they have reached their highest point since that time.

In 2007, the food price index calculated by the Food and Agriculture Organization of the United Nations (FAO) rose by nearly 40 per cent, compared with 9 per cent the year before, and in the first months of 2008 prices again increased drastically. Nearly every agricultural commodity is part of this rising price trend. Since 2000, a year of low prices, the wheat price in the international market has more than tripled and maize prices have more than doubled.

The price of rice jumped to unprecedented levels in March 2008. Dairy products, meat, poultry, palm oil, and cassava also experienced price hikes. When adjusted for inflation and the dollar's decline (by reporting in euros, for example), food price increases are smaller but still dramatic, with often serious consequences for the purchasing power of the poor.

National governments and international actors are taking various steps to try to minimize the effects of higher international prices for domestic prices and to mitigate impacts on particular groups. Some of these actions are likely to help stabilize and reduce food prices, whereas others may contain elements of exclusivity which help certain groups at the expense of others or actually make food prices more volatile in the long run and seriously skew trade patterns.

BEHIND THE PRICE INCREASES

The combination of new and ongoing forces is driving the world food situation and, in turn, the prices of food commodities. One emerging factor behind rising food prices is the high price of energy. Energy and agricultural prices have become increasingly intertwined. With oil prices at an all-time high of more than US$ 120 a barrel and the U.S. government subsidizing farmers to grow crops for energy (conversion into ethanol), U.S. farmers have massively shifted their cultivation towards biofuel feedstocks, especially maize, often at the expense of soybean and wheat cultivation. It is claimed that it takes a ton of grain to make 40 litres of ethanol.

About 30 per cent of U.S. maize production will go into ethanol in 2008 rather than into world food and feed markets. High energy prices have also made agricultural production more expensive by raising the cost of mechanical cultivation, inputs like fertilizers and pesticides and transportation of inputs and outputs. At the same time, the growing world population (and growing affluent middle class) is demanding more and different kinds of food.

Rapid economic growth in many developing countries has pushed up consumers' purchasing power, generated rising demand for food and shifted that demand away from traditional staples towards higher-value foods like meat and milk. This dietary shift is leading to increased demand for grains used to feed livestock.

Poor weather and speculative capital have also played a role in the rise of food prices. Severe drought for three consecutive years in Australia, one of the world's largest wheat producers, has cut into global wheat production.

THE IMPACT

Higher food prices have radically different effects across countries and population groups. At the country level, nations that are net food exporters will benefit from improved terms of trade, although some of them are missing out on this opportunity by banning exports to protect domestic consumers. Net food importers, however, will struggle to meet domestic food demand. Given that almost all countries in Africa are net importers of cereals, they will be the hardest hit by rising prices, followed by many Asian countries.

At the household level, surging and volatile food prices hit those who can afford it the least – the poor and food insecure. The few poor households that are net sellers of food will benefit from higher prices, but households that are net buyers of food – which represent the large majority of the world's poor – will be harmed. Adjustments in the rural economy, which can create new income opportunities, will take time to reach the poor. The nutrition of the poor is also at risk when they are not shielded from the price rises.

Higher food prices lead poor people to limit their food consumption and shift to even less-balanced diets, with harmful effects on health in the short and long-term. At the household level, the poor spend about 50 to 60 per cent of their overall budget on food. For a five-person household living on the equivalent of US$ 1 per person per day, a 50 per cent increase in food prices removes up to US$ 1.50 from their US$ 5 budget, besides the added burden of growing energy costs.

Given below are some expert opinions on the situation:

- Growing consumption can lead to major environmental damage. The emergence of over one billion new consumers, people in 17 developing and three transition countries with a total spending capacity, in purchasing power terms, that matches that of the U.S.A., is especially significant. Two consumption-related activities – meat consumption and the growing number of personal automobiles – probably have the most impact on the environment.
- Global food security will remain a worldwide concern for the next 50 years and beyond. Recently, crop yield has fallen in many areas because of declining investments in research and infrastructure, as well as increasing water scarcity. Climate change and HIV/AIDS are also crucial factors affecting food security in many regions.
- Non-communicable diseases have become a major health problem not just in developed but also in developing countries. Already 79 per cent of the deaths attributed to the non-communicable diseases occur in developing countries. The rising trends are a consequence of the demographic and dietary transition, and the globalization of economic processes.

According to Nobel Laureate R. K. Pachauri, the rural poor are facing a range of climate-related problems. First, changes in precipitation patterns and increases in the intensity and frequency of floods and droughts have major implications for agriculture, water availability, and human health. For instance, whenever a flood occurs, health officials face a major challenge in preventing and minimizing the outbreak of diseases. The impact of climate change on agricultural yield also directly affects the livelihoods of the poor.

A study was conducted by TERI on the effects of two sets of influences on agriculture. The first related to globalization and international trade in agricultural produce, and the second assessed the impacts of climate change on agriculture. Poor farmers are often not able to compete against subsidized food coming from developed countries and are therefore suffering from the unfavourable effects of globalization on their livelihoods.

Climate change only exacerbates some of these stresses. In fact, during the World Summit on Sustainable Development held in Johannesburg in 2002, several African farmers demonstrated against agricultural subsidies in the developed countries because they found themselves unable to compete with the resulting prices of imports.

The relevant issue to be considered in this context is the fact that the rural poor are already subjected to several stresses for a variety of reasons. Climate change would only add to these stresses.

The poor are also unable to adapt to the impacts of climate change because often they do not have the technical or financial capacity to be able to take essential measures—for instance, creating infrastructure for storage of water.

CHAPTER 2

THE 2007–08 WORLD FOOD PRICE CRISIS

THE years 2007–08 saw dramatic world food price rises, bringing a state of global crisis and causing political and economical instability and social unrest in poor and developed nations.

Systemic causes for the worldwide food price increase continue to be the subject of debate. Initial causes of the late 2006 price spikes included unseasonable droughts in grain producing nations and rising oil prices. Rising oil prices further heightened the costs of fertilizers, food transport and industrial agriculture.

Other causes may be the increasing use of biofuels in developed countries and an increasing demand for a more varied diet (especially meat) across the expanding middle-class populations of Asia. These factors, coupled with falling world food stockpiles have all contributed to the dramatic worldwide rise in food prices.

Long-term causes remain a topic of debate. These may include structural changes in trade and agricultural production, agricultural price supports and subsidies in developed nations, diversions of food commodities to high input foods and fuel, commodity market speculation, and climate change.

Since the start of 2006, the average world price for rice has risen by 217 per cent, wheat by 136 per cent, maize by 125 per cent and soybeans by 107 per cent. In late April 2008, rice prices hit 24 cents a pound, twice the price that it was seven months earlier.

CONTRIBUTING FACTORS

Analysts attributed the price rises to a perfect storm of poor harvests in various parts of the world, increasing biofuel usage, lower food reserves, the U.S. Federal Reserve decreasing interest rates so that money is no longer a means to preserve wealth over the long-term (people invest in food commodities which causes an increase in demand and therefore price), growing consumer demand in Asia, oil price rises, and changes to the world economy.

IMPACT OF BIOFUELS

One systemic cause for the price rise is held to be the diversion of food crops (maize in particular) for making first-generation biofuels. An estimated 100 million tonnes of grain per year are being redirected from food to fuel. It is estimated that one ton of maize converts into 40 litres of enthanol. Total worldwide grain production for 2007 was just over 2,000 million tonnes. As farmers devoted larger parts of their crops to fuel production than in previous years, land and resources available for food production were reduced correspondingly. This has resulted in less food available for human consumption, especially in developing and least developed countries, where a family's daily allowances for food purchases are extremely limited. The crisis can be seen, in a sense, to dichotomize rich and poor nations since, for example, filling a tank of an average car with biofuel, amounts to as much maize (Africa's principal food staple) as an African person consumes in an entire year.

Since late 2007, 'agflation,' caused by the increased diversion of maize harvests in biofuels, the tying of maize prices to rising oil prices by commodity traders and the resulting price rise, has caused a market substitution with price rises cascading through other commodities: first wheat and soy prices, then later rice, soy oil and a variety of cooking oils.

Brazil, the world's second largest producer of ethanol after the U.S.A., is considered to have the world's first sustainable biofuels economy and its government claims Brazil's sugarcane-based ethanol industry has not contributed to the 2008 food crises.

Second- and third-generation biofuels (such as cellulosic ethanol and algae fuel, respectively) may some day ease the competition with food crops, as non-food energy crops can grow on marginal lands unsuited for food crops, but these advanced biofuels require further development of farming practices and refining technology; in contrast, ethanol from maize uses mature technology and the maize crop can be shifted between food and fuel use quickly.

CHANGE IN GLOBAL DIET

Growth in food production has been greater than population growth. Food per person increased during the 1961-2005 period.

2005/1990 Ratios of Per Capita Consumption

	India	China	Brazil	Nigeria
Cereals	1.0	0.8	1.2	1.0
Meat	1.2	2.4	1.7	1.0
Milk	1.2	3.0	1.2	1.3
Fish	1.2	2.3	0.9	0.8
Fruits	1.3	3.5	0.8	1.1
Vegetables	1.3	2.9	1.3	1.3

Although some commentators have argued that this food crisis stems from rapid global population growth,world population growth rates have dropped dramatically since the 1980s,and grain availability has continued to outpace population. Aggregate food production per capita has risen since the 1960s, and this trend has not changed dramatically with the 2006-07 harvests.

April 2008 analyses by the United Nations' Food and Agriculture Organization maintained that while food consumption of grains has gone up one per cent since 2006, most of this increase has gone to developed countries. Where food utilization has increased, it has largely been in value added (processed) foods, sold in developing and developed nations. Total grain utilization growth since 2006 (up three per cent, over the 2000-06 per annum average of two per cent) has been greatest in non-food usage, especially in feed and biofuels. One kilogram of beef requires seven kilograms of feed grain. These reports, therefore, conclude that usage in industrial feed, and input intensive foods, not population growth among poor consumers of simple grains, has contributed to the price increases.

Middle-class populations have grown throughout Asia over the last 20 years. Although the vast, overwhelming majority of the population in

Asia remains rural and poor, the growth of the middle class in the region has been dramatic, and is projected to continue to be so. For comparison, in 1990, the middle class grew by 9.7 in India and 8.6 in China, as a percentage of their populations; whereas in 2008 it has reached a growth rate of nearly 30 per cent and 70 per cent, respectively.

The corresponding increase in affluence has also brought with it a change in lifestyle and eating habits, particularly a demand for greater variety and more meat in the diet, leading to greater demand for agricultural resources. This demand has also been responsible for dramatic increases in commodity prices, as well as the oil price increases since 2003.

Joachim von Braun, Head of the International Food Policy Research Institute, has stated that the gradual change in diet among newly prosperous populations is the most important factor underpinning the rise in global food prices. However, the World Bank lists changing diet as secondary to the effect of biofuels.

IMPACT OF OIL PRICE INCREASES

The rise in the price of oil has affected the costs of fertilizers (in some instances doubling the price within the six months before April, 2008), the majority of which require petroleum or natural gas during the manufacturing process. Although the main fossil fuel input for fertilizer comes from natural gas to generate hydrogen for the Haber-Bosch process, natural gas has its own supply problems similar to those for oil. Because natural gas can substitute for petroleum in some uses (for example, natural gas liquids and electricity generation), increasing prices for petroleum lead to increasing prices for natural gas and thus for fertilizer.

Costs for fertilizer raw materials other than oil have themselves been increasing as increased production of staples increases demand. This is causing a boom (with associated volatility) in agriculture stocks. Oil also provides most energy for mechanized food production and transport. Higher prices for liquid fuels from petroleum increase the demand for biofuels, which may result in diverting some crops from food to energy. Even though per-capita petroleum consumption among the world's poorest people is very low, what petroleum the poor do consume, is disproportionately in the form of fossil fuel inputs to the food they eat, especially to any food imported from industrial agriculture powerhouses such as the United States. People who were already living at a subsistence level when oil was relatively cheap are extremely vulnerable when oil prices rise, and may simply lack the means to afford enough daily food calories to survive.

DECLINING WORLD FOOD STOCKPILES

In the past, nations tended to keep comparably larger food stockpiles, but more recently, due to the pace at which food could be grown and the ease with which it could be imported, less emphasis was placed on maintaining stockpiles. Therefore, for example, in February 2008, wheat stockpiles hit a 60-year low in the United States.

FINANCIAL SPECULATION

Destabilizing influences, including indiscriminate lending and real estate speculation, led to a crisis in January 2008 and eroded investment in food commodities. The United States, specifically, has been facing an economic crisis which, it is claimed, is likely to lead to recession. Financial speculation in commodity futures following the collapse of the financial derivatives markets has contributed to the crisis due to a 'commodities super-cycle.' Financial speculators seeking quick returns have removed thousands of millions of dollars from equities and mortgage bonds for investment into food and raw materials. That American commodities speculation could have a worldwide impact on food prices is reflected in the globalization of food production.

It represents the concentration of wealth throughout the world which Frances Moore Lappé equates to a weakening in fundamental democracy. In a recent article for *The Nation*, she suggests that there is no food shortage but that as long as food is merely a commodity in societies that don't protect people's right to participate in the market, and as long as farming is left vulnerable to consolidated power off the farm, many will go hungry, farmers among them—no matter how big the harvests.

IMPACT OF TRADE LIBERALIZATION

Some theorists, such as Martin Khor of the *Third World Network*, point out that many developing nations have gone from being food independent to being net food importing economies since the 1970s and 1980s International Monetary Fund (and later the World Trade Organisation's Agreement on Agriculture) free market economics directives to debtor nations. In opening developing countries to developed world food imports which continue to be subsidised by Western governments, developing nations have become dependent upon food imports which are cheaper than those which can be produced by local small farmers, even in the poorest regions of the world.

While developed countries pressured the developing world to abolish subsidies in the interest of trade liberalization, rich countries largely kept subsidies in place for their own farmers. In recent years, United States government subsidies have been added which pushed production towards biofuel rather than food.

The U.S.A., committed at the Uruguay Round of the WTO in 1995 to reduce by 20 per cent its trade-distorting farm subsidy. According to latest reports in 2008, the U.S.A., in fact, doubled its farm subsidy since 1995.

BIOFUEL SUBSIDIES IN THE U.S.A.

The FAO has reported that world land usage for agriculture has declined since the 1980s and subsidies, excluding those of the United States and the EU, have dropped since the year 2004, leaving supply, while sufficient to meet 2004 needs, vulnerable when the United States began converting agricultural commodities to biofuels. According to the United States Department of Agriculture, global wheat imports and stocks have decreased, domestic consumption has stagnated, and world wheat production has decreased from 2006-08.

In the United States, government subsidies for ethanol production have prompted many farmers to switch to production for biofuel. Maize is the primary crop used for the production of ethanol, with the United States being the biggest producer of maize ethanol. As a result, 23 per cent of United States maize crops were being used for ethanol in 2006-07 (up from 6 per cent in 2005-06), and the USDA expects the United States to use 81 million tonnes of maize for ethanol production in the 2007-2008 season, up 37 per cent. This not only diverts grains from food, but it diverts agricultural land from food production.

IDLE FARMLAND

According to the *New York Times* of April 9, 2008, the United States government pays farmers to idle their cropland under a conservation programme. This policy reached a peak of 36.8 million acres idled in 2007, that is 8 per cent of the cropland in United States, representing a total area bigger than the state of New York.

CROP SHORTFALLS FROM NATURAL DISASTERS

Several distinct weather- and climate-related incidents have caused disruptions in crop production. Perhaps the most influential is the extended drought in Australia, in particular the fertile Murray-Darling Basin, which produces large amounts of wheat and rice. The drought has caused the annual rice harvest to fall by as much as 98 per cent from pre-drought levels. Australia is historically the second-largest exporter of wheat after the United States, producing up to 25 million tons in a good year, the vast majority for export. However, the 2006 harvest was 9.8 million.

Other events that have negatively affected the price of food include the 2006 heat wave in California's San Joaquin Valley, which killed large numbers of farm animals and unseasonal 2008 rains in Kerala, India, which destroyed swathes of grain. Scientists have stated that several of these incidents are consistent with the predicted effects of climate change.

The effects of Cyclone Nargis on Myanmar in May 2008 caused a spike in the price of rice. Myanmar has historically been a rice exporter, though yields have fallen as government price controls have reduced incentives for farmers. The storm inundated rice paddies up to 20 kilometres inland in the Irrawaddy Delta, raising concern that salinity could make the fields infertile.

The FAO had previously estimated that Myanmar would export up to 600,000 tons of rice in 2008, but concerns were raised in the cyclone's aftermath that it may be forced to import rice for the first time, putting further upward pressure on global rice prices.

SOIL AND PRODUCTIVITY LOSSES

It has been pointed out that large areas of croplands are lost year after year due mainly to soil erosion, water depletion and urbanisation. According to a report '60,000 km^2/year of land becomes so severely degraded that it loses its productive capacity and becomes wasteland, and even more is affected to a lesser extent, adding to the crop supply problem.'

Additionally, agricultural production is also lost due to water depletion. Northern China in particular has depleted much of its non-renewable aquifers, which now impacts negatively on its crop production.

Urbanisation is another, smaller, difficult to estimate, cause of annual cropland reduction.

EFFECTS ON DEVELOPING COUNTRIES

From the beginning of 2007 to early 2008, the prices of some of the most basic international food commodities increased dramatically in international markets. The international market price of wheat doubled from February 2007 to February 2008 hitting a record high of over $ 10 a bushel. Rice prices also reached ten-year highs. In some nations, milk and meat prices more than doubled, while soy (which hit a 34 year high price in December 2007) and maize prices have increased dramatically.

Total food import bills rose by an estimated 25 per cent for developing countries in 2007. Researchers from the Overseas Development Institute have suggested this problem will be worsened by a likely fall in food aid. As food aid is programmed by budget rather than volume, rising food prices mean that the World Food Programme (WFP) needs an extra US$ 500 million just to sustain the current operations.

To ensure that food remains available for their domestic populations and to combat dramatic price inflation, major rice exporters, such as China, Brazil, India, Indonesia, Vietnam, Cambodia and Egypt, have imposed strict export bans on rice. Conversely, several other nations, including Argentina, Ukraine, Russia, and Serbia have, as well, either imposed high tariffs or blocked the export of wheat and other foodstuffs altogether, driving up prices still further for net food importing nations and reducing the incentives for exporting farmers to increase production.

CHAPTER 3

GLOBAL AGRICULTURE AND THE ENVIRONMENT

RECENT attention to the threat of global environmental change has tended to focus on the possible impacts of a changing environment on agriculture and the implications for global and regional food security. From a policy viewpoint, however, it is also critical to understand the degree to which agriculturally related activities may contribute to global-scale environmental change and the extent to which policies to prevent, mitigate, or adapt to environmental change may themselves affect agriculture and hunger. These two issues are likely to become especially important in making decisions not only about how to reduce the magnitude of human perturbations to the environment but also about how to improve both food security and environmental quality in the more crowded world of the future.

The primary focus here is on global-scale changes in the environment, including possible changes in the earth's climate induced by increasing atmospheric concentrations of active trace gases such as carbon dioxide (CO_2), methane (CH_4), and nitrous oxide (N_2O) and depletion of the stratospheric ozone (O_3) layer caused by releases of chlorofluorocarbons (CFCs) and other ozone-depleting substances. Interactions between agriculture and local, or regional-scale changes in the environment, which may also have important implications for human health and welfare, are not considered in detail.

THE ORIGINS OF AGRICULTURE

Humanity has relied solely on hunting, fishing, and gathering for food for most of its two million years of existence. Agriculture, the domestication of plants and animals, appeared only about 10,000 years ago, roughly coincident both with a period of widespread climatic and ecological fluctuations and with an acceleration of population growth to the order of 0.1 per cent per year. Whether the spread of agriculture was a trigger for more rapid population growth or was itself a response to increasing population or environmental pressures remains a controversial question. For example, anthropologic evidence, including indicators of nutritional status derived from skeletal remains, suggests that the health of hunter-gatherers tended to be better than that of subsequent farmers in the same region.

One explanation for this observation is that agriculture and related technological and social innovations may have emerged initially as a way to compensate for an unreliable or declining resource base arising from population pressures, environmental fluctuations, or both. In a sense, such 'stress' models of the origins of agriculture suggest that hunger and a changing environment may have helped motivate the development and adoption of agriculture, even though in the short-term, agriculture apparently provided less output per unit of labour input than hunting and gathering.

An alternative viewpoint, no longer widely held by anthropologists, is that plant domestication and social and cultural innovations such as sedentism did not begin among those subject to stress, but rather among hunting and gathering populations, that had the resources and energy to experiment. Environmental and other stresses leading to hunger, therefore, they would have been an impediment to the development of agriculture. As in the stress models, hunger and malnutrition should still have decreased with increasing success in agriculture.

A third 'ecologic' view is that human use of plants and animals naturally led to significant impacts on the local or even regional environment, for example, through the spread of seeds, selective harvesting of 'wild' species and deposit of waste matter. Such modifications to plant and animal habitats and genotypes resulted eventually in a variety of symbiotic, co-evolutionary relationships that we now term domestication. In essence, the ecologic model raises the possibility of important two-way interactions between environmental stresses and humanity's demographic and technological development and perhaps even its social development.

These alternative models of the origins of agriculture are instructive because they highlight the intimate links that may have persisted for many millennia among environmental fluctuations, agriculture and human welfare. In the long-term, agriculture has clearly brought the potential for larger populations, expanded exploitation of climatic and other natural resources and reduced vulnerability to many forms of environmental fluctuation, such as drought and other extremes of weather and climate. At the same time, however, agriculture and the increasing globalization of food systems may have increased vulnerability to other problems, such as market failures and the unequal distribution of food. For example, nutritional levels as indicated by estimates of human height have been marked by variations of comparable magnitude on time scales of 50–10,000 years. Although it seems likely that environmental factors are now relatively less important contributors to such variations than they were in past millennia, human history provides no guarantee that new forms of environmental change might not emerge as dominant influences on human nutrition and well-being.

THE PRESENT: THE GLOBAL FOOD SYSTEM

Some time after the World War II, probably during the early 1960s, humanity surpassed what may have been an unprecedented threshold. It collectively produced enough food calories for the world's population, assuming that all calories were distributed evenly and utilized directly by humans, that is, not for animal feed or non-food uses. Since then, the size of the theoretic 'surplus' calories has grown to as much as 20 per cent above world food requirements as determined by United Nations (UN) nutritional standards, although during 1987 and 1988 it decreased to less than 10 per cent above aggregate requirements in part because of weather-related production shortfalls in North America and continuing rapid population growth around the world. Current world 'carryover' stocks of cereals are extremely low, constituting only about 17 per cent of aggregate cereal consumption, roughly the minimum level considered safe by the UN's Food and Agriculture Organization.

Of course, since food production, buying power, and consumption are not distributed evenly with population, large surpluses and deficits exist at regional, national, and subnational levels. For example, in the mid- to late 1980s, as many as 1.5 billion people lived in countries where dietary energy supplies were inadequate to meet national nutritional needs, and some 350–500 million people lived in households too poor to obtain enough calories for minimal adult activity and the healthy growth of children. In contrast, dietary energy supplies in the developed world averaged more than 3,300 calories per person in 1984-86, of which 30 per cent were derived from animal products. Assuming conservatively that four calories of animal feed are needed to produce one calorie of animal product, the developed world, with only 25 per cent of the world's population, in effect consumes at least 40 per cent of the total world 'primary' food supply in caloric terms.

Growth in food production in recent decades has resulted primarily from increased crop yields per unit of land and to a lesser extent from expansion of cropland. Between 1964-66 and 1983-85, total world cropland increased by only 9 per cent, but total agricultural production grew nearly 60 per cent. Global mean yields of cereals increased by nearly two-thirds during this period and those of roots and tubers by about one-fourth. These improvements in yield stemmed from a combination of increased agricultural inputs, more intensive use of land and the spread of improved crop varieties. For example, global mean fertilizer use more than doubled from 34 kg/ha of cropland in 1964-66 to 86 kg/ha in 1983-85 and irrigation expanded from 13 to 15 per cent of the world's arable land between 1974-76 and 1984-86. It is estimated that, in 1986, improved varieties of maize were planted on more than 70 per cent of all maize-growing cropland.

Marine catches averaged nearly 80 million metric tons in 1985-87, an increase of 30 per cent over 1975-77 levels. Freshwater catches grew more than 60 per cent to 11 million mt during this period. Roughly 70 per cent of world fish production is used for food, with the remainder going into fish meal and oil.

Concurrent with these production and yield increases has been significant growth of world trade in food and agriculture. Food imports grew from 8 per cent of total world production in 1961-63 to 12 per cent in 1983-85. In 93 developing countries (excluding China), the share of food imports in production doubled from 5 per cent to nearly 10 per cent of production during this period. Imports of nitrogenous and phosphate fertilizers grew by more than 27 per cent in tonnage between 1982-83 and 1985-86 and constituted 20-25 per cent of world consumption. About 12.5 million metric tons of fish products were traded internationally in 1985 or about one-third of local fish production. One consequence of this 'emerging' global food system may be a decrease in local vulnerability to famine in developing countries through increased reliance on food imports including food aid, but an increase in vulnerability to problems stemming from international trade and integration into the global economy.

INFLUENCE OF THE GLOBAL FOOD SYSTEM ON THE ENVIRONMENT

The global food system may influence the global environment in a variety of ways. The direct impacts of agriculture on the environment include modification of land for agricultural purposes and byproducts of production such as methane released by rice paddies and livestock. Activities such as food processing, distribution, and preparation use fossil fuels, fuelwood, refrigerants, and other inputs and generate wastes. Indirect impacts include the effects of energy, materials and pollution entailed in constructing and maintaining equipment, transportation and storage facilities and other infrastructure used in food production, fisheries, and related activities and in supporting the populations involved in them. Of course, it is especially difficult to quantify such indirect impacts, to attribute them consistently to particular activities, and to ascertain whether alternative uses of resources would have resulted in greater or lesser impacts.

As noted previously, the primary focus is on global scale effects, principally the emissions of active trace gases affected by agriculture and other food-related activities. The most important trace gases from the standpoint of cumulative temperature change given an assumed scenario of trends in trace gas concentrations are CO_2, CH_4, N_2O, and various CFCs.

Land Use and Conversion

About 11 per cent of all land worldwide is used for crops and another 25 per cent for pasture. On a regional basis, crop areas range from as low as 6 per cent of Africa and 8 per cent of South America to 17 per cent of Asia and 30 per cent of Europe. About 15 per cent of all cropland is irrigated, ranging from 6 per cent in Africa and South America to 31 per cent in Asia.

As noted previously, cropland expanded only 9 per cent between 1964-66 and 1984-86. The area of permanent pasture remained constant. World population grew by some 45 per cent during this period, leading to a decrease in cropland per capita from 0.4 to 0.3 ha/person.

The potential environmental impacts of cropland depend largely on

(a) the type of crop production, and

(b) the land use that crop production replaces.

Net changes in albedo and evapotranspiration associated with crop production are probably modest on the global scale, in part because snow-free land constitutes only about one-fourth of the earth's total surface area. Past conversion of tropical forests into agricultural lands is estimated to have resulted in an average increase in land albedo of about 0.02, equivalent to about one-fifth of the radiative effect of doubling atmospheric CO_2. Further changes in land albedo during the next century are not expected to exceed this amount. Evapotranspiration rates for tropical forests are higher than those for rainfed agriculture and grassland, but lower than those for irrigated agriculture. Net effects on the global scale may therefore depend largely on the mix of land uses on deforested lands. Drastic changes in evapotranspiration rates and other land surface properties could certainly have significant regional or even global climatic impacts, but more realistic and detailed studies of the climatologic effects of projected land surface changes are needed using global climate models. Other mechanisms for large-scale environmental change, such as dust production and various biogeochemical feedbacks, have been suggested but remain speculative.

Of greater concern are changes in biomass and emissions of trace gases associated with deforestation. Estimates of deforestation rates vary widely, primarily because of data limitations and definitional problems. As much as seven million hectares of closed tropical forests may have been cleared annually for agriculture around 1980 and an additional four million hectares of open woodland deforested annually to meet agricultural or fuelwood needs. The extent of shifting cultivation and the nature of subsequent land uses are important uncertainties; estimates of closed primary and secondary forests affected by shifting cultivation range from about 5 to 44 million hectares per year. Recent studies suggest even higher rates of deforestation in some countries, although there may be considerable year-to-year variability because of weather, political and economic factors.

The net contribution of deforestation to total CO_2 emissions also remains controversial, not only because of disagreement on deforestation rates but also because of uncertainties in the amounts of CO_2 released from vegetation and soils recovered in subsequent land use. Estimates of annual emissions range from 400 million metric tons of carbon up to 2,500 million metric tons, or as much as one-third of total annual CO_2 emissions. One later estimate places current annual emissions as high as 2,800 million metric tons per year.

Much deforestation and other land conversion occurs through burning of biomass, which releases CO_2, CO, N_2O, CH_4, soot and other trace gases into the atmosphere. Once forests are removed, emissions of CH_4, N_2O, and other trace gases may continue from exposed soils. For example, high CH_4 fluxes have been associated with both flooding and the spread of termites on deforested lands. The net environmental impacts of biomass burning depend to a large degree on the subsequent use of the land, which in turn may depend on the objectives and actions of those who initiated the burning.

Releases of N_2O are of particular concern because N_2O is not only a long-lived and radiatively active trace gas, but it is also a precursor to NO, a catalytic species that is thought to play an important role in depleting stratospheric O_3. N_2O concentrations are increasing some 0.2–0.3 per cent per year. Estimates of the size of N_2O sources vary widely, but biomass burning, natural soils and fertilized and unfertilized fields are all thought to be important contributors.

Emissions of CO are also important, since CO reacts with OH radicals in the atmosphere. OH radicals help to cleanse the atmosphere of a variety of trace gases, including CH_4 and CFCs. Higher levels of CO may therefore reduce scavenging of these trace gases, leading to their more rapid accumulation in the atmosphere. Data on CO sources are limited, but rough estimates indicate that forest clearing and burning of savannahs and wood account for more than one-third of anthropogenic CO emissions and about one-fourth of all CO emissions.

Conversion of wetlands may also contribute to trace gas emissions. Draining wetlands releases stored carbon and, if such lands are converted to paddy rice production, net methane emissions may increase rather than decrease.

CROP PRODUCTION AND FERTILIZER APPLICATION

Various forms of agricultural production may lead to significant trace gas emissions. Tilling of soils permits oxidation of organic matter, producing CO_2. Even with no application of nitrogen fertilizers, cultivated soils may emit large amounts of N_2O, perhaps as much in the aggregate as that released from fertilized fields. Application of fertilizers increases N_2O release by plants, although emission rates vary greatly with soil conditions. As noted previously, world fertilizer consumption is growing rapidly, and its use is widespread in a variety of different socioeconomic and technologic settings.

Some 20–30 per cent of CH_4 emissions result from anaerobic production in the paddy fields used in wet rice production. Rapid expansion of paddy area and increasing cropping intensities have helped accelerate growth in CH_4 emissions to some 1 per cent per year. Measured atmospheric concentrations are increasing at or near this rate, or about 0.8–1.0 per cent per year as of the mid-1980s.

Livestock Production

Animals constitute a second major source of CH_4 emissions, which result from microbial breakdown of cellulose and other carbohydrates in their digestive tracts. Cattle in developed countries and Argentina and Brazil produce an estimated 55 kilograms of CH_4 per head per year. Cattle in other developing countries are thought to produce less, about 35 kilograms per year, because of lower feed intakes despite poorer feed quality. Estimated cattle populations of some 570 million in the first group of countries and 650 million in the second, yield a total production of at least 54 million metric tons of CH_4 per year. Another 20 million metric tons are produced by more than 120 million buffaloes, 1.1 billion sheep, 470 million goats, 17 million camels, 770 million pigs, 64 million horses, and 54 million mules and asses. Applying this emission rates to country-specific data on animal populations, the World Resources Institute estimated total CH_4 emissions from livestock to be 76 million metric tons, of which some 60 per cent occured in developing countries. Just six countries—India, the U.S.S.R., Brazil, the United States, China, and Argentina—account for more than half of all CH_4 emissions from livestock. These estimates, together with the estimates for CH_4 emissions from biomass burning and paddy fields, indicate that activities primarily associated with food production generate some two-thirds of annual CH_4 emissions.

Other environmental impacts of livestock include overgrazing of pasture and rangelands, leading to changes in albedo and evapotranspiration, soil erosion, and reductions in biomass. Overgrazing is evident throughout Asia, Latin America and Africa. Animal wastes may also release large amounts of ammonia (NH_3), which is thought to contribute to acidification of soils and aquatic systems.

Water Use

Agriculture is the largest single consumer of fresh water, although its share of total use has declined significantly during the past century and is expected to continue to decline through the year 2000. On a global basis, total water withdrawals for all purposes constitute less than one tenth of total river runoff and consumption uses only one-twentieth of this total. Withdrawal rates are much higher in some river basins, leading to significant regional-scale impacts on water level and quality in rivers, lakes and enclosed seas such as the Aral. Irrigation has led to high salinity and waterlogging in millions of hectares of irrigated land in arid and semi-arid areas of South Asia, the Middle East, the United States, and the U.S.S.R.

Water quality and quantity problems are critical from the viewpoint of human health and environmental quality on local and regional scales and they undoubtedly have global-scale implications for food production and food security – especially if projected hydrologic and sea level changes do occur. However, they do not as yet appear to have significant influences on the likelihood or timing of global environmental change. This conclusion could change if various proposed mechanisms for biogeochemical feedback prove significant. For example, it has been suggested that aquifers polluted by agricultural, livestock and other effluents may emit large amounts of N_2O and that changes in marine productivity could result from nitrogen pollutants.

Energy Use

Agriculture is a modest user of energy relative to other economic sectors, accounting for an estimated 3.5 per cent of commercial energy use in developed countries and 4.5 per cent in developing countries. These estimates take into account energy used in irrigation, pesticide and fertilizer production and machinery production and operation, but not energy used in food processing, storage, and transportation. When the latter are taken into account along with other food system activities, their share of energy consumption increases significantly. For example, some analysts attribute 17 per cent of United States fossil-fuel consumption to food-system activities, divided equally between food production, processing and preparation. Since the U.S.A. itself generates about one-fifth of annual world CO_2 emissions, its food-related activities alone contribute a not insignificant 3-4 per cent to total annual CO_2 emissions. Energy use in food processing, marketing, and distribution appears to be growing at relatively high rates in the U.S.A., reaching about half of energy consumed in the commercial food and fibre sector.

Modern agricultural systems are especially energy intensive and generally require large quantities of fossil fuels to run machinery and irrigation pumps. The ratio of food energy output to total energy inputs in California rice production is 1.6, compared with 2.5 for Japanese production,

3.3 for Philippine production using animal power, and 7.0 for the Iban of Borneo, who use little more than their own labour. Resulting yields of food energy per hectare are two to three times higher for California and Japan than for the Philippines and Borneo.

In developing countries, fertilizers require the highest commercial energy inputs, followed by machinery and irrigation. An FAO report assumed that significant increases in commercial energy application will be needed to boost agricultural yields and farm earnings. Its two scenarios for the year 2000 project an average increase of 7.5 per cent per year in commercial energy use in agriculture in 90 developing countries. Given the high costs of importing fertilizers and fossil fuels, it seems likely that developing countries may increasingly turn to alternatives such as biogas and animal power. Biogas consists mostly of methane and hydrogen gases produced by anaerobic fermentation of crop and animal wastes. Usable nitrogen, phosphorus and potassium are byproducts, Of course, widespread use of biogas would presumably lead to significant methane and N_2O emissions.

Other Food-System Activities

Other aspects of the food system are expected to have relatively limited impacts on the global environment. CFC releases associated with refrigeration of foodstuffs are relatively small; in the United States, they amounted to less than 6 per cent of total CFC emissions in the last century. Recovery of CFCs from large refrigeration units may already be economical and alternate refrigerants do exist for small home refrigerators and freezers.

THE FUTURE

Recent population data suggest that birth rates have not fallen as quickly as expected in the 1980s. By the year 2025, world population is projected to reach nearly 8.5 billion. Providing adequate nutrition for this larger population will require at least a comparable increase in effective food availability and probably a much higher increase to allow for unequal distribution and better diets. Key issues are

(a) whether existing production can be used more efficiently,

(b) whether production can be increased without increasing impacts on the global environment, and

(c) whether the global food system can adapt to any environmental changes that do occur?

Although firm conclusions about any of these issues are not yet possible, a brief discussion of each of them is instructive.

Can Existing Production be More Efficiently Used?

The present global food system entails a high degree of waste of potentially usable food products. Estimates of 'post harvest' losses—that is, losses between harvest and delivery of food at the retail level range from 10 to 30 per cent or more. However, large losses also occur both before harvest and after food distribution to retail outlets. Crop losses were estimated at 35 per cent prior to harvest and 20 per cent after harvest, implying a total loss of nearly half of potential food supply. Post retail losses may exceed 10 per cent according to one order-of-magnitude estimate.

Poor utilization of food calories after food has been consumed may also result in the effective waste of food. For example, even a mild episode of diarrhoea in adults may lead to a loss of food calories equivalent to 1–2 per cent of annual food requirements and diarrhoea and associated infections among infants and small children can result in weight loss equivalent to 5–10 per cent of annual food requirements. One probe estimates that small children in the developing world average on the order of three episodes of diarrhoea per year, or more than 1.4 billion episodes annually. Intestinal parasites such as *Schistosoma, Giardia lamblia, Ascaris lumbricoides, Trichuris trichiura, Strongyloides stercoralis* and hookworm may also cause or enhance malnutrition through a combination of reduced food intake, malabsorption, anaemia, and other nutrient loss. Schistosomiasis alone is estimated to affect some 200 million people in the developing world.

Large effective losses of food calories also occur because of inefficiencies in converting raw animal feed into edible animal food products. Net conversion efficiencies observed in breeding populations of farm animals range from 3 to 6 per cent for sheep and beef cattle to 11–12 per cent for pig meat, milk, and eggs. Overall efficiencies are at best about 17 per cent, that is, about 600 calories of feed are needed to produce 100 calories of animal products. Of course, animal production may produce foods with higher contents of protein, minerals and fats, than the raw feed could have provided and may also generate other benefits such as the work performed by animals and a mechanism for storing food and household assets.

Nevertheless, these estimates of losses and inefficiencies suggest that there may be substantial room for improvement in the delivery of nutrition, which is presumably one of the primary objectives of the global food system. As recognized in the energy field in earlier decades, it is important to focus on the end use efficiency of production—in this case, the level of food production and associated inputs needed to provide a desired set of 'services', such as a minimum number of calories per person each day and some degree of dietary quality and diversity. The most practical and cost-effective way to increase delivered nutrition may not be to increase gross production but to reduce pre- and post-harvest losses, find lower-input methods for producing high-protein and other desired food products and improve the capability of households and individuals to process and utilize food efficiently. A major benefit of such a 'food conservation' strategy, akin to present-day energy conservation efforts, should be the overall reduction of the environmental stresses stemming from use of agricultural inputs, disposal of agricultural wastes and other food-system activities.

More effective utilization of agricultural inputs and reduction of 'on-farm' losses—a major focus of traditional agricultural research—constitute one area for efficiency improvements. This includes methods for more precise and timely application of fertilizers, pesticides, herbicides and irrigation water and reductions in crop damage and loss caused by pests, diseases, weather and harvesting methods. Improvements in the efficiency of 'secondary' production, i.e., production of more desirable food products using primary foodstuffs as inputs, are also possible through more efficient breeds of animals, reduced exposure of animals to adverse environmental conditions, diseases and parasites and use of feed substitutes that could not otherwise be used for human foods. In the long run, it may well be possible to eliminate the animals and to produce desired foods, or nutritionally and aesthetically equivalent substitutes, through sophisticated food processing or even direct culturing of animal cells. The former is essentially what Buddhist vegetarians have done for centuries in creating meatlike foods from soy and other plant products.

Other opportunities for improving the efficiency of food use include improvement in post harvest food storage, more efficient food preparation at the household level and improvements in the health of individuals to minimize losses caused by diarrhoea, parasites, and incomplete digestion. For example, new storage methods such as a hermetically sealed 'cube' developed by the Volcani Institute in Israel promise reduced grain losses caused by pests and moisture while at the same time lowering pesticide use. In the United States, a number of organizations utilize volunteer labour to 'glean' crops missed by mechanical harvesters, thereby salvaging foodstuffs that would otherwise go to waste. New types of cooking stoves in developing countries can significantly reduce the firewood needed for food preparation and help improve food digestibility. More widespread use of oral rehydration therapy, promotion of breastfeeding and other efforts to combat diarrhoeal-related diseases help reduce nutritional losses even after food consumption.

Improving overall end use efficiency will not only require recognition of opportunities of this kind, but also, as evident from ongoing efforts to promote energy conservation around the world, restructuring of market and regulatory incentives, for example, to reflect more realistically the environmental 'externalities' of agricultural production and to remove explicit and implicit subsidies of limited resources and entrenched technologies. Resulting changes in markets and food prices would undoubtedly have significant distributional effects, both between and within countries—but how levels and patterns of hunger might change is difficult to predict.

Can Production be Increased without Increasing Impacts on the Global Environment?

As noted earlier, efforts to improve the efficiency of agricultural production and the utilization of food products may themselves lead to reduced levels of pollutants and resource use. However, significant increases in total food production are still likely to be needed in the future, in part because efficiency improvements could easily take decades to implement. An important issue, therefore, is whether future increases in production are possible with lower levels of impact on the global environment.

From this perspective, expansion of cropland appears to have a relatively high level of impact. Much of the untapped reserve of available land is covered with tropical forest, so that agricultural development would likely lead to net reductions in biomass. Soil quality is generally poor, so that large amounts of fertilizer, energy and other inputs would probably be necessary to maintain yields and prevent soil erosion. Pests and diseases affecting plants, animals and humans are common, so that efficient production and utilization of food would be difficult. Some of these lands are in areas of poor or erratic rainfall, so that irrigation may be required—but even with irrigation, production in these areas may be especially sensitive to any environmental changes that do occur.

Similarly, expansion of rangeland for livestock production is also likely to have high levels of impact, especially to the extent that tropical forests are replaced and overgrazing occurs, contributing to land degradation, soil erosion and desertification. Increased livestock numbers may of course increase methane emissions, unless new breeds of animals with lower emission rates are introduced.

Increased production on existing cropland has in the past been achieved primarily through more intensive application of fertilizer, expansion of irrigation and improved crop varieties. As noted previously, the first option may entail releases of N_2O and the second, especially for wet rice production, releases of methane. Clearly, new methods for providing nitrogen such as intercropping with nitrogen-fixing plants or genetic manipulation to add nitrogen-fixing abilities to crops could significantly reduce the use of nitrogen fertilizers. Reducing methane emissions from wet rice production is more problematic, since present methods for dry rice production have significantly lower yields. However, new strains of rice may reduce the need for flooding and therefore lower emissions of methane.

The third option, improved crop varieties, will depend greatly on the pace and direction of agricultural research, the availability and diversity of genetic resources, advances in genetic manipulation, success in disseminating new varieties and other factors. Concern is growing over recent trends towards more modest yield gains—or even small declines—in areas such as the United States and Pakistan. On the other hand, present-day agriculture relies on only 15 species of plants and 8 species of livestock for 90 per cent of world food production, out of millions of plant and animal species and at least 75,000 edible plants. Both, improved forms of existing foods and entirely new foods, are possible. Triticale, for example, is a hybrid of wheat and rye that performs significantly better than wheat in areas of marginal soils and climate.

Alternative agricultural methods that deserve more attention from the viewpoint of potentially lower environmental impacts include various forms of low-input and rotational cropping methods such as agroforestry and alley cropping, trickle or drip irrigation methods, integrated pest management, perennial grain crops, low-intensity animal production systems, higher-yield forage crops, and aquaculture. Low-input alternatives for corn production are estimated to produce roughly twice the food-energy output from a given energy input as conventional corn production, primarily because of lower fertilizer requirements. Trickle irrigation reduces percolation and evaporative water losses, helps to prevent salinization, and can save energy used in lifting and delivering water. Possibilities exist to improve the quality and yield of forage crops, including reduction in cellulose content, which would presumably lower methane emissions by ruminants. Further assessments of the potential environmental benefits, and tradeoffs, of techniques of this kind are clearly warranted.

Can the Global Food System Adapt to Environmental Change?

The potential impacts of environmental change on the global food system and the responses and adaptations that could mitigate such impacts are not well understood. Research to date has focused largely on a small set of environmental changes (for example, in atmospheric CO_2 and in temperature and precipitation patterns), a narrow range of agricultural impacts (for example, impacts on grain yields), a limited repertoire of technologic and socio-economic adjustments (for example, increased irrigation), a sprinkling of countries and regions (for example, the U.S.A. or climatically 'marginal' regions) and a relatively short time frame (for example, impacts on present-day agricultural technologies and food systems). Many important issues have been addressed only in qualitative terms. For example, little is known about the combined impact of climatic changes, higher levels of atmospheric CO_2, increased ultraviolet radiation, increasing acid deposition and air pollution on crops, animals, plant and animal pests and diseases. Only limited attention has been given to potential changes in international agricultural competitive advantage, differential vulnerability to environmental change, implications for food access and hunger within countries and the full range of technological, economic and social responses available to farmers and other socioeconomic units. Not much is known about the potential impacts of changing atmospheric and oceanic conditions on marine ecosystems and fisheries, including possible effects of increased ultraviolet radiation on krill and other Antarctic species.

Even more poorly understood are the many complex links and feedbacks that are likely to exist between :

(a) food system activities that contribute significantly to environmental change,

(b) food system activities that would be directly or indirectly affected by environmental change,

(c) impacts in related activities such as energy production and transportation, and

(d) actions taken to reduce or modify the effects of any of these activities.

For example, a traditional response to climatic variability has been to increase irrigation, but the latter often requires large amounts of energy to move irrigation water and may lead to increased methane emissions. Irrigation also competes for water supplies with municipal and industrial water demands and evaporative losses, all of which could grow even faster than expected in a warming climate. Without enough water, both the effectiveness of other agricultural inputs, such as fertilizers, and the yield benefits from CO_2 enrichment may be reduced.

Complex linkages of this kind may exist throughout the food system. Higher air temperature and humidity imply increased refrigeration loads at the same time that potentially less energy-efficient refrigerants may be in widespread use to limit emissions of CFCs thought to damage the stratospheric O_3 layer. Increased prices for fossil fuels or restrictions on fossil fuel use would increase input costs throughout the food system but should, among other things, lower crop damage caused by air pollution and acid deposition. Efforts to promote production of biomass fuels as a substitute for fossil fuels and reforestation to sequester atmospheric CO_2 could lead to displacement of food production, reduced income and standards of living on the part of farmers and labourers and increased levels of environmental stress and resource degradation. Biogas production, which may make sense in terms of reduced fossil fuel and fuelwood. demands and increased fertilizer availability, could increase CH_4 and N_2O emissions. In developing new crop varieties, complex trade offs will be necessary to deal with changes in climatic variability and stresses, altered patterns of plant pests and diseases, changing availability of various agricultural inputs and evolving food production, harvesting, storage and processing methods. However, the genetic diversity, upon which new varieties depend, may itself be threatened by deforestation and other land use changes and by local, regional and global environmental change.

Thus, it is clear that the problem of providing more food to more people during the next several decades is greatly complicated by the threat of global environmental change. Measures to prevent such change or to improve adaptive capabilities could conceivably have effects on the global food system as profound as some of the expected effects of global environmental change itself. Whether larger or smaller numbers of people would end up hungry is difficult to predict. For example, efforts to protect forests and species diversity might well limit access to important common resources on the part of landless and land-short populations in developing countries. Limits on livestock and irrigation and increases in energy prices could affect the livelihood and food security of billions of people in both rural and urban areas. Moreover, since preventive measures may not succeed in preventing environmental change immediately and completely—or at all—it is certainly plausible that the global food system might have to adapt not only to significant changes in energy and fertilizer consumption, land use and production methods, but also to some degree of local, regional, and global environmental change.

Developing robust alternatives that simultaneously :

(a) stabilize or reduce contributions on the part of the global food system to global environmental change, and

(b) permit increased levels of delivered nutrition to the growing world population in the face of substantial environmental and other uncertainties will not be an easy task.

However, failure to develop such alternatives could have dire consequences for hunger and world food security. To draw a lesson from the origins of agriculture, increased hunger could be inevitable if human society is only able to adapt under conditions of stress or evolutionary pressure. Instead, it may well be necessary to respond now to the perceived threat of global environmental change and to find and implement solutions before any changes or their adverse impacts become too damaging or irreversible. This is likely to be the best hope for reducing hunger and maintaining a livable environment in the more crowded world of the future.

CHAPTER 4

THE CURRENT STATUS OF WORLD HUNGER

WHERE does starvation exist in the world today? What are some of the causes of world hunger? Are citizens of developed countries donating monetarily to the ongoing relief efforts? In this chapter I will address these questions with the hope that by creating an understanding of the current world hunger situation, morally conscious individuals will do their part in contributing to the eradication of this unseen suffering.

It is a well known fact that there is enough food in the world to feed every human being on earth. Sadly, malnutrition and hunger still afflict one out of every seven people in the world today. Or, from a slightly different statistical perspective, the current world population is 4,712,200,000. The number of malnourished is 797,900,000. Therefore 17 per cent of the world population is currently malnourished or starving. No matter how you examine the issue, a current crisis is at hand. Why is this so?

The causes of starvation are complex, but there are some common threads that seem to be associated with this problem. First and foremost, starvation is caused by poverty. To address the problem of world hunger, the problem of global poverty must be addressed. Therefore, we should examine the causes of poverty. A thorough discussion on the causes of global poverty is outside the purview of this chapter. Entire textbooks have been written on the subject. For our discussion, it will suffice to say that one of the major causes of poverty is the governments pursuing policies, that inhibit self-sufficiency.

Areas of starvation are also characterized by persistent problems in cultivating food from lack of seed, arable land, and tools. Those that can grow food, must deal with insects, drought, floods, and war, which can result in complete destruction of crops. Historically, areas of Africa have experienced periodic locust infestations, which can completely destroy crops.

Other causes of world hunger are related to the globalized system of food production. The globalized system of food production and trade favours a reliance on export crops while discriminating against small-scale farmers and subsistence crops. Many Third World countries export so much food while concomitantly not keeping enough food to sustain their own people.

AIDS is a significant cause of hunger. In societies affected by AIDS, famine is more deadly and difficult to combat. Why is this so? AIDS attacks the most productive individuals within society. Fewer productive people within society means fewer individuals to work the jobs that involve food production. This is one contributor to the starvation currently taking place in Africa.

Weather plays a major role in terms of the prevalence of starvation. Areas of drought leads to non-useable land with subsequent famine. This is a well known fact. But what is less well known is that floods can also lead to starvation. Crops can be flooded and therefore destroyed, which in essence produces the same result as drought. In both cases, weather can produce a complete lack of self-sufficiency.

Military conflicts, both internal and between neighbouring countries, can lead to starvation. These conflicts can result in destruction of crops. Government money is directed at funding the conflict at the expense of the starving people. Funds are diverted from social and economic development. Military conflicts can also result in the displacement of large groups of people, removing them from their farms and their way of life. People can end up in refugee camps, completely dependent on relief aid.

The causative factors of world hunger are numerous, and certain factors change from year to year; therefore at any given time, some areas may be more prone than others. The extent of drought, flood, internal conflicts, and war with neighbouring countries can vary over time. Therefore, these factors incorporate a variable affect on the degree to which inhabitants of susceptible countries suffer from starvation.

A combination of these causative factors in a particular region is a formula for disaster. When this occurs, large-scale starvation can take place.

A case in point. The Horn of Africa has seen severe drought coupled with internal conflicts. This is leading to the development of a tragedy. In this region currently 11 million people are on the brink of starvation.

Historically, certain areas of the world have had a high prevalence of hunger and starvation. These areas are the central region of South America, large areas of East, Central, and Southern Africa, and regions of South Asia. As of 2006, the current hot spots, those areas which are suffering the greatest degree of starvation, are as follows:

Niger

This area in central Africa has been struggling to cope with the devastating impact of drought and locust infestations.

Haiti

In this region extreme poverty has been further exacerbated by a political crisis, floods, tropical storms, and hurricanes.

Horn of Africa

An estimated 11 million people in the Horn of Africa "are on the brink of starvation" because of severe drought and war. Somalia, Kenya, Djibouti and Ethiopia need food aid, water, new livestock and seeds. This is a major hunger crisis in development.

Afghanistan

Poverty in Afghanistan, made worse by drought, has contributed greatly to their hunger problem.

Pakistan

The recent earthquake coupled with a severe winter have produced starvation conditions. Recently, mudslides have hampered relief efforts.

North Korea

Food insecurity caused by the country's economic problems, is compounded by unpredictable and severe weather conditions. To date, the North Korean government has failed in its duty to provide for its starving people. The North Korean government has actually refused foreign aid.

Colombia

A 40-year civil conflict and the illegal drug trade have caused mass displacement and poverty.

Democratic Republic of Congo

Over 3.4 million people have been internally displaced as a result of a continuing internal conflict.

Mali

They are struggling to cope with the devastating impact of a recent drought.

Southern Africa

Erratic weather, lack of seed and fertilizer, chronic poverty, and AIDS have been contributing factors to starvation.

These are the areas of the world which are currently suffering the highest levels of malnutrition and hunger. With this understanding of where relief efforts are needed, we must address the question of individual response. Are individuals of developed countries donating to relief efforts? Most morally conscious individuals donate to relief efforts when the problem is presented to them.

A major problem in the relief effort is the general population of developed countries not knowing about the current hunger crisis. News organizations, more specifically television news, are not giving enough attention to the global hunger situation. While an in-depth discussion as to the reasons for this is outside the purview of this chapter, a few points can be made.

Evidently, the American TV news organizations do not think world hunger is much of a story since starvation is a daily occurrence. I suspect, from the perspective of these news organizations, that 24,000 people per day dying from hunger is not a big enough news story. When 1,386 people died from hurricane Katrina, the news coverage was enormous. Five months after hurricane Katrina hit New Orleans, TV news organizations were still squeezing all they could out of this story. Granted this was an obvious tragedy, but an even bigger tragedy, much bigger, is going on in Africa and the general public does not even know about it.

I have seen little to almost no coverage given by American TV news organizations on the devastating hunger crisis in the Horn of Africa. I have only learned of this crisis through RSS feeds on the Internet. Television news organizations such as CNN, ABC, CBS, and NBC are thus far not reporting on this crisis. Hopefully this will change.

It is evident that the American TV news organizations do not really provide total and complete news, rather they screen the events and only provide what they feel may be interesting to their audience. News organizations should present the news and concomitantly maintain high journalistic standards. Maybe these news organizations need to incorporate a higher level of moral obligation into their decision making process, when deciding which stories to cover. In any case, people can not donate if they do not know the problem exists.

We have addressed some key questions in order to characterize the current status of the world hunger situation. We have examined where hunger is the most prevalent in the world today, and we have identified some of the causative factors which contribute to malnutrition, hunger, and starvation. We have concluded that most morally conscious individuals would contribute to the elimination of hunger, if they knew about the crisis. Finally, we have observed that the degree of world hunger coverage by TV news organizations is very much lacking.

Even though TV news organizations have not been covering the current world hunger crisis, by reading this chapter, you have developed an understanding of the degree to which starvation is prevalent in the world today. If you are reading this in a developed country, which is highly likely since you are reading it on a computer which has Internet access, you have a moral obligation to donate either time or money to help in the elimination of unseen suffering. Winston Churchill once said "we make a living by what we get, but we make a life by what we give." We must all do our part to eliminate world hunger.

CHAPTER 5

THE MARKET PUSHES PRICES AND HUNGER

ANGER at rapidly rising food prices has now been surpassed in the U.S.A. by anger at the high cost of gas and getting to work. For the 2 billion ordinary people around the globe that live on less than $ 2 a day, the current global food crisis is having a huge impact. It is likely that more people will starve to death in the coming months than die as a result of all the current wars on the planet combined. How did this situation arise?

There has been a worldwide increase in prices in certain food commodities especially cereals, which are the staple foods for a huge proportion of the world's population. Primarily affected are wheat, corn, rice and soybeans. These price increases in turn are affecting the prices of other foods like dairy products and eggs. Slightly less affected at this point are the prices of meats and vegetables.

For example, globally, food prices have increased by 83 per cent in the past 36 months, with the greatest price increase happening since the summer of 2007.

Rice prices in Asia have increased two to threefold in the recent period and specifically doubled this year. Thai rice at the end of 2007 was $ 320 per metric ton, in May 2008 it was $ 1,100 per metric ton. In May of 2008, corn in the U.S.A. was priced at $ 5.50 a bushel, which is double the 2007 price and at the Minneapolis Grain Exchange in February wheat prices had quadrupled in one year to over $ 15 a bushel. Even food commodities that have primarily local markets have increased in price: lentils in India have increased from $ 300 to $ 800 per ton during this same period. In Burundi a product called farine noir, a combination of black flour and mouldy cassava, which is sold as a subsistence food to the very poor, saw its price triple in eight weeks.

In China, food inflation was estimated at about 18 per cent for last year. In the Middle East, which is a net food importer, the food import bill has increased 170 per cent since 2000. In Egypt and Yemen alone food prices have increased almost 60 per cent in one year. In Pakistan, food and beverage prices increased by over 20 per cent in March of 2008 alone.

WORLDWIDE STARVATION, INCREASED REVOLTS

The biggest impact from price increases are on the world's poorest people. There are many references to the 'world's bottom billion,' which is generally the population that lives on less than $ 1 per day and is currently about 880 million people. This is an arbitrary dividing line; in fact, 2.1 billion people live on less than $ 2 a day. The UN estimates that with the 2008 rise in food prices 100–13C million more people are at risk from hunger than they were eight months ago. In the world's underdeveloped countries the poorest people spend about 40–70 per cent of their incomes on food, compared to 10–15 per cent in the industrialized nations. It is clear how this food crisis is greater for those living in poverty.

In response to these dramatic price increases, there has been increased unrest in dozens of countries in the form of strikes and riots. Haiti, Egypt, Yemen and the Philippines have had some forms of rioting. In Haiti, the Prime Minister was forced to resign in response to the unrest over food prices. In Lebanon, a general strike was organized in response to price increases and calls for strikes in Egypt have been aggressively suppressed by the US-backed regime there.

Some countries, desperate to prevent food-related unrest, have introduced increased price controls for food. India and Vietnam, the No. 2 and No. 3 rice exporters in the world, have begun export restrictions. Also countries such as Argentina, China, Cambodia and Indonesia have introduced similar measures.

A MARKET PHENOMENA

India, under pressure from its population's rising anger, shut down its food futures markets to try to dampen price fluctuations. Indonesia, Thailand, and Cambodia are providing subsidized rice to their populations and the government of the Philippines has been buying up massive amounts of rice which it plans to provide to its population at a lower cost. However, when the Philippines government tried to buy up 500,000 tons of rice on the global market, only 300,000 tons were available for purchase.

ENERGY AND FOOD CRISIS CONVERGE

There are multiple reasons why food prices are increasing, primary among these is the increase in fuel costs. Currently oil is selling at about $ 135 a barrel, which has more than doubled since last year's high price. This is a huge additional expense for food production, especially for factory farming practices. These are very fuel-intense and highly mechanized, with the use of tractors and other heavy machinery. Also, with globalized food production, there is increased shipping of food around the globe, which is consuming more fuel. This is entirely a market-driven process. Food production is geared towards producing large volumes of food cheaply, which is then shipped to where they are most likely to be sold for the most profit.

This process increases the dependence on cash crops for many farmers in the developing world who hope to produce enough to make a meagre living for themselves. However, this makes many poor rural dwellers more vulnerable to the market. Inherent in capitalism's inequality, they will never be paid the full value of the food products they are producing, so they can never afford to buy back what they are producing. In areas where farm productivity is relatively low it is impossible for them to make enough income from what they produce to buy back enough basic food for themselves and their families. This just puts them at a further disadvantage compared to their counterparts in more developed countries whose farming techniques are more productive per acre: simply irrigating land doubles its productivity compared to non-irrigated land. In the U.S.A., farmers can often obtain a yield of 150 bushels of corn per acre, compared to farms in the underdeveloped world which average about 30 bushels per acre.

On top of increased fuel prices, there is increased demand for food worldwide. With rising economic growth in China and India swelling the ranks of the middle class in those countries, there is increased demand for meat. Every kilogram of beef produced requires 10 kilograms of grain, and each kilogram of pork requires about 4.16 This grain is being diverted to animal feed, or the land is being diverted away from human food production to animal food production.

FOOD FOR CARS

Other food crops, especially corn, and soy to a lesser extent, are also being diverted to biofuel production. In 2007, a record 13.1 billion bushels of corn was grown in the U.S.A. on 85 million acres; 22 per cent of that was diverted to ethanol production. U.S. farmers get a 51 cent tax credit per gallon of ethanol produced. The current farm bill in Congress will likely decrease this to 45 cents, but this is unlikely to have a major effect on the colossal production of ethanol from corn. This push for biofuels is a huge subsidy to big corn growers and not necessarily a greener source of fuel.

Increased demand for corn for biofuels will lead to diversion of land from growing other crops which will in turn increase the cost for animal feeds and other food production. The UN estimates that the diversion of corn to biofuels has already contributed 10 per cent to the current rise in food prices, while the IMF estimates it at 20-30 per cent. Patrick Schnable, an agronomy professor at Iowa State University made this point: "Crops will go to the highest bidder, and we in the Western world are willing to pay more for fuel than poor people are able to pay for food."

Global warming is also likely contributing a small amount to the price increase through the effects of climate change on changing crop patterns. An ongoing drought in Australia for the last few years has significantly decreased its wheat production.

Finally, financial speculation on food prices has also contributed to the increase. It is discounted as a significant factor in the capitalist press. They are very quick to rule it out as a possible contributor to escalating prices. However, in an interview with the *Financial Times,* the head of the UN Development Programme argued: "We are seeing excessively expansionary economic policies, just as we did when the dotcom bubble burst" and, "We face a new phenomenon of commodity prices going through the roof at a time of recession, or at least slowdown, in the advanced economies.... I cannot help feeling that liquidity in the system is looking for an outlet."

SPECULATION FUELS RUNAWAY PRICES

An important element of capitalism is that it always seeks to maximize its profits. The current housing and credit crisis means that real estate is not as attractive as a source of profits and consequently food futures have become more appealing. Food futures, which are the basis of this speculation, are when food is bought before it is harvested and delivered.

Those who buy the futures at one price can turn around and sell at whatever the market price is later. There is a huge speculative element in this, as those buying the food futures are hoping that food prices will rise. A senior grain analyst from a major Chicago trading company said: "I've never seen a rice (futures) market until this year in my three decades of trading grains."

Middlemen stand to make huge amounts of money, just as we have seen in recent years in the housing market. Grains are being stockpiled, not just by traders, but by governments, which fuels panic buying and further increases the mammoth potential for profiteering. Around Christmas of 2007, fuelled by the low dollar, investors staged a run on the U.S. wheat harvest. The price skyrocketed.

The Chairman of the Kansas City Board of Trade, said: "We have never seen anything like this before. Prices are going up more in one day than they have in entire years in the past. But no matter what the price there always seems to be a buyer... this isn't just any commodity. It is food, and people need to eat."

Meanwhile, according to the European Commission, two-thirds of the recent rise in food prices can be attributed to increased costs of ingredients. Bread increased 10 per cent between February 2007 and 2008, but doubling the price of wheat should only have led to a price increase of 3 per cent. From their report, "energy, transport, and labour costs have risen. But it is possible that somewhere along the food chain someone may be doing well out of this."

SHORT-TERM PERSPECTIVES

There is no perspective for a short-term decrease in food prices. None of the fundamental causes are likely to change soon. A *Financial Times* analyst argues, "prices are likely to remain relatively elevated, by historical standards, unless (or until) energy prices tumble."

It is hard to imagine any perspective of energy prices tumbling. Energy is likely to continue to become more expensive. This will, in turn, increase worldwide suffering, poverty, starvation and social unrest, particularly in the under-developed world, but capitalism will continue to push to maximize profits as long as it can get away with it.

Increased prices of their commodities will still fail to help poor cash crop farmers, and the general price increases will only make it harder for them. In fact, the UN notes that "we have been saying Africans cannot grow food or cotton because of low world prices, in a sense, there is an opportunity here. But on the negative side you have to remember that higher energy prices affect the prices of fertilizer and other inputs. Farmers cannot produce more because the inputs are so expensive."

Once again we are facing the undeniable fact of capitalism that there will always be an underclass, and those on the bottom need to stay on the bottom for capitalism to maximize its profits.

CAPITALISM'S ALTERNATIVE

Capitalism's solutions to the global food crisis would be aimed at the preservation of the market and maintaining maximum profits. Their answers would include an increased use and reliance on genetically modified foods. In Japan, where the population has a deep aversion to genetically modified foods, manufacturers have started importing GM foods for use in processed foods for the first time.

The capitalists will push also to eliminate subsidies and tariffs to decrease regulations and allow the market to 'work things out.' This will be at the expense of poor countries and to the benefit of richer ones. Big Business will also push to increase production per acre, which is more energy and water intensive, more chemically reliant, more destructive to the environment, and ultimately unsustainable.

The market is driven by profits and ignores the needs of humanity. It depends on and perpetuates massive imbalances and inequality worldwide. To solve the global food crisis the market system itself must be destroyed. In the midst of rising global food prices there is also extreme global caloric imbalances with massive levels of starvation in the underdeveloped world and unprecedented levels of obesity in the developed world. Calories are put into the global market place and then they follow the Dollar or Euros. In the developed world it is common to throw food calories away. Bulimics flush them down the toilet, while others exercise hard to get rid of them. Capitalism pushes them our way and we are desperate to get rid of them. Meanwhile, there is brutal starvation and malnutrition across the entire globe. As long as the market exists the imbalance will continue.

We also need to focus on decreasing consumption in developed nations, not just of unnecessary calories, but also of consumer goods. A change in lifestyles will decrease the general strain on global resources, making more resources available for food production.

SOCIALISM, DEMOCRACY AND ENDING THE MARKET

By replacing capitalism with democratic Socialism we can begin to plan food production according to the needs of people worldwide and with a better understanding of resources worldwide to try to decrease the global shipping of food. This may mean any of the following: do we eat foods only when they are locally in season? Do we only eat foods grown in our geographic area? Do we discourage development in places such as deserts where there is inadequate soil and water to produce enough food to support large populations? Do we try to increase food production within urban areas. These questions need to be discussed, and will only be seriously taken up once the market itself is eliminated.

Cuba, after the fall of the Soviet Union, lost access to cheap Soviet oil, and essentially became close to a post-petroleum economy. As combine harvesters were left to rust, wheat production collapsed and the caloric intake of Cubans also collapsed. In response, the Stalinist regime led the development of infill urban organic gardens all over the island. These were able to produce a massive increase in food for the population. Local organic gardens in Havana supply 90 per cent of all the fruit and vegetables consumed by the city's two million residents. Similarly, where lawns were abandoned for agriculture during World War II, Victory Gardens provided the U.S.A. with 40 per cent of all its vegetables.

We can see that under democratic socialist planning there is a perspective to better provide for the world's food needs in a way that capitalism has failed to do. Big business will never be able to feed the world because the profit motive can never be separated from capitalism.

CHAPTER 6

MAJOR HURDLES TO FOOD SUFFICIENCY

MOST countries, democratic or otherwise, give at least lip credence to providing food, shelter and livelihood to all their citizens. However, *access to food,* strangely enough, is still more a privilege than a basic human right. It is estimated that about 35,000 people around the world die each day from hunger. An even larger number of people (mainly women, children, and the elderly) suffer from malnutrition.

Despite breakthrough technology advances in agriculture and optimum modern parameters being set up for distribution and production of food, hunger and malnutrition are on the increase, even in advanced industrialized countries like Canada, where each year an estimated 2.5 million people depend on food banks. About 30 million people in the United States are reported to be unable to buy enough food to maintain good health. The continuing reality of hunger and the unsustainability of current practices, both locally and globally, make food security an essential concern.

The United Nations Food and Agriculture Organization's (FAO's) definition of food security is widely accepted:

> "Food security" means that food is available at all times; that all persons have means of access to it; that it is nutritionally adequate in terms of quantity, quality and variety; and that it is acceptable within the given culture. Only when all these conditions are in place can a population be considered "food secure."

In recent years, most of the research initiatives for food security have focused on the four key components of the FAO's definition:

1. **Availability**—Providing an adequate supply of food for all people at all times has historically been a major challenge. Although technical and scientific innovations have made important contributions focused on quantity and economies of scale, little attention has been paid to making such practices sustainable in the long-term.

2. **Accessibility**—The equality of access to food is a dimension of food security. Intra- and inter-societies, there have been wide inequities which have resulted in serious entitlement problems, reflecting class, gender, ethnic, racial, and age differentials, as well as national and regional gaps in development. Most measures to provide emergency food aid have attempted to help the disadvantaged but, despite efforts, have not been able to change the structural conditions that perpetuate such inequities.

3. **Acceptability**—As essential ingredients in human health and well-being, food and food practices reflect the social and cultural diversity of humanity. Efforts to provide food without paying attention to the symbolic role of food in people's lives have failed to solve food-security problems. This dimension of food security is also important in determining whether information and food-system innovations will be accepted in a country, given the social and ecological concerns of its citizens.

4. **Adequacy**—Food security also requires that suitable and adequate measures are put in place at all levels of the food system to guarantee the sustainability of production, distribution, consumption and waste management. A sustainable food system should help to satisfy basic human needs, without compromising the ability of future generations to meet their needs. It must therefore maintain ecological integrity and integrate conservation and development.

Unfortunately, a number of global economic and ecological problems continue to limit the prospect of global food security. World per capita cereal production (62 per cent of least-developed countries' food consumption), for example, has been increasing only marginally in recent years. In fact, it has even been on the decline in sub-Saharan Africa and in Latin America and the Caribbean, particularly in low-income countries struck by economic reforms, natural and other disasters and other factors. The LDCs' dependence on net food imports has been growing and is set to continue to grow; currently, 104 of 132 LDCs are net importers, although imports have brought little relief overall.

In sub-Saharan Africa, the number of chronically undernourished people more than doubled in 1970–91, notwithstanding that this region depended on food aid for half its total food imports. The population of this region is expected to more than double by 2020.

Regional and global economic crises and chronic problems of underdevelopment make the situation particularly bad in the developing world. The overall mean per capita income of so-called Black Africa, for example, is, maximally, no higher than it was in 1960, and the region has less weight in the global economy today than it did in the 1960s. Economic ad-hocism clearly leads to an economy's disintegration. Real prices in domestic food markets have increased over the last few years and are set to increase further. To improve food security and global food supplies, policy scenarios of the 2020 Vision Initiative require increased exports of staple foods from industrialized countries to the LDCs. But insufficient purchasing power among the world's poorest 800 million people remains a primary obstacle to such strategies.

Multilateral agreements in trade and investment further threaten the availability and accessibility of food for large segments of the world's population. Many experts agree that the reduction in world surpluses and the increase in international prices encouraged by the Uruguay Round of the General Agreement on Tariffs and Trade posed a real threat to regions already suffering severe food insecurity. Currently, however, in the latest round of WTO talks, the poorer countries are finding support from many countries, especially the BRIC countries, for their demand for a more just social order.

Global prospects for improving food security are further threatened by environmental limitations on production increases, even in Green Revolution countries, and by growing poverty. In Asia, a large share of the population will soon be without access to adequate food supplies. So, despite the technical modernization of food production and distribution, hunger and malnutrition still undermine the health and well-being of millions of people and actually seem to be worsening, particularly among low-income urban residents. This led Dr. Uwe Werblow of the European Commission in Brussels to recommend favouring production of more traditional food crops in rural areas and developing non-land-using production in semi-urban and urban areas.

FOOD SECURITY AND URBAN POPULATIONS

Although the consequences are visible, as far as urban populations are concerned, it is difficult to realistically pinpoint the causes and scope of food-security problems. From production to consumption, the food system comprises complex interrelated and interdependent parts: social and economic elements, agencies, processes, and structures. Their interdependent relationship requires a structural and systemic analysis focusing on global as well as local linkages.

The rural-urban and local-global interrelationships make it impossible to study urban food-security issues in isolation. Yet, it is also clear that the extraordinary urban growth, which started in the latter decades of the 20th century and is still continuing, poses increasing threats to the food security for millions of urban dwellers. The scope and urgency of the problems require analyses of food-security questions for urban areas and new policies and practices to encourage the adoption of sustainable urban food systems.

Food security has become an increasing concern of urban populations. Four major challenges can be identified. First, urban centres have expanded enormously in population and in size. In the late 20th century, urban growth reached unprecedented levels in most parts of the world. In the last three decades of the century alone, the urban population in developed countries, doubled from 448 million in 1950 to 875 million in 1990. In the same period, the urban population in developing countries more than quintupled from 280 million to 1.6 billion. In 1990, over 33 per cent of the world's urban population was living in cities with 1 million or more inhabitants.

By the end of the century, six of the largest cities were found in the developing world. Having urban settlements approaching 30 million people will strain already overburdened services in countries with limited resources and extreme income inequalities. Urban expansion has converted a significant portion of green space and good-quality, often scarce, agricultural land. It has already increased water and air pollution and created serious waste-disposal problems. Also, speculative land markets, and soil and water contamination, have created obstacles to effective local food systems and urban agriculture.

Another obstacle lies in the inequality of access. Poverty has always been largely a rural phenomenon. Yet, as the majority of the world's population moves to urban areas, there has been a reversal in the regional distribution of poverty. World Bank figures indicated that in 1988 about 25 per cent of the poorest segments of the developing world were living in urban areas. The World Bank also had estimated that by 2000 this would reach 50 per cent. In developing countries, the numbers of the urban poor have risen as a result of such factors as the continuous migration of the rural poor into the cities, the limited ability of the urban informal sector to absorb the unemployed, the inadequate employment opportunities in formal labour markets, negative impacts of the global economic crisis and the austerity measures adopted to deal with foreign debt.

In Eastern Europe and the industrialized West the situation is not much better. A decline in full-time, secure, well-paid employment (the result of economic downsizing), the dismantling of the welfare state and social programmes, and the feminization of poverty have turned urban poverty into a truly global phenomenon.

Most analysts claim that the increase in poverty has been the biggest threat to food security. Unfortunately, most of the solutions have been limited to patchwork remedies, such as food banks, food aid, and similar emergency responses. There are no long-term strategies in evidence, on the ground, to enhance food security, perhaps because of the serious negative impact of the present insecurity which demands immediate short-term sops.

Overcoming the inability of the existing market and service agencies to respond to the highly diverse social and cultural mosaic of the urban population is also a major problem. The complexity of cities—the multiplicity of their class, gender, ethnic, and demographic characteristics and their corresponding needs and access problems—have led to new challenges to attempts to enhance urban food security. Although the markets and traditional service agencies target certain 'consumers,' thousands of others are marginalized.

Food retail chains often ignore poor neighbourhoods in the North and South alike and the location of bulk-produce stores in suburbs limits the access of smaller families, elderly people, people with disabilities and those who depend on public transport. The diversity of food practices arising from most cities' complex ethnic composition also creates distinct access problems. Unfortunately, most retailers, food banks, and public-service agencies fail to respond to the unique traditions and demands of cultural minorities and thereby pressure people into making significant dietary changes to conform to what the dominant food system makes available.

THE DANGERS OF GLOBALISATION

Another obstacle in the path of ensuring food security is the growing 'commodification' and globalization of the agrifood system. The majority of people in urban populations have very little understanding of how their food is produced, transported, processed, or distributed. The dominant structures of production, distribution, and marketing of food often ignore local solutions for efficient and accessible production and distribution.

Although the global food system claims to offer more choice at an affordable cost for the individual consumer, it has actually created obstacles for more sustainable local food systems. In many places, even during the season, locally grown foods tend to be more expensive or more difficult to find than those shipped in from thousands of miles away.

Often, food grown locally is exported while thousands of local residents may be enduring hunger and malnutrition. Questions can be (and have been) raised about the long-term economic, ecological, and political sustainability of the so-called success of the current food system, with its global division of labour, commodified food economy, increasing regional specialization, industrialized agriculture, and transcontinental networks of distribution.

Among the fiercest, and first, critics of the globalisation of agriculture is Vandana Shiva. Dr. Shiva is Director of the Research Foundation for Science, Technology and Natural Resource Policy in New Delhi, India, and winner of the Alternate Nobel (The Right Livelihood Award) in 1993. Over the past decade and a half she has vociferously attacked *laissez faire* policies in food and agriculture and her arguments have been acknowledged to have considerable force. The rest of this chapter is largely based on her arguments condemning globalisation in food.

Trade liberalisation and the globalisation of agriculture is supposed to increase the production of food and improve the economic situation of farmers across the world. However, in country after country the process is leading to a decline in food production and productivity, a decline in conditions for farmers and a decline in food security for consumers. Globalisation is deepening food insecurity the world over.

The globalisation of agriculture is in fact merely the commercialisation of agriculture. According to Kristin Dawkins, Director of the Research Institute for Agriculture and Trade Policy of the United States, the U.S. government has led the world in promoting globalised monopolies through international trade agreements, assisted by such arm-twisting tactics as the unilateral leveraging of its vast markets. Under encouragement from the U.S. government, says Dawkins, the food corporations controlling U.S. agriculture are attempting to control world agriculture.

This corporatisation of agriculture, which is being pushed as a successor to the Green Revolution of the 1960s and 1970s, is leading to new areas of poverty for small farmers, as unequal and unfair contracts lock them into a new form of bondage. Farmers in the Indian state of Punjab contracted by Pepsico to grow tomatoes received only 0.75 rupees per kilo, while the market price was 2.00 rupees. First the farmers rejected Pepsico and Pepsico then abandoned Punjab, selling its tomato processing plant to a subsidiary of Levers.

The liberalisation of agriculture can be either external or internal. External liberalisation is driven by foreign trade and foreign investment; it serves external interests. Agricultural liberalisation under the IMF's structural adjustment programmes is an example of such external liberalisation. It includes liberalising fertiliser imports and deregulating the domestic manufacture and distribution of fertilisers; the removal of subsidies on irrigation, electricity and credit; the deregulation of the wheat, rice, sugarcane, cotton and oilseed industries; and the dismantling of the food security system. These elements are recipes for concentrating control over agriculture in the hands of transnational agribusiness corporations such as Cargill and Pepsico.

Internal liberalisation liberates agriculture for ecological sustainability and social justice. It includes freeing agriculture from high external inputs such as chemical fertilisers and pesticides, making a transition instead to sustainable agriculture based on internal inputs for ecological sustainability. It means freeing farmers from debt and the fear of dispossession, whether of land, water or biodiversity. It means freeing peasants from landlessness, freeing rural people from water scarcity by ensuring inalienable and equitable water rights, freeing the poor from the spectre of starvation and rebuilding local markets and local food security.

The globalisation of agriculture is violating all these components of food-related human rights. The rights of small producers to land, water and biodiversity are being violated by undoing land reform, by the privatisation of water and the monopolisation of seed and plant resources. The ecological rights of the people are being violated by the spread of ecologically destructive industrial and factory farming methods.

THE BOTTOM LINE

Everywhere across the world less food is being produced and less diverse food is being grown, and less is reaching the poor and hungry. Fewer farmers are finding a place in agriculture, and even privileged consumers have no food security in the sense of access to safe and nutritious food.

The centralised and chemical-intensive production and distribution system linked with the Green Revolution model has proved itself to be undemocratic, wasteful and non-sustainable. The globalisation of corporate agriculture is aggravating all the problems linked with the centralised system of food production and distribution. It is increasing the use of chemicals through conventional methods as well as by genetic engineering. It is increasing transport and 'food miles', and fuelling food insecurity through climate change. It is promoting the mining of water and soil fertility by putting profitability above sustainability. It is giving primacy to trade and undermining domestic production.

CHAPTER 7

BROAD STRATEGIES

THE current world food and agricultural policy system is in disarray. The symptoms include incoherent or inadequate responses to exploding food prices; the slowdown in agricultural productivity growth; looming water problems; a disorderly response to higher energy prices; rapid concentration in multinational agribusiness corporations without the necessary institutional innovation to guide them; lack of progress in addressing scarcity; adverse impacts of climate change on agriculture; widespread nutrition problems, including hunger, obesity, and chronic diseases; and agriculture-related health risks, such as avian influenza.

THE GLOBAL OUTLOOK

Governments and international institutions have notoriously underinvested in public goods related to agriculture, food, and nutrition, such as rural infrastructure, agricultural research and rural institutions, which have international spillover effects and global impact. National policies are central, but the increasing globalization of the agrifood system calls for collaboration across country borders to adequately address new opportunities and challenges.

The world food system that has evolved over recent decades has not effectively achieved food safety, good health and sound nutrition for the poor and hungry. Improved institutional architecture and governance is needed to ensure that the following functions in the agriculture, food, and nutrition system operate effectively and efficiently at the global level:

1. Research, innovation, and intellectual property rights (IPRs);
2. Trade and standards;

3. Food safety and health;
4. Private investment and competition policy;
5. Climate change, adaptation, and mitigation;
6. Cross-boundary water management; and
7. Natural resource use related to, for instance, soils and biodiversity.

For most of these functions, some institutions, conventions, declarations, and organizations already exist. But there is ample room for scaling them up, efficiently coordinating them or increasing their effectiveness. Current global investments in these areas, so vital for the international community, are clearly suboptimal.

Too little research and development (R&D) is taking place on the crops and technologies of most interest to poor farmers. Trade policies and standards are in some cases harming poor countries' capacity to develop their own agricultural systems. Food safety standards are not sufficiently harmonized. The absence of appropriate international institutions to guide competition has resulted in non-competitive markets and trade behaviour, private and public, at the global level. The world is investing far too little in mitigating and adapting to climate change in agriculture. Cross-boundary disputes over water are almost certain to become worse in the future as resources come under increasing pressure. And patterns of natural resource use too often pose threats to the global commons, such as biodiversity.

The roles and structures of the global organizations addressing agriculture, food, and related health issues, the Food and Agriculture Organization of the United Nations (FAO), the World Food Programme (WFP), the International Fund for Agricultural Development (IFAD), the World Health Organization (WHO), the World Bank, the World Trade Organization (WTO), and the Consultative Group on International Agricultural Research (CGIAR), have evolved over the past six decades. Individually, they all serve important functions, but collectively they may now require rethinking and adjustment to meet new and emerging challenges related to agriculture, food, and nutrition in a comprehensive fashion in the coming decades.

THE HARD OPTIONS

For a worthwhile debate on the future global institutional architecture and governance of agriculture, food and nutrition, it is necessary to find answers to some important questions. These are:

1. If we were to design a global governance system for agriculture, food, and nutrition, what would it look like?
2. How should the governance system be designed so that it can adapt well to the changing needs for global public goods in the future?
3. What type of structure should the international governance system have?
4. How should the current governance system be reformed?
5. What are the roles of the different actors, including new actors such as the private sector and civil society, in a future global governance system for agriculture, food, and nutrition?
6. How would the system of existing international organizations, including their structure and interrelationships, be changed?
7. What role should the United Nations (UN), the Group of 8, and various groups of developing countries play in such a reform process?

THERE ARE THREE OPTIONS—NOT MUTUALLY EXCLUSIVE—FOR CHANGE

The first option is to maintain the current institutions and make marginal improvements. This option could involve, for example, strengthening the UN and CGIAR systems for agriculture, food, and nutrition in terms of their effectiveness, their governance, and their resources, as they are clearly under-funded.

The second option is to form an innovative government network, that is, to strengthen government-to-government systems for decision-making in the areas of agriculture, food and nutrition through a set of agreements and conventions. More structured networks could be created between institutions within governments. Such steps are beginning to be taken in some fields, such as public health, but not much in the areas of agriculture, food, and nutrition.

A third option is to expand the current system to explicitly engage the new players in the global food system, the private sector and civil society, including large private foundations, together with national governments in new or significantly reorganized international organizations and agreements. Given that the global food system is in reality no longer governed only by governments, this inclusive approach seems worthwhile now.

The three options cover the gamut from realistic to utopian. Moving forward may require a combination of these three options. One approach to implementation might be to establish a superstructure (for example, a panel appointed by the UN leadership) to guide changes in the global governance of agriculture, food and nutrition across the existing specialized institutions and organizations. To obtain a meaningful synthesis of the three options will require leadership on the part of the governments of the world. Countries with leading roles in the global agricultural system now go beyond just European nations and the United States to include Brazil, China, India, and others. Leadership could well come from the developing countries and not only the largest ones.

It is clearly time to re-examine the global architecture and system for governing agriculture, food, and nutrition to determine how best to address the challenges the world now faces. Small adjustments will not achieve the needed changes. The ultimate goal must be to quickly come closer to a world that provides each person with enough food, on a sustainable basis, to live a healthy and productive life as envisioned in the Millennium Development Goals. The current system does not live up to this task. The leading global organizations involved with agriculture, food, and nutrition themselves should explore these issues further and invite a global dialogue for change.

THE NATIONAL OUTLOOK

Various countries have already taken a number of steps to try to minimize the effects of higher prices on their populations. Argentina, Bolivia, Cambodia, China, Egypt, Ethiopia, India, Indonesia, Kazakhstan, Mexico, Morocco, Russia, Thailand, Ukraine, Venezuela, and Vietnam are among those that have taken the easy option of restricting food exports, setting limits on food prices, or both.

For example, China has banned rice and maize exports; India has banned milk powder exports and imposed heavy export duties on rice and other food products; Bolivia has banned the export of soy oil to Chile, Colombia, Cuba, Ecuador, Peru, and Venezuela; and Ethiopia has banned exports of major cereals. Other countries are reducing restrictions on imports: Morocco has reduced tariffs on wheat imports from 130 per cent to 2.5 per cent; Nigeria cut its rice import tax from 100 per cent to just 2.7 per cent.

How effective are these responses likely to be? Price controls and changes in import and export policies may to some extent address the immediate problems of poor consumers who find that they can no longer afford an adequate diet for a healthy life. But some of these policies are also likely to boomerang by reducing the boundaries of the global market and, thus, add volatility to it. Price controls reduce the price that farmers receive for their agricultural products and thus reduce their motivation to produce more food. Any long-term strategy to stabilize food prices *must* include increased agricultural production, but price controls push farmers to produce less. In addition, by benefiting all consumers, even those who can afford higher food prices, blanket price controls divert resources towards even the affluent who do not really need it. In the process, the target group, the poor, gets less than it needs.

Export restrictions and import subsidies have harmful effects on trading partners dependent on imports and also give incorrect incentives to farmers by reducing their potential market size. These national agricultural trade policies weaken the benefits of global integration, as the rich countries' longstanding trade distortions with regard to developing countries are joined by developing countries' interventions against each other.

POLICIES NEEDED FOR SHORT- AND LONG-TERMS

The increases in food prices have a dominant role in increasing inflation in many countries now. It would be injudicious to address these specific inflation causes with general macroeconomic instruments. Specific policies are needed to deal with the causes and consequences of high food prices. Although the current situation poses policy challenges on several fronts, there are effective and coherent actions that can be taken to help the most vulnerable people in the short-term while working to stabilize food prices by increasing agricultural production in the long-term.

In the short run, developing country governments should expand social protection programmes (that is, safety net programmes like food or income transfers and nutrition initiatives focused on children) for the poorest people—both urban and rural. Some of the poorest people in developing countries are not well connected to markets and thus will feel few effects from rising food prices, but the much higher international prices could mean serious hardship for millions of poor urban consumers and rural residents who are net food buyers, when they actually are exposed to them.

These people need direct assistance. Some countries, such as India and South Africa, already have social protection programmes in place that they can be expanded to meet new and emerging needs. Countries that do not have such programmes in place will not be able to create them rapidly enough to make a difference in the current food price situation. They may feel forced to rely on cruder measures like export bans and import subsidies. Aid donors should expand food-related development aid, including social protection, child nutrition programmes and food aid, where needed.

Next, developed countries should eliminate domestic biofuel subsidies and open their markets to biofuel exporters like Brazil. Biofuel subsidies in the United States and ethanol and biodiesel subsidies in Europe have proven to be ill-advised policies that have distorted world food markets. Subsidies on biofuel crops also act as an implicit tax on staple foods, on which the poor depend the most. Developed country farmers should make decisions about what to cultivate based not on subsidies, but on world market prices for various commodities.

Also, the developed countries should take this opportunity to eliminate agricultural trade barriers. Although some progress has been made in reducing agricultural subsidies and other trade-distorting policies in developed countries, many remain, and poor countries cannot match them. This issue has been politically difficult for developed country policymakers to address, but the political risks may now be lower than in the past. A level playing field for developing country farmers will make it more profitable for them to increase production in response to higher prices.

To achieve long-term agricultural growth, developing-country governments should increase their medium and long-term investments in agricultural research and extension, rural infrastructure, and market access for small farmers. Rural investments have been sorely neglected in recent decades, and now is the time to reverse this trend. Farmers in many developing countries are operating in an environment of inadequate infrastructure such as roads, electricity and communications; poor soils; lack of storage and processing capacity; and little or no access to agricultural technologies that could increase their profits and improve their livelihoods.

The growing unrest over food prices in a number of countries may tempt policymakers to put the interests of urban consumers over those of rural people, including farmers, but this approach would be short-sighted and counterproductive. Given the scale of investment needed, aid donors should also expand development assistance to agriculture, rural services and science and technology.

Food being an essential part of life, food security concerns require public awareness. In these last years of the first decade of the second millennium, public awareness has increased drastically. Unfortunately, this resulted not from prior warnings of scientists and agricultural administrators of the growing threats to global food security but to the actual onset of the tragic consequences of food insecurity – growing poverty, lack of access or affordability to nutritious food, sweeping and rapid rise in the price of food items and commercialization of the production, distribution and delivery of foodgrains.

It is now very clear that ushering in food security cannot be left to the vagaries of the market. There has to be public regulation. To be fair, the *laissez faire* food system has had remarkable achievements to its credit. However, it has been at the cost of fairness and sustainability of the system. The food security needs, especially of urban populations, will require comprehensive government intervention to avoid catastrophe. To avert disaster, it is essential to be prepared and understand the nature of the problems and the available solutions, even if it is rather late in the day.

A large number of concerns and solutions have been presented by scientists, social scientists and administrators. Among them:

- ⌘ Local food systems often offer long-term sustainable solutions for improving the environment and for local and regional development. By linking the productive activities in the surrounding bioregion to the consumers in metropolitan centres, local food systems can reduce greenhouse gases and other pollutants caused by long distance haulage and storage. They can also reduce the vulnerability of food supply systems to the impacts of weather and market related supply problems of distant producers; offer greater choice through regional variations in biodiversity; provide fresher and more nutritious products in season; allow more effective regional control of quality and chemical inputs and create the potential for local development and employment opportunities. A regional or national network of local food systems does not necessarily diminish the possible advantages of the global food system for food security; rather, it enhances these advantages.

- ⌘ Cities need to encourage urban and semi urban agriculture, aquaculture, forestry and animal husbandry, as well as safe waste recycling; all elements of self reliant local food system initiative.

- ⌘ Food and non-feed production can tap idle resources and, through income and savings, improve food security, local employment and urban resource management. From a food democracy perspective, one's right to food must include the right to feed oneself. Future plans for the flexible, creative and combined use of urban space and form need to include permanent and temporary food production within metropolitan regions and create land reserves for productive green space (see Appendix II: Food Security and Human Rights).

⌘ Cities and metropolitan regions need to give priority to the availability and accessibility of food and develop their own food security plans as part of their social and economic planning. Food policy councils should be formed to advise local governments and planners.

⌘ Food banks and other community assistance programmes should only be relied upon as emergency measures, rather than institutionalising them as permanent mechanisms for food access. Food banks often serve two goals: to assist low income consumers and to distribute surplus food. To reduce poverty and inequities in access, structural measures need to be undertaken to provide long-term food security. At the same time, mechanisms for distribution of surplus food can be developed to respond to specific community needs, without stigmatizing the poor.

CHAPTER 8

MILLENNIUM DEVELOPMENT GOALS

'THE MDGs are still achievable if we act now. This will require inclusive sound governance, increased public investment, economic growth, enhanced productive capacity, and the creation of decent work.'

– United Nations Secretary General Ban-Ki Moon

THIS comment was made by the UN Secretary General in 2008. He could have added that had countries performed better in attaining the Millennium Development Goals, today's food security crisis may have been of much less critical proportion. While the first Goal directly connects to food security, the ramifications of the problem indicate that many of the other Goals are also critical, to a higher or lesser degree, to the attainment of food security. An audit of how countries affected by the food security crisis faired in achieving the targets is provided in Appendix I.

The Millennium Development Goals (MDGs) are eight goals to be achieved by 2015 that respond to the world's main development challenges. The MDGs are drawn from the actions and targets contained in the Millennium Declaration that was adopted by 189 nations and signed by 147 heads of state and governments during the UN Millennium Summit in September 2000. The targets are benchmarked to 1990.

The eight MDGs break down into 18 quantifiable targets that are measured by 48 indicators.

Goal 1: Eradicate extreme poverty and hunger

Goal 2: Achieve universal primary education

Goal 3: Promote gender equality and empower women
Goal 4: Reduce child mortality
Goal 5: Improve maternal health
Goal 6: Combat HIV/AIDS, malaria and other diseases
Goal 7: Ensure environmental sustainability
Goal 8: Develop a Global Partnership for Development.

The eight Goals are a package in themselves; no single Goal is fully achievable unless the others are achieved in whole or in part. The first Goal, by implication, embraces global food security.

The MDGs, while synthesising in a single package many of the most important commitments made separately at the international conferences and summits of the 1990s, recognise explicitly the interdependence between growth, poverty reduction and sustainable development; they acknowledge that development rests on the foundations of democratic governance, the rule of law, respect for human rights and peace and security.

IMPLEMENTATION OF THE MDGS

In 2001, in response to the world leaders' request, UN Secretary General presented the 'Road Map Towards the Implementation of the United Nations Millennium Declaration', an integrated and comprehensive overview of the situation, outlining potential strategies for action designed to meet the goals and commitments of the Millennium Declaration.

The road map has been followed up since then with annual reports. In 2002, the annual report focused on progress made in the prevention of armed conflict and the treatment and prevention of diseases, including HIV/AIDS and Malaria.

In 2003, emphasis was placed on strategies for development and strategies for sustainable development. In 2004, it was on bridging the digital divide and curbing transnational crime.

In 2005, the Secretary-General prepared the first comprehensive five-yearly report on progress towards achieving the MDGs The report reviews the implementation of decisions taken at the international conferences and special sessions on the least developed countries, progress on HIV/AIDS and financing for development and sustainable development.

The first Millennium Development Goal (MDG) sets targets for poverty and hunger. In contrast to the bewildering variety of definitions of poverty adopted in country strategies, the benchmark for hunger is consistently based on an average daily intake of 2,100 kilocalories.

Where groups of people are coping below this threshold, they are food insecure and will experience the symptoms of malnutrition, that is, impaired ability to learn or to work, and reduced resistance to disease. Hunger is therefore a cause as well as a consequence of poverty.

In adopting a target to reduce by half the proportion of people experiencing hunger by 2015, governments signing the Millennium Declaration were overriding a commitment made just four years earlier at the World Food Summit of 1996 which applied the same target to the number of people. Rising population figures mean that 170 million fewer people will be targeted by the MDG programme than would otherwise have been the case.

The MDG progress report published in 2005 was pessimistic about the prospects for achieving the hunger-related Goal, an assessment that was found true over the past three years. Rapid progress over two decades to the early 1990s has ground to a halt to the extent that hunger is currently increasing by about 4 million people each year.

'The State of Food Insecurity in the World 2006', published by the Food and Agriculture Organization (FAO), identifies 32 countries of particular concern, where prevalence of hunger is 42 per cent and average calorie intake is lower than it was 30 years ago.

Amongst the success stories, Ghana has reduced the prevalence of hunger from 37 per cent to 12 per cent over the MDG period; Ethiopia and Mozambique have also been commended for their relative recovery from desperate situations.

Although Sub-Saharan Africa has proportionately the greatest food insecurity with 33 per cent of its people undernourished, many countries in South Asia appear to be moving backwards.

Food security in rural India has deteriorated over the last 10 years with wheat production falling and the largest number (212 million) of undernourished people in the world—this in a country trumpeted as a modern economic powerhouse. Likewise, China's economic miracle is yet to reach out to 150 million hungry citizens.

A discussion of the various factors affecting food security is appropriate here in that they are intimately related to the Millennium Development Goals.

CLIMATE CHANGE AND FOOD SECURITY

Surprisingly, neither the MDG, nor the FAO report, makes any reference to climate change. Yet the 'Intergovernmental Panel on Climate Change (IPCC) Working Group 2007' report paints an almost cataclysmic picture in which 'for even small temperature increases of 1–2 degrees, access to food in many African countries is projected to be severely compromised by climate variability and change. In some countries, yields for rainfed agriculture could be reduced by up to 50 per cent by 2020. As well as falling yields in hotter temperatures, agriculture will suffer from the predicted increase in drought and floods, already a serious short-term cause of food insecurity. In South Asia, climate change threatens to upset the stable monsoon pattern around which farming has evolved.

At the global level, adaptation of agriculture to climate change will typically involve selection of alternative crops, revised planting dates, improved irrigation and modified chemical inputs. Investment on this scale however is likely to be beyond the poorest countries, whose economies are predominantly dependent on agriculture. For this reason they 'will be hit earliest and most severely', according to the UK Stern Review Report published in 2006.

Developing countries are instead undertaking National Adaptation Programmes of Actions (NAPAs) as directed by the UN Framework Convention on Climate Change. Recognising the urgency of the situation and the limited capacity for major adjustment programmes, NAPAs focus on community-based low-cost options for dealing with climate variability.

BIOTECHNOLOGY AND GM CROPS

Climate change is not the only seemingly unstoppable force assailing developing countries in their search for food security. Scientific advances in agriculture have brought great benefits, notably in the 'green revolution' originating in the 1970s. However, unlike the green revolution which was largely driven by state funding, today's biotechnology puts seed management and patents in the hands of a small number of very large international companies, such as Monsanto, Dow and Syngenta.

One consequence has been a rapid decline in food crop varieties as favoured seeds are mass-marketed. Industrial crops are now limited to about 150 varieties, rendering superfluous the inherited local wisdom acquired over generations. The implications of the loss of biodiversity in both seeds and local ecosystems, for resistance to disease or climate change, are uncertain.

Genetically-modified (GM) crops, in which a gene of desired characteristic is transposed from one plant to another, are the most extreme and controversial output of the biotechnology companies. Offering higher yields, lower chemical inputs and higher nutritional value, GM crops sound like the panacea to food insecurity. The snag is that under the current global regime of intellectual property rights, local farmers lose control over their own produce. There are doubts as to whether developing countries have the capacity to establish regulatory frameworks to manage inevitable conflicts of interests between the local stakeholders (farmers, consumers and governments) and global shareholders.

Governments therefore face difficult policy decisions to achieve food security. Led by Brazil, South Africa, China and India, the majority of developing countries have adopted GM crops, accounting for over 40 per cent of world production. The African Union endorses the technology as does the Alliance for the Green Revolution in Africa, the $ 150 million programme announced jointly by the Bill and Melinda Gates Foundation and the Rockefeller Foundation. Worries about contamination and the wider loss of biodiversity have enhanced the importance of local seed banks now established by many developing countries to protect their national assets.

BIOFUELS AND FOOD SECURITY

Production of petrol additives such as ethanol and biodiesel from plant crops has surged in popularity as a means of reducing dependence on fossil fuels and cutting carbon dioxide emissions. The EU has announced that these biofuels will contribute 10 per cent of transport fuels by 2020 and both U.S.A. and China have similar targets.

The consequence is that land and crops, which might otherwise contribute to global food security will be devoted to satisfying travel-rich Western lifestyles. By coincidence, the number of vehicles in the world, 800 million, is almost the same as the number of undernourished people in developing countries, but the similarity ends there. One tank of ethanol for a Sports Utility Vehicle consumes corn that could feed a man for a year.

As with GM crops, it is possible that biofuel production could benefit developing countries, but the U.S.A. holds the purse-strings to a global biofuel economy. Bottom line politics will underpin the payment of subsidies to U.S. corn farmers and impose tariffs on the more efficient sugar-based ethanol, such as that produced in Brazil. The suspicion remains that the U.S.A. and other governments have espoused the virtues of biofuels as a knee-jerk reaction to the spiralling climate change crisis without full impact assessment. Many observers consider that such an explicit exchange of food for fuel will trigger a public backlash against the craze for biofuels. In China already a shortage of pork has prompted the government to block approval of new ethanol plants, which are indirectly forcing up prices of animal feed.

CAUSES OF FOOD INSECURITY

External pressures associated with climate change and biotechnology are acting on local structural shortcomings, which already render developing countries prone to food insecurity. Foremost is the pattern of small farms (not dissimilar to the pattern in pre-industrial Europe), whose output is typically a mix of subsistence and surplus for market. There are 500 million farms of less than 2 hectares in the developing world, many of uncertain land tenure or title and many dependent on the labour of women and marginalised groups, whose low status weakens the agriculture lobby.

This profile of livelihoods rarely escapes poverty, lacks capital to invest, and is chronically vulnerable to fluctuating prices or unfavourable weather, especially drought-factors, which all contribute to food insecurity. Africa has been further affected by the distortion of labour resources created by HIV/AIDS. The two countries, which currently prompted the highest state of food security alerts, Swaziland and Lesotho, both experienced drought and high HIV prevalence.

Governments themselves have compounded weaknesses through prolonged lack of investment in rural economies, which account for about 75 per cent of world hunger—African governments are yet to meet their 2003 Maputo Declaration commitment, which called for 10 per cent of national budgets to be dedicated to agriculture and rural economies by 2008.

Those farmers who have been encouraged to switch to cash crops for export find themselves at the mercy of unpredictable world food prices, with competitiveness undermined by distorting subsidies for rich country farmers. The Doha round of world trade negotiations was supposed to open new markets for developing country agriculture, but the protective governments of the U.S.A. and Europe have baulked at the compromises involved.

Whilst overall population growth creates pressure on food security, it is not an underlying cause. World production of food has outpaced population growth and is projected to reach record levels in 2007, more than sufficient to feed the 6.7 billion population if sufficient political will could be summoned. The human weakness for violent conflict does however invariably lead to extreme food insecurity—nine of the twelve lowest ranking countries in the 2006 Global Hunger Index were conflict regions, such as the Democratic Republic of Congo and Angola. Collapsed economies such as North Korea and Zimbabwe also generate food crises.

SEARCH FOR SOLUTIONS

There are two longstanding and opposing philosophies for addressing the structural weaknesses that lead to food insecurity. The neo-liberal model advocates that small farms should be consolidated as has been the case in richer countries, with minimum state involvement and alternative livelihoods found for surplus labour. Farms can then afford to invest in higher technologies and compete in export markets.

Critics of this open market approach feel that it can succeed only in conditions of strong transport and storage infrastructure of efficient local markets and high standards of governance-conditions which rarely exist in poorer countries. The alternative model of 'food sovereignty' gives priority to local ownership of the full chain of resources. It accepts small farms for what they are and encourages their sustainability through pro-poor policies such as subsidies, tax breaks and protection against big business.

Neither model has yet absorbed the urgency of climate change. The open market approach fails to recognise the extreme sensitivity of tropical ecosystems and the pro-poor model may have to acknowledge the expediency of seeking help from the latest technologies in a potentially frightening environment.

FOOD AID

Food aid alone is not a sustainable solution to hunger, but compassion demands that action be taken in the most critical circumstances. The balance of food supply and demand throughout the world is monitored by the FAO's Global Information and Early Warning System. Where a situation is deemed serious, the World Food Programme (WFP) becomes involved and prepares an appeal to governments and other donors for aid—there have been 30 emergency appeals since 2000.

As the principal agency responsible for food aid, the WFP supports 100 million people and about the same number are assisted by international aid agencies. This leaves over 600 million dependent on highly variable or non-existent domestic safety net arrangements such as the Indian Public Distribution Scheme.

The U.S.A. is the largest donor country but insists not only in donating surplus grain from US stocks rather than cash, but also that the chain of delivery to the recipient country must be handled entirely by US contractors. The result is often months of delay for a service which is time critical. Agencies are pressing donors instead to purchase food direct from the beneficiary country—high prices typically being the deterrent to the poor rather than availability.

Donors also increasingly favour a twin-track approach of providing both cash and food to individuals—food, as the emergency component to ensure nutrition, and cash, as the development component to transfer sustainability decisions to the household and ward off a culture of dependency.

WORLD FOOD PRICES AND FOOD SECURITY

There is consensus in rich countries that retail food prices are about to increase sharply, in fact, the uptrend is already alarmingly visible. The reasons given include rising demand from countries such as India and China whose new middle classes can afford a diet of greater meat content and the tightening of food production from the expansion of biofuels. Fluctuation of Western supermarket prices would normally have little bearing on the battle for food security in developing countries. But there are ominous signs of knock-on effects; the WFP has announced that it will struggle to feed its target beneficiaries due to higher world prices and the disappearance of surpluses. A July 2007 leading article in the U.K. *Financial Times* concluded that 'for those in poor countries, (the effects of higher food prices) are potentially devastating.'

The latest available review of the Millennium Development Goals (2007) is excerpted in Appendix I.

CHAPTER 9

LONG-TERM POLICY OPTIONS

THE Secretary-General of the United Nations Conference on Trade and Development (UNCTAD), in April 2008, called for long-term strategies and policy options to manage global food shortages and rising commodity prices threatening the world in recent time. Advising against hasty responses to manage the food crises and skyrocketing commodity prices affecting the world, he said measures such as scaling up investments in agricultural research and development are long-term solutions to the problem of food shortages.

He declared: 'while we certainly must focus on urgent immediate relief, we would be jumping from one crises to another without restructuring the global aid delivery systems to ensure more coherent and consistent focus on boosting the agriculture sector.'

In the hope that stakeholders will find common grounds in identifying long-term measures to address 'this crippling crisis,' the Secretary-General claimed that rising food prices were driven by world population growth, especially in the developing world, climate change and extreme weather conditions, soaring energy costs, coupled with shortages in key staples such as rice and maize among others.

Some governments have responded to the crisis by restricting food imports and setting limits on commodity prices. However, those stop-gap measures were not the best solution and could prove to be more damaging in the long run, since global food shortages could be linked to agricultural development, which had long been neglected in least developed countries in Africa and other parts of the world. This had led almost to a state of permanent starvation and malnutrition in these countries and called for medium and long-term measures to alleviate the situation.

The international development community had always emphasised social sector and emergency aid at the expense of investment in productive sectors such as agriculture. However, current trends show that total share of official development assistance earmarked for economic infrastructure and productive sectors had decreased from nearly 50 per cent during mid 1990s to 24 per cent between 2002 and 2004.

The immediate need is to focus on economies that might be suffering the most or on those with little means to extricate themselves from the situation, where much more official development assistance should be earmarked for initiatives to enhance agricultural productivity and boost science and technology in agricultural research and development as well as irrigation.

NEEDED NATIONAL STRATEGIES

Most parts of the developing world are facing a food crisis. Unless two things are done, officials of any country cannot convince the public that there is no need for fear. On the short-term, the first task is to provide the actual figure of the country's grain stocks and to guarantee a good harvest of the new crops in 2008. Thankfully, reports to date, forecast a bumper harvest in 2008.

The other is a long-term task. Since farm products have become more expensive, government have to come up with a programme to give the right incentives to farmers and to cushion consumers at the same time.

For this governments have to determine a reasonably accurate estimate of available stocks. Where there is central procurement, as in India, the task is somewhat easier, but where most stock lies in the barns of small farmers, the task becomes very difficult. However, this first move is the base from which a strategy can be developed. How much governments can depend on the figure when it comes to planning for contingencies would require a double check. The next task is to estimate whether there will be a normal output.

However, even if these questions are not satisfactorily answered, the exercise will help the setting up of a domestic strategy. The world food price level will still continue to rise, due mainly to the increasing use of land for biofuels, and the dampening effect of rising prices of inputs on farm production. If an increasing share of the world's energy is to be provided by farms, then sooner or later, the general price of farm produce will edge towards, if not exceed, that of oil products. And not many people are prepared for that kind of 'new equilibrium', as economists would call it. Between now and then, as the World Bank has warned, some countries may even go through serious social unrest. With or without social unrest, in no country, will the farm sector and the food market remain unchanged.

Officials often tend to imagine that the current inflationary cycle is only temporary, or leave such an impression on their audience, while in fact, this can hardly be the case. A more realistic way to prepare for the future is to offer higher prices to encourage farmers to produce more, while developing some strategies to help low-income groups. Instead of a general ration, coupons on certain designated items may be a practical solution.

Global food security has been estimated to remain a worldwide concern for the next fifty years and beyond. Recently, crop yield has fallen in many areas because of declining investments in research and infrastructure, as well as increasing water scarcity. Climate change and HIV/AIDS are also crucial factors affecting food security in many regions.

Although agro-ecological approaches offer some promise for improving yields, food security in developing countries could be substantially improved by increased investment and policy reforms. The ability of agriculture to support growing populations has been a concern for generations and continues to be high on the global policy agenda. The eradication of poverty and hunger was included as one of the United Nations Millennium Development Goals adopted in 2000. One of the targets of the Goals is to halve the proportion of people who suffer from hunger between 1990 and 2015.

Meeting this food security goal will be a major challenge. Predictions of food security outcomes have been a part of the policy landscape since Malthus' *An Essay on the Principle of Population* written in 1798. Over the past several decades, some experts have expressed concern about the ability of agricultural production to keep up with global food demands, whereas others have forecast that technological advances or expansions of cultivated area would boost production sufficiently to meet rising demands.

Nevertheless, crop yield growth has slowed in much of the world because of declining investments in agricultural research, irrigation, and rural infrastructure and increasing water scarcity. New challenges to food security are posed by climate change and the morbidity and mortality of human immunodeficiency virus/acquired immuno-deficiency syndrome (HIV/AIDS). Many studies predict that world food supply will not be adversely affected by moderate climate change, assuming farmers take adequate steps to adjust to climate change and that additional CO_2 will increase yields. However, many developing countries are likely to fare badly. In warmer or tropical environments, climate change may result in more intense rainfall events between prolonged dry periods, as well as reduced or more variable water resources for irrigation.

Such conditions may promote pests and disease on crops and livestock, as well as soil erosion and desertification. Increasing development into marginal lands may in turn put these areas at greater risk of environmental degradation. The HIV/AIDS epidemic is another global concern, with an estimated 42 million cases worldwide at the end of 2002 with the developing countries alone accounting for 95 per cent. In addition to its direct health, economic and social impacts, the disease also affects food security and nutrition. Adult labour is often removed from affected households, and these households will have less capacity to produce or buy food, as assets are often depleted for medical or funeral costs. The agricultural knowledge base will deteriorate as individuals with farming and science experience succumb to the disease. Can food security goals be met in the face of these old and new challenges?

Several organizations have developed quantitative models that project global food supply and demand into the future. According to recent baseline projections of the International Food Policy Research Institute's (IFPRI's) International Model for Policy Analysis of Agricultural Commodities and Trade (IMPACT), global cereal production is estimated to increase by 56 per cent between 1997 and 2050 and livestock production by 90 per cent. Developing countries will account for 93 per cent of cereal demand growth and 85 per cent of meat-demand growth by 2050.

Income growth and rapid urbanization are major forces driving increased demand for higher valued commodities, such as meats, fruits, and vegetables. International agricultural trade will increase substantially, with developing countries' cereal imports doubling by 2025 and tripling by 2050. Child malnutrition will persist in many developing countries, although overall, the share of malnourished children is projected to decline to 14 per cent in 2050.

Nevertheless, this represents a nearly 35-year delay in meeting the Millennium Development Goals. In some places, circumstances will deteriorate, and in sub-Saharan Africa, the number of malnourished preschool children will increase between 1997 and 2015, after which they will only decrease slightly until 2050. South Asia is another region of concern—although progress is expected in this region, more than 30 per cent of preschool children will remain malnourished by 2030, and 24 per cent by 2050.

Achieving food security needs policy and investment reforms on multiple fronts, including human resources, agricultural research, rural infrastructure, water resources, and farm- and community-based agricultural and natural resources management. Progressive policy action must not only increase agricultural production, but also boost incomes and reduce poverty in rural areas where most of the poor live. If we take such an approach, we can expect production by 2050 to increase by 71 per cent for cereals and by 131 per cent for meats.

A reduction in childhood malnutrition would follow; the number of malnourished children would decline from 33 to 16 million in 2050 in sub-Saharan Africa, and from 85 million to 19 million in South Asia.

Increased investment in people is essential to accelerate food security improvements. In agricultural areas, education works directly to enhance the ability of farmers to adopt more advanced technologies and crop-management techniques and to achieve higher rates of return on land. Moreover, education encourages movement into more remunerative non-farm work, thus increasing household income. Women's education affects nearly every dimension of development, from lowering fertility rates to raising productivity and improving environmental management.

Research in Brazil shows that 25 per cent of children were stunted if their mothers had four or fewer years of schooling; however, this figure fell to 15 per cent if the mothers had a primary education and to 3 per cent if mothers had any secondary education. Poverty reduction is usually enhanced by an increase in the proportion of educational resources going to primary education and to the poorest groups or regions. Investments in health and nutrition, including safe drinking water, improved sewage disposal, immunization and public health services also contribute to poverty reduction. For example, a study in Ethiopia shows that the distance to a water source, as well as nutrition and morbidity, all affect agricultural productivity of households.

When rural infrastructure has deteriorated or is nonexistent, the cost of marketing farm produce and thus escaping subsistence agriculture while improving incomes, can be prohibitive for poor farmers. Rural roads increase agricultural production by bringing new land into cultivation and by intensifying existing land use, as well as consolidating the links between agricultural and non-agricultural activities within rural areas and between rural and urban areas. Government expenditure on roads is the most important factor in poverty alleviation in rural areas of countries like India and China because it leads to new employment opportunities, higher wages and increased productivity.

In addition to being a primary source of crop and livestock improvement, investment in agricultural research has high economic rates of return. Three major yield-enhancing strategies include research to increase the harvest index, plant biomass and stress tolerance (particularly drought resistance). For example, the hybrid 'New Rice for Africa,' which was bred to grow in the uplands of West Africa, produces more than 50 per cent more grain than current varieties when cultivated in traditional rainfed systems without fertilizer. Moreover, this variety matures 30 to 50 days earlier than current varieties and has enhanced disease and drought tolerance. In addition to conventional breeding, recent developments in non-conventional breeding, such as marker-assisted selection and cell and tissue culture techniques, could be employed for crops in developing countries, even if these countries stop short of transgenic breeding. To date, however, application of molecular biotechnology has been mostly limited to a small number of traits of interest to commercial farmers, mainly developed by a few global life science companies.

Although much of the science and many of the tools and intermediate products of biotechnology are transferable to solve high-priority problems in the tropics and subtropics, it is generally agreed that the private sector will not invest sufficiently to make the needed adaptations in these regions with limited market potential. Consequently, the public sector will have to play a key role, much of it by accessing proprietary tools and products from the private sector.

Irrigation is the largest water user worldwide, but also the first sector to lose out as scarcity increases. The challenges of water scarcity are heightened by the increasing costs of developing new water sources, soil degradation in irrigated areas, groundwater depletion, water pollution and ecosystem degradation. Wasteful use of already developed water supplies may be encouraged by subsidies and distorted incentives that influence water use. Hence, investment is needed to develop new water management policies and infrastructure. Although the economic and environmental costs of irrigation make many investments unprofitable, much could be achieved by water conservation and increased efficiency in existing systems and by increased crop productivity per unit of water used. Regardless, more research and policy efforts need to be focused on rainfed agriculture.

Exploiting the full potential of rainfed agriculture will require investment in water harvesting technologies, crop breeding, and extension services, as well as good access to markets, credit and supplies. Water harvesting and conservation techniques are particularly promising for the semi-arid tropics of Asia and Africa, where agricultural growth has been less than one per cent till recently. For example, water harvesting trials in Burkina Faso, Kenya, Niger, Sudan and Tanzania show increases in yield of a factor of 2 to 3, compared with dryland farming systems.

Agro-ecological approaches that seek to manage landscapes for both agricultural production and ecosystem services are another way of improving agricultural productivity. A study of 45 projects, using the agro-ecological approaches in 17 African countries showed cereal yield improvements of 50 to 100 per cent. There are many concomitant benefits to such approaches, as they reduce pollution through alternative methods of nutrient and pest management, create biodiversity reserves, and enhance habitat quality through careful management of soil, water and natural vegetation. Important issues remain about how to scale up agro-ecological approaches. Pilot programmes are needed to work out ways to mobilize private investment and to develop systems for payment of ecosystem services. All of these issues require investment in research, system development, and knowledge sharing.

To implement agricultural innovation, we need collective action at the local level, as well as the participation of government and non-governmental organizations that work at the community level. There have been several successful programmes, including those that use water harvesting and conservation techniques. Another priority is participatory plant breeding for yield increases in rainfed agrosystems, particularly in dry and remote areas. Farmer participation can be used in the very early stages of breed selection to help find crops suited to a multitude of environments and farmer preferences. It may be the only feasible route for crop breeding in remote regions, where a high level of crop diversity is required within the same farm, or for minor crops that are neglected by formal breeding programmes.

Making substantial progress in improving food security will be difficult, and it does mean reform of currently accepted agricultural practices. However, innovations in agro-ecological approaches and crop breeding have brought some documented successes. Together with investment in research and water and transport infrastructure, we can make major improvements to global food security, especially for the rural poor.

However, an oversight of how countries have responded to the food security crisis so far (given below), seems to indicate that immediate relief to the affected is predominant. This is as it should be. However, it should not preclude resorting to long-term options as early as possible.

So far, national policy responses to soaring food prices have varied in nature and effectiveness. In general, the focus has been on guaranteeing an adequate and affordable food supply for the majority of consumers, providing safety nets for the most food insecure and vulnerable and, to a much lesser degree, fostering agricultural supply response.

Approximately half of the governments in the 77 countries surveyed reduced grain import taxes, reflecting both the ease of use and political expediency of this measure. Fifty-five per cent of the countries used price controls or consumer subsidies in an attempt to reduce the transmission of price increases to the consumer. One-quarter of the governments imposed some type of export restriction and roughly the same proportion took action to increase supply, drawing on foodgrain stocks. Only 16 per cent of countries surveyed showed no policy activities whatsoever.

Policy actions vary considerably by region. The governments sampled in East Asia, South Asia and the Middle East and North Africa have undertaken significant activities in all four areas of intervention. In every geographical region except sub-Saharan Africa, 50 per cent or more of the countries reported using price controls or consumer subsidies. Sub-Saharan Africa and Latin America and the Caribbean regions showed the lowest policy activity, with roughly 20 per cent and 30 per cent of their countries, respectively, reporting no activity in any of the policy categories.

ASSESSING POLICY OPTIONS

The current situation serves as a reminder of the fragility of the balance between global food supplies and the needs of the world's inhabitants, and of the fact that earlier commitments to accelerate progress towards the eradication of hunger (especially through agricultural and rural development) have not been met. The immediate need is to prevent human suffering due to hunger and malnutrition and to induce a rapid supply response to restore a better balance between food supply and demand, especially in developing countries.

But, if these immediate measures are to have a sustained impact, they must be followed up by actions in the medium term that will result in an accelerated and permanent reduction in the number of people suffering from hunger and malnutrition. These actions must take place not only at the national but also the global level, in relation to public goods, trade policies, markets and responses to the impact of climate change. The focus for the longer term must be on generating and enabling farmers to apply sustainable technologies for agricultural intensification that will continue to meet the food needs of future generations in the face of rising population and effective demand, tightening availability of land and water resources and increased risks associated with climate change processes.

NATIONAL RESPONSES

High food prices are associated with both threats and opportunities. Analyses have shown that for the poorest net buyer households, high food prices of principal staple foods are associated with potentially serious welfare losses, at least in the short run. At the same time, high food prices increase the value of agricultural assets and have the potential of stimulating private sector investment in agriculture if the necessary public goods are present. In order to prevent the potential negative effects of high food prices on the extremely poor and a further increase in undernourishment and to simultaneously take advantage of the potentially positive effects on agricultural investment, productivity and food production, a twin track approach will be essential.

The twin track approach addresses the dichotomy between needed actions to protect the welfare of the most poor and hungry by providing direct support on an emergency basis and beyond, while at the same time providing public resources and designing policies to re-launch agriculture and revitalize rural economies over the medium and long-term plans. In the case of high food prices, emergency measures also include those intended to boost short-term supply response by facilitating small landholder access to essential production inputs.

Policy measures available in the short run include the provision of safety nets and social protection to the most vulnerable consumers in both rural and urban areas, as well as the enhancement of short-term supply response by small landholder farmers. Improved trade policies can also yield important gains. In the longer run, it will be important to address the fundamentals that increase investment in agriculture, both public and private, and improve the functioning of markets. Implementation of these policies offers the best option for putting the world on track to reach the World Food Summit target despite price increases.

SAFETY NETS, SOCIAL PROTECTION AND RAPID RECOVERY OF AGRICULTURE

Those most vulnerable to food price shocks need to be protected from nutritional deprivation, asset shedding and reductions in their real purchasing power. Such protection not only saves lives, it can also strengthen livelihoods and promote longer-term development. Safety nets and social protection can reduce malnutrition that has lifelong consequences, prevent distress sales of assets, and allow investments in education and health that high food prices make more difficult, all of which help keep households from falling into poverty traps.

In the very short run, protecting the most vulnerable may require direct food distribution, targeted food subsidies and cash transfers and nutritional programmes including school feeding. The precise choice will depend on the extent to which some form of safety net or social protection mechanisms are already in place and can be mobilized.

In the short to medium run, social protection programmes must be set up or expanded and strengthened, allowing countries to phase out more generalised subsidies while making sure that all their people are able to meet their essential food needs. In order to become part of national development priorities, they must be integrated into national development plans such as national food security strategies and poverty reduction programmes. Successful implementation will generate beneficial impacts on the overall diet and nutritional status, an outcome which would not arise with input subsidies aimed at a single staple food crop. Well organized and targeted social protection systems are potentially capable of providing direct support to the neediest at a cost that is substantially lower than more broad-based actions which, in turn, makes them more sustainable.

Because cash economies are more prevalent and social networks are generally weaker in urban areas, strengthening of safety nets is especially important for the urban poor. Safety nets will also be especially important for nutritionally vulnerable groups, including children, pregnant women and the elderly.

For rural households, an integrated approach to social protection should be taken that combines traditional transfers (social safety nets) and policies that enable small landholders to respond quickly to the market opportunities created by higher prices. In the very short run, however, the supply response to higher price incentives, especially by small landholders, may be limited by their lack of access to essential inputs such as seeds and fertilizers. In these cases, social protection measures, including the distribution of seeds and fertilizers, directly or through a system of vouchers and 'smart subsidies', may be an appropriate short-term response. If implemented effectively, such a programme will increase the income of small producers and may reduce price increases in local markets, thereby contributing to improvements in the nutritional status of net food-buying families.

However, safety net programmes must be carefully designed. They may place large demands on institutional capacity, especially in countries where such programmes are most needed. Indeed, the implementation of various forms of transfer programmes has proven to be a major challenge. Particular risks include leakage of benefits to non-target groups, resale of vouchers by the target group and rent seeking by officials.

One of the risks of subsidies on purchased farm inputs is that they draw farmers' attention away from making better use of the resources already available to them, such as the use of manure, compost and rotations involving nitrogen fixing legumes or cover crops to improve soil fertility and structure.

IMPROVING TRADE POLICIES

As elaborated above, many countries have restricted exports in attempts to ensure domestic food security. While such barriers sometimes help to contain pressures on domestic prices, they can also signal problems and lead to panic buying on domestic markets. On the other hand, in some countries where the barriers are effective, farmers have reduced planting of cereals in the face of low domestic prices for their products coupled with high prices for inputs such as fuel, seeds and fertilizers.

Export restrictions also exacerbate price instability on world markets, especially when they are implemented in an *ad-hoc* and uncoordinated manner. Increased world market volatility in turn will then often worsen food security in other countries. Fortunately for world food markets, some countries have started to relax those restrictions. Ukraine has recently increased the quantities of wheat exports that will be allowed, and, so far, Thailand has avoided government restrictions on rice exports.

Export restrictions have been given substantially less attention in the WTO than import barriers, but the current situation argues strongly that trade negotiations give more serious attention to export barriers. Indeed, many countries resort to import barriers out of fear that exporting nations may be unreliable suppliers. Thus, legal restraints on the use of export barriers may provide some spur to the reduction of import tariffs, which will lead to longer term welfare gains. Given that many of the poorest countries will have difficulties in implementing safety net programmes (as noted above), export barriers may have a role to play in providing food security, but the use of such instruments should be restricted to the poorest countries.

Subsidies to, and tariff protection of biofuel production may also need to be re-examined in light of their effects on food security. China and South Africa have already restricted the use of grains for ethanol production based on food security concerns and some observers have called for other countries to also include food security considerations in the policymaking process.

While actions to free import restrictions and release foodgrain stocks into the market have had mostly immediate and favourable effects on consumers and on economic efficiency in general, these measures do have some shortcomings. First, they provide only one-time relief. Once the tariff or tax has been reduced to zero, no further reductions in price can take place through this measure. Second, they entail revenue losses for the government, which in some countries could be substantial. On the positive side, tariff reductions may make good policy sense in any case, especially if the original tariffs unduly distorted the trade regime. But if tariff reductions are to be sustainable, the government would need to undertake complementary reforms in the medium term, for example, tax reform measures to help recoup at least part of the revenue loss. In addition, since tariff reductions imply a loss of protection for domestic producers, complementary measures (with credible exit strategies) may be needed to support and ease their transition to a liberalized environment. Such measures could include strengthening safety nets, public investment in rural infrastructure, improved extension services or other policies that facilitate response to the new market signals.

STIMULATING AGRICULTURAL INVESTMENT AND SUPPLY RESPONSE

In the medium term, there is a need for renewed attention to the agricultural sector. High food prices constitute an important element in the effort to re-launch agriculture since they provide incentives to the private sector to invest and produce. There is ample scope for substantial increases in agricultural production and productivity. Productivity increases will require significant and sustained improvements in long neglected areas such as research, extension, agricultural and general infrastructure along with credit and risk management instruments, all of which will complement increased price incentives. These initiatives will need to consider the challenges from possible long-term impact of climate change as well as more short-term effects of increased demand for biofuel feedstock.

Support needs to focus particularly on enabling poor rural producers—those least able to respond to changing market signals—to expand their production and market supply. The main areas of support include fostering agricultural research focused on the needs of poor rural producers, many of whom farm in increasingly marginal areas; enhancing access to agriculture services, including research, extension and financial services and strengthening their capacity to take advantage of these; securing their access to natural resources such as land and water; and fostering their participation in non-agricultural sources of income including payments for environmental services. It is also important to assist poor rural households in strengthening their livelihoods in conditions of ever greater climatic uncertainty and their awareness of ways to benefit from new approaches to managing weather and other risks, including new forms of insurance.

THE WAY AHEAD

The risks to food security posed by the present regime of low worldwide food stocks and high food prices are substantial. The challenges of 'managing' this crisis over the coming years are daunting. However, the costs of failure will be measured in terms of increased poverty and hunger, reversals in hard-earned gains in nutrition, health, education and social protection and, more broadly, social unrest and insecurity. The world community must ensure that governments have the human, financial, technical and material resources they need to implement the priority reforms listed above.

These include avenues for—and access to—increased budgetary and technical support, strong policy guidance, heightened advocacy in international negotiations to reduce international trade barriers and market distortions and the creation of new international protocols and agreements surrounding biofuels. Good governance and the support of the private sector are essential for improving effectiveness and for any measures to succeed domestically.

A fundamental economic incentive for stimulating the agricultural sector (higher prices) is in place for the first time in 25 years. Global attention is also now focused on the plight of the poor and hungry. At the national level, governments, supported by their international partners, must now undertake the necessary public investment and provide a suitable environment for private investments, while at the same time ensuring that the most vulnerable are protected from hunger. They must initiate actions to ensure accelerated progress towards the permanent eradication of chronic hunger and malnutrition in the world, making this a fundamental element of their development policies and poverty reduction strategies. For as long as a large number of people remain hungry, the threat of a repetition of the current crisis will remain.

The international community must take immediate steps to increase its capacity to respond in a coordinated and expeditious way to requests from countries for professional assistance and financial support to enable them to meet the costs of emergency interventions without unduly compromising their economic and growth potential. It should be noted that these funding needs for agricultural investment are already in need of updating as the cost of investment has risen and food prices have increased. Further, the time period in which the target needs to be achieved is substantially shorter and therefore the effort needs to be stepped up. A mere inflation adjustment will bring the required amount to more than US$ 30 billion.

At the same time, it is necessary to set in motion steps towards ensuring long-term global food security, taking into account the probable risks to global food supplies posed by climate change. Amongst the big issues to be addressed are how to develop a new generation of technologies for agricultural intensification that is sustainable from financial, environmental and social perspectives and is resilient to climate change and how to prevent further reductions in the availability of fresh water and land resources for future food production.

CHAPTER 10

AGRICULTURAL REFORM OPTIONS

THE options for agricultural reforms delineated below might sound impressive; there is no denying that they are based on sound principles. What is likely to be found disturbing by most people is the 'either/or' approach. Either we commercialise agriculture or we go in for more hefty nationalisation of farming. In a perfect world, both approaches are realisable; however, we don't live in a perfect world. In fact the more critical the situation, the more people tend to inject sentiment and emotion into the problem and its solution. Granted that compassion is a desirable human attribute and the principle of the 'survival of the fittest' is not always acceptable, this anomaly allows room for dissent which provides a tool for their manipulation, both socially and politically. Perhaps the acceptable but necessarily less efficient solution lies somewhere in between.

As the tragic reality of food insecurity dawns upon the world, a number of analysts and some social scientists have given up looking at the problem through the rosy spectacles of the 'romantic' small farmer. They see many gains in introducing 'commercial' farming in Africa and Asia which, they claim, has the flexibility of meeting potential food crises because of their reach into credit sources. The argument in Case I below exemplifies this belief.

CASE I

The sharp increase in the world price of staple foods is an inconvenience for consumers in the rich world, but for consumers in the poorest countries, especially in Africa, it is a catastrophe. Despite the predominance of peasant agriculture, most African and many Asian countries are net food importers and food accounts for over half of the budget of low-income households. This is the result of decades of agricultural stagnation combined with growing populations.

Although many of the net purchasers are rural, evidently the problem is at its most intense in the urban slums. These slums are political powder kegs and rising food prices have already triggered riots. Indeed, they sow the seeds of an ugly and destructive populist politics.

Paradoxically, this squeeze on the poorest has come about as a result of the success of globalization in reducing world poverty. As China and India develop, helped by massive exports to Western markets, millions of Chinese and Indian households have started to eat better. Better means not just more food but more meat, the new luxury. But to produce a kilo of meat takes six kilos of grain. Livestock reared for meat to be consumed in Asia is now eating the grain that would previously have been eaten by the poor.

The best solution to a problem is often not closely related to its cause (a proposition that that might be recognized in the climate change debate). The Chinese and Indian long march to prosperity is something to be celebrated. The remedy to high food prices is to increase food supply, something that is entirely feasible. The most realistic way to raise global supply is to replicate the Brazilian model of large, technologically sophisticated agro-companies supplying for the world market. To give one remarkable example, the time between harvesting one crop and planting the next, in effect the downtime for land, has been reduced by an astounding thirty minutes. There are still many areas of the world that have good land which could be used far more productively if it was properly managed by large companies. For example, almost 90 per cent of Mozambique's land, an enormous area, is idle.

Unfortunately, large-scale commercial agriculture is frowned upon. The production style of the peasant is lauded as environmentally sustainable and human in scale. In respect of manufacturing and services, commercialisation was accepted years ago, but in agriculture it continues to shape policies. In Europe, Japan, India and other southeast Asian countries huge public resources have been devoted to propping up small farms. The best that can be said for these policies was that they were affordable by the countries involved.

But in Africa, which cannot afford them, development agencies have oriented their entire efforts on agricultural development to peasant style production. As a result, Africa has less large-scale commercial agriculture than it had 50 years ago. Unfortunately, peasant farming is generally not well-suited to innovation and investment: the result has been that African agriculture has fallen further and further behind the advancing productivity frontier of the globalised commercial model. Indeed, during the present phase of high prices, the FAO is worried that African peasants are likely to reduce their production because they cannot finance the increased cost of fertilizer inputs.

While there are partial solutions to this problem through subsidies and credit schemes, large-scale commercial agriculture simply does not face this problem. If output prices rise by more than input prices, production can be expanded because credit lines are well-established.

This longstanding agricultural tendency has been compounded by a new-found environmental 'romanticism.' In the United States, fears of climate change have been manipulated by shrewd interests to produce grotesquely inefficient subsidies for biofuel. Around a third of American grain production has rapidly been diverted into energy production.

This switch demonstrates both the superb responsiveness of the market to price signals and the shameful power of subsidy-hunting lobby groups. Given the depth of anti-Americanism in Europe and Asia it is, of course, fashionable to criticize the American folly with biofuel. But Europe has its equivalent follies.

The European Commission is now imitating the American biofuel policy. At present the programme is small enough to be unimportant, but over time it has the potential for real damage. But the true European equivalent of America's folly with biofuel is the ban on GM. Europe's distinctive and deep-seated fears of science have been manipulated by the agricultural lobby into yet another form of protectionism. The ban on both the production and import of genetically modified crops has obviously retarded productivity growth in European agriculture: again, the best that can be said of it is that the continent is rich enough to afford such folly.

But Europe is a major agricultural producer, so the cumulative consequence of this reduction in the growth of productivity has affected world food markets. Further, and most cruelly, as an unintended side-effect the ban has terrified African governments into themselves banning genetic modification in case by growing modified crops they would permanently be shut out of selling to European markets. Africa definitely cannot afford this self-denial. It needs all the help it can possibly get from genetic modification. Not only is Africa currently being hit by rising food prices, over the longer term it will face climatic deterioration in the context of a rapidly growing population.

While the policies needed for the long-term have been befuddled by 'emotional' thinking, the short-term global response has been pure beggar-thy-neighbour. It is easier for urban slum dwellers to riot than for farmers: riots need streets, not fields. And so, in the internal tussles between the interests of poor consumers and poor producers, the interests of consumers have prevailed. Governments in grain-exporting countries have swung prices in favour of their consumers and against their farmers by banning exports.

These responses further politicize and fragment an already confused global food market. They increase the risks of investing in commercial-scale food production and drive up prices further in the food-importing countries. Unfortunately, trade in agriculture has been the main economic activity to have resisted being subject to global rules. We need stronger and fairer globalization, not less of it.

Then there are the votaries of the small farmers who are vociferously against the commercialisation of agriculture, are not convinced of the benefits of GM crops and see 'romanticism' not in small holdings but in the markets and in large scale agriculture. They bemoan the dismantling of traditional credit and marketing institutions and urge a revisit to primary causes of poverty.

Their case is given below:

CASE II

The current food price crisis presents opportunities for structural change to address the causes of food vulnerability of the poorest people in the world. To make the right changes, however, requires that we get the analysis of the problem right.

The real issue is not the rise in food prices—market prices, after all, go up and down. We would be foolish indeed to try to prevent that phenomenon. While some of the underlying causes relate to policy errors (unthinking support for mass production of biofuel for export, for example), and these should be corrected, the focus should instead be on the causes of food vulnerability. It is this that makes food price volatility costly in terms of deepening hunger and poverty.

The causes of this vulnerability are complex, but include the rash discarding of those institutions, that although not functioning perfectly, did provide some reduction in uncertainty for producers and consumers alike in the poorest countries. Christian Aid's analysis ('Farmers left behind', 2007) shows that this is the underlying cause of the fall in staple food yields and phenomena like the limited usage of available land in Mozambique.

Two institutions in particular were discarded in the period of dogmatic liberalisation from the 1980s. First, state banks rushed into privatisation. While this yielded some benefits by addressing inefficiencies, it also generally led to sharp falls in rural lending of the sort that helped smooth consumption across volatile harvests and provide investment funds for basics such as seed and fertiliser.

Second, agricultural marketing boards were dismantled. While these again had often not functioned perfectly, they had nonetheless provided an important degree of stability and improved access to markets for marginal producers who typically sell little into the market but for whom that little can be pivotal in determining whether they can continue and prosper over time.

Finally, the expansion of long-run supply will not come about through the careless embrace of GM technology. The recently launched International Agriculture Assessment on Science and Technology for Development, supported by around 60 governments, the World Bank and all UN institutions, concluded that 'assessment of [genetic modification] technology lags behind its development, information [on its impact] is anecdotal and contradictory, which has led to uncertainty about the possible benefits and damage'. In other words, transgenetic crops cannot feed the world and there is no evidence to support the emotive assertion that the only choice is between adoption of genetically modified crops or mass starvation.

It has been argued that 'romanticism' (see Case I) about agriculture and the environment has clouded the judgment of policymakers. That may be true. But romanticism about the role of the market and the potential for large-scale agriculture has to take some of the blame for this. Ultimately, there is no scope for, nor likelihood of, the latter making a great change to the production and consumption possibilities of the poorest people on the planet. Staple food yields will instead be improved by providing a little more security to marginal producers, by replacing and improving institutions that were rashly abandoned, and by giving these producer-consumers some prospect of food security.

Finally, there are views that falling poverty in China and India, for example, is partly responsible for the rise in food prices—thus arguing that deepening poverty for some is a consequence of a few successes of globalization. This is certainly true. An obvious feature of the current form of globalization, dominated by trade and financial liberalization, whose basis is primarily ideological rather than supported by evidence, has been one of deepening inequality. So falling poverty in one country or income group is entirely compatible with deepening poverty elsewhere.

The solution is not, of course, more liberalization, but rather more thought and more policy space for countries to pursue alternative options.

And, lastly, we have those who, while agreeing with Case I and Case II votaries that the major issues are on the supply side, feel that demand issues cannot be ignored altogether. They buttress their argument by pointing to the alacrity with which demand side votaries have found scapegoats in higher food consumption by the people of China and India who are now experiencing hitherto unrealised and unexpected levels of affluence. The Case III group are also more pragmatic about the securitisation of food items—seeing both the good and evil of the system.

CASE III

The opinions above quite rightly draw attention to the supply-side issues that characterize the current food crisis and the need for policy reforms to strengthen food production. Indeed, it has been disturbing to see how quickly many experts have found a scapegoat in such demand factors as the increased consumption in emerging economies. On their own, demand factors cannot fully explain the abrupt skyrocketing of many prices over the past 15—and particularly the past three—months (first quarter, 2008). Other commentators, who put the blame solely on speculation or on the recent growth of managed futures as an asset class, ignore the fact that a significant amount of price pressure has been building up for several years, before the recent shooting up of prices started.

We need to examine the two phenomena—increased shortages due to a decline in the growth of supply, and price increases related to speculation and securitization of several commodities—in conjunction to fully understand what has happened and what is likely to happen next. There is no question that the securitization of various food commodity markets in early 2007 has played an important role in this crisis, especially over recent months. The mean of the price increases of securitized agricultural commodities (including coffee, cotton, soybean oil, soybeans, sugar, wheat, and corn) was 49 per cent in the 15 months from January 2007 to April 2008, compared to 20 per cent in the preceding 12 months. In comparison, prices of non-securitized agricultural commodities (including, rice, tea, cocoa and rubber) increased by only 14 per cent in the last 15 months, compared to 11 per cent in the 12 months before.

Despite the slower average price increase, the effects of speculation do appear to have spilled over into some of these non-securitized commodities, for example, to rice (69 per cent since January 2007) and palm oil (88 per cent). One should also ask: If this is truly a speculative bubble, where are the stocks of these goods? The answer is, in part, still out in the fields, as future contracts deal with future harvests. In all likelihood, some of the recent price jumps stem from the perception among hedgers and investors, that the harvests will disappoint. (If this is true, they will be disappointed as 2008 is going to see a bumper harvest of grains.)

The supply side of this crisis stems from much more, and potentially much more enduring issues, than natural causes like droughts, floods and untimely rains. A strong focus for many years on development of manufacturing and services in many emerging economies, notably in Asia, has come at the cost of improving agricultural productivity. World production of rice and wheat has barely increased in the past 10 years and agricultural productivity has severely slowed in several key producing countries in Asia, including China (2 per cent per year from 1996–2003, compared to 4 per cent from 1989–96), India (around 1 per cent from 1995–2005 compared to almost 2 per cent from 1985–95, and Indonesia (only 1 per cent from 1995–2004 compared to more than 3 per cent in 1985–95).

The causes of this productivity slowdown include a relative neglect of agricultural R&D, low investment in rural extension services and even a failure to extend infrastructure such as roads and irrigation to rural areas. There is enormous potential to increase both food supply and agricultural productivity in these countries, but it will take time to bring production back up to the levels needed to meet demand.

The protectionist backlashes in important producing countries such as Thailand, Vietnam and Argentina and now India and Thailand will be difficult to reverse even after the bubbles have burst. Restrictions of exports, higher import subsidies to protect domestic supplies and taxes to support consumer subsidies, will be difficult to remove even when the crises are past. More frequent mismatches between demand and supply will keep prices at a higher level and produce only more volatility Even with higher prices, these measures create more uncertainty for farmers to expand food production and will limit the growth potential of international markets. In emerging economies, many of the price declines from productivity growth before the mid 1990s will be reversed, and it will become harder for poorer people to move up the consumption ladder. Such increases in inequality could reduce the growth potential further.

In the end, it would appear that the different approaches typified by the Cases above (and their variants) all have their points. It is a matter of selecting the right mix of measures, not being inflexible if there is need for change and maintaining a well thought-out in depth real time grasp of the situation. The grain-to-ethanol subsidies, however, have been decried by all. This is an important pointer to the fact that the surging prices of crude are, and will probably remain, a major factor in extending and expanding food insecurity across the globe.

CHAPTER 11

NEW VISIONS OF SUSTAINABILITY

AGRICULTURE has changed dramatically, especially since the end of World War II. Food and fibre productivity soared due to new technologies, mechanization, increased chemical use, specialization and government policies that favoured maximizing production. These changes allowed fewer farmers with reduced labour demands to produce the majority of the food and fibre in developed countries such as the U.S.A.

The concept of sustainable development which primarily focused on sustainable agriculture first came into prominence in the second half of the 20th century. Even as unprecedented agricultural surpluses in countries such as the U.S.A. were leading to complacency on the farm front, doubts were being expressed in scientific circles, at first guardedly then more openly, on whether increased agricultural output obtained by industrial management methods on farms could be sustained for any length of time. The costs inherent in industrialised agriculture were, among others, topsoil depletion, groundwater contamination, the decline of family farms, continued neglect of the living and working conditions for farm labourers, increasing costs of production, and the disintegration of economic and social conditions in rural communities.

CONCERTED EFFORTS REQUIRED

Attaining sustainability will require concerted interactive efforts among disciplines, many of which have not yet recognized, and internalized, the relevance of environmental issues to their main intellectual discourse. The inability of key scientific disciplines to engage interactively is an obstacle to the actual attainment of sustainability. For example, in the list of Millennium Development Goals from the United Nations World Summit on Sustainable Development, 2002, the seventh of the eight goals, to 'ensure environmental sustainability,' is presented separately from the parallel goals of reducing fertility and poverty, improving gains in equity, improving material conditions, and enhancing population health. A more integrated approach to sustainability is urgently needed.

For human populations, sustainability means transforming our ways of living to maximize the chances that environmental and social conditions will indefinitely support human security, well-being, and health. In particular, the flow of non-substitutable goods and services from ecosystems must be sustained.

The contemporary stimulus for exploring sustainability is the accruing evidence that humankind is jeopardizing its own longer term interests by living beyond Earth's means, thereby changing atmospheric composition and depleting biodiversity, soil fertility, ocean fisheries, and fresh-water supplies.

Much early discussion about sustainability has focused on readily measurable intermediate outcomes such as increased economic performance, greater energy efficiency, better urban design, improved transport systems, better conservation of recreational amenities, and so on.

However, such changes in technologies, behaviours, amenities, and equity are only the means to attaining desired human experiential outcomes, including autonomy, opportunity, security and health. These are the true ends of sustainability—and there has been some recognition that their attainment and their sharing will be optimized by reducing the rich-poor divide.

Some reasons for the failure to achieve a collective vision of how to attain sustainability lie in the limitations of, and disjunction between, disciplines we think should be central to our understanding of sustainability: demography, economics, ecology and epidemiology.

These disciplines bear on the size and economic activities of the human population, how the population relates to the natural world and the health consequences of ecologically injudicious behavior. Sustainability issues are of course not limited to these four disciplines, but require the engagement and interdisciplinary collaboration of other social and natural sciences, engineering, and the humanities.

Neither mainstream demography nor economics, for the most part, incorporates sufficient appreciation of environmental criticalities into their thinking. They implicitly assume that the world is an open, steady-state system within which discipline-specific processes can be studied. Although contemporary ecology has broadened its perspectives significantly, there is a tendency to exclude consideration of both human influence and dependence on ecosystem composition, development, and dynamics. Epidemiologists focus mainly on individual-level behaviors and circumstances as causes of disease. This discounts the underlying social, cultural, and political determinants of the distribution of disease risk within and between populations and has barely recognized the health risks posed by today's global environmental changes.

These four disciplines share a limited ability to appreciate that the fate of human populations depends on the biosphere's capacity to provide a continued flow of goods and services. The assumption of human separateness from the natural world perpetuates a long-standing premise of Western scientific thought of Man as master, with dominion over Nature.

A growing movement emerged during the past two decades of the 20th century on the role of the agricultural establishment in promoting practices that contribute to these social problems. This movement for sustainable agriculture garnered increasing support and acceptance within mainstream agriculture. Not only does sustainable agriculture address many environmental and social concerns, but it offers innovative and economically viable opportunities for growers, labourers, consumers, policymakers and many others in the entire food system. This concern has deepened drastically with the current threat to the world's food security. While fiscal policy and monetary measures are being taken by many countries to afford a degree of immediate relief from the hazards of food insecurity, focus has now returned to sustainable measures which will provide long-term relief from this threat.

CONCEPT

Sustainable agriculture integrates three main goals—environmental health, economic profitability and social and economic equity. A variety of philosophies, policies and practices have contributed to these goals. People in many different capacities, from farmers to consumers, have shared this vision and contributed to it. Despite the diversity of people and perspectives, the following themes commonly weave through definitions of sustainable agriculture.

Sustainability rests on the principle that we must meet the needs of the present without compromising the ability of future generations to meet their own needs. Therefore, stewardship of both natural and human resources is of prime importance. This includes consideration of social responsibilities such as working and living conditions of labourers, the needs of rural communities and consumer health and safety both in the present and the future. Stewardship of land and natural resources involves maintaining or enhancing this vital resource base for the long-term.

Next, a systems perspective is essential to understanding sustainability. The system is envisioned in its broadest sense, from the individual farm, to the local ecosystem, reaching out to communities affected by this farming system both locally and globally. An emphasis on the system allows a larger and more thorough view of the consequences of farming practices on both human communities and the environment. A systems approach provides the tools to explore the interconnections between farming and other aspects of our environment.

Also, a systems approach also implies interdisciplinary efforts in research and education. This requires not only the input of researchers from various disciplines, but also farmers, farm workers, consumers, policymakers and others.

Making the transition to sustainable agriculture is a process. For farmers, the transition to sustainable agriculture normally requires a series of small, realistic steps. Family economics and personal goals influence how fast or how far participants can go in the transition. It is important to realize that each small decision can make a difference and contribute to advancing the entire system further on the 'sustainable agriculture continuum,' The key to moving forward is the will to take the next step.

Finally, reaching towards the goal of sustainable agriculture is the responsibility of all participants in the system, including farmers, labourers, policymakers, researchers, retailers, and consumers. Each group has its own part to play, its own unique contribution to make to strengthen the sustainable agriculture community.

We now consider specific strategies for realizing these broad themes or goals. The strategies are grouped according to three separate though related areas of concern: Farming and Natural Resources, Plant and Animal Production Practices and the Economic, Social and Political Context. They represent a range of potential ideas for individuals committed to interpreting the vision of sustainable agriculture within their own circumstances.

FARMING AND NATURAL RESOURCES

Water

When the production of food and fibre degrades the natural resource base, the ability of future generations to produce and flourish decreases. The decline of ancient civilizations in Mesopotamia, the Mediterranean region, pre-Columbian southwest U.S. and Central America is believed to have been strongly influenced by natural resource degradation from non-sustainable farming and forestry practices. Water is the principal resource that has helped agriculture and society to prosper and it has been a major limiting factor when mismanaged.

Water Supply and Use

In California, an extensive water storage and transfer system was established which has allowed crop production to expand to very arid regions. In drought years, limited surface water supplies prompted overdraft of groundwater and consequent intrusion of salt water or permanent collapse of aquifers. Periodic droughts, some lasting up to 50 years, occurred in California. Several steps can be taken to develop drought-resistant farming systems even in 'normal' years, including both policy and management actions, such as:

1. improving water conservation and storage measures,
2. providing incentives for selection of drought-tolerant crop species,
3. using reduced-volume irrigation systems,
4. managing crops to reduce water loss, or
5. not planting at all.

Water Quality

The most important issues related to water quality involve salinisation and contamination of ground and surface waters by pesticides, nitrates and selenium. Salinity has become a problem wherever water of even relatively low salt content is used on shallow soils in arid regions and/or where the water table is near the root zone of crops. Tile drainage can remove the water and salts, but the disposal of the salts and other contaminants may negatively affect the environment depending upon where they are deposited. Temporary solutions include the use of salt-tolerant crops, low-volume irrigation, and various management techniques to minimize the effects of salts on crops. In the long-term, some farmland may need to be removed from production or converted to other uses.

Other uses include conversion of row crop land to production of drought-tolerant forages, the restoration of wildlife habitat or the use of agroforestry to minimize the impacts of salinity and high water tables. Pesticide and nitrate contamination of water can be reduced using many well known practices.

Wildlife

Another way in which agriculture affects water resources is through the destruction of riparian habitats within watersheds. The conversion of wild habitat to agricultural land reduces fish and wildlife through erosion and sedimentation, the effects of pesticides, removal of riparian plants, and the diversion of water. The plant diversity in and around both riparian and agricultural areas should be maintained in order to support a diversity of wildlife. This diversity will enhance natural ecosystems and could aid in agricultural pest management.

Energy

Modern agriculture is heavily dependent on non-renewable energy sources, especially petroleum. The continued use of these energy sources cannot be sustained indefinitely, yet to abruptly abandon our reliance on them would be economically catastrophic. However, a sudden cut-off in energy supply would be equally disruptive. In sustainable agricultural systems, there is reduced reliance on non-renewable energy sources and a substitution of renewable sources or labour to the extent that is economically feasible.

Air

Many agricultural activities affect air quality. These include smoke from agricultural burning; dust from tillage, traffic and harvest; pesticide drift from spraying; and nitrous oxide emissions from the use of nitrogen fertilizer. Options to improve air quality include incorporating crop residue into the soil, using appropriate levels of tillage and planting wind breaks, cover crops or strips of native perennial grasses to reduce dust.

Soil

Soil erosion continues to be a serious threat to our continued ability to produce adequate food. Numerous practices have been developed to keep soil in place, which include reducing or eliminating tillage, managing irrigation to reduce runoff, and keeping the soil covered with plants or mulch.

PLANT PRODUCTION PRACTICES

Sustainable production practices involve a variety of approaches. Specific strategies must take into account topography, soil characteristics, climate, pests, local availability of inputs and the individual grower's goals. Despite the site-specific and individual nature of sustainable agriculture, several general principles can be applied to help growers select appropriate management practices:

- ⌘ Selection of species and varieties that are well suited to the site and to conditions on the farm;
- ⌘ Diversification of crops (including livestock) and cultural practices to enhance the biological and economic stability of the farm;
- ⌘ Management of the soil to enhance and protect soil quality;
- ⌘ Efficient and humane use of inputs; and
- ⌘ Consideration of farmers' goals and lifestyle choices.

SELECTION OF SITE, SPECIES AND VARIETY

Preventive strategies, adopted early, can reduce inputs and help establish a sustainable production system. When possible, pest-resistant crops should be selected which are tolerant of existing soil or site conditions. When site selection is an option, factors such as soil type and depth, previous crop history, and location (for example, climate, topography) should be taken into account before planting.

Diversity

Diversified farms are usually more economically and ecologically resilient. While monoculture farming has advantages in terms of efficiency and ease of management, the loss of the crop in any one year could put a farm out of business and/or seriously disrupt the stability of a community dependent on that crop. By growing a variety of crops, farmers spread economic risk and are less susceptible to the radical price fluctuations associated with changes in supply and demand.

Properly managed, diversity can also buffer a farm in a biological sense. For example, in annual cropping systems, crop rotation can be used to suppress weeds, pathogens and insect pests. Also, cover crops can have stabilizing effects on the agro-ecosystem by holding soil and nutrients in place, conserving soil moisture with mowed or standing dead mulches, and by increasing the water infiltration rate and soil water holding capacity. Cover crops in orchards and vineyards can buffer the system against pest infestations by increasing beneficial arthropod populations and can therefore reduce the need for chemical inputs. Using a variety of cover crops is also important in order to protect against the failure of a particular species to grow and to attract and sustain a wide range of beneficial arthropods.

Optimum diversity may be obtained by integrating both crops and livestock in the same farming operation. This was the common practice for centuries until the mid-1900s when technology, government policy and economics compelled farms to become more specialized. Mixed crop and livestock operations have several advantages. First, growing row crops only on more level land and pasture or forages on steeper slopes will reduce soil erosion. Second, pasture and forage crops in rotation enhance soil quality and reduce erosion; livestock manure, in turn, contributes to soil fertility. Third, livestock can buffer the negative impacts of low rainfall periods by consuming crop residue that in 'plant only' systems would have been considered crop failures. Finally, feeding and marketing are flexible in animal production systems. This can help cushion farmers against trade and price fluctuations and, in conjunction with cropping operations, make more efficient use of farm labour.

Soil Management

A common philosophy among sustainable agriculture practitioners is that a 'healthy' soil is a key component of sustainability; that is, a healthy soil will produce healthy crop plants that have optimum vigour and are less susceptible to pests. While many crops have key pests that attack even the healthiest of plants, proper soil, water and nutrient management can help prevent some pest problems brought on by crop stress or nutrient imbalance. Furthermore, crop management systems that impair soil quality often result in greater inputs of water, nutrients, pesticides, and/or energy for tillage to maintain yields.

In sustainable systems, the soil is viewed as a fragile and living medium that must be protected and nurtured to ensure its long-term productivity and stability. Methods to protect and enhance the productivity of the soil include using cover crops, compost and/or manures, reducing tillage, avoiding traffic on wet soils, and maintaining soil cover with plants and/or mulches. Conditions in most soils (warm, irrigated and tilled) do not favour the build-up of organic matter. Regular additions of organic matter or the use of cover crops can increase soil aggregate stability, soil tilth, and diversity of soil microbial life.

Efficient Use of Inputs

Many inputs and practices used by conventional farmers are also used in sustainable agriculture. Sustainable farmers, however, maximize reliance on natural, renewable, and on-farm inputs. Equally important are the environmental, social, and economic impacts of a particular strategy. Converting to sustainable practices does not mean simple input substitution. Frequently, it substitutes enhanced management and scientific knowledge for conventional inputs, especially chemical inputs that harm the environment on farms and in rural communities. The goal is to develop efficient, biological systems which do not need high levels of material inputs.

Growers frequently ask if synthetic chemicals are appropriate in a sustainable farming system. Sustainable approaches are those that are the least toxic and least energy intensive, and yet maintain productivity and profitability. Preventive strategies and other alternatives should be employed before using chemical inputs from any source. However, there may be situations where the use of synthetic chemicals would be more 'sustainable' than a strictly non-chemical approach or an approach using toxic 'organic' chemicals. For example, one grape grower switched from tillage to a few applications of a broad spectrum contact herbicide in the vine row. This approach may use less energy and may compact the soil less than numerous passes with a cultivator or mower.

FARMER GOALS AND LIFESTYLE CHOICES

Management decisions should reflect not only environmental and broad social considerations, but also individual goals and lifestyle choices. For example, adoption of some technologies or practices that promise profitability may also require such intensive management that one's lifestyle actually deteriorates. Management decisions that promote sustainability nourish the environment, the community and the individual.

ECONOMIC, SOCIAL AND POLITICAL CONTEXT

In addition to strategies for preserving natural resources and changing production practices, sustainable agriculture requires a commitment to changing public policies, economic institutions, and social values.

Strategies for change must take into account the complex, reciprocal and ever-changing relationship between agricultural production and the broader society.

The 'food system' extends far beyond the farm and involves the interaction of individuals and institutions with contrasting and often competing goals including farmers, researchers, input suppliers, farm workers, unions, farm advisors, processors, retailers, consumers and policymakers. Relationships among these actors shift over time as new technologies spawn economic, social and political changes.

A wide diversity of strategies and approaches is necessary to create a more sustainable food system. This will range from specific and concentrated efforts to alter specific policies or practices, to the longer-term tasks of reforming key institutions, rethinking economic priorities and challenging widely-held social values. Areas of concern, where change is most needed, include the following:

Food and Agricultural Policy

Existing federal state and local government policies often impede the goals of sustainable agriculture. New policies are needed to simultaneously promote environmental health, economic profitability and social and economic equity.

For example, commodity and price support programmes could be restructured to allow farmers to realize the full benefits of the productivity gains, made possible through alternative practices.

Tax and credit policies could be modified to encourage a diverse and decentralized system of family farms rather than corporate concentration and absentee ownership.

Government and land grant university research policies could be modified to emphasize the development of sustainable alternatives. Marketing orders and cosmetic standards could be amended to encourage reduced pesticide use. Coalitions must be created to address these policy concerns at the local, regional and national level.

Land Use

Conversion of agricultural land to urban uses is a particular concern in many developed as well as developing nations as rapid growth and escalating land values threaten farming on prime soils. Existing farmland conversion patterns often discourage farmers from adopting sustainable practices and a long-term perspective on the value of land. At the same time, the close proximity of newly developed residential areas to farms is increasing the public demand for environmentally safe farming practices. Comprehensive new policies to protect prime soils and regulate development are needed. By helping farmers adopt practices that reduce chemical use and conserve scarce resources, sustainable agriculture research and education can play a key role in building public support for agricultural land preservation. Educating land use planners and decision-makers about sustainable agriculture is an important priority.

Labour

The conditions of agricultural labour are generally far below accepted social standards and legal protections in other forms of employment. Policies and programmes are needed to address this problem, working towards socially just and safe employment that provides adequate wages, working conditions, health benefits and chances for economic stability. The needs of migrant labour for year-round employment and adequate housing are a particularly crucial problem needing immediate attention. To be more sustainable over the long-term, labour must be acknowledged and supported by government policies, recognized as important constituents of land grant universities and carefully considered when assessing the impacts of new technologies and practices.

Rural Community Development

Rural communities are currently characterized by economic and environmental deterioration. Many are among the poorest locations in the nation. The reasons for the decline are complex, but changes in farm structure have played a significant role. Sustainable agriculture presents an opportunity to rethink the importance of family farms and rural communities. Economic development policies are needed that encourage more diversified agricultural production on family farms as a foundation for healthy economies in rural communities. In combination with other strategies, sustainable agriculture practices and policies can help foster community institutions that meet employment, educational, health, cultural and spiritual needs.

CONSUMERS AND THE FOOD SYSTEM

Consumers can play a critical role in creating a sustainable food system. Through their purchases, they send strong messages to producers, retailers and others in the system about what they think is important. Food cost and nutritional quality have always influenced consumer choices. The challenge now is to find strategies that broaden consumer perspectives, so that environmental quality, resource use, and social equity issues are also considered in shopping decisions. At the same time, new policies and institutions must be created to enable producers using sustainable practices to market their goods to a wider public. Coalitions organized around improving the food system are one specific method of creating a dialogue among consumers, retailers, producers and others.

CHAPTER 12

FOOD SECURITY AND POLITICS

GROWING demand for more food—in terms of quality and quantity—as well as general rising living standards in India, Brazil, Russia and China, where vast new middle classes are emerging, has been partly responsible for the price increases.

Oil demands are up, leading to the US$ 130+ per barrel costs, as more people can afford to own a car, which in turn fuels the food price ramp-up by increasing transport costs and making fertilizer more expensive. That the US dollar is weakening is also a major reason for the rising price of crude as it is priced in dollars—at least so far.

Thomas Friedman's flat-world thesis seems relevant here—consumers in emerging economies seeking to match Western affluence. This means more cars, more meat and more high calorie, high protein foods—all of which puts pressure on oil supplies and prices, not least as more meat equals more fuel consumption for cooking, as well as increased demand for the grain feed for livestock and chickens.

Dominique Strauss-Kahn, the chief of the International Monetary Fund (IMF), got no argument from the 24 finance ministers on his steering committee when he warned on April 12, 2008, that ongoing price inflation could undermine much of the recent pro-poor development gains in many countries. This echoed fears outlined in a World Bank policy paper *Rising Food Prices—Policy Options and World Bank Response*—released on April 9. Group President Robert B. Zoellick was quoted as saying: 'In some countries, hard-won gains in overcoming poverty may now be reversed.'

'THE POLITICS OF THE BELLY'

This treatise by Jean Francois Bayart took its title as a metaphor for the corrupt and patronage-addled nature of post-colonial African politics. But there seems to be a more literal application these days. Politics has at least partly caused the food price increases, with corrupt administrations unwilling to maximize food-production potential, and other developing economies unable as yet to improve yields—with the worst performers squandering their thriving agriculture systems.

More directly, producer governments are restricting exports, notably rice, to meet domestic demand, but leaving neighbouring importers in a quandary. C. Peter Timmer, visiting professor at Stanford University's Food Security and Environment Institute, wrote: 'The newly elected populist government in Thailand did not want consumer prices for rice to go up, so they started talking about export restrictions.... On March 28, rice prices in Thailand jumped US$ 75 per metric tonne. They have risen another US$ 200 per metric tonne since. This is the stuff of panics....'

David King is secretary-general of the International Federation of Agricultural Producers. He said, 'for example, only one-quarter of the irrigation potential along the Niger river valley is being exploited' and that 'yields in Africa are very low compared with other regions, but there is massive potential for improvement.'

In 1998, food price increases brought people onto Zimbabwe's streets, accelerating Robert Mugabe's turn to demagoguery as a diversion from his regime's frailties and sparking his ruthless suppression of any political opposition. Zimbabwe was once called 'the breadbasket of Africa,' but now cannot feed its own people, much less function as a swing supplier, helping meet demand and reduce prices.

Myanmar was once the world's biggest rice exporter, now many of its people hunger under the quixotic and brutal dictatorship ensconced in its jungle hideaway-fortress capital in Napyidaw.

Politically expedient choices made by governments, donors and recipients alike, contribute to the structural issues undermining food supply in vulnerable locations. As David King puts it, 'it is much easier for developed countries to send their food surpluses as aid to somewhere like Ethiopia, than it is to make focused long-term investments in water management technology to reduce that country's drought vulnerability. It is also easier for any recipients to divert attention from their own administration to external factors—such as food aid—when things go wrong.'

EATEN BREAD IS SOON FORGOTTEN

The impact of food price increases could well be serious instability in many countries.

Pakistan's pivotal parliamentary elections were depicted as a litmus-test for Muslim democracy and counterterrorism policy. But ordinary people voted for who they thought best able to help them make ends meet. The incumbent coalition led by President-General Pervez Musharraf took a hammering, as voters fused his anti-democratic policies with rising inflation now hitting consumers in the pocket.

These days, Pakistani troops are reported to be guarding rice warehouses against looting, with similar scenes in Thailand and Vietnam—the world's number one and three rice exporters, respectively—and in the Philippines and Indonesia, both rice importers.

In Manila, President Gloria Macapagal-Arroyo recently jailed nine coup plotters, but legitimately expressed disaffection with her administration, continues. She recently admonished rice traders against hoarding, saying that 'anyone who steals rice from the people' will be jailed. Arroyo is clearly hoping that rice supply can be maintained on the domestic market, heading off any further price increase or shortage, which could bring people onto the streets.

Such 'people power' manifestations have twice changed governments in the Philippines, in 1986 and 2001, the latter bringing the incumbent Mrs. Arroyo to power.

But with Thailand, India and Vietnam all more or less halting rice exports and China rebuffing Manila's request for additional wheat, urgent calls were being made for high-level pan-Asian talks on the food price crisis. David King's timely warning, 'this type of thing can bring down a government in a developing country,' was realized on Saturday, April 12, 2008, with Haiti's Senate sacking the prime minister in a deliberate snub to President Rene Preval over his response to Port-au-Prince's deadly food riots.

THE MOST VULNERABLE

The price spike provoked 'tortilla riots' in middle-income Mexico, and wealthy consumer groups in Italy staged a one-day protest at the price of pasta. But it is the world's poor who are feeling the pinch. Most vulnerable could be the aid-dependent in Darfur, Somalia, North Korea and elsewhere. The WFP appealed to donors for an extra half-billion dollars—just to enable it to meet the needs projected back in June 2007. 'This does not even account for any emergency or contingency funding needed, say, if another Niger-type scenario came about,' a WFP official said, referring to the August 2005 near-famine in that impoverished Sahelian country, which left over three million people on the brink of starvation.

THE HEAT IS ON

'Green' subsidies for biofuel crops are diverting agri-output away from food. American farmers have diverted over 30 per cent of corn as part of a government-sponsored ethanol production scheme. The U.S.A. was the world's fourth largest rice producer, the result of divestment into corn is lifting rice prices amid greater demand, while reduced U.S. corn-for-food output has put pressure on corn importer countries to diversify into ever more expensive wheat and sorghum, the latter needed to replace corn as animal feed.

All four agencies that track the earth's temperature—the U.K.-based Hadley Climate Research Unit, NASA's Goddard Institute for Space Studies in New York, the Christy Group at The University of Alabama (U.S.A.) and Remote Sensing Systems Inc. in California—report that it cooled by about 0.7 degrees C in 2007. A German study published in the journal *Nature* (May 1, 2007) projected that the planet may cool until 2015 "while natural variations in climate cancel out the increases caused by man-made greenhouse gas emissions."

While the *Nature* article outlines that the planet will likely resume warming by about 2020, the warming gap is at odds with continuous warming projections outlined by the UN's Intergovernmental Panel on Climate Change (IPCC) that, 'for the next two decades, a warming of about 0.2° C per decade is projected for a range of SRES emission scenarios. Even if the concentrations of all greenhouse gases and aerosols had been kept constant at year 2000 levels, a further warming of about 0.1° C per decade would be expected.'

With natural factors seemingly overriding human impact on climate, and after bitterly cold winters in China, its coldest in a century, in Central Asia and across North America, the biofuels gambit thus seems doubly-questionable, as it fuels food price increases more efficiently than its does environment-friendly automobiles.

WHAT MORE CAN HAPPEN?

The impact on the global economy remains to be seen—but the IMF has warned that commodity price increases were feeding inflation, curtailing what policy options were available to deal with an overall global slowdown. This too can have political ramification. China's communist rulers, now shaken by Olympics and Tibet protests, doubtlessly also recall the inflation-driven unrest culminating in the 1989 Tiananmen Square massacre.

Experts believe that policymakers should use this (price increase) as a catalyst to develop agriculture, especially in low-yield, high-potential regions, which echoes a call from the International Rice Research Institute for 'a second Green Revolution,' replicating the improvements in the 1960s and 1970s in agricultural technologies that boosted production across Asia.

A cautionary note is that there is already substantial evidence that significant increases in production, if they are attainable at all, will require development of new crop technologies that are not on the shelf or even in the pipeline. The prospect is that very high food prices, perhaps near current levels, will be a market reality for many years.

In the first four months of 2008, protests over food have taken place in Indonesia, Peru, Mauritania, Yemen, Burkina Faso, Bolivia and Uzbekistan. In Egypt and Haiti, riots turned deadly, with seven and four people killed, respectively, in both countries over 10 days, while over 40 died in Cameroon's February food unrest. Even as far back as August 2007, the quashed Saffron Revolution in Myanmar was sparked in the first instance by the junta's overnight doubling of essential food and fuel prices.

Despite government attempts to shelter domestic food from soaring global cereal prices, essentials such as bread, rice, maize products, milk and soybean have continued to become more expensive all over the world.

The facts are stark: The global price of wheat has risen by 130 per cent in the past year, and dairy prices have doubled since 2005. A combination of factors is making basic food and fuel too expensive for people in poorer countries—even as projected world cereal production for 2008 is a record 2,164 million tonnes, up almost 3 per cent from last year.

But with across-the-board world food price rises averaging over 80 per cent during the last 24 months, this volatility could acquire a dangerous political counterpart, in countries where 60 to 75 per cent of people's income is spent on food. On Saturday, 12 April, 20,000 Bangladeshis took to the streets—angered over low wages and high food costs—wrecking vehicles and attacking police, after last year's rice crop was ruined by another of that country's periodic floods.

Anger and political unrest over escalating world food prices is becoming increasingly violent. Higher prices for the basic food commodities used by developing countries have produced clashes in Egypt and several African states. The government of Haiti has fallen from a political segue that started with a protest against food prices. An international food expert has warned of more fighting with no short-term relief in sight.

According to an article from the *Washington Times*, 'World food prices have risen 45 per cent in the last nine months and there are serious shortages of rice, wheat and corn,' said Jacques Diouf, head of the Rome-based U.N. Food and Agriculture Organization (FAO) at a conference in New Delhi. 'There is a risk that this unrest will spread in countries where 50 to 60 per cent of income goes to food.'

Several people have been reported killed in disturbances as unrest in Haiti continues amid a doubling of the price of rice. A supermarket, several gas station marts and a government rice warehouse have been looted.

The Prime Minister of Egypt promised concessions to workers in the industrial city of Mahalla al-Kobra after days of rioting over rising food prices resulted in the death of one protestor. These clashes were described as the most serious anti-government demonstrations since riots in 1977 erupted over soaring bread prices. Unrest has also been reported by the FAO in Burkina Faso, Cameroon, Indonesia, Ivory Coast, Mauritania, Mozambique, Bolivia and Uzbekistan, among other countries.

The world's largest rice importer, the Philippines, has moved to head off protests following the global price doubling of rice. Higher rice prices would cut the country's gross domestic product by at least one per cent this year according to Credit Suisse. Controls of domestic rice sales have been tightened and security of government storehouses has been strengthened. President Gloria Macapagal Arroyo warned that anyone convicted of stealing rice would be jailed. The President of the World Bank, has said that close to three dozen countries face social unrest as a result of rising food and fuel prices. He sees the countries most at risk as having 'no margin for survival.'

This crisis has been building for months spurred by a confluence of events. Among them are higher fuel prices that make the transport of food more expensive, and the rotation of farmers from food crops to biofuel. Food demand is also rising as the emerging populations in China, India and other Asian countries gain wealth with which to purchase better quality food containing higher levels of protein. Weather has also been a factor as drought has hit some major producers such as Australia. Commodity market speculators have helped sustain the higher prices. Although speculators are often discounted during extreme price moves, the fact that they seldom take delivery of the actual commodity prevents market prices from reflecting true market conditions.

The chief U.N. humanitarian official predicted that the situation would continue to produce political repercussions. 'The security implications should not be underestimated, as food riots are already being reported across the globe,' he said.

According to analysts, price increases are across the board, not just focused on a few crops or markets. A recent survey found that the price of staple food has risen by 80 per cent since 2005, including a 40 per cent increase in 2008. The real price of rice is at a 19 year high, with the price of wheat at a 28 year high.

Along with the conversion of huge segments of farm lands to biofuels, it is also believed that demographic trends, changing diets, energy prices and climate changes predict higher food prices for years to come. It is not just the poor who will be pushed into extreme behaviour.

Food security is the condition in which everyone has access to sufficient and affordable food; it can relate to a single household or to the global population. The first Millennium Development Goal (MDG) falls short of food security aspirations in seeking only to reduce by half the proportion of the world's population experiencing hunger.

Furthermore, governments signing the Millennium Declaration were overriding a commitment made just four years earlier at the World Food Summit of 1996 which applied the same target to the *number* of people. Rising population figures mean that 170 million fewer will be targeted by the MDG programme than would otherwise have been the case.

The first of two benchmarks for measuring progress is the 'minimum dietary energy requirement' for each person as stipulated by the UN Food and Agriculture Organization (FAO). This naturally varies by age and sex so that a weighted average is calculated for each country based on its population profile; typically this average is just below 2,000 kilocalories per day. Despite the promises of the MDGs, over 50 million people have been added to the 800 million falling below this benchmark in 2000. Malnutrition impairs the ability to learn or to work and reduces resistance to disease, these problems increasing in severity with the shortfall from the minimum dietary requirement. Hunger is therefore a cause as well as a consequence of poverty.

Children's health and cognitive development is especially sensitive, to the extent that the majority of child mortality is attributed to malnutrition. The second MDG indicator is therefore the proportion of children under age five who are underweight in relation to their age. This figure has reduced from 32 per cent to only 27 per cent in the period 1990–2006. UNICEF says that 51 countries are unlikely to reach this MDG target by 2015. Moreover, these progress assessments predate the explosion in world food prices that has rocked global development agencies in 2008. UN Secretary-General Ban Ki-Moon has warned that 'high food prices threaten to undo the gains achieved so far in fighting hunger and malnutrition'.

CLIMATE CHANGE AND FOOD SECURITY

As recently as 2006, progress reports on malnutrition published by UN agencies made no reference to climate change. Yet it was no surprise when, in preparation for the Bali Climate Change Conference in 2007, the Intergovernmental Panel on Climate Change (IPCC) painted an almost cataclysmic picture for Africa in which 'for even small temperature increases of 1–2 degrees.....yields for rain-fed agriculture could be reduced by up to 50 per cent by 2020'. In addition, the predicted increase in drought and floods will aggravate what is already a serious short-term cause of food insecurity. In South and East Asia climate change threatens to upset the stable monsoon pattern around which rice production in particular has evolved.

The UN supports the 50 Least Developed Countries (LDCs) in preparation of National Adaptation Programmes of Actions (NAPAs) and the Bali Conference launched an Adaptation Fund which may in time support these programmes. Recognising that funding is likely to be scarce, NAPAs limit their scope to community-based low-cost options for dealing with climate variability. Adaptation of agriculture will include the use of alternative seed varieties, improved soil management, maintenance of water management systems and reforestation. These NAPA reports convey universal concern for the sensitivity of food security to a less predictable climate and for the very limited capacity of poor communities to respond. Seed scientists acknowledge the extreme difficulty of climate adaptation even where research funding is available.

BIOFUELS AND FOOD SECURITY

Under pressure to take action on climate change in the run up to the Bali Conference, politicians resorted to knee-jerk policymaking, seduced by the claims of the biofuel industry. Petrol additives such as ethanol and biodiesel are manufactured from plant crops as a means of reducing dependence on fossil fuels and cutting carbon dioxide emissions. Apparently oblivious to the mathematics that one tank of ethanol for a Sports Utility Vehicle consumes corn that could feed a man for a year, the EU announced that these biofuels will contribute 10 per cent of transport fuels by 2020 whilst the U.S.A. plans to quadruple output in that period.

Quite apart from the flawed assumption that these products create a net reduction in greenhouse gas emissions, the use of land and food crops to cater for rich motorists at a time of global food insecurity has provoked outrage amongst groups campaigning for poverty reduction.

Oxfam predicts that biofuel targets could create 600 million additional hungry people by 2025. In 2008, one third of the U.S. maize crop will be diverted to biofuel production, showering corn farmers with subsidies of far greater value than U.S. food aid. As these realities sink in, there are initial signs of back-pedalling on biofuel targets and subsidies amongst EU and U.S. officials.

THE RIGHT TO FOOD

Promotion of biofuels has been cited as a breach of the right to sufficient food enshrined in the Universal Declaration of Human Rights and other international treaty commitments. The UN Special Rapporteur for the Right to Food, Olivier de Schutter, has urged the UN to respond to the food crisis as a human rights emergency and called for a freeze on new investment in converting food into fuel.

In contrast to the half-speed MDG vision, a human rights approach to food security places immediate and inclusive obligations on governments to create capacity for their people to feed themselves. Ideally the right to food should take its place in national laws or constitutions, with guarantees of non-discriminatory and non-political strategies.

Many of the world's food security problems stem from the absence of an overriding goal to honour the right to food. A set of world trade rules might look very different if governed by such an objective rather than the focus on absolute volumes of trade.

CAUSES OF FOOD INSECURITY

The aftermath of the World War II saw strategies which did indeed award priority to food security. The European Common Agricultural Policy and the U.S. Farm Bill combined subsidies and tariffs to support the pattern of small family farms which were dominant at that time. These policies proved successful, generating colossal internal food surpluses.

Not surprisingly, the poorer countries of the modern world were keen to copy this successful protectionist model, not least because of their similar profile of agriculture – there are 500 million farms of less than 2 hectares in developing countries. Such ambitions remain unfulfilled largely because in 1995 the richer countries were successful in their efforts to include agriculture in the system of open market rules governed by the World Trade Organisation, whilst simultaneously refusing to unravel their own protectionist model. Attempts by developing countries to build their agriculture sectors have been undermined, both in domestic markets undercut by cheap imports from rich countries and in exports which encounter trade barriers erected in Europe and the U.S.A.

Countries in Africa and South Asia are also to blame for their prolonged lack of investment in rural economies which account for about 75 per cent of world hunger. For example, African governments are yet to meet their 2003 Maputo Declaration commitment which called for 10 per cent of national budgets to be dedicated to agriculture by 2008. Rural economies have therefore failed to grow. Poor farmers, often holding uncertain land tenure and lacking capital, plant for a mix of subsistence and surplus for market, a model chronically vulnerable to fluctuating prices or unfavourable weather. The majority of developing countries have food deficits, a serious problem for those lacking foreign currency to purchase expensive imports.

Whilst overall population growth creates pressure on food security, it is a relatively minor factor. Since 1961, world production of food has trebled, whilst the population has doubled. Feeding more than half of the world's grain production to animals, is the more significant indicator. As 7 kg of grain is required to produce 1 kg of beef, there is an argument that meat production on this scale impedes the goal of global food security. Another human weakness, for violent conflict, invariably leads to extreme food insecurity. The 2007 Global Hunger Index reports that 'almost all' of its worst ranking countries have been involved in violent conflict in the last decade. Collapsed economies such as North Korea and Zimbabwe also generate food crises.

THE SEARCH FOR SOLUTIONS TO FOOD INSECURITY

Disagreement over trade rules reflects the two longstanding and opposing philosophies for addressing structural weaknesses that lead to food insecurity. The neo-liberal model advocates that food should be subject to the same market forces as manufactured goods with minimum state involvement. It denies any value to 'romantic peasant farming' which should be consolidated, with alternative livelihoods found for surplus labour. Larger farms can then raise capital and compete in export markets. Foreign aid would have a role to play in developing transport and storage infrastructure, creating efficient local markets and improving standards of governance. Advocates of this model put a price of $ 8–10 billion per annum on doubling farm output in Africa.

The alternative philosophy of 'food sovereignty' restores the priority for food security over trade volume. This model favours local ownership and control of the full chain of resources, accepting small farms for what they are and encouraging their sustainability through subsidised inputs and credit, as has been followed successfully in Malawi's recent transformation from shortage to surplus. New communications technologies can also play an innovative role in supporting small farmers.

WORLD FOOD PRICES AND FOOD SECURITY

These competing philosophies are undergoing intense scrutiny in reaction to recent dramatic increases in world food prices, which on average have doubled over the year to April 2008. As the world's poorest households already spend 60 to 100 per cent of their incomes on food, they have no mechanism to cope with rising prices other than to reduce the volume or nutritional quality of their consumption. The World Food Programme (WFP) says that 100 million people will be added to those below the hunger threshold, taking the global total to almost one billion and creating a new class of urban poor unable to afford sufficient food.

There is little consensus as to the underlying cause of such sudden price adjustments. Each of the most favoured explanations is open to challenge: global production of grain increased by 4 per cent in 2007, casting doubt on claims of poor harvests; biofuel production does not involve rice or wheat and therefore should not impact those prices; and the increasing demand for meat is neither new nor confined to China. The parallel doubling of the price of oil does have a significant impact on the cost of farm inputs and transportation and is a reminder that the last serious world food crisis of the early 1970s coincided with the oil price shocks of that period. The finger of suspicion is also being pointed at speculative rich country traders in commodities. The increasingly complex and opaque world of derivative financial products has been exposed as rotten to the core in the context of the global credit crisis. Governments in India and Ethiopia have banned futures trading in their agricultural commodities markets.

Although the UN has set up a task force and world leaders promise discussions, national interests have so far dominated the response to a crisis which requires coordinated global action. Many countries have resorted to stockpiling food and blocking exports in order to keep down domestic prices. The U.S. Farm Bill currently under discussion ignores the golden opportunity presented by high prices to abolish farm subsidies. Without global food security today, adaptation to future climate change will have no foundation on which to build.

FOOD AID

Rising prices create a pincer movement on food aid programmes by increasing the numbers in need whilst reducing the amount of food that can be purchased with fixed budgets. Although food aid alone is not a sustainable solution to hunger, it has a vital humanitarian role to play in the most critical circumstances. Monitoring the balance of food supply and demand throughout the world is the core mandate of the FAO, delivered by its Global Information and Early Warning System. Based on this information the World Food Programme (WFP) draws up its programmes, giving priority to regions where the depth of hunger is most serious. Currently the agency supports 70–100 million people and about the same number is assisted by international aid agencies. This leaves over 750 million dependent on highly variable or non-existent domestic safety net arrangements such as the Indian Public Distribution Scheme.

BIOTECHNOLOGY AND GM CROPS

The current crisis in food security will strengthen the hand of those who believe that biotechnology is the way forward. The great advances in crop yields since the 1970s, symbolised by the 'green revolution', have to be weighed against their ecological and structural consequences. The FAO says that 75 per cent of food biodiversity was lost in the 20th century whilst 80 per cent of the world's dietary energy is now supplied by just 12 industrial crops, such is the dominance of a small number of very large international 'agribusiness' corporations. The green revolution has also been responsible for significant degradation of soil quality and severe depletion of water resources, a worrying loss of environmental capital with which to satisfy the projected doubling of demand for world food production in the next 25-50 years.

Genetically-modified (GM) crops, in which a gene of desired characteristic is transposed from one plant to another, are the most extreme and controversial output of the biotechnology companies. Offering higher yields, lower chemical inputs and higher nutritional value, GM crops sound like the panacea to food insecurity. Led by Brazil, South Africa, China and India, many developing countries have adopted GM crops. However, there are doubts as to whether the poorer countries have the capacity to establish regulatory frameworks to manage inevitable conflicts of interests between the local stakeholders (farmers, consumers, and governments) and global shareholders who control the intellectual property rights.

CHAPTER 13

BUYER-SELLER POLITICS OF FOOD SCARCITY

FOR more than 40 years, international trade negotiations have been dominated by grain-exporting countries, principally the United States, Canada, Argentina, and Australia, pressing for greater access to markets in importing countries. Now the world may be moving into a period dominated not by surpluses but by shortages. In this case, the issue becomes not exporters' access to markets but importers' access to supplies.

The behaviour of exporters very early in the decade, shows why grain-importing countries should be concerned. In early September of 2002, Canada, following a harvest decimated by heat and drought, announced that it would export no more wheat until the next harvest. Two months later, Australia, another key exporter, said that because of a short harvest it would supply wheat only to its traditional buyers. And in the summer of 2003, during the crop-withering heat waves in Europe, the European Union announced that it would not issue any grain export permits until the supply situation improved.

A similar situation developed in Russia following a poor harvest in 2003. Facing a rise in bread prices of more than 20 per cent, in January 2004, the government imposed an export tax of 24 euros ($ 30) per ton on wheat, effectively ending wheat exports.

In late August 2004, China approached Vietnam to buy 500,000 tons of rice. The leaders in Hanoi responded by saying that the rice could not be supplied until the first quarter of 2005 at the earliest. This is because the Vietnamese government had imposed export limits of 3.5 million tons for the year, or just under 300,000 tons per month, out of fear that growing external demand for its rice would lead to over-exporting and thus to rising domestic prices.

This response is of interest because Vietnam is the world's second-ranking rice exporter after Thailand. Thailand, Vietnam, and the United States account for 16 million of the 25 million tons of world exports. In addition to China, more than 30 other countries import substantial amounts of rice, ranging from 100,000 tons a year for Colombia and Sri Lanka to 1.8 million tons for Indonesia.

If substantially higher grain prices are needed to bring additional agricultural resources into play, whether in boosting water productivity, which effectively expands the supply, or bringing new land into play in Brazil, how will the world adjust? It may be that the *laissez-faire*, independent decision-making of national governments will have to blend into a more coordinated approach to managing food supplies in a time of scarcity.

Unfortunately, the government of China contributes to global food insecurity by refusing to release data on its grain stocks, leaving the international community to try and estimate them independently. This leads to a great deal of uncertainty and confusion, as can be seen in three substantial revisions of estimates for China's grain stocks in the last four years by the U.S. Department of Agriculture (USDA) and the Food and Agriculture Organization (FAO). While holding this information close to the vest gives Chinese grain buyers an advantage in the world market, it makes it extremely difficult for the world to plan for, and thus respond to, potentially huge future import needs.

Because the last half-century has been dominated by excessive production and market surpluses, the world has had little experience in dealing with the politics of scarcity outside a brief period in 1972–74. In 1972, with a poor domestic harvest in prospect, the Soviets entered the world wheat market secretively and managed to tie up almost all the world's exportable supplies of wheat, before governments of either exporting or importing countries realized what was happening.

CHAPTER 14

FORESTRY AND FOOD SECURITY

FOOD security is a fundamental problem facing the world today. Despite substantial increases in food production in many countries, over 800 million people still suffer from malnutrition. According to FAO figures, approximately 20 million people are dying of starvation or related diseases each year. It has become imperative to go look beyond the evident corrective measures that can be taken. One such measure is forestry.

For many foresters, the issue of food security may seem to be a concern which goes far beyond the domain of their profession. And yet, in many rural areas, forests and farm trees provide critical support to agricultural production (for example, in maintaining and improving soil conditions, and maintaining hydrological systems), they provide food, fodder and fuel, and they provide a means of earning cash income. Thus, both directly and indirectly, forestry activities may have an impact on people's food security.

Within the community of forestry professionals, food security has emerged in the last few years as a new focus for forestry development and planning. While it is recognized that forests contribute to food security in many ways, these links have seldom been studied in depth and there have been few attempts to assess their significance. At the policy and planning level, very little has been done to incorporate food security as a specific objective in forestry strategies and programmes.

An Expert Consultation on forestry and food security sponsored by the FAO Forestry Department illuminates some of the links between forestry and food security, and shows how forestry activities can and do have an impact on food security. In this report, forestry is defined in a broad sense to include management and use of trees and shrubs on farms and grazing areas, as well as within established forest reserves. Drawing on many different sources, it pieces together a picture of the complex interactions between people, trees, forests, agriculture and food production.

It looks at negative as well as positive effects of forestry activities, and it aims to distinguish links between forestry and food security that are well proven from those that are still speculative or disputed. Going beyond this, the report also sets out some initial ideas about how forestry policies and programmes can be directed to improving food security, especially for the poor.

PUTTING FORESTRY IN PERSPECTIVE

The part played by forestry in food security must be kept in perspective. Forests are just one element within the complex fabric of rural life, and food security depends on a whole range of factors quite apart from forests and forestry activities.

It is clearly wrong, for example, to suggest that forestry can replace agriculture as a food production system to any significant extent. It must also be recognized that forestry initiatives, by themselves, cannot remove the underlying pressures caused by population growth. Neither can they fundamentally alter the social, economic and political factors that create inequalities and separate the rich from the poor; the hungry from the well-fed.

The premise, however, is that forests and trees do have an important role to play in food security. It is a role that has been ignored in the past, and is currently being eroded as forests in many parts of the world are cleared and the remaining trees on farmland come under increasing pressure. These trends are undermining existing agricultural systems and jeopardising their long-term productivity.

But these trends are not irreversible. Through better management of forests and by supporting tree growing on farms, the contribution of forestry to food security can be both strengthened and enhanced. Forestry initiatives have the potential for providing a range of benefits—augmenting food production, increasing the sustainability of food supplies and improving access to food for the landless and poor by providing subsistence products, income and employment.

THE LINKS BETWEEN FORESTRY AND FOOD SECURITY

It is clear that many links between forestry and food security are interrelated. To simplify the discussion, however, they can be divided into three main groups: environmental, production, and socio-economic factors.

Environmental Links

Trees and forests influence both their immediate surroundings and the stability of the larger environment, and as a result have several important links to food security. Both at the micro and the macro-level, they help provide the stable environmental conditions on which sustainable food production depends.

For many communities in tropical regions forests provide the only means for restoring soil productivity (through systems of forest fallowing). Forest areas also represent the single largest storehouse of genetic diversity, a resource of great importance to future agricultural production.

The effects of trees are most easily seen at the farm level, where they can play an important role in improving the microclimate, reducing the damage caused by wind, protecting against soil erosion, and restoring soil productivity.

At the watershed level, forests can reduce sedimentation and improve water quality; they may also have an effect on water availability downstream, and may assist to some extent in reducing the incidence of floods. All of these factors have a major influence on downstream agriculture. At a regional and global level, forests may also affect climate and rainfall patterns, although the detailed interactions are controversial and still only partly understood.

Production Links

The most direct connection between forestry and food security is the food items produced by trees. Fruits, nuts, leaves, roots and gums are just some of the huge array of edible foods, that are obtained from trees and shrubs, either growing naturally in the wild or cultivated on farms and around the home. Forests also provide a habitat for many animals, birds, insects and other forms of wildlife, that are hunted and consumed, often as delicacies. While these forest foods rarely provide staples, they do provide important supplements as well as seasonal and emergency substitutes when food supplies dwindle.

Links with Household Food Security

In addition, forests can have an important indirect influence on food production. By maintaining and improving soil fertility, trees grown on farms can help sustain crop yields. In pastoral production systems, trees and shrubs provide an essential source of livestock fodder, especially during the dry season. And in mangrove areas, the forests are a habitat and breeding ground for many fish, crustacea and other marine animals that support coastal and off-shore fisheries.

Socio-economic Links

Food security is fundamentally a social issue. The socioeconomic links between forestry and food security are those that link the products and 'services' of forests to the people who depend on them. From the point of view of individual households, forests may affect their food security in several ways.

Foods obtained from trees and forests make an important direct contribution to family diets, providing a tasty and nutritious supplement to otherwise bland staple foods. Although the quantities involved may be small, their nutritional contribution is often critical, especially at certain times of the year and during droughts or other emergency periods when cultivated foods are unavailable.

Even more important for many families is the fact that forests provide a source of income and employment. Millions of rural people depend on money earned from gathering, processing and selling forest products to buy food and other basic necessities. For the poor, and also for women, these are often one of their only sources of cash income. Trees grown on the farm are also used as savings, that can be harvested and sold to meet large or emergency cash needs.

OPPORTUNITIES FOR ACTION

There is much that can be done by foresters to enhance household food security. Some of the most obvious opportunities for action include:

- ⌘ Directing forest management objectives to people's food security needs;
- ⌘ Broadening the range of products produced by forests – food and other items – and improving their supply to local people through new management approaches and access arrangements;

- Encouraging tree growing on farms using species and management approaches that complement crop and livestock production, help protect the environment, provide income to farmers, and assist them to spread risks;
- Supporting small-scale forest-based enterprises by ensuring a sustainable supply of input materials, providing managerial and technological assistance, and improving access to credit; and
- Providing market support to help rural people get a better price for the forest products they sell and secure a more sustainable livelihood.

While a number of promising approaches of this kind can be identified, experience in putting them into practice is still limited. Local circumstances will inevitably play a big part in determining their relevance and a great deal will depend on local people's needs, available resources and careful planning.

SETTING A POLICY FRAMEWORK

Forests and farm trees contribute to food security in many rural regions throughout the world. In order to strengthen and develop these contributions, forestry programmes and foresters need to review the goals and devise new approaches for their activities. Existing institutional structures, and the traditional focus of forestry training, research and extension work, are not at all well matched to the task of addressing food security objectives.

Support at the policy level is a prerequisite for change. This means reorganising the specific role of existing forests and of trees in the food security of rural people and their effectiveness in sustaining land-use and food production systems.

It will also require support for staff, resources and training. Addressing problems of food security will require a shift in emphasis away from traditional goals of production and protection forestry to gearing forestry activities to meet local people's needs.

It could mean, for example, upgrading of the status of so-called 'minor forest products' to recognise the extremely important contribution they already make to local incomes and livelihoods and to exploit the potential for enhancing their production and use. It will involve exploring new approaches to forest management, which address issues of access and control of forest resources and which acknowledge the rights of local people to benefit from the forests.

Clearly this will involve putting a lot more effort into understanding local circumstances, and the problems, food security being just one of them, that people face, especially those who are poor. To this end forestry planners will need to build from the considerable traditional knowledge of forest resources that exists in many communities and on methods of managing their local environment.

New types of training will be required for forestry professionals and extension workers to broaden their outlook and provide them with the skills needed to work more closely with local people. There is a need to bring in other professionals such as nutritionists and social-scientists. Special emphasis must be placed on incorporating the needs and perspectives of women in the planning and implementation of projects.

Much can be gained if forestry services can collaborate more effectively with agriculture departments and agencies involved in fisheries, livestock and other related professions. Food security crosses over conventional sectoral boundaries and can only be tackled effectively through cooperative endeavours.

More fundamentally, the social, economic and political factors that create and maintain inequalities and lie behind poverty and hunger, must be recognized. Forestry initiatives cannot change these realities. Even so, there is much that can be done to channel benefits towards poor and disadvantaged groups, provided their needs are properly identified and the necessary commitment exists.

There are many challenges to be faced if forestry is to contribute more effectively to food security. However, there are solid grounds for optimism. Forestry philosophy and practice have changed radically over the last few decades, moving away from a narrow traditional view to broader and more people-oriented goals. Incorporating food security concerns can be seen as the logical next step in making forestry more responsive to people's needs, and more relevant to the development process.

CHAPTER 15

GOVERNMENT INTERVENTIONS

GLOBAL food supplies are sufficient to meet the calorie requirements of all people if food were distributed according to needs. Per capita food supplies are projected to increase further over the next twenty years. Thus, the world food problem now and in the foreseeable future is not one of global shortage. Instead, the world is faced with three main food-related challenges: widespread hunger and malnutrition, mismanagement of natural resources in food production and obesity. This section deals with the first two only.

While rapidly increasing yields per unit of land in large parts of East and Southeast Asia, the United States and parts of Europe reduced the expansion of agriculture into new lands and had positive effects on biodiversity, wildlife, soils and forests, they also introduced large quantities of chemical pesticides and caused water and soil degradation. In many other areas, including sub-Saharan Africa, stagnating yields combined with rapid population growth forced farmers into new lands poorly suited for agriculture, causing deforestation and land degradation. The challenge confronting us is to continue the expansion of food production to meet future demand without negative effects on the environment.

The other challenge is to assure that everyone has access to sufficient food to live a healthy and productive life. Elimination of food insecurity, hunger and malnutrition, in a manner consistent with an ecologically sustainable management of natural resources, is of critical importance. The failure of about 800 million people to meet food needs, is a reflection of widespread poverty, which in turn is associated with a very skewed and deteriorating relative income distribution.

Although some progress has been made during the last 20 years, the future is not bright. At the World Food Summit in 1996, high-level policy makers from more than 180 countries agreed to the goal of reducing the number of food-insecure people by half, to 400 million, between 1990 and 2015.

At the follow-up Summit in 2002, policy makers from the same countries reaffirmed the goal. Unfortunately, action does not seem to follow rhetoric. In the 1990s, less than one third of the countries managed to reduce the number of food-insecure people, while one half experienced an increase.

The design and implementation of food and agricultural policies for the future should pay particular attention to eight driving forces:

1. Increasing globalization.
2. Technological change.
3. Degradation of natural resources and water scarcity.
4. Rapidly changing consumer behaviour.
5. Emerging and re-emerging health crises.
6. Rapid urbanization.
7. National and international instability and conflict.
8. Changing roles and responsibilities of key actors.

The eight listed factors embrace practically all areas of the food economy. Determining the policy to embrace all these factors can be best left to scientists, economists and environmentalists. But to implement and monitor such a policy is impossible without government intervention.

Globalization has benefited hundreds of millions of people, but many others have been made worse off. Effective food and agricultural policy and institutions are needed to complement and guide globalization to achieve sustainable food security. It is of critical importance that the industrialized countries phase out trade-distorting agricultural policies, including those providing subsidies based on quantity produced or acreage used. Industrialized countries have repeatedly committed themselves to open their markets for exports from the world's poorest countries. However, very little progress has been made.

In addition to high tariffs, countries of the Organization for Economic Cooperation and Development impose a variety of non-tariff barriers, including food safety and sanitary levels that few developing countries can meet. These barriers for commodities and products from developing countries, such as foods and textiles, should be eliminated gradually, along with subsidized exports and non-emergency related food aid. It is particularly critical that tariff escalation related to the degree of processing of agricultural commodities be phased out as soon as possible. Tariff escalations are in stark contrast to efforts by development assistance agencies and national governments of developing countries to promote employment-generating, value-adding processing of agricultural commodities as a tool for development and poverty reduction.

In the case of developing countries, investments in public goods and institutions to promote effective and efficient private markets, rural infrastructure, credit and savings institutions, primary education, primary health care and publicly funded agricultural research to generate knowledge and technology for the smallholder farming community, are essential for them to facilitate economic growth and poverty alleviation and to reap the benefits from trade liberalization and other aspects of globalization. Policies and institutions are needed to facilitate access by women to land and purchased inputs. The *de facto* importance of women in agriculture should be recognized by eliminating discriminatory policies and practices in land tenure and providing access to credit, inputs, technology, extension and education.

Under-investment by developing countries in agricultural research is another serious bottleneck to productivity increases and competitiveness. These countries invest 0.6 per cent of the value of agricultural output on research, compared to 2.6 per cent in industrialized countries, if only public funding is considered. If private research funding is added, the difference becomes much larger.

Rapid scientific and technological developments in molecular biology, information, communication and energy are placing new demands on government policy to guide the design and utilization of these new scientific and technological opportunities for the benefit of farmers, consumers and natural resources while, at the same time, managing new risks and uncertainties. The impact of the new technology on people and their food security will, to a very large extent, depend on accompanying policies. Currently, action by governments, the for-profit private sector and civil society tends to be excessively influenced by ideology and unsubstantiated claims about risks and opportunities. The lack of appropriate facilitating and regulatory policies and related low levels of public investment in public goods-creating research is a major reason why potential benefits from the new technology are not reaching low-income people in developing countries.

Much of the technology needed by small landholders is of a public goods nature and unlikely to be produced by the private sector. There is an urgent need for substantial increases in public funding of agriculture research for small landholder farming in developing countries. Research aimed at biofortification, for example, improving the nutritional value of staple foods, offers a particularly exciting opportunity for reducing micronutrient deficiencies.

Policies and new institutions are urgently needed on intellectual property rights questions, biosafety and food safety regulations, facilitation of markets for improved seed, solar panels, cell phones and other information and communications technology, and a variety of facilitation and regulatory policy issues.

Failure to achieve yield increases on land that is well suited for agricultural cultivation has pushed farmers into areas less suited for agriculture, causing deforestation, land degradation and the unsustainable exploitation of surface and ground water. On the other hand, efforts to expand yields have frequently been based on the excessive and inappropriate use of fertilizers and pesticides, which in turn has damaged the environment. The challenge to policy makers is to put in place institutions and incentives that will guide farmers towards productivity increases compatible with sustainable management of natural resources.

Concerns are growing about the extent and rate of soil degradation and its effects on agricultural productivity and the preservation of natural resources, including biodiversity. Overgrazing, soil mining for nutrients, deforestation and inappropriate agricultural practices account for most of the degradation. These problems often result from inadequate property rights, poverty, population pressure, inappropriate government policies and lack of access to markets, credit and technologies appropriate for sustainable agricultural development.

Competition for water is becoming more acute, increasing the potential for conflicts between sectors, and water wars between countries. Efficiency of water use in agriculture, industry and urban areas is generally low. Degradation of land and water resources through waterlogging, salination and groundwater mining is mounting, while the excessive use of water in some locations causes a lack of access to water elsewhere. In many locations, water is still treated as goods, with little or no clearly defined property and user rights. Policy reforms are needed to provide secure water rights vested in individuals or groups of water users that increase incentives for investment, improve water use efficiency, reduce the degradation of the environment and encourage flexibility in resource allocation. Irrigation infrastructure and management should be turned over to water user associations where well-defined rights provide incentives for user groups to economize on water. Governments should reform distorted price incentives and reduce or remove subsidies to prevent overuse or misuse.

Much of the current debate about agriculture and the environment is based on the implicit or explicit premise that productivity increases in agriculture must necessarily harm the environment. This is a false premise. In fact, when productivity fails to increase, the resulting poverty and struggle for survival are much more likely to result in negative environmental effects. Improved production methods and appropriate use of inputs and technology, can boost productivity and benefit the environment, whether in developing or industrialized countries. The challenge is to help farmers design and implement such win-win solutions.

While population growth, increasing urbanization and changes in prices and household incomes continue to be the principal driving forces behind changes in food demand in developing countries, other factors are taking on increasing importance among the non-poor in both developing and industrialized countries. The most important are increasing concerns about food safety and the related increases in demand for organically produced food, identity preservation, natural foods and the increasing desire to consume locally produced food. European and to a lesser extent American consumers are complementing their market power with the exercise of power over the regulatory and other policy processes. Nowhere is this more obvious than in the case of European consumer reaction to genetically modified food. These changes in consumer behaviour raise a number of policy issues.

Within the context of increasing globalization, one of the policy questions deserving additional analysis, relates to food safety concerns as a function of income level. While food safety problems are more severe among the poor in developing countries, one of the ironies of recent developments is that high-income people in industrialized countries express much more concern about food safety than the poor. They are frequently facing a trade-off between food safety and food security in the sense that higher levels of safety are likely to be translated into higher prices and therefore lower real purchasing power among the poor who frequently spend 50 to 80 per cent of their income on food. When these trade-offs occur at a level above the most basic requirements for food safety, one of the globalization-related policy questions is whether different standards are compatible with globalization, and if not, who sets the standard. A related question is whether very high levels of food safety standards in industrialized countries are in fact being used as non-tariff barriers towards developing countries that wish to export but cannot meet the high standards.

The tragic pandemic of HIV/AIDS, persisting threats from malaria, re-emergence of tuberculosis, widespread prevalence of micronutrient deficiencies, and epidemic expansion of overweight and obesity causing a variety of chronic diseases, compromise food and nutrition security in both developed and developing countries. In addition to the welfare effects on those affected, the global health crisis contributes to rising healthcare costs, labour shortages and declining asset bases. Labour scarcity and low productivity among people affected by HIV/AIDS, along with the disintegration of rural and urban households, call for very different food and agricultural policies and research priorities, with focus on labour-saving rather than labour-using technologies and food safety nets for displaced individuals as well as affected households.

Innovative policy research and interventions are urgently needed to slow down and reverse the strong trend of increasing overweight and obesity. Such interventions should focus on changing consumer behaviour through the dissemination of information, price incentives and peer pressure similar to those used to reduce smoking. Research to alter the composition and taste of food, along with regulation of corporate behaviour on advertising and promotion, should also be pursued.

During the next 20 years, the urban population of developing countries will double, while the rural population will increase by only 4 per cent. In 1975, about a quarter of the population of developing countries resided in urban areas; by 2015, it will have increased to one half. This rapid urbanization will present new challenges to providing employment, education, health care and food in urban areas. Poverty and under-nutrition are also increasing at a faster rate in urban areas. Policies and programmes are needed to reduce the cost of food to urban consumers and create income-generating opportunities for them, provide low-cost efficient safety nets and stimulate the generation of social capital, provide acceptable and affordable child-care substitutes, ensure the safety of prepared and processed foods sold in the streets, improve primary health care, water and sanitation services, and enforce property rights for low-income urban people. Government intervention may also be needed to counter dietary changes towards excessive sugar, oils and fats resulting from more severe time constraints, greater exposure to advertising and easier access to fast food and processed foods.

Armed conflicts continue to cause severe human misery in a large number of developing countries. About half of the African countries are currently experiencing some form of instability or armed conflict. While humanitarian assistance may be effective in providing food and shelter for the many millions of refugees and displaced persons, policy action is needed to deal with the underlying causes. Recent research shows a clear causal link between poverty, hunger and natural resource degradation on the one hand, and the probability of armed conflict and instability on the other. While these studies have been undertaken at the national level, it is reasonable to hypothesize that continued extreme inequalities and poverty among nations, along with further information on globalization, will lead to similar relationships at the international level. Widespread hunger, hopelessness and lack of social justice generate anger and provide a perceived justification for international instability and terrorism instigated and supported by non-poor individuals and groups. Failure to recognize and deal with these underlying causes of instability will render ineffective much of the current investments in military solutions, intelligence and other protective measures.

The roles of the State, market, private voluntary organizations and for-profit private sector have changed markedly both internationally and in countries exposed to globalization, structural adjustment and related policy and market reforms. However, lack of knowledge about the proper role of each of these agents in the new socioeconomic and political environments within which many countries find themselves, is a major bottleneck to successful transformation. The failure to arrive at proper roles and appropriate institutions is a major reason why reforms have been disappointing in many developing countries.

The role of the public sector appears to be shrinking in many aspects of food security, while civil society and the private sector have taken on increasing importance. While such a shift may be appropriate, recent research and experience clearly show the importance of an effective public sector in many areas related to food security. Among the areas affected are agricultural research to develop appropriate technology for small farmers, rural infrastructure, healthcare, education, development and enforcement of a legal system, and the creation of public goods in general. Market liberalization and globalization require new institutions, rules and regulations. An effective government is needed to facilitate privatization and guide the transformation of the agricultural sector in a direction beneficial to the poor.

The impact of governance, including democracy, adherence to human rights principles, the rule of law and empowerment of civil society, on transaction costs and efficiency of food systems and poor people's access to food should take high priority, and efforts should be made to identify appropriate governance structures. Current efforts in many developing countries to decentralize public sector decision-making and resource allocation are hampered by a lack of understanding of how best to implement local government action.

Market liberalization often assumes that the private sector is capable and willing to take over the roles traditionally managed by the government. In economies where that assumption has been taken too far, the elimination of inefficient government agencies and institutions have not been replaced by effective public goods creation and the private-sector performance has been disappointing. In the economies, where market fundamentalism has directed economic reforms, the results have also been disappointing. Strong and effective public sectors are essential for successful privatization. Private sector agents and non-governmental organizations must be held accountable for their actions nationally and internationally and institutional innovation is urgently needed for this purpose.

Eliminating hunger, food insecurity and malnutrition is humankind's foremost challenge. Failure to meet the challenge will result in continued high levels of unnecessary human suffering, forgone economic opportunities for both poor and non-poor, and an increasingly unstable world.

MACROECONOMIC POLICY MECHANISMS

The macro-economic environment is determined by certain crucial parameters and rules, often set by government, which affect the basis on which nations trade with one another, and the conditions for longer-term economic growth within the economy. These parameters can be classified into three broad areas: those affecting international resource flows, such as exchange rate regulations; those concerned with the monetary regime, such as the rate of interest; and those set by government to finance its own operation, fiscal mechanisms such as taxation and public expenditure levels.

These parameters and policy options may well have as much, or more effect, on food security as policies aimed specifically at the food and agricultural sectors, yet the links between the macro-economy and food security are often not well understood. Even where they are, the longer term objectives of achieving more permanent food security for all citizens and the short-term issue of protecting existing levels of food security often have to take second or third place to what are seen as more immediate concerns of controlling a balance of payments crisis or tackling high levels of inflation.

However, these different objectives need not always be incompatible. Governments can make choices between alternative strategies for achieving economic growth in ways which are sustainable, some of which may be more beneficial to their most vulnerable citizens than others. If major policy decisions have to be made in ways which have a negative impact on those who are already food insecure, then there may be ways of offsetting that damage by implementing specially designed and targeted welfare programmes.

To do this, there must be a clear understanding of how macro-economic policy affects those suffering from food insecurity, based on a well developed analysis of policy linkages for the specific country concerned. The general nature and direction of the linkages concerned will conform to a broad pattern for all countries, but the precise interpretation and implications will vary according to elements such as the degree of monetisation in the economy, the nature of international markets for the commodities produced in the national economy, the degree of urbanisation, the capacity of state administration and the overall philosophy of the government in power.

Most government economic policy has one overriding policy objective: to maximise the welfare of its citizens. This would typically involve aiming for stable growth levels through such intermediary objectives as low inflation rates, sustainable budgets and balance of payments, low unemployment and high levels of investment. This view of government objectives puts far too much emphasis on economic issues to be a complete explanation of the basis on which governments make decisions. Government policy is also heavily influenced by social and political concerns. It does, however, encompass all the main elements of macroeconomic policy.

In each country, the government will pursue its own balance between all these different policy elements, according to its own political philosophy: the importance it puts on its own role as a provider of goods and services; the priority it puts on the welfare of different sectors of the population; and its own self-interest. When governments change, these views will also change, and along with that, economic policy.

However, governments and their economic policies do not exist in a vacuum. External and domestic economic shocks can make existing policies unsustainable, or extremely difficult to maintain. Governments may be forced to make abrupt changes in policy, which in turn may have a damaging impact on the food security of its citizens.

MACROECONOMIC SHOCKS

Imbalances can be caused by macroeconomic shocks or by the continuous pursuit of domestic policies which fail to achieve internal balance (full employment and price stability), such as governments persisting in running high budget deficits. Major macroeconomic shocks can be both external or internal in source. Combinations of some or all of these causes of structural imbalance have been faced by many developing countries in the past few decades.

External macroeconomic shocks have been critical in disrupting trading patterns for many poor countries. Perhaps the most dramatic shock was the oil price rise of the mid-1970s and later, more serious, in 2007-08, which brought about a major increase in the import bill and the domestic cost structure of many countries. However, all violent changes in international prices can cause problems. Commodity price booms (which, unfortunately coincided with the 2008 oil price surge) encourage large spending programmes in exporting countries which become unsustainable when the boom ends. Increases in international interest rates lead to sharp rises in debt service payments.

Domestic shocks have also been disruptive to market function and economic growth in some countries. Drought has ravaged some of the poorest economies in Sub-Saharan Africa. Civil war and the influx of refugees has disrupted economic activity in others. In some countries economic policy has encouraged rent-seeking rather than productive activity. In other words, entrepreneurs have seen greater opportunity for profit in manipulating regulations governing access to resources, such as import licences, than in producing agricultural or industrial output.

Bureaucracies have flourished at the expense of the manufacturer and entrepreneur.

In summary, one can state that internal and external shocks and unfavourable trends in foreign trade, in conjunction with inappropriate policies, have caused a decline in economic growth and exposed many developing countries to a vicious circle of growing internal and external macroeconomic disequilibria.

CHAPER 16

WHAT'S IN STORE FOR ASIA?

FOOD security is a concept that often needs different definitions. No one definition seems to apply to all situations. Many economists doubt that it has any precise meaning at all. Having enough to eat on a regular basis, however, is a powerful human need, and satisfying this need drives household behaviour in both private and public markets in predictable ways. Indeed, the historical record suggests that policy initiatives by central governments to satisfy this need for food security at the level of both households and national markets can speed economic growth in countries where a substantial proportion of the population does not get enough to eat.

Paradoxically, in most successfully developing countries, especially those in the rice-based economies of Asia, the public provision of food security ignores its essential role as an economic stimulus and becomes a political response to the pressures of rapid structural transformation, thereby becoming a drag on economic efficiency. The long-run relationship between food security and economic growth thus tends to switch from positive to negative over the course of development. Because of inevitable inertia in the design and implementation of public policy, this switch presents a serious challenge to the design of an appropriate food policy.

Food security and economic growth interact with each other in a mutually reinforcing process over the course of development. It is only in modern times that entire societies have achieved food security. Earlier, only privileged members of society were able to escape from chronic hunger and the constant threat of famine. Many countries in the developing world, especially in Africa and South Asia, have not managed this escape. In these countries, understanding the factors that cause widespread hunger and vulnerability to famines, and the mechanisms available to alleviate their impact, remain important intellectual challenges.

There is a different way, however, to pose the question. Rather than asking how to cope with hunger and famine, the question might be how to escape from their threat altogether. Fogel (1991) emphasized that this is a modern question which is only partly answered by the institutional and technological innovations that are at the heart of modern economic growth. Without these innovations, the modern escape from hunger to food security would not have been possible. But the record of economic growth for the developing countries since the 1950s shows that even in countries with relatively low levels of per capita income, government interventions to enhance food security can lift the threat of hunger and famine. The countries most successful at this task are in East and Southeast Asia, although the experience in South Asia has been instructive as well.

CONCEPTUALIZING THE ISSUES

That the rich countries have little to fear from hunger, is a simple consequence of Engel's Law; consumers have a substantial buffer of non-food expenditures to rely on, even if food prices rise sharply. In a market economy, the rich do not starve. Wars, riots, hurricanes, and floods, for example, can disrupt the smooth functioning of markets, and all in their wake can perish. But rich societies usually have the means to prevent or alleviate such catastrophes, social or natural. Food security in rich societies is simply part of a broader net of social securities.

PUBLIC ACTION

Without the buffer of Engel's Law, consumers in poor countries are exposed to continued hunger and vulnerability to shocks that set off famines. And yet, several poor countries have taken public action to improve their food security. The typical approach reduces the numbers of the population facing daily hunger by raising the incomes of the poor, while simultaneously managing the food economy in ways that minimize the shocks that might trigger a famine. These countries, some of them quite poor, have managed the same 'escape from hunger' that Fogel documents for Europe during the 19th and early 20th centuries.

An early escape from hunger, achieving food security at the societal level, is not just the result of one-way causation from economic growth

Engel's law is an observation stating that, with a given set of tastes and preferences, as income rises, the proportion of income spent on food falls, even if actual expenditure on food rises. In other words, the cost of food is less than 1.

The law was named after the statistician Ernest Egel (1821-96)

Engel's Law does not imply that food spending remains unchanged as income increases: It suggests that consumers increase their expenditures for food products (in percentage terms) less than their increases in income.

generated by private decisions in response to market forces. Improved food security stems directly from a set of government policies that integrates the food economy into a development strategy that seeks rapid economic growth with improved income distribution. With such policies, economic growth and food security mutually reinforce each other. Countries in East and Southeast Asia offer evidence that poor countries using this strategy can escape from hunger in two decades or less, that is, in the space of a single generation.

Although two decades may seem an eternity to the hungry and those vulnerable to famine, it is roughly the same as the time between the first World Food Summit Conference in 1974 and the second one in 1996. Despite much well-meaning rhetoric at the earlier summit, including Henry Kissinger's pledge that no child would go to bed hungry by 1985, the failure to place food security in a framework of rural-oriented economic growth, in combination with policies to stabilize domestic food economies, meant that those two decades were wasted in many countries. And despite the global community's pledge to reach the Millennium Development Goals by 2015, goals which place an end to hunger at the centre of the objectives, there is still no widespread understanding that food security needs to be connected directly to economic growth strategies if these goals are to be achieved.

The focus here is on food security as an objective of national policy. The emphasis is on food security at the 'macro' level. At that level, policymakers have an opportunity to create the aggregate conditions in which households at the 'micro' level can gain access to food on a reliable basis through self-motivated interactions with local markets and home resources. The perspective taken is, thus, primarily an economic one.

At first glance, economics seem to have had little influenced over food security strategic in Asia . The dominance of rice in the diets of most Asians, coupled to the extreme price instability in the world market for rice, forced all Asian countries to buffer their domestic rice price from the world price. This clear violation of the border price paradigm, and the accompanying restrictions on openness to trade, seems to have escaped many advocates of the East Asian miracle, who saw the region's rapid growth as evidence in support of free trade.

In addition, most Asian governments have paid little attention to formal efforts to define food security as a prelude to government interventions that would be seen as their approach to 'food security.'

THE STRATEGIC APPROACH

The rate and distribution of economic growth are primarily matters of macroeconomic and trade policy (once asset distributions are given as an initial condition). Although there is now widespread controversy over what role Asian governments played in stimulating growth and channelling its distribution, there is no disagreement that high rates of savings and investment, coupled with high and sustained levels of capital productivity, in combination with massive investments in human capital, explain most of the rapid growth that occurred up to 1997. Growth that reached the poor—what is now termed 'pro-poor growth'—was one component of the food security strategy.

In the second element of the strategy, Asian governments sought to stabilize food prices, in general, and rice prices, in particular. Engel's Law ensures that success in generating rapid economic growth that includes the poor is the long-run solution to food security.

In the language of Dreze and Sen, such economic growth provides 'growth-mediated security.' In the meantime, stabilization of food prices in Asia ensured that short-run fluctuations and shocks did not make the poor even more vulnerable to inadequate food intake than their low incomes required.

Most economists are highly dubious that such food price stability is financially feasible or economically desirable. It is not a key element of the 'support-led security' measures outlined by Dreze and Sen. In a review of food security and the stochastic aspects of poverty, Anderson and Roumasset essentially dismiss efforts to stabilize food prices using government interventions:

Given the high costs of national price stabilization schemes and their effectiveness in stabilizing prices in rural areas, alternative policies decreasing local price instability need to be considered. The most cost-effective method for increasing price stability probably is to remove destabilizing government distortions. Government efforts to nationalize grain markets and to regulate prices across both space and time have the effect of eliminating the private marketing and storage sector. Rather than replacing private marketing, government efforts should be aimed at enhancing private markets through improving transportation, enforcing standards and measures in grain transactions, and implementing small-scale storage technology.

Although this condemnation of national price stabilization schemes might well be appropriate for much of the developing world, it badly misinterprets both the design and implementation of interventions to stabilize rice prices in East and Southeast Asia. For food security in this region, the stabilization of domestic rice prices was in fact feasible in the context of an expanding role for an efficient private marketing sector. The resulting stability was not an impediment, but was actually conducive to economic growth. The stabilization scheme and economic growth worked in tandem to achieve food security as quickly as possible.

MICRO DIMENSIONS

For the purposes of government policy, food security can be thought of as a continuous spectrum, that is, from the micro perspective of nutritional well-being of individuals all the way to the macro perspective that assures regular supplies of food in national, regional, and local markets. The challenge, and one important objective of food policy, is to create an environment where access to purchasing power, nutritional knowledge, and health care within each individual household assures adequate demand for food in those markets, thus guaranteeing food security at both ends of the micro-macro spectrum. Creating food security at both the micro and macro levels is a complicated task in an open, market-oriented economy; but it is only this kind of economy that can generate rapid growth and reduction of poverty.

Both elements of the Asian strategic approach to food security, rapid economic growth and food price stability, address the 'macro' dimensions of food security, not the 'micro' dimensions found within the household. Governments can do many things to improve food security at the household and individual level, and most countries in Asia have programmes to do so. Rural education accessible to females and the poor, family planning and childcare clinics in rural areas, nutrition education and extension specialists helping to improve home gardens are just a few of the possibilities. Most of the literature on food security deals with approaches at this level, but problems of definition, measurement, project design, and management vastly complicate strategies that rely on direct household interventions.

These complications, in turn, effectively limit the number of households that can be reached with a micro approach. Without dismissing the potential effectiveness of these approaches to enhancing food security in particular circumstances, it is still important to realize the scale of the problem. Hundreds of millions of people still do not have food security in Asia. Programmes delivering food directly to households cannot bring it in a sustainable fashion. Only food security at the macro level can provide the appropriate facilitative environment for households to ensure their own food security.

GROWTH, POVERTY AND STABILITY

The close historical connection seen in much of East and Southeast Asia between improvements in food security and reduction of poverty has been a result of government efforts to link market-led economic growth to interventions that improve food security at both the household and national levels. This strategic connection is not an accident. A coherently designed macro food policy couples a strategy for food security with a strategy for growth that reaches the poor. Establishing this link to food security from the macro side allows a country to capture growth opportunities, some quite subtle, that are missed otherwise. Such a macro food policy has three components which, in turn, reinforce the country's food security: rapid growth in the macro economy, poverty reduction through rural economic growth, and stability of the food system. Agriculture and a dynamic rural economy are the keys to integrating all three components.

This 'macro' perspective on the food economy helps integrate a country's food security at the household level with national food markets. In turn, food security at both levels enhances the prospects for rapid economic growth, poverty reduction and broad-based participation by citizens in higher living standards. The complexity for food policy arises because the achievement of each of the goals depends on the simultaneous pursuit of the other two strategies, which interact through market and behavioural mechanisms. For example, rapid growth in the macro economy must be designed to reach the poor. Otherwise, poverty reduction is delayed. Likewise, more direct interventions to reach the poor, such as a targeted rice distribution programme, cannot be sustained. Similarly, raising poor households above the poverty line does not guarantee their food security if food supplies disappear from markets or prices rise beyond their means.

Rapid economic growth has been the main vehicle by which most Asian countries have reduced poverty and enhanced food security. Most countries have averaged growth rates in per capita incomes of between 3 and 4 per cent per year, rates that double living standards every two decades or so. When such growth reaches the poor (that is, income distribution does not deteriorate significantly during the growth process), poverty rates can fall from over half the population – the poverty incidence in extremely poor countries – to less than an eighth of the population in just one generation.

REACHING THE POOR

Such rates of decline in poverty rates were achieved in Indonesia, China and Vietnam since the 1970s, and earlier in Thailand, Malaysia and Northeast Asia. Income distribution tended to be stable, or even improve somewhat, during periods of extremely rapid growth in average incomes per capita, in addition to the average growth experience for eight Asian countries since the 1960s.

Despite this long-run stability in income distribution, there is considerable variance in how well the poor connect to economic growth during shorter episodes. This variance tends to be explained by initial conditions, especially land distribution, and by the sector of economic growth. At least in most of Asia, agricultural growth has tended to be much more pro-poor than growth in the modern industrial or service sectors. Finally, rice prices are influential in explaining changes in income distribution. Sharply rising rice prices are bad for the poor.

STABILIZING FOOD PRICES

All government leaders recognize the impact of rice prices on the poor, and most countries stabilized their rice economy by keeping domestic rice prices more stable than border prices. Economic growth, poverty reduction, and stability are linked to each other through the virtuous circles. Greater stability of the food economy contributes to faster economic growth by reducing signal extraction problems, lengthening the investment horizon and reducing political instability. In the other direction, stability contributes to equity and poverty reduction by reducing the vulnerability of the poor to sudden shocks in food prices or availability. Greater equity also stimulates investment in human capital, especially in rural areas thus speeding up economic growth, at least in the long run.

By implementing a simple policy objective of stabilizing the real domestic price of rice, the operational definition of food security in these societies, most Asian countries saw the level of protection of their rice farmers rise sharply from the 1970s to the mid-1990s. Pro-poor economic growth and stable rice prices were the recipe for food security in Asia. The high levels of agricultural protection and the failure to diversify and modernize their agricultural sectors were largely unanticipated side-effects from the strategy of growth with stability. Efforts to reduce these high levels of agricultural protection, especially for rice farmers; by directly confronting the political forces defending this 'Asian' approach to food security have been repeatedly rebuffed since the 1980s.

AGRICULTURE AND THE RURAL ECONOMY

For the large countries of Asia, investments since the 1960s to raise the productivity of domestic rice producers brought greater stability to the rice economy at the macro level, mostly because reliance on the world market had been destabilizing in relation to domestic production. Expanded rice production and greater purchasing power in rural areas, stimulated by the profitable rice economy, improved the level and stability of food intake of rural households. The dynamic rural economy helped to reduce poverty quickly by inducing higher real wages. The combination of government investments in rural areas, stable prices at incentive levels, and higher wages helped reduce the substantial degree of urban bias found in most development strategies. Growth in agricultural productivity has been seen also to stimulate more rapid economic growth in the rest of the economy.

RURAL ECONOMIC GROWTH

The agricultural revolution that swept through East and Southeast Asia since the 1960s dramatically improved the living standards of most people, despite the setbacks from the Asian financial crisis in 1997. By the 1990s, far fewer people were trapped in poverty than in the mid-1960s, food security had been enhanced by surpluses available in an expanded

Asian rice market, economies had become highly diversified as the manufacturing sector had outgrown the agricultural sector, and export-oriented companies became competitive in international markets.

The historical and comparative lessons from Asia are clear. They show conclusively that growth of the rural economy has helped the poor more than growth in the urban industrial sector and that such growth has also contributed to more rapid growth in the overall economy. An entire body of literature exists that analyzes the role of agriculture in economic growth. Specific linkages that have been identified in this literature work through the capital and labour markets; through product markets; and through a variety of non-market connections that involve market failures and endogenous growth mechanisms.

These are difficult issues. Designing and coordinating relationships among sectors so that the growth process is rapid, equitable, and sustainable has become a complicated process. The complexity is especially clear in the example of food security, which requires an integration of macroeconomic policies that affect the speed of economic growth, sectoral policies and institutional changes that affect the distribution of that growth and implementation of food distribution and stabilization schemes that guarantee continued access to food by the poor.

AGRICULTURAL PRODUCTIVITY

Improvements in agricultural productivity that have been stimulated by government investment in rural infrastructure, agricultural research and extension, irrigation and appropriate price incentives have contributed directly to economic growth, poverty reduction and stability. Throughout Asia, however, rice is no longer the engine of growth in most rural areas. The difficult task has been to conduct research, on a country-specific basis, to discover ways to raise productivity in agriculture per hectare and per worker, to sustain that productivity and to maintain adequate incentives to ensure continued investment in the sector.

Embracing all three issues is the need to manage a smooth structural transition by ensuring that the productivity of the rural labour force and its per capita income keep pace with productivity and per capita income in the urban sector. It is no coincidence that all of these issues revolve around productivity. Higher productivity is the only way to achieve and sustain higher living standards in the long run. Income transfers, whether through price policy or direct government subsidies, do not build the economic foundation to support broad-based increases in welfare. Food policy, thus, must stimulate increases in productivity in the rural economy. Concern for the short-run food intake of the poor and their nutritional well-being, is also important. But the vehicles that will solve the problem of poverty all involve higher productivity of resource use in the economy.

After the significant gains from the first 'Green Revolution' of the 1960s, Asia has had a particularly difficult task in raising agricultural productivity. Since 1990, rice yields on IRRI's (International Rice Research Institute) best experimental plots have stagnated and there has been only limited evidence of gains in other crops or in the livestock sector.

The sources of growth for the higher yields that could form the basis of a second 'Green Revolution' have not been identified. Fertilizer and labour have been used very intensively. New biological technologies and improved management of all inputs at the farm level will be needed for the next round of productivity gains.

Both the technologies and the management techniques have had to be fine-tuned to local environments—a process that already has put great stress on central research centres to develop locally appropriate varieties and cultivation practices from the basic scientific breakthroughs that have been promised by IRRI and other centres in the CGIAR (Consultative Group on International Agricultural Research) system.

In the first instance, this need for technologies to fit local environments has fit nicely with the efforts by many governments to decentralize political decision making and resource management. But the human and scientific resources to implement such an effort have been grossly inadequate and it will take time to build the local institutions that can carry out these tasks.

Almost every component of the gains in agricultural productivity since the 1960s has raised concerns about its sustainability. It is possible that soil fertility has been declining. The conversion of fertilizer into useful output has become less efficient. There is less biodiversity. Long-run problems are emerging in managing pests, weeds and diseases in highly productive ecosystems. There has been increased instability of weather and rainfall patterns, which is possibly a function of global climate change.

Despite these emerging problems of sustainability, the real prices of agricultural commodities in world markets have declined to very low levels in historical terms and this decline has reduced incentives to fund research that raises agricultural productivity and its sustainability. It has been difficult to justify investments whose payoff has been increased production of exactly these low-value commodities. The real price of rice in world markets has dropped from $ 1,000 per metric ton to $ 200 per metric ton since 1975. Many other agricultural commodity prices have followed a similar trend. Since average farm size has decreased in most countries in Asia because of population growth, finding a technology package and farm-gate price that could raise farm household incomes above the poverty line

> Real price is a price that has been adjusted to remove the effect of changes in the purchasing power of the currency involved. Real prices, which are expressed in constant currency units, usually reflect buying power relative to a base year.

has become more than four times harder than in the mid-1970s. Agricultural policies in OECD countries have made both tasks even harder.

THE RURAL ECONOMY AND FOOD SECURITY

One important outcome of a rural-oriented growth strategy is the achievement of food security. Political pressures to achieve this goal are one of the main driving forces behind the strategy itself. From this political perspective, food security is achieved when economic growth has raised the poor above a meaningful poverty line and when stabilization of the food economy prevents exogenous shocks from threatening their food intake.

In this approach, food security is sustained by the productivity of the poor themselves, but this security continues to depend on public action to maintain a stable macro environment, including the food economy, as an essential complement to that productivity.

Once this process of rapid growth is under way, political tensions inevitably emerge from a structural transformation that takes place too rapidly for resources to move smoothly from the rural to the urban sector. The entire society is less prone to these tensions if the gap between rural and urban incomes does not widen too much. All successfully growing countries have had to find ways to keep this gap from widening so much that it destabilizes the political economy and jeopardizes continued investment. Managing the transition from 'getting agriculture moving' to 'manufactured export-led growth' has been a very difficult process throughout Asia, partly because of the very speed of the transition.

RURAL-URBAN RELATIONSHIPS

Integrating the three components of the strategy for food security—rapid growth in the macro economy, poverty reduction through rural economic growth and stability of the food system—is greatly complicated by the changing relationship between the rural and urban economies during the process of industrialization. In all successful economies, incomes earned from farming tend to lag behind those earned in other occupations. Rural labour productivity can increase in two ways: directly in agricultural activities, through the application of new technologies; and indirectly, as workers shift from agriculture to manufacturing or the modern service sector. Both processes are part of the structural transformation, but productivity of urban workers tends to run ahead of rural productivity, causing a pronounced structural lag. In most of Asia, from China to Indonesia to India, there has been a growing spread between the wages earned by unskilled agricultural workers and new entrants into labour-intensive manufacturing sectors, such as garments and electronics. At the same time, rice growing has been kept profitable through subsidies, virtually free irrigation water, price support and stabilization programmes, as well as a well-developed rural infrastructure that ensured low marketing margins for rice. Investments in rural education and health helped build human capital, but accumulation of other assets by farmers has been limited.

MANAGING FOOD POLICY

The challenge throughout Asia is to modernize agriculture, reduce its heavy dependence on rice through diversification, integrate the entire rural economy more fully into the industrial sector, especially through greater processing activities and still keep rural incomes high enough to avoid rapid migration of workers to cities. This challenge is not unique to Asia. It is the heart of the tension generated by all successful structural transformations. But the political pressures to resolve the tension can quickly distort policy making and cause massive budget losses, burdens on consumers and conflicts with trading partners.

In particular, efforts to reduce the incomes of rice farmers by bringing domestic prices closer to world prices are seen as worsening the situation, not helping it. A food policy that helps smoothen the transition from a poor and rural economy to a rich and urban economy would pay very high dividends, but it must be formulated with a clear understanding of why the structural lag exists and its political link to food security.

Managing policy during the structural transformation thus becomes the organizing framework for food policy analysis. The advantage of this perspective is the need to keep long-run objectives and economic forces in focus, at the same time that short-run crises receive urgent attention. For example, even as governments in the region attempt to cope with the problem for rice farmers of low prices in world markets, the structural transformation has reduced the significance of rice to national economies, to consumers and even to rural incomes. Throughout Asia, most rice-producing families now earn more income from non-rice sources, including non-farm sources, than they do from producing and selling rice. Growing rice is a source of income that is competitive with non-farm wages for only a small share of rural households and the proportion will continue to fall in the future. If efforts to raise incomes of rice farmers are not consistent with these longer-run forces, the efforts will at best be expensive palliatives that slow down the movement of resources to more highly paid alternatives.

THE POLITICAL ECONOMY OF AGRICULTURAL PROTECTION

It is a sign of great progress that policy makers throughout Asia have come to worry more about keeping rice prices high rather than keeping them low. Historically, in those societies in which poverty has remained untouched or even deepened, the agricultural sector has been seriously undervalued by both the public and private sectors. In addition to an urban bias in most domestic policies, the root cause of this undervaluation was a set of market failures. Commodity prices, by not valuing reduced hunger or progress against poverty, failed to send signals with appropriate incentives to decision makers. These inappropriate signals tend to cause several problems.

First, low values for agricultural commodities in the marketplace are reflected in low political commitments. But political commitments to rural growth are needed to generate a more balanced economy. The developing world has already seen a notable reduction in the macroeconomic biases against agriculture, such as overvalued currencies, repression of financial systems, and exploitive terms of trade. Further progress might be expected as democracy spreads and empowers the rural population in poor countries (although agricultural policies in most democracies make economists cringe, a point discussed below).

The second problem with low valuation of agricultural commodities is that rural labour is also undervalued. This weakens the link between urban and rural labour markets, which is often manifested in the form of seasonal migration and remittances. There is no hope of reducing rural poverty unless real wages for rural workers rise. Rising wages have a demand and a supply dimension and migration can affect both in ways that support higher living standards in both parts of the economy. Migration of workers from rural to urban areas raises other issues, of course, but those issues depend fundamentally on whether this migration is driven by the push of rural poverty or the pull of urban jobs. Whatever the cause, the implications for food security are clear: a greater share of food consumption will be sourced from urban markets. Whether these urban markets are supplied by domestic farmers or international trade is one of the key food security debates under way in most Asian countries.

So far, the typical response has been for both of these problems to be addressed by trade and subsidy policies that increasingly protect farmers from foreign competition, especially rice farmers. How does urban bias turn so quickly to agricultural protection? The question has fascinated political scientists and economists for some time. Building on Krueger's (1974) and Olsen's (1965) theories of rent-seeking and collective action, Anderson and Hayami (1986) attempted to explain the rapid rise of agricultural protection in Asia in terms of the changing role of agriculture in the structural transformation and the costs of free-riding in political coalitions. A broader effort followed the same approach, which is now formalized as 'positive political economy' Actors in both economic and political spheres make rational (personal) choices with respect to policies, using political action, lobbying and even bribery as mechanisms of influence.

These 'rational choice' models of agricultural protection, while illuminating, are not entirely satisfactory. An alternative model that builds on Asian societies' deep desire for food security, manifested as stable rice prices, does a much better job of explaining changes in the nominal degree of protection of rice farmers in Asia. It is this deep-seated desire for food security that explains the rapid flip from urban bias to high protection. Newly well-off urban workers no longer need cheap rice in order to survive, but they still must buy all of their rice in local markets. They want to be certain it is available. For societies deeply distrustful of the world market as a source of reliable supplies, it is a very short step to protecting their own rice farmers as the surest vehicle to ensure the availability of rice.

FOR AN EFFICIENT TRANSITION

Efficient paths to providing food security which are politically feasible have been hard to find. Any such path will involve greater diversification of agricultural production and consumption, including a greater role for international trade, continued commercialization and market orientation, and a balance between the roles of the public and private sectors. At the core will be the welfare of farm households as they struggle with these issues. Mechanisms to enhance asset accumulation, including land consolidation and larger farm enterprises, will be needed for at least some of these households to remain competitive as agricultural producers. Others will exit agriculture. More effective rural credit systems will help this process, but institutional changes in land tenure are also likely to be needed, even if these are mostly in the form of long-term rental arrangements.

HUMAN CAPITAL AND TECHNOLOGY

A key role of the government in developing a dynamic rural economy is the creation of human capital through the provision of education and the improvement of health care. These investments improve the welfare of rural citizens directly through improved life expectancy and a better quality of life. Indirectly, they are keys to increasing productivity. Only workers who are knowledgeable and healthy can participate effectively in the development process and choose how best to contribute productively to society, including exiting rural areas altogether by migrating to urban jobs. Education and health care in rural areas are particularly important because the incidence of poverty in rural areas is higher than in urban areas. Furthermore, research has shown that rural education has more beneficial effects on the growth process than does education in urban areas. Rural health care is also important because rural labour is physically demanding.

Technology is an obvious means of increasing productivity in rural areas. Provided the government does not force farmers to use them, new technologies also give farmers and producers a wider range of choices. In rural industry, trade and services, much of this new technology comes from the private sector, and the primary role of the government is to avoid impeding this process with unnecessary rules and regulations. Even in agriculture, often the best thing the government can do is to remove obstacles to dissemination of private-sector research, as with hybrid corn seed.

In many countries, public sector agricultural research has made important contributions to productivity growth, with rates of return on investment often much greater than the social opportunity cost of capital. Malaysia's agricultural research system has made tremendous progress in oil, palm and rubber, among other crops. In Indonesia, the agricultural research system has created many rice varieties that are planted by farmers throughout the country. Even before the monetary crisis in 1997, rice pesticide sales declined during the 1990s due to the efforts to develop integrated pest management strategies. Yet many challenges remain. Since 1990, rice yields have been virtually stagnant at the major rice research centres. Research institutions need support to make Asian agriculture internationally competitive and allow it to contribute to improved rural, as well as urban, welfare.

MARKETS AND INFRASTRUCTURE

In a market economy, macroeconomic stability is essential to long-term poverty reduction in rural areas that are far from the offices of central governments in capital cities, where macro policy is determined. Sustained increases in labour productivity require the accumulation of more physical and human capital per worker. Without a stable real exchange rate and a low rate of inflation, these investments will not be forthcoming and there will be inadequate job creation in urban and rural areas to absorb a growing labour force with aspirations for a better life. A stable macroeconomic environment is essential for the creation of more job opportunities that mean more choices for rural citizens, that is, farmers, traders, and workers in small- and medium-size enterprises. This increased range of employment choices is the foundation of a dynamic rural economy.

Once macro stability is assured, the provision of infrastructure widens choices for rural dwellers, including the poor. Better roads allow the landless access to a wider range of employment and higher wages through opportunities for migration. Roads offer farmers a greater choice of locations in which to market their produce. One study of a group of 45 farmers in a Philippine village well served by infrastructure found that they sold their output to 37 different traders. Such competition makes it far less likely that traders will be able to take advantage of farmers. Roads also give a private firm more freedom to choose its location, allowing the decentralization of industry away from urban areas and providing rural inhabitants with more job choice in rural areas without the need to resort to migration. Rural electrification provides rural citizens access to more information that allows them to participate in the modern economy. In general, physical infrastructure such as roads, ports, and communication networks cause production and marketing systems to become more integrated and function more effectively, providing the base upon which an efficient rural economy can be built. Thailand has had a dynamic rural economy that could compete in a wide range of international markets partly because of its dense road network which connects agricultural production areas with consumption centres and export markets.

Marketing systems need to be predominantly or completely in the hands of the private sector, because only private marketing agents have the necessary detailed knowledge of both producers and consumers. Nevertheless, there is a strong role for government in providing the infrastructure that allows the private sector to perform its services efficiently. While the private sector should not be prevented from building infrastructure, it cannot be relied upon exclusively to perform this task because it typically does not have the ability to capture all the returns from such investments. Thus, it is important for the government to undertake these investments in public goods.

In addition to integrated markets for commodities and inputs, such as fertilizer, efficient and well-functioning rural credit markets are also important if farmers are to be able to reduce the impact of risk and have an effective instrument for asset accumulation. The most important role that government can play in integrating rural credit markets is to ensure macroeconomic stability, which reduces risk and uncertainty and thereby lowers costs in the financial system. Regulations can encourage the formation of rural branch banks, but requiring them is usually counterproductive.

Creation of a dynamic rural economy can occur only in a market-driven environment. Government plays a crucial role in fostering growth, but government cannot be the main engine of productivity growth in rural areas. This lesson has been learned many times over, often at great cost. The rural economies of the former Soviet Union and Eastern Europe were grossly inefficient and did not serve to improve the living standards of their people. Government monopolies on trade in agricultural products inevitably harm farmer interests, as is clearly shown by the experience with commodity boards in Latin America and Africa. In Indonesia and the Philippines, local and national monopolies enjoyed by special interest groups (either inside or outside government) produced the same result, i.e. less choice and lower living standards for farmers.

Fortunately, there are many positive results as well. Productivity growth in agriculture surged when China abandoned its control of the rural economy in 1978. As Vietnam began to introduce market-oriented reforms in agriculture in 1989, productivity growth accelerated so quickly that Vietnam moved from being a rice importer to the world's second-leading rice exporter.

Recent history has shown conclusively that a network of well-functioning markets is the only mechanism that allows rural citizens to realize their full potential as productive members of society. Governments cannot directly make farmers productive because agriculture is exceedingly complex, heterogeneous and risky. Farmers operate in a constantly changing physical and economic environment that requires a wealth of micro-level information for efficient decision-making. The amount of information required makes it impossible for bureaucrats to design sensible micro-level interventions. Farmers must be free to make these choices, both on grounds of economic efficiency and because freedom itself is an important component of human welfare.

THE ROLE OF GOVERNMENT

The new emphasis in development economics on governance as a key factor affecting the rate and distribution of economic growth brings the opportunity to link powerful political forces, such as the deep desire on the part of both urban and rural populations for food security, to the growth process itself. The obvious link is through policy analysis, where the analysis systematically utilizes 'neoclassical political economy' to use Srinivasan's nomenclature. Understanding the role of markets and the state, and their mutual interaction, will be key.

Within a framework where economic decision makers are free to make choices based on their own knowledge and conditions, the role of government remains critical. In particular, government investments that allow markets to function efficiently are essential to fostering a dynamic rural economy, especially in agriculture. But the government role also spans a wide range of other activities, from macroeconomic policy at the national level to providing immunizations to poor children in remote areas. The key areas where government must provide support to the rural economy are growth-oriented economic policies and macroeconomic stability, the generation of new technologies, facilities for the creation of human capital and the provision of infrastructure to lower transactions costs. All are essential components of a dynamic rural economy. Large gains in agricultural productivity come from such public investments, which create new wealth for all members of society to share. Gains in productivity do not come from changes in price policy (for example, tariffs), which merely shift income from one group in society to another. From society's point of view, income transfers do not contribute to gains in productivity. The efficient provision of public goods, however, does stimulate such gains.

AN ASIAN PERSPECTIVE

Rice is different and the difference has powerfully influenced economics and politics throughout much of Asia. The difference is manifested in three ways:

- ⌘ First, rice is the dominant food staple throughout the region, often accounting for more than half of normal food energy intake. Daily access to rice is essential for survival.
- ⌘ Second, rice is grown predominately by small holders who have been adept at adopting new technologies when market signals were favourable. In many countries, rice farmers are the single largest identifiable voting group.
- ⌘ Third, international rice markets have been historically thin and unstable, causing all Asian countries to buffer their own farmers and consumers from fluctuating world prices (and thus making the fluctuations worse in an even thinner market). This buffering requires that governments actively control the flow of rice across their borders.

These characteristics of rice-based food systems forge a strong link between politics and economics, a link that policy makers, elected or not, see as a public mandate to deliver food security. Without understanding this link, it is impossible to understand Asia's record of economic growth, driven historically by dynamic rural economies, and the subsequent, seemingly inevitable, rise of agricultural protection. Although some of the forces driving this protection are similar to those in Europe and the United States, the speed, level, and early onset are unique to Asia.

The way forward is to make rice less 'different' to consumers, farmers and in world markets, by making it more of an economic commodity and less of a political commodity. As noted above, much progress has actually been made in this direction since the 1980s, but that progress has not been clearly recognized or incorporated into new, politically viable strategies for food security in Asia. Still, the ingredients of such a strategy are clear: greater investment in rural human capital to improve labour productivity and mobility; more efficient rural financial markets to facilitate farm consolidation and even rural exit; and coordinated international efforts to open the world rice market to freer trade in order to deepen and stabilize price formation. This is a big agenda, to be sure, but implementing it—even gradually—will ensure a more prosperous and equitable future for Asia's farmers and greater food security for its consumers.

CHAPTER 17

IMPACT OF CLIMATE CHANGE

IT is found that of the four main elements of food security, that is, availability, stability, utilization, and access, only the first is usually addressed in simulation studies. The Food and Agriculture Organization (FAO) defines food security as:

> 'a situation that exists when all people, at all times, have physical, sccial, and economic access to sufficient, safe, and nutritious food that meets their dietary needs and food preferences for an active and healthy life.'

This definition comprises four key dimensions of food supplies: availability, stability, access, and utilization. The first element relates to the availability of sufficient food, that is, to the overall ability of the agricultural system to meet food demand. Its sub-categories include the agro-climatic fundamentals of crop and pasture production and the entire range of socio-economic and cultural factors that determine where and how farmers perform in response to markets.

The second element, stability, relates to individuals who are at high risk of temporarily or permanently losing their access to the resources needed to consume adequate food, either because these individuals cannot ensure in advance against income shocks or they lack enough 'reserves' to smoothen future consumption shocks. An important cause of unstable access is climate variability, for example, landless agricultural labourers, who almost wholly depend on agricultural wages in a region of erratic rainfall and have meagre savings, would be at high risk of losing their access to food. However, there can be individuals with unstable access to food even in agricultural communities where there is no climate variability, for example, landless agricultural labourers who fall sick and cannot earn their daily wages would lack stable access to food if, for example, they cannot take out insurance against illness.

The third element covers access by individuals to adequate resources (entitlements) to acquire appropriate foods for a nutritious diet. Entitlements are defined as the set of all those commodity bundles over which a person can establish command, given the legal, political, economic and social arrangements of the community of which he or she is a member. Thus, a key element is the purchasing power of consumers and the evolution of real incomes and food prices. However, these resources need not be exclusively monetary but may also include traditional rights, for example, to a share of common resources.

Finally, utilization encompasses all food safety and quality aspects of nutrition; its sub-categories are therefore related to health, including the sanitary conditions across the entire food chain. It is not enough that someone is getting what appears to be an adequate quantity of food, if that person is unable to make use of the food because he or she is always falling sick. Agriculture is not only a source of food but, equally importantly, also a source of income. In a world where trade is possible at reasonably low cost, the crucial issue for food security is not whether food is 'available,' but whether the monetary and non-monetary resources at the disposal of the population are sufficient to allow everyone access to adequate quantities of food.

An important corollary to this is that national self-sufficiency is neither necessary nor sufficient to guarantee food security at the individual level. Hong Kong and Singapore are not self-sufficient (agriculture is non-existent) but their populations are food-secure, whereas India is self-sufficient but a large part of its population is not food-secure. Numerous measures are used to quantify the overall status and the regional distribution of global hunger. None of these measures covers all dimensions and facets of food insecurity described above.

This also holds for the FAO indicator of under-nourishment. The FAO measure, however, has a number of advantages. First, it covers two dimensions of food security, availability and access; second, the underlying methodology is straightforward and transparent; and third, the parameters and data needed for the FAO indicator are readily available for past estimates and can be extrapolated without major difficulties into the future.

CLIMATE CHANGE IMPACT ON FOOD PRODUCTION, AVAILABILITY AND SECURITY

Climate change affects agriculture and food production in complex ways. It affects food production directly through changes in agro-ecological conditions and indirectly by affecting growth and distribution of incomes, and thus demand for agricultural produce. Impacts have been quantified in numerous studies and under various sets of assumptions. It is useful to summarize the main alterations in the agro-ecological environment that are associated with climate change.

Continued emissions of greenhouse gases will bring changes in land suitability and crop yields. In particular, the Intergovernmental Panel on Climate Change (IPCC) considers four families of socio-economic development and associated emission scenarios, known as Special Report on Emissions Scenarios. Of relevance here, the 'business-as-usual scenario,' corresponds to the highest emissions. Depending on the emission scenario and climate models considered, global mean surface temperature is projected to rise in a range from 1.8°C to 4.0°C by 2100.

In temperate latitudes, higher temperatures are expected to bring predominant benefits to agriculture: the areas potentially suitable for cropping will expand, the length of the growing period will increase, and crop yields may rise. A moderate incremental warming in some humid and temperate grasslands may increase pasture productivity and reduce the need for housing and for compound feed. These gains have to be set off against an increased frequency of extreme events, for instance, heat waves and droughts in the Mediterranean region or increased heavy precipitation events and flooding in temperate regions, including the possibility of increased coastal storms.

They also have to be balanced against the fact that semiarid and arid pastures are likely to see reduced livestock productivity and increased livestock mortality. In drier areas, climate models predict increased evapotranspiration and lower soil moisture levels. As a result, some cultivated areas may become unsuitable for cropping and some tropical grassland may become increasingly arid. Temperature rise will also expand the range of many agricultural pests and increase the ability of pest populations to survive the winter and attack spring crops.

Another important change for agriculture is the increase in atmospheric carbon dioxide (CO_2) concentrations. Depending on the emission scenario, the atmospheric CO_2 concentration is projected to increase from 379 ppm today to 550 ppm. Higher CO_2 concentrations will have a positive effect on many crops, enhancing biomass accumulation and final yield. However, the magnitude of this effect is less clear, with important differences depending on management type (for example, irrigation and fertilization regimes) and crop type. Experimental yield response to elevated CO_2 show that under optimal growth conditions, crop yields increase at 550 ppm CO_2 in the range of 10 to 20 per cent for crops such as wheat, rice, and soybean), and only 0–10 per cent for crops such as maize and sorghum.

Yet the nutritional quality of agricultural produce may not increase in line with higher yields. Some cereal and forage crops, for example, show lower protein concentrations under elevated CO_2 conditions. Finally, a number of recent studies have estimated the likely changes in land suitability, potential yields, and agricultural production on the current mix of crops and cultivars available today. These estimates implicitly include adaptation using available management techniques and crops, but excluding new cultivars from breeding or biotechnology. These studies are in essence based on the FAO/International Institute for Applied Systems Analysis. For instance, pioneering work suggested that total land and total prime land would remain virtually unchanged at the current levels of 2,600 million and 2,000 million hectares (ha), respectively.

The same study also showed, however, more pronounced regional shifts, with a considerable increase in suitable cropland at higher latitudes (developed countries—160 million ha) and a corresponding decline of potential cropland at lower latitudes (developing countries—110 million hectares). An even more pronounced shift within the quality of cropland is predicted in developing countries. The net decline of 110 million hectares is the result of a massive decline in agricultural prime land of 135 million hectares, which is offset somewhat by an increase in moderately suitable land of 20 million hectares.

This quality shift is also reflected in the shift in land suitable for multiple cropping. In sub-Saharan Africa alone, land for double cropping would decline by between 10 million and 20 million hectares and land suitable for triple cropping would decline by 5 million to 10 million hectares.

At a regional level, similar approaches indicate that under climate change, the biggest losses in suitable cropland are likely to be in Africa, whereas the largest expansion of suitable cropland is in the Russian Federation and Central Asia.

IMPACTS ON THE STABILITY OF FOOD SUPPLIES

Global and regional weather conditions are also expected to become more variable than at present, with increases in the frequency and severity of extreme events such as cyclones, floods, hailstorms, and droughts. By bringing greater fluctuations in crop yields and local food supplies and higher risks of landslides and erosion damage, they can adversely affect the stability of food supplies and thus food security.

Neither climate change nor short-term climate variability and associated adaptation are new phenomena in agriculture, of course. Some important agricultural areas of the world like the Midwest of the United States, the northeast of Argentina, southern Africa, or southeast Australia have traditionally experienced higher climate variability than other regions such as central Africa or Europe. They also show that the extent of short-term fluctuations has changed over longer periods of time. In developed countries, for instance, short-term climate variability increased from 1931 to 1960 as compared with 1901 to 1930, but decreased strongly in the period from 1961 to 1990. What is new, however, is the fact that the areas subject to high climate variability are likely to expand, whereas the extent of short-term climate variability is likely to increase across all regions.

Furthermore, the rates and levels of projected warming may exceed in some regions the historical experience. If climate fluctuations become more pronounced and more widespread, droughts and floods, the dominant causes of short-term fluctuations in food production in semiarid and sub-humid areas, will become more severe and more frequent. In semiarid areas, droughts can dramatically reduce crop yields and livestock numbers and productivity. Again, most of this land is in sub-Saharan Africa and parts of South Asia, meaning that the poorest regions with the highest level of chronic under-nourishment will also be exposed to the highest degree of instability in food production.

How strongly these impacts will be felt will crucially depend on whether such fluctuations can be countered by investments in irrigation, better storage facilities, or higher food imports. In addition, a policy environment that fosters freer trade and promotes investments in transportation, communications and irrigation infrastructure can help address these challenges early on.

IMPACTS OF CLIMATE CHANGE ON FOOD UTILIZATION

Climate change will also affect the ability of individuals to use food effectively by altering the conditions for food safety and changing the disease pressure from vector, water, and food-borne diseases. Various forms of diseases, including vector-borne diseases such as malaria, are likely to spread or recede with climate change. We are concerned, however, with a narrow selection of diseases that affect food safety directly, that is, food and water-borne diseases.

The main concern about climate change and food security is that changing climatic conditions can initiate a vicious circle where infectious disease causes or compounds hunger which, in turn, makes the affected populations more susceptible to infectious disease. The result can be a substantial decline in labour productivity and an increase in poverty and even mortality. Essentially, all manifestations of climate change, be they drought, higher temperatures, or heavy rainfall have an impact on the disease pressure and there is growing evidence that these changes affect food safety and food security.

Increases in daily temperatures will also increase the frequency of food poisoning, particularly in temperate regions. Warmer seas may contribute to increased cases of human shellfish and reef-fish poisoning (ciguatera) in tropical regions and a pole-ward expansion of the disease. However, there is little new evidence that climate change significantly alters the prevalence of these diseases. Several studies have confirmed and quantified the effects of temperature on common forms of food poisoning, such as salmonellosis. These studies show an approximately linear increase in reported cases for each degree increase in weekly temperature.

Moreover, there is evidence that temperature variability affects the incidence of diarrhoeal disease. A number of studies found that rising temperatures were strongly associated with increased episodes of diarrhoeal disease in adults and children. These findings have been corroborated by analyses based on monthly temperature observations. Several studies report a strong correlation between monthly temperature and diarrhoeal episodes on the Pacific Islands.

In Australia and Israel, for instance, extreme rainfall events can increase the risk of outbreaks of water-borne diseases particularly where traditional water management systems are insufficient to handle the new extremes. Likewise, the impacts of flooding will be felt most strongly in environmentally degraded areas and where basic public infrastructure, including sanitation and hygiene, is lacking. This will raise the number of people exposed to water-borne diseases (for example, cholera) and thus lower their capacity to effectively use food.

IMPACTS OF CLIMATE CHANGE ON ACCESS TO FOOD

Access to food refers to the ability of individuals, communities, and countries to purchase sufficient quantities and qualities of food. Over the last 30 years, falling real prices for food and rising real incomes have led to substantial improvements in access to food in many developing countries. Increased purchasing power has allowed a growing number of people to purchase not only more food but also more nutritious food with more protein, micronutrients, and vitamins. East Asia and to a lesser extent the Near-East/North African region have particularly benefited from a combination of lower real food prices and robust income growth. From 1970 to 2001, the prevalence of hunger in these regions, as measured by FAO's indicator of under-nourishment, declined from 24 to 10.1 per cent and 44 to 10.2 per cent, respectively, in the two regions.

In East Asia, it was endogenous income growth that provided the basis for the boost in demand for food, which was largely produced in the region; in the Near-East/North African region demand was spurred by exogenous revenues from oil and gas exports, and additional food supply came largely from imports. But in both regions, improvements in access to food have been crucial in reducing hunger and malnutrition.

FAO's longer-term outlook to 2050 suggests that the importance of improved demand side conditions will become even more important over the next 50 years. The regions that will see the strongest reductions in the prevalence of under-nourishment are those that are expected to see the highest rates of income growth. South Asia stands to benefit the most. Spurred by high income growth, the region is expected to reduce the prevalence of under-nourishment from 22 per cent currently to 12 per cent by 2015 and to just 4 per cent by 2050.

Progress is also expected in sub-Saharan Africa, but improvements will be less pronounced and are expected to set in later. Over the next 15 years, for instance, the prevalence of under-nourishment will decline less than in other regions, from 33 per cent to a still worrisome 21 per cent, as significant constraints (soil nutrients, water, infrastructure, etc.) will limit the ability to further increase food production locally, while continuing low levels of income rule out the option of importing food. In the long run, however, sub-Saharan Africa is expected to see a more substantial decline in hunger; by 2050, six per cent of its total population is expected to suffer from chronic hunger.

It is important to note that these FAO projections do not take into account the effects of climate change. By coupling agro-ecologic and economic models, others have gauged the impact of climate change on agricultural gross domestic product (GDP) and prices. At the global level, the impacts of climate change are likely to be very small; under a range of climate-change scenarios, the estimates range from a decline of 1.5 per cent to an increase of 2.6 per cent by 2080. At the regional level, the importance of agriculture as a source of income can be much more important. In these regions, the economic output from agriculture itself (over and above subsistence food production) will be an important contributor to food security.

The strongest impact of climate change on the economic output of agriculture is expected for sub-Saharan Africa, which means that the poorest and already most food-insecure region is also expected to suffer the largest contraction of agricultural incomes. For the region, the losses in agricultural GDP, compared with no climate change, range from 2 to 8 per cent for one model and 7 to 9 per cent for other projections.

IMPACTS ON FOOD PRICES

Essentially, all development paths describe a world of robust economic growth and rapidly shrinking importance of agriculture in the long run and thus a continuation of a trend that has been underway for decades in many developing regions. This growth will allow the largest part of the world's population to address possible local production shortfalls through imports and, at the same time, find ways to cope with safety and stability issues of food supplies. It is also a world where real incomes rise more rapidly than real food prices, which suggests that the share of income spent on food should decline and that even high food prices are unlikely to create a major dent in the food expenditures of the poor.

However, not all parts of the world perform equally well in the various development paths and not all development paths are equally benign for growth. Where income levels are low and shares of food expenditures are high, higher prices for food may still create or exacerbate a possible food security problem. There are a number of studies that have ventured to measure the likely impacts of climate change on food prices. The basic messages that emerge from these studies are: first, on average, prices for food are expected to rise moderately in line with moderate increases of temperature (until 2050); some studies even foresee a mild decline in real prices until 2050.

Second, after 2050 and with further increases in temperatures, prices are expected to increase more substantially. In some studies and for some commodities (rice and sugar) prices are forecast to increase by as much as 80 per cent above their reference levels without climate change. Third, price changes expected from the effects of global warming are, on average, much smaller than price changes from socio-economic development paths. For instance, one scenario would imply a price increase in real cereal prices by 170 per cent. The (additional) price increase caused by climate change would only be 14.4 per cent.

Overall, this appears to be the sharpest price increase reported and it is not surprising that this scenario would imply a stubbornly high number of undernourished people until 2080. However, it is also needless to say that a constant absolute number of undernourished people would still imply a sharp decline in the prevalence of hunger and, given the high population assumptions, (13.6 billion people globally and 11.6 billion in the developing world) this would imply a particularly sharp drop in the prevalence from currently 17 to 7 per cent by 2080.

However, as the stabilizing effects of mitigation measures can take several decades to be realized from the moment of implementation, the benefits for crop production may be realized only in the second half of this century. Importantly, even in the presence of robust global long-term benefits, regional and temporal patterns of winners and losers that can be projected with current tools, are highly uncertain and depend critically on the underlying projections.

UNCERTAINTIES AND LIMITATIONS

The finding that socio-economic development paths have an important bearing on future food security and that they are likely to top the effects of climate change should not, or at least not only, be interpreted as a probability-based forecast. This is because scenarios offer a range of possible outcomes 'without any sense of likelihood.' Yet these scenarios, like all scenarios, do not overcome the inability to accurately project future changes in economic activity, emissions and climate. Second, the existing global assessments of climate change and food security have only been able to focus on the impacts on food availability and access to food, without quantification of the likely important climate change effects on food safety and vulnerability(stability).

This means that these assessments neither include potential problems arising from additional impacts due to extreme events such as drought and floods, nor do they quantify the potential impacts of changes in the prevalence of food-borne diseases (positive as well as negative) or the interaction of nutrition and health effects through changes in the proliferation of vector-borne diseases such as malaria.

On the food availability side, they also exclude the impacts of a possible sea-level rise on agricultural production or those that are associated with possible reductions of marine or freshwater fish production.

Third, it is important to note that even in terms of food availability, all current assessments of world food supply have focused only on the impacts of mean climate change, that is, they have not considered the possibility of significant shifts in the frequency of extreme events on regional production potential, nor have they considered scenarios of abrupt climate or socio-economic change; any of these scenario variants is likely to increase the already negative projected impacts of climate change on world food supply.

Models that take into account the specific biophysical, technological and market responses necessary to simulate realistic adaptation to such events, are not yet available.

Fourth, this review finds that recent global assessments of climate change and food security rest essentially on a single modelling framework. This has important implications for uncertainty, given that the robustness of all these assessments strongly depends on the performance of the underlying models.

Finally, assessments that do not only provide scenarios, but also attach probabilities for particular outcomes to come true could provide an important element for improved or at least better-informed policy decisions. One option would be to produce such estimates with probability-based estimates of the (key) model parameters. Alternatively, the various scenarios could be constructed so that they reflect expert judgements on a particular issue.

CONCLUSIONS

Climate change will affect all four dimensions of food security, namely food availability (that is, production and trade), access to food, stability of food supplies, and food utilization. The importance of the various dimensions and the overall impact of climate change on food security will differ across regions and over time and, most importantly, will depend on the overall socio-economic status that a country has achieved as the effects of climate change set in.

Essentially, all quantitative assessments show that climate change will adversely affect food security. Climate change will increase the dependency of developing countries on imports and accentuate the existing focus of food insecurity on sub-Saharan Africa and to a lesser extent on South Asia. Within the developing world, the adverse impacts of climate change will fall disproportionately on the poor. Many quantitative assessments also show that the socio-economic environment in which climate change is likely to evolve is more important than the impacts that can be expected from the biophysical changes of climate change.

Less is known about the role of climate change on food stability and utilization, at least in quantitative terms. However, it is likely that differences in socio-economic development paths will also be the crucial determinant for food utilization in the long run and that they will be decisive for the ability to cope with problems of food instability, be they climate-related or caused by other factors.

Finally, all quantitative assessments reviewed show that the first decades of the 21st century are expected to see low impacts of climate change, but also lower overall incomes and still a higher dependence on agriculture. During these first decades, the biophysical changes as such will be less pronounced but climate change will affect those particularly adversely that are still more dependent on agriculture and have lower overall incomes to cope with the impacts of climate change. By contrast, the second half of the century is expected to bring more severe biophysical impacts but also a greater ability to cope with them. The underlying assumption is that the general transition in the income formation away from agriculture toward non-agriculture will be successful.

How strong the impacts of climate change will be felt over all decades will crucially depend on the future policy environment for the poor. Freer trade can help to improve access to international supplies; investments in transportation and communication infrastructure will help provide secure and timely local deliveries; irrigation, a promotion of sustainable agricultural practices, and continued technological progress can play a crucial role in providing steady local and international supplies under climate change.

There is a new urgency to improve the accuracy of predicting climate change impact on crop yields because the balance between food supply and demand is shifting abruptly from surplus to deficit. This reversal is being driven by a rapid rise in petroleum prices and, in response, a massive global expansion of biofuel production from maize, oilseed, and sugar crops.

Soon the price of these commodities will be determined by their value as feedstock for biofuel rather than their importance as human food or livestock feed. The expectation is that petroleum prices will remain high. Supportive government policies in several major crop producing countries are providing strong momentum for continued expansion of biofuel production capacity and the associated pressures on global food supply.

Farmers in countries that account for a majority of the world's biofuel crop production will enjoy the promise of markedly higher commodity prices and incomes. In contrast, urban and rural poor in food-importing countries will pay much higher prices for basic food staples and there will be less grain available for humanitarian aid. For example, the developing countries of Africa import about 10 million tons of maize each year; another 3-5 million tons of cereal grains are provided as humanitarian aid. In a world where more than 800 million are already undernourished and the demand for crop commodities may soon exceed supply, alleviating hunger will no longer be solely a matter of poverty alleviation and more equitable food distribution, which has been the situation in the past.

Instead, food security will also depend on accelerating the rate of gain in crop yields and food production capacity at both local and global scales. Given this situation, the question of whether global climate change will have a net positive, negative, or negligible impact on crop yields takes on a larger significance because additional hundreds of millions of people could be at risk of hunger and the window of opportunity for mounting an effective response is closing.

To answer this question, Lobell and Field use an innovative empirical/ geostatistical approach to estimate the impact of increased temperature since 1980 on crop yields, a period when global mean temperature increased 0.4°C. For three major crops, maize, wheat, and barley, there was a significant negative response to increased temperature. For all six crops evaluated (also including rice, soybean, and sorghum), the net impact of climate trends on yield since 1980 was negative. While the approach used by Lobell and Field can be questioned on several points, the body of their work represents an ambitious global assessment of recent climate impact on crop yields. Most noteworthy is their conclusion that the combined effects of increased atmospheric CO_2 concentration and climate trends have largely cancelled each other over the past two decades.

While there appears to be agreement on the predicted impact of atmospheric CO_2 enrichment on crop yields across a wide range of studies conducted using different approaches, there is less convincing evidence on the impact of warming temperatures. There are three reasons for greater uncertainty about temperature effects.

First, it is logistically more difficult to control temperature at elevated levels in studies that allow crops to grow in an 'open-air' environment comparable to field-grown plants. The 'free-air carbon dioxide enrichment' (FACE) systems were specifically designed to avoid such problems for study of CO_2 effects and appear to have been largely successful. In contrast, growth chamber, greenhouse, and small-enclosure studies used for temperature-effect experiments have confounding effects associated with differences in humidity, air turbulence, and reduced light intensity that result from the need to more fully enclose experimental units with a transparent barrier, to achieve adequate temperature control.

Second, unlike CO_2 effects, yield response to temperature is often discontinuous. In many crops, pollination fails if temperatures rise above a critical threshold, which can result in dramatic yield reductions due to very small changes in temperature. Also, because climate change is predicted to increase both average temperature and temperature variability, changes in both factors must be evaluated in experiments with realistic growth conditions to fully understand climate change impact on crop yields. Such experiments would require expensive infrastructure with creative new designs—studies that have yet to be conducted, in part due to lack of adequate funding.

A third factor is the interactive effect of temperature on respiration, which is poorly understood. In the absence of such studies, it is sobering to note that one long-term field study in which the effect of temperature on rice yield could be isolated from other factors documented a 15 per cent decrease in yield for every 1°C increase in mean temperature. The magnitude of this decrease is considerably larger than predictions of yield decreases from higher temperature obtained from crop simulation models. Like the results of Lobell and Field, we see a discrepancy between estimates of the effects of warmer temperatures on crop yields, based on the relationship between crop yields and temperature under field conditions versus those derived from modelling and experiments conducted under controlled conditions.

As we make the historic transition from an extended period of surplus food production to one in which demand for staple crop commodities exceeds supply, there is a vital need to better understand the impact of warming temperatures on current and future crop yields.

THE UN GLOBAL WARMING REPORT 2007

First, the facts as outlined by the report. Global warming is a reality and 'very likely' human-induced. Although the term 'very likely' may seem vague, it is as close as 700 scientists, 2,500 reviewers and countless government officials can get to consensus about if humanity is to blame.

Greenhouse gases in our atmosphere have increased since 1750 due to the consumption of fossil fuels, new forms of land use, and agriculture. While atmospheric pollution has had a cooling effect during the last centuries, the massive increase in greenhouse gases has led to a rise of average temperatures by 0.74 degrees Celsius since 1901.

Scientists are 90 per cent sure that the last half of the 20th century has been the hottest period in the Northern Hemisphere since 500 years.

Numerous long-term changes in climate have been observed. These include changes in Arctic temperatures and ice, widespread changes in precipitation amounts, ocean salinity, wind patterns and aspects of extreme weather including droughts, heavy precipitation, heat waves and the intensity of tropical cyclones.

Scientists have refined their simulations and now have a fairly good idea of the effects of carbon dioxide emissions. A doubling of carbon dioxide levels in the atmosphere, relates to a surface warming of some 3 degrees Celsius plus/minus one degree.

Even if we manage to reduce carbon emissions to year 2000 levels such a doubling of carbon dioxide is unpreventable. Warming, the report reads, will not be equally distributed. Effects will be more pronounced in the northern latitudes.

Critics often referred to changes in the sun's radiation to account for global warming. Although scientists have found fluctuations in the sun's radiation, its effects are nearly 20 times weaker than human-induced warming. Meanwhile glaciers all over the world are declining, an effect that is also perceivable at the fringes of the vast Antarctica ice shield. Scientists say that sea levels have already risen 17 centimetres during the 20th century, most of it due to the simple fact that warm water has a larger volume than cold water.

With the melting of icecaps and glaciers, the annual rise has nearly doubled since 1993 to a rate of about 3.1 mm. Even if carbon dioxide emissions can be stabilized, sea levels will keep on rising for centuries until the temperature gain will have reached the deep oceans.

CLIMATE CHANGE SCENARIOS

Three different scenarios for global warming have been presented. In the worst case global average temperatures could rise up to 6.4 degrees Celsius by the end of the 21st century. An increase of more then 10 degrees is possible in the northern latitudes.

Findings also show that the atmosphere now holds more water vapour, one of the driving forces of tropical storms and floods. Since the 1960s, westerly winds have gained in strength all over the planet. The Atlantic was particularly affected by more frequent and severe tropical cyclones, a phenomenon in line with rising surface water temperatures. The report says that there is a chance of six out of 10 that recent severe storms were boosted by global warming.

Arctic temperatures have increased twice as fast as global average temperatures. Summer ice in the Arctic Ocean is decreasing by 7.4 per cent per decade. By the end of the century, the Arctic might well be ice-free in summer. Meanwhile permafrost is on the retreat. Since 1900, the seasonally frozen ground in the Northern Hemisphere has shrunk by some 7 per cent. This has freed large amounts of methane, another potent greenhouse gas. To what extent such side-effects amplify ongoing global warming is not yet properly understood. The IPCC's scenarios, therefore, do not account for eventual runaway effects that would speed up global warming.

Precipitation patterns, too, changed over the last century. There is significantly more rain in the eastern parts of North and South America, northern Europe and northern and central Asia. On the other hand, dry spells are more frequent in the Sahel, the Mediterranean, southern Africa and parts of southern Asia.

THE IPCC SCENARIOS

The world's leading scientists have put together data and expertise available and devised seven climate scenarios for the 21st century. It all depends, they say, on the level of demographic and economic development, and how serious we are about the fight against global warming.

Level 2000

If we manage to stabilize our greenhouse gas emissions to the levels attained in the year 2000, we will still feel the heat, but the increase will be less than a degree over the next hundred years. Unfortunately, this option is not even considered a real scenario but rather a benchmark to compare with more realistic models.

Global Service Economy

Scenario B1 presents the most optimistic outlook: by mid-century, global population will hit a peak and decline thereafter. Rapid economic changes will bring about a service and information economy based on clean and efficient technologies.

The international community will unite around policy solutions—such as the Kyoto Protocol—for the reduction of greenhouse gases. While all this sounds promising, global warming will still occur, albeit not beyond a range of 1.1 to 2.9 degrees Celsius. Sea level rises between 18 and 38 centimetres until the end of the century are forecast.

Population Growth

Scenario B2 is less rosy: global population will constantly grow while climate change mitigation efforts have a regional focus. This translates into a temperature rise of some 1.4 to 3.8 degrees Celsius. Sea levels increase some 20 to 40 centimetres by 2100.

Rapid Economic Growth

The A1 scenario has been split up in three sub-divisions. Each of them is based on rapidly growing economies and a growing number of people, albeit populations will decline towards the second half of the century.

A1FI represents 'business-as-usual'—a world that still runs on coal and gas. It is here that predictions are most shocking: temperature gains of some 2.4 to 6.4 degrees Celsius are within reach. The sea would rise some 26 to 50 centimetres until the end of the century flooding large coastal cities and numerous islands.

A1B, the most probable scenario given current trends, is also alarming. While fossil fuels are still widely used, they are part of a more balanced energy mix. Still, by the end of the century, temperatures will have risen some 1.7 to 4.4 degrees Celsius, with the oceans gaining some 21 to 48 centimetres. Rainfall is likely to decrease by some 20 per cent in the subtropics, while more rain will fall in the northern and southern latitudes. The Gulf Stream will not stop, but it will lose about a quarter of its force.

Finally, A1T is a world that has lived through a third industrial revolution—a widespread conversion to 'green' energy sources. It is similar to B1 in the sense that temperatures and oceans will rise, but to an extent that experts such as Hans Joachim Schellnhuber call 'manageable'. (See text of report in Appendix IX)

FIGHTING CLIMATE CHANGE

The United Nations Development Programme's Human Development Report has warned that the world should focus on the development impact of climate change that could bring unprecedented reversals in poverty reduction, nutrition, health and education (see also *The International Development Agenda and the Climate Change Challenge:* Appendix IX).

The report, *Fighting Climate Change: Human Solidarity in a Divided World*, provides a stark account of the threat posed by global warming. It argues that the world is drifting towards a 'tipping point' that could lock the world's poorest countries and their poorest citizens in a downward spiral, leaving hundreds of millions facing malnutrition, water scarcity, ecological threats and a loss of livelihoods.

'Ultimately, climate change is a threat to humanity as a whole. But it is the poor, a constituency with no responsibility for the ecological debt we are running up, who face the immediate and most severe human costs,' commented UNDP Administrator Kemal Dervis.

The report comes at a key moment in negotiations to forge a multilateral agreement for the period after 2012—the expiry date for the current commitment period of the Kyoto Protocol. It calls for a 'twin track' approach that combines stringent mitigation to limit 21st century warming to less than 2°C (3.6°F), with strengthened international cooperation on adaptation.

On mitigation, the authors call on developed countries to demonstrate leadership by cutting greenhouse gas emissions by at least 80 per cent of 1990 levels by 2050. The report advocates a mix of carbon taxation, more stringent cap-and-trade programmes, energy regulation, and international cooperation on financing for low-carbon technology transfer. Turning to adaptation, the report warns that inequalities in ability to cope with climate change are emerging as an increasingly powerful driver of wider inequalities between and within countries. It calls on rich countries to put climate change adaptation at the centre of international partnerships on poverty reduction.

'We are issuing a call to action, not providing a counsel of despair,' commented lead author Kevin Watkins, adding: 'Working together with resolve, we can win the battle against climate change. Allowing the window of opportunity to close would represent a moral and political failure without precedent in human history." He described the talks as a unique opportunity to put the interests of the world's poor at the heart of climate change negotiations.

The report provides evidence of the mechanisms through which the ecological impacts of climate change will be transmitted to the poor. Focusing on the 2.6 billion people surviving on less than US$ 2 a day, the authors warn that forces unleashed by global warming could stall and then reverse progress built up over generations. Among the threats to human development identified are:

- The breakdown of agricultural systems as a result of increased exposure to drought, rising temperatures, and more erratic rainfall, leaving up to 600 million more people facing malnutrition. Semi-arid areas of sub-Saharan Africa with some of the highest concentrations of poverty in the world face the danger of potential productivity losses of 25 per cent by 2060.
- An additional 1.8 billion people facing water stress by 2080, with large areas of South Asia and northern China facing a grave ecological crisis as a result of glacial retreat and changed rainfall patterns.
- Displacement through flooding and tropical storm activity of up to 332 million people in coastal and low-lying areas. Over 70 million Bangladeshis, 22 million Vietnamese, and six million Egyptians could be affected by global warming-related flooding.
- Emerging health risks, with an additional population of up to 400 million people facing the risk of malaria.

Setting out the evidence from a new research exercise, the authors of the Human Development Report argue that the potential human costs of climate change have been understated. They point out that climate shocks such as droughts, floods and storms, which will become more frequent and intense with climate change, are already among the most powerful drivers of poverty and inequality—and global warming will strengthen the impacts.

'For millions of people, these are events that offer a one-way ticket to poverty and long-run cycles of disadvantage,' says the report. Apart from threatening lives and inflicting suffering, they wipe out assets, lead to malnutrition, and result in children being withdrawn from school. In Ethiopia, the report finds that children exposed to a drought in early childhood are 36 per cent more likely to be malnourished—a figure that translates into 2 million additional cases of child malnutrition.

While the report focuses on the immediate threats to the world's poor, it warns that failure to tackle climate change could leave future generations facing ecological catastrophe. It highlights the possible collapse of the West Antarctic ice sheets, the retreat of glaciers, and the stress on marine ecosystems as systemic threats to humanity.

'Of course there are uncertainties, but faced with risks of this order of magnitude uncertainty is not a case for inaction. Ambitious mitigation is in fact the insurance we have to buy against potentially very large risks. Fighting climate change is about our commitment to human development today and about creating a world that will provide ecological security for our children and their grandchildren,' Dervis said.

AVOIDING DANGEROUS CLIMATE CHANGE

The authors of the Human Development Report call on governments to set a collective target for avoiding dangerous climate change. They advocate a threshold of 2°C (3.6°F) above pre-industrial levels (the current level is 0.7°C, 1.3°F). Drawing on a new climate model, the report suggests a '21st century carbon budget' for staying within this threshold.

The budget quantifies the total level of greenhouse gas emissions consistent with this goal. In an exercise that captures the scale of the challenge ahead, the report estimates that business-as-usual could result on current trends in the entire carbon budget for the 21st century being exhausted by 2032. The authors warn that on current trends the world is more likely to breach a 4°C threshold than stay within 2°C (3.6°F).

The Human Development Report addresses some of the critical issues facing negotiators. While acknowledging the threat posed by rising emissions from major developing countries, the authors argue that northern governments have to initiate the deepest and earliest cuts. They point out that rich countries carry overwhelming historic responsibility for the problem, have far deeper carbon footprints, and have the financial and technological capabilities to act.

'If people in the developing world had generated per capita CO_2 emissions at the same level as people in North America, we would need the atmosphere of nine planets to deal with the consequences,' commented Watkins. Using an illustrative framework for an emissions pathway consistent with avoiding dangerous climate change, the Human Development Report suggests that:

- ⌘ Developed countries should cut greenhouse gas emissions by at least 80 per cent by 2050 and 30 per cent by 2020 from 1990 levels.
- ⌘ Developing countries should cut emissions by 20 per cent by 2050 from 1990 levels. However, these cuts would occur from 2020 and they would be supported through international cooperation of finance and low carbon technology transfer.

Measured against this benchmark, the authors find that many of the targets set by developed country governments fall short of what is required. It notes also that most developed countries have failed to achieve even the modest reductions – averaging around 5 per cent from 1990 levels – agreed under the Kyoto Protocol. Even where ambitious targets have been set, the report argues, few developed countries have aligned stated climate security goals with concrete energy policies.

Scenarios for future emissions reinforce the scale of the challenge ahead. On current trends, CO_2 emissions are projected to increase by 50 per cent by 2030, an outcome that would make dangerous climate change inevitable. 'The bottom line is that the global energy system is out of alignment with the ecological systems that sustain our planet,' commented Watkins, adding: 'realignment will take a fundamental shift in regulation, market incentives, and international cooperation.'

Fighting climate change identifies a range of policies needed to close the gap between climate security statements and energy policies for avoiding dangerous climate change. Among the most important:

Pricing carbon : The report argues that both carbon taxation and cap-and-trade schemes have a role to play. Gradually rising carbon taxes would be a powerful tool to change incentive structures facing investors. It also stresses that carbon taxes need not imply an overall greater tax burden because they could be compensated by tax reductions on labour income.

Stronger regulatory standards: The report calls on governments to adopt and enforce tougher standards on vehicle emissions, buildings and electrical appliances.

Supporting the development of low carbon energy provision: The report highlights the unexploited potential for an increase in the share of renewable energy used and for breakthrough technologies such as carbon capture and storage (CCS).

International cooperation on finance and technology transfer: The authors note that developing countries will not participate in an agreement that provides no incentives for entry, and which threatens to raise the costs of energy. The report argues for the creation of a Climate Change Mitigation Facility (CCMF) to provide $ 25–50 billion annually in financing the incremental low-carbon energy investments in developing countries consistent with achieving shared climate change goals.

Drawing on economic modelling work, the Human Development Report argues that the cost of stabilizing greenhouse gases at 450 parts per million (ppm) could be limited to an average to 1.6 per cent of world GDP to 2030. 'While these are real costs, the costs of inaction will be far greater, whether measured in economic, social or human terms,' warned, Dervis. The report points out that the cost of avoiding dangerous climate change represents less than two-thirds of current world military spending.

ADAPTATION EFFORTS OVERLOOKED

While stressing the central medium-term role of mitigation, *Fighting Climate Change* warns against neglecting the adaptation challenge. It points out that, even with stringent mitigation, the world is now committed to continued warming for the first half of the 21st century. The report warns that adaptation is needed to prevent climate change leading to major setbacks in human development—and to guard against the very real danger of insufficient mitigation.

The report draws attention to extreme inequalities in adaptation capacity. Rich countries are investing heavily in climate-change defence systems, with governments playing a leading role. By contrast, in developing countries 'people are being left to sink or swim with their own resources,' writes Desmond Tutu, Archbishop Emeritus of Cape Town, in the report, creating a 'world of adaptation apartheid.'

'Nobody wants to understate the very real long-term ecological challenges that climate change will bring to rich countries,' Watkins commented. 'But the near-term vulnerabilities are not concentrated in lower Manhattan and London, but in flood prone areas of Bangladesh and drought prone parts of sub-Saharan Africa.'

The Human Development Report shows that international cooperation on adaptation has been slow to materialize. According to the report, total current spending through multilateral mechanisms on adaptation has amounted to $ 26 million to date – roughly one week's worth of spending on UK flood defences. Current mechanisms are delivering small amounts of finance with high transaction costs, the authors say.

The report argues for reforms including:

- ⌘ Additional financing for climate proofing infrastructure and building resilience, with northern governments allocating at least $ 86 billion annually by 2015 (around 0.2 per cent of their projected GDP).
- ⌘ Increased international support for the development of sub-Saharan Africa's capacity to monitor climate and improve public access to meteorological information.
- ⌘ The integration of adaptation planning into wider strategies for reducing poverty and extreme inequalities, including poverty reduction strategy papers (PRSPs).

Fighting Climate Change concludes that 'one of the hardest lessons taught by climate change is that the historically carbon intensive growth and the profligate consumption in rich nations that has accompanied it, is ecologically unsustainable.' But the authors argue, 'with the right reforms, it is not too late to cut greenhouse gas emissions to sustainable levels without sacrificing economic growth. Rising prosperity and climate security are not conflicting objectives.'

CHAPTER 18

BIOFUELS DIVIDE THE WORLD

THERE'S little doubt that subsidies have diverted some agricultural production from food crops to biofuels for ethanol. This is just one of several factors contributing to the rise in food costs, but this factor is amenable to influence, unlike some other factors, such as extreme weather and droughts for instance. However, the biofuel controversy does raise the ethical question of food or fuel: is it right to grow fuel for food when so many go hungry? Unfortunately, parochial issues of security of fuel supply confound and complicate this debate.

Cellulosic fuels, also called second generation biofuels, are beginning to be recognized as acceptable alternatives. They can be derived from non-food materials such as food wastes or perennial grasses. Sawdust, scrap wood and urban wastes can be converted to biofuels, but the net energy benefit is uncertain when all collecting and processing costs are factored in.

This sort of comprehensive accounting shows, for example, that biofuel from corn residues is environmentally harmful. Corn production needs large applications of fertilizer and water so that removing stalks and leaves will degrade soil quality by removing nutrients and organic matter; and this deficit is quite apart from consideration of the net energy yield.

Grasses, like switch grass, can be used both as an energy source and soil improver. Harvesting in the autumn when nutrients have been returned to the roots from the foliage minimizes soil nutrient depletion, and several grass species develop extensive root systems, which contribute significantly to soil organic and nutrient content. Many of them will grow adequately on degraded soils, thus again performing a dual function of site amelioration and biofuel production.

Such focus on biofuel alternatives to fossil fuels unfortunately diverts attention away from addressing the possibilities of reducing demand for these fuels. We have the situation where Canadian-manufactured electric ZENN cars, acceptable in several countries, cannot be driven on Canadian urban roads!

They could substitute very well for petrol-powered commuting. Inter-city high-speed trains are an energy-preferable alternative to short-haul aircraft, yet many countries are still to adopt this strategy. Recently published research has produced yet another argument against vehicle use and the consequent air pollution. It's been known for some time that breathing in small particulate matter from car and truck engines poses a risk of heart disease and stroke.

The overall message seems clear; fewer vehicles on our roads and at least as much effort devoted to reducing our dependence on petrol or diesel-powered vehicles as is expended on improving their fuel-efficiency or finding alternative fuels. In other words, address the causes of air pollution, not just the symptoms.

In this context, it is not surprising that participants at the UN summit on the world's food crisis held in June 2008, differed drastically over how much the rush for environmentally friendly biofuels is contributing to the rocketing prices that are causing hunger and unrest in much of the globe. The prediction that an agreement on the role of biofuels would not be achieved at the summit proved true. The declaration effectively deferred the issue by calling for more 'indepth' studies (see Appendix V: 'Text of Resolution').

Most countries and international organizations meeting at the Rome-based U.N. Food and Agriculture Organization cited multiple causes, but biofuels was the most hotly debated issue. The UN line was that biofuel production should be studied in the context of food production and called for a balanced view.

Discussion of whether to scale back or push ahead with the introduction of biofuels weighed heavily on attempts to come up with a global strategy to solve the crisis, but the final declaration failed to achieve consensus on the issue. The main objections to scaling back biofuel production were from the two biggest biofuel producing countries, Brazil and the U.S.A. The EU, which had laid down a programme for a biofuel road map up to 2020, preferred to remain neutral.

Brazil has been using sugarcane to produce ethanol as fuel for cars and trucks for many years. It said it was 'frightening' to see attempts to draw a cause-and-effect relationship between biofuels and the rise of food prices and flayed countries who 'pointed fingers' at the clean biofuels—fingers which were 'soiled with oil and coal.'

Fuels made from sugarcane, corn and other crops have been seen as a way to combat climate change and rising oil prices. The United States has been heavily subsidizing corn-based ethanol production. In 2007, the 27-nation European Union endorsed a plan calling for biofuels to make up 10 per cent of the fuel for road vehicles by 2020.

However, environmentalists, international groups and some countries are becoming increasingly wary of biofuels, which they say could accelerate global warming by encouraging deforestation and contribute heavily to the commodities price hike by diverting production from food crops to biofuel crops.

Several speakers at the Rome meeting criticized government policies that diverted food crops to energy use, particularly at a time of increasing hunger. There were calls for 'an urgent international dialogue' on the food crisis that 'sets standards for the responsible utilization of agricultural crops as food for human beings, not as fuel for human beings. Brazil pointed the finger at U.S. ethanol production, saying that corn-based ethanol could obviously only compete with sugarcane ethanol when it is 'shot up with subsidies and shielded behind tariff barriers.'

Brazil and the United States are the world's largest producers of ethanol. Most of Brazil's ethanol comes from sugarcane and all of the production in the United States comes from corn. Brazil went on to differentiate between 'good' and 'bad ethanol. 'Good ethanol helps clean up the planet and is competitive. Bad ethanol comes with the fat of subsidies.' Of course the U.S.A. dismissed the charge, saying Brazil could be planting food crops like corn and soybeans on the acres it devotes to sugar cane for ethanol. Brazil chose to grow sugarcane and we chose to grow corn, the U.S. delegate said and added that he was unable to understand the distinction.

Studies by international organizations, including the International Monetary Fund, show that the increased demand for biofuels is contributing 15–30 per cent to food price increases. Food stocks are at their lowest in 25 years, so the market is very vulnerable to any policy changes such as U.S. subsidies and the EU's mandate on greater use of this energy source.

Some countries, Japan for instance, categorically claimed that biofuel production competed with food supply. Asking for a study on the 'sustainability' of biofuel production, they called for accelerating research into production of second-generation biofuels out of plants other than food crops.

The U.S.A. agreed that sustainability and innovation were needed but insisted that biofuels contribute only 2 or 3 per cent to a predicted 43 per cent rise in prices this year. It claimed that the use of sustainable biofuels can increase energy security, foster economic development especially in rural areas and reduce greenhouse gas emissions without weighing heavily on food prices.

Earlier, the U.S. Congress enacted a farm bill that reduced a tax credit for refiners by about 10 per cent per gallon. The credit supports the blending of fuel with the corn-based additive. More money would go to cellulosic ethanol, made from plant matter. But even between the United States and Brazil, both of which tried to exonerate biofuels of the charge of raising food prices, there was little agreement on the best way to tap the energy source.

The Summit Declaration, obviously taking all viewpoints on the contentious issue of biofuels into consideration, compromised with a resolution that: 'It is essential to address the challenges and opportunities posed by biofuels, in view of the world's food security, energy and sustainable development needs.' It called for in-depth studies to ensure that production and use of biofuels is sustainable in accordance with the three pillars of sustainable development and take into account the need to achieve and maintain global food security.

TIME TO REVISIT FOOD-TO-FUEL MANDATE

Over the past several months, a healthy debate has begun in the U.S.A. and around the world about the current crisis of rising food prices and the role America's overly aggressive food-to-fuel policy plays in that crisis. Congressional hearings have been held, studies have been released—all in an effort to get to the bottom of the food-to-fuel problem. America is indeed the bread basket of the world, and takes great pride in providing America and the world with an abundant, affordable and safe food supply. However, recent events—driven in part by the U.S.A.'s food-to-fuel policy—are driving up the cost of food at an alarming rate. According to the United States Department of Labour's Bureau of Labour Statistics, the price of food is rising at twice the rate of inflation. In the past three years, egg prices are up 78 per cent, bread prices are up 37 per cent and milk prices are up 18 per cent.

Consumers in America and around the world are taking it on the chin as food prices are rising the fastest they have in 17 years. Overseas shortages of food have sparked riots in developing countries. All of this is happening as the environmental benefits of corn ethanol are coming into question as never before. A broad coalition of organizations has begun to speak out on this issue. This includes some of the largest and most respected anti-hunger organizations in the U.S.A., as well as some leading environmental groups. In addition, organizations representing a wide range of vitally important industries, including livestock and poultry producers, restaurants and retailers, are asking Congress to revisit the issue.

Unfortunately, a small group of those who ardently support turning food into fuel is working hard to put an end to the discussion. The group wants to stifle debate and distract the American public from the issue at hand by spreading disinformation, dragging food companies through the mud and painting the antagonist viewpoint as somehow 'anti-farmer.' The fact is, there is nothing anti-farmer about the proposals. Indeed, livestock and poultry farmers are at the vanguard of efforts to get Congress to revisit these policies. The effort is not about undermining farmers. It is about making sure biofuels policy is not unintentionally undermining food security, adding to the economic burden of working families or creating new environmental harm.

That is why Congress must reopen this debate and think carefully about all aspects of the current biofuels policy, including mandates that require turning one-third of our corn into fuel, taxpayer subsidies that distort food and energy markets and tariffs that block the importation of ethanol from countries such as Brazil. These are steps that could reduce costs for American consumers.

Revisiting this policy is consistent with the overwhelming factual evidence. According to the U.N., food prices around the world have jumped more than 80 per cent in just the past three years. In the U.S.A., food prices are rising faster than at any time in the past two decades. With t he economy softening, food banks nationwide are reporting record demand, even as they struggle to afford to buy enough food to meet the need.

To be absolutely clear, biofuels policy is not the sole driver of food price inflation. Population growth, weather and oil prices all contribute. But the biofuels policy is one of the contributing factors. That is the conclusion of the U.N., the World Bank, the International Monetary Fund, the Congressional Research Service and the International Food Policy Research Institute, not to mention the view expressed by Barack Obama and John McCain. Moreover, it is the one factor in the food inflation equation that Congress can actually control.

GROWING STRENGTH OF ANTI LOBBY

A newly formed 'Food Before Fuel Campaign' bills itself as a cooperative effort urging Congress to revisit the nation's food-to-fuel policies.

According to the campaign's statement of principles, the members will encourage policymakers to 'revisit and restructure policies that have increased our reliance on food as an energy source, and to carefully address how to develop alternative fuels that do not pit our energy needs against affordable food and environmental sustainability.'

Supporters of this campaign blame corn-based ethanol and American government fuel policies, including the Energy Independence and Security Act of 2007, for the skyrocketing price of food. These supporters believe that food-to-fuel policies led to expanded corn planting, which set off a cascade of changing land use at home and around the world that threatens crucial ecosystems. At the same time, rising demand for corn set off global food price spikes that are destabilizing nations and driving millions of people deeper into poverty.

These arguments against corn-based ethanol are not new. But what is striking is the wide spectrum of organizations who have signed on to this new campaign. They include the following:

- American Bakers Association
- American Beverage Association
- American Conservative Union
- American Frozen Food Institute
- American Meat Institute
- Competitive Enterprise Institute
- Earth Policy Institute
- Environmental Working Group
- Food For All

- Grocery Manufacturers Association
- International Dairy Foods Association
- International Foodservice Distributors Association
- MANA (A National Latina Organization)
- National Cattlemen's Beef Association
- National Chicken Council
- National Council of Chain Restaurants
- National Restaurant Association
- National Retail Federation
- National Turkey Federation
- Pilgrim's Pride Corporation
- Popeye's Chicken & Biscuits
- Snack Food Association
- The Hispanic Institute
- Tortilla Industry Association
- Women Impacting Public Policy.

This wide-ranging membership, which includes cultural organizations, such as The Hispanic Institute, shows just how quickly the battlefield is expanding in the food *vs.* fuel war.

CHAPTER 19

RIGHT TO FOOD AS AN ALTERNATIVE APPROACH

THE term 'right to food, and its variations, is derived from the International Covenant on Economic, Social and Cultural Rights (ICESCR). The UN Special Rapporteur on the Right to Food in 2002 defined it as follows:

> 'Right to adequate food is a human right, inherent in all people, to have regular, permanent and unrestricted access, either directly or by means of financial purchases, to quantitatively and qualitatively adequate and sufficient food, corresponding to the cultural traditions of people to which the consumer belongs, and which ensures a physical and mental, individual and collective fulfilling and dignified life free of fear.'

This definition entails all normative elements explained in detail in the General Comment 12 of the ICESCR, which states:

> '....the right to adequate food is realized when every man, woman and child, alone or in community with others, have the physical and economic access at all times to adequate food or means for its procurement.'

THE RIGHT TO FOOD IN THE ICESCR

The ICESCR recognizes the 'right to an adequate standard of living, including adequate food', as well as the 'fundamental right to be free from hunger'. The relationship between the two concepts is not straightforward.

For example, 'freedom from hunger' (which General Comment 12 designates as more pressing and immediate) could be measured by the number of people suffering from malnutrition and at the extreme, dying of starvation. The 'right to adequate food' is a much higher standard, including not only absence of malnutrition, but to the full range of qualities associated with food, including safety, variety and dignity, in short all those elements needed to enable an active and healthy life.

The ICESCR recognises that the right to freedom from hunger requires international cooperation and relates to matters of production, the agriculture and global supply.

Article 11 states that:

'The States Parties to the present Covenant... shall take, individually and through international co-operation, the measures, including specific programmes, which are needed:

(a) To improve methods of production, conservation and distribution of food by making full use of technical and scientific knowledge, by disseminating knowledge of the principles of nutrition and by developing or reforming agrarian systems in such a way as to achieve the most efficient development and utilization of natural resources;

(b) Taking into account the problems of both food-importing and food-exporting countries, to ensure an equitable distribution of world food supplies in relation to need.'

DEVELOPMENT OF THE RIGHT TO FOOD

⌘ **1941:** The Four Freedoms speech by Franklin D. Roosevelt. In this speech Roosevelt set out four points as fundamental freedoms humans 'everywhere in the world' ought to enjoy: Freedom of speech and expression, Freedom of religion, Freedom from want, and Freedom from fear.

⌘ **1948:** Universal Declaration of Human Rights recognises in Article 25 that 'Everyone has the right to a standard of living adequate for the health and well-being of himself and of his family, including food, clothing, housing and medical care and necessary social services, and the right to security in the event of unemployment, sickness, disability, widowhood, old age or other lack of livelihood in circumstances beyond his control.'

⌘ **1966:** International Covenant on Economic, Social and Cultural Rights (ICESCR) reiterates the Universal Declaration of Human Rights with regard to the right to an adequate standard of living, including food, and specifically recognises the right to be free from hunger.

- ⌘ **1976:** ICESCR comes into force.
- ⌘ **1993:** Human Rights Congress in Vienna, establishment of the Office of the High Commissioner for.Human Rights.
- ⌘ **1996:** World Food Summit.
- ⌘ **1999:** General Comment 12.
- ⌘ **2004:** Voluntary Guidelines.

CHAPTER 20

WORLD FOOD SECURITY SUMMIT 2008

UNNERVED by food prices that rose 53 per cent in just months, 191 nations gathered in Rome on June 3, 2008, for a Summit on World Food Security. Convened by the Food and Agriculture Organization of the United Nations, the gathering sought ways to halt runaway food bills before the 862 million who barely get enough to eat today are joined by millions more. The delegates worried over price hikes in cereals, oil seeds, meat and fish. There was more than a hint that many delegates were worried by the political implications of the global food price rise. Food riots in Africa and Asia and rationing of rice in some Western countries lent urgency to the need to find a practical, workable solution to the problem of growing food insecurity.

Rice rationing in the West represents just shortage of one item in a large basket of edibles: fruits, vegetables, meats, wheat, corn, maize and much more. In Asian countries, however, the shortage and high prices of rice are a matter of life and death. In most of these countries, polished rice is being retailed at more than twice the price of government-subsidized rice, which itself is not available to most consumers.

FAO's *Food Outlook* for June 2008 provides the context. Bad weather and export curbs jacked up rice prices by as much as 71 per cent between January and April 2008. Cyclone Nargis in Myanmar spurred international price quotations into rising 10 per cent in one week. By early May 2008, prices were more than double their May 2007 level.

Even small exporting nations, Brazil, Ecuador, Cambodia and Thailand, curbed sales. This came when rice-short countries, notably the Philippines and Bangladesh, shopped for sizeable volumes abroad. This further propelled international prices skyward. Despite tapering supplies, Thailand kept its export window open. So did the United States. These are among the few sources of supplies that remained open – the U.S.A. because rice is not a staple there and Thailand because it is the largest producer of rice. Prices of Thai white rice which represent world prices more than doubled. This strengthened prices in Vietnam and Pakistan.

It's not all bad news, however. The signs are that 2008 harvests will top record levels. Stocks should bring down prices. But not overnight. October-November is when the bulk of 2008 paddy will be sold. Until then, 'world rice quotations are likely to remain extremely strong,' according to FAO However, availability might ease and granaries overflow, but prices are not likely to come down to pre-2007 levels, although they are expected to drop somewhat from the June 2008 peaks.

Food prices do not operate in a vacuum, and crude oil (fuel) is the one input which underpins most farming costs. In June 2008 crude was around $ 125 a barrel, a four-fold rise from 2004. Expectations are that, as in the case of food, the days of low-cost crude will not return. This will spur food production costs, especially for small farmers in poorer countries. Fuel is all over the food scenario.

Fertilizer is oil-based. It takes fuel to move crops from farms to tables and inputs to farms. To add to the distress, neglect of agriculture over the decades has made the achievement of higher productivity a long-term goal (see chapter 18: Biofuels Divide the World).

Ban Ki-Moon, UN Secretary General, in his opening remarks at the Rome summit said that food production needed to rise by 50 per cent by 2030 if the projected demand was to be met. (The cost for this is variously estimated at between $ 20 to 30 billion annually).

He emphasized the need to revitalize agriculture productivity. Moon succinctly laid out the causes and remedies of food insecurity. The first step, he said, was the short-term need to improve the access to food of the vulnerable populations and increase food availability. He suggested:

In the short-term

- ⌘ expanding food assistance through food, vouchers or cash;
- ⌘ scaling up nutritional support and improving safety nets and social protection programmes to help the most vulnerable;

- ⌘ boosting small landholder farmers' food production through an urgent insertion of key inputs (including seeds and fertilizers) in time for the 2008 planting seasons;
- ⌘ improving rural infrastructure and links to markets and expanding micro-credit programmes;
- ⌘ adjusting trade and taxation policies to minimise export restrictions and import tariffs and help free flow of agricultural goods;
- ⌘ skillfully managing the impact of rising food prices on inflation and macroeconomic policy;
- ⌘ supporting balance of payments of net food importing countries; and
- ⌘ helping to ensure that short-term measures to respond to food price rises are financially sustainable by governments.

The UN Secretary General cautioned against recourse to limiting exports or imposing price controls. They only distort markets and spur food prices even higher, he said.

In the long-term

To achieve longer term resilience, sustainability and to contribute to global food security, he recommended:

- ⌘ addressing structural issues that impede agricultural development;
- ⌘ ensuring long-term investment in small landholder farming in developing countries, including technical and financial support;
- ⌘ helping governments to reinforce social safety nets for the neediest and most vulnerable people;
- ⌘ looking at rural infrastructure needs, as well as new financing mechanisms;
- ⌘ eliminating trade and taxation policies that distort markets—not least through rapid resolution of the Doha round; and
- ⌘ supporting promising research into optimal food crops and better animal production systems, and adapting known technologies to existing food chains.

Another issue which created some amount of heat at the Summit was the action of many nations in imposing food export controls with a view to increasing food security for their poorer population. Some food-producing countries had been opposed to the declaration that calls on governments 'not to institute trade actions, such as export limits or bans that could threaten stability of food supply,' as stated in a revised draft. At the outset of the summit, U.N. chief Ban Ki-moon warned against export restrictions by food-exporting nations.

World Bank President Robert Zoellick joined Moon in warning against the trade practice, terming it as encouraging hoarding, driving up prices and hurting the poorest people in the world.

As short-term remedial steps, the declaration called on governments to provide food and financial aid to countries facing food shortages. As for medium- to long-term measures, it urged governments to step up international cooperation to expand investments in the agricultural sector and to bolster agricultural production.

THE REAL TRAGEDY

Whether the resolutions taken by the nearly 200 countries that gathered for the summit will bring an end to the food crisis remains to be seen. However, it is doubtful whether notable results can be expected in the short-term.

Perhaps the most tragic thing about the global food crisis is that it takes riot police and violent deaths to expose a crisis that has been with us all along. Before prices started to jump, an estimated 850 million people were living with extreme hunger. More than 30,000 children were dying every day from hunger-related diseases.

Hunger compromises every stage of human development. It perpetuates poverty by stunting mental and physical capacities. Hunger is a scourge. It has no place in a world in which governments spend hundreds of millions of dollars each day on war.

At the World Food Conference in 1974, governments pledged to eradicate child hunger in a decade. At the World Food Summit in 1996, governments settled for halving the number of people living with hunger by 2015. In 2000, governments made halving hunger one of the Millennium Development goals.

In 2008, not only are the world's governments failing to make headway on this objective, but even to halve the number of people living with hunger just got a lot harder because so many cracks in the existing food and agriculture system have burst open at once.

THE TRAGEDY WAS ALREADY THERE, BENEATH THE SURFACE

For 30 years, governments, aid donors and development agencies have neglected agriculture. The sector was seen as backward, unproductive and a poverty trap. The result is a shocking investment deficit that will take years to recover. At the same time, an ideological obsession with the world market as the best insurance policy for food security led to a dramatic reduction in publicly held food stocks.

Global rice and corn stocks have shrunk by almost half since 2000. Governments abdicated their responsibility for public stocks to the private companies that dominate world markets. The companies' priorities lie elsewhere. When harvests fail, as too many did in 2006–07, governments now depend on a volatile market to replenish their stocks. 2007–08 is expected to provide a bumper harvest, but it may not have much impact on food insecurity because prices of foodgrains are expected to remain high, if not increase.

In other words, availability and accessibility to food might improve but prices will not as incomes of the poor will certainly not rise proportionately.

So more investment in agriculture and more responsible storage policies—is that the answer? In part. But other aspects of the crisis also need attention. In particular, it is essential to determine if the crisis is about high prices, or in fact about price shocks, in which extreme price movements go both up and down, making risk management and agricultural planning more difficult.

For several decades, many analysts have argued that agricultural prices, especially commodity prices paid to farmers, are too low. Farmers and farm labourers were unable to make a decent living from their production, which in turn kept millions of people in poverty. Many small farmers were forced off their land.

Low food prices are not the answer. Instead, policy-makers should be thinking about how to reallocate the profits within the food system, to increase the return to farmers and reduce the burden on consumers. Support for farmer organizations and investment in infrastructure to strengthen local markets is also needed.

Stronger regulation of corporate activity, especially where they have monopoly or oligopoly power, is essential. Better documentation of corporate influence and the creation of national and international competition laws would be a good first step. Finally, consumer subsidies, like those set up in Mexico, may be required, to stimulate demand for increased local production to meet local demand for food.

While world leaders at the Rome meet agreed to a slew of measures to avert the food crisis, increasing humanitarian assistance must find a high on the agenda. This is only the tip of the iceberg. The time is ripe for a break with the past and the start of a radically new vision for food and agriculture.

CHAPTER 21

GLOBAL FOOD SITUATION: PRESENT AND PROJECTED

THE world food situation is currently being rapidly redefined by new driving forces. Income growth, climate change, high energy prices, globalization, and urbanization are transforming food consumption, production, and markets. The influence of the private sector in the world food system, especially the leverage of food retailers, is also rapidly increasing. Changes in food availability, rising commodity prices, and new producer-consumer linkages have crucial implications for the livelihoods of poor and food-insecure people.

Analyzing and interpreting recent trends and emerging challenges in the world food situation is essential in order to provide policymakers with the necessary information to mobilize adequate responses at the local, national, regional, and international levels. It is also critical for helping to appropriately adjust research agendas in agriculture, nutrition, and health. Not surprisingly, renewed global attention is being given to the role of agriculture and food in development policy, as can be seen from the World Bank's World Development Report, accelerated public action in African agriculture under the New Partnership for Africa's Development (NEPAD), and the Asian Development Bank's initiatives for more investment in agriculture, to name just a few examples.

THE WORLD FOOD EQUATION

Many parts of the developing world have experienced high economic growth in recent years. Developing Asia, especially China and India, continues to show strong sustained growth. Real GDP in the region increased by 9 per cent per annum between 2004 and 2006. Sub-Saharan Africa also experienced rapid economic growth of about 6 per cent in the same period. Even countries with high incidence and prevalence of hunger reported strong growth rates. Of the world's 34 most food-insecure countries, 22 had average annual growth rates ranging from 5 to 16 per cent between 2004 and 2006.[1] Global economic growth, however, is projected to slow from 5.2 per cent in 2007 to 4.8 per cent in 2008. Beyond 2008, world growth is expected to remain in the 4 per cent range while developing-country growth is expected to average 6 per cent. This growth is a central force of change on the demand side of the world food equation. High income growth in low-income countries readily translates into increased consumption of food.

Another major force altering the food equation is shifting rural-urban populations and the resulting impact on spending and consumer preferences. The world's urban population has grown more than the rural population; within the next three decades, 61 per cent of the world's populace is expected to live in urban areas. However, three-quarters of the poor remain in rural areas, and rural poverty will continue to be more prevalent than urban poverty during the next several decades.

Agricultural diversification toward high-value agricultural production is a demand-driven process in which the private sector plays a vital role. Higher incomes, urbanization, and changing preferences are raising domestic consumer demand for high-value products in developing countries. The composition of food budgets is shifting from the consumption of grains and other staple crops to vegetables, fruits, meat, dairy, and fish. The demand for ready-to-cook and ready-to-eat foods is also rising, particularly in urban areas. Consumers in Asia, especially in the cities, are also being exposed to nontraditional foods. Due to diet globalization, the consumption of wheat and wheat-based products, temperate-zone vegetables, and dairy products in Asia has increased.

Today's shifting patterns of consumption are expected to be reinforced in the future. With an income growth of 5.5 per cent per year in South Asia, annual per capita consumption of rice in the region is projected to decline from its 2000 level by 4 per cent by 2025. At the same time, consumption of milk and vegetables is projected to increase by 70 per cent and consumption of meat, eggs, and fish is projected to increase by 100 per cent. In China, consumers in rural areas continue to be more dependent on grains than consumers in urban areas (Table 1). However, the increase in the consumption of meat, fish and aquatic products, and fruits in rural areas is

TABLE 1
China: Per Capita Annual and Household Consumption

	Urban			Rural		
Product	**1990 (kg)**	**2006 (kg)**	**2005-1990 ratio**	**1990 (kg)**	**2006 (kg)**	**2006-1990 ratio**
Grain	131	76	0.6	262	206	0.8
Pork, beef, mutton	22	24	1.1	11	17	1.5
Poultry	3	8	2.4	1	4	2.8
Milk	5	18	4.0	1	3	2.9
Fish, aquatic prodicts	8	13	1.7	2	5	2.4
Fruits	41	60	1.5	6	19	3.2

Source: National Bureau of Statistics of China, 2007a, 2007b.

even greater than in urban areas.

In India, cereal consumption remained unchanged between 1990 and 2005, while consumption of oil crops almost doubled; consumption of meat, milk, fish, fruits, and vegetables also increased (Table 2). In other developing countries, the shift to high-value demand has been less obvious. In Brazil, Kenya, and Nigeria, the consumption of some high-value products declined, which may be due to growing inequality in some of these countries. (Table 2)

TABLE 2
Change in Food Consumption Quantity, Ratios 2005-1990

Type	India	China	Brazil	Kenya	Nigeria
Cereals	1.0	0.8	1.2	1.1	1.0
Oil crops	1.7	2.4	1.1	0.8	1.1
Meat	1.2	2.4	1.7	0.9	1.0
Milk	1.2	3.0	1.2	0.9	1.3
Fish	1.2	2.3	0.9	0.4	0.8
Fruits	1.3	3.5	0.8	1.0	1.1
Vegetables	1.3	2.9	1.3	1.0	1.3

Source: FAO, 2007a.

WORLD FOOD PRODUCTION

Wheat, coarse grains (including maize and sorghum), and rice are staple foods for the majority of the world's population. Cereal supply depends on the production and availability of stocks. World cereal production in 2006 was about 2 billion tons—2.4 per cent less than in 2005. Most of the decrease is the result of reduced plantings and adverse weather in some major cereal producing and exporting countries. Between 2004 and 2006, wheat and maize production in the European Union and the United States decreased by 12 to 16 per cent. On the positive side, coarse grain production in China increased by 12 per cent and rice output in India increased by 9 per cent (based on data from FAO, 2006b and 2007b). In 2007, world cereal production is expected to rise by almost 6 per cent due to sharp increases in the production of maize, the main coarse grain.

In 2006, global cereal stocks,[2] especially wheat, were at their lowest levels since the early 1980s. Stocks in China, which constitute about 40 per cent of total stocks, declined significantly from 2000 to 2004, and have not recovered in recent years. End-year cereal stocks in 2007 are expected to remain at 2006 levels.

As opposed to cereals, the production of high-value agricultural commodities such as vegetables, fruits, meat, and milk is growing at a fast rate in developing countries. Climate-change risks will have adverse impacts on food production, compounding the challenge of meeting global food demand. Consequently, food import dependency is projected to rise in many

TABLE 3
Expected Impacts of Climate Change on Global Cereal Production

Region	1990-2080 (% change)
World	–0.6 to –0.9
Developed countries	2.7 to 9.0
Developing countries	–3.3 to –7.2
Southeast Asia	–2.5 to –7.8
South Asia	–18.2 to –22.1
Sub-Saharan Africa	–3.9 to –7.5
Latin America	5.2 to 12.5

Source: Adapted from Tubiello & Fischer, 2007.

regions of the developing world. With the increased risk of droughts and floods due to rising temperatures, crop-yield losses are imminent. In more than 40 developing countries, mainly in Sub-Saharan Africa, cereal yields are expected to decline, with mean losses of about 15 per cent by 2080. Other estimates suggest that although the aggregate impact on cereal production between 1990 and 2080 might be small, a decrease in production of less than 1 per cent, large reductions of up to 22 per cent are likely in South Asia (Table 3).

In contrast, developed countries and Latin America are expected to experience absolute gains. Impacts on the production of cereals also differ by crop type. Projections show that land suitable for wheat production may almost disappear in Africa. Nonetheless, global land use due to climate change is estimated to increase minimally by less than 1 per cent. In many parts of the developing world, especially in Africa, an expansion of arid lands of up to 8 per cent may be anticipated by 2080.

World agricultural GDP is projected to decrease by 16 per cent by 2020 due to global warming. Again, the impact on developing countries will be much more severe than on developed countries. Output in developing countries is projected to decline by 20 per cent, while output in industrial countries is projected to decline by 6 per cent. Carbon fertilization[3] could limit the severity of climate-change effects to only 3 per cent. However, technological change is not expected to be able to alleviate output losses and increase yields to a rate that would keep up with growing food demand. Agricultural prices will thus also be affected by climate variability and change.

Temperature increases of more than 3°C may cause prices to increase by up to 40 per cent.

DEVELOPING COUNTRIES NATIVE INSURANCE MECHANISMS

This is an area for new institutional exploration in globalization and trade. A more open trade regime in agriculture would benefit developing countries in general. Research by the International Food Policy Research Institute (IFPRI) has shown that the benefits of opening up and facilitating market access between member countries of the Organisation for Economic Co-operation and Development (OECD) and developing countries, as well as among developing countries, would bring significant economic gains. However, large advances in poverty reduction would not occur except in some cases. Multilateral discussions towards further trade liberalization and the integration of developing countries into the global economy are currently deadlocked.

The conclusion of the World Trade Organization (WTO) Doha Development Round has been delayed due to divisions between developed and developing countries and a lack of political commitment on the part of key negotiating parties. In the area of agriculture, developed countries have been unwilling to make major concessions. The United States has been hesitant to decrease domestic agricultural support in its new farm bill, while the European Union has been hesitant to negotiate on its existing trade restrictions on sensitive farm products. Deep divisions have also emerged regarding the conditions for nonagricultural market access proposed in Potsdam in July 2007. In reaction to the lack of progress of the Doha Round, many countries are increasingly engaging in regional and bilateral trade agreements.

The number of regional arrangements reported to the WTO rose from 86 in 2000 to 159 in 2007. Increasingly, South-South and South-North regional initiatives have emerged, such as the Central American Free Trade Agreement (CAFTA) between the United States and Central America and the negotiations between the African, Caribbean, and Pacific (ACP) states and the European Union, and they may create more opportunities for cooperation among developing countries and for opening up their markets. Another development has been the improvement of the terms of trade for commodity exporters as a result of increases in global prices.

The share of developing countries in global exports increased from 32 per cent in 2000 to 37 per cent in 2006, but there are large regional disparities. Africa's share in global exports, for example, increased only from 2.3 to 2.8 per cent in the same period.

CHANGES IN THE CORPORATE FOOD SYSTEM

The growing power and leverage of international corporations are transforming the opportunities available to small agricultural producers in developing countries. While new prospects have arisen for some farmers, many others have not been able to take advantage of the new income-generating opportunities since the rigorous safety and quality standards of food processors and food retailers create high barriers to their market entry. Transactions along the corporate food chain have increased in the past two years. Between 2004 and 2006, total global food spending grew by 16 per cent, from US$ 5.5 trillion to 6.4 trillion. In the same period, the sales of food retailers increased by a disproportionately large amount compared to the sales of food processors and of companies in the food input industry. The sales of the top food processors and traders grew by 13 per cent, and the sales of the top 10 companies producing agricultural inputs (agrochemicals, seeds, and traits) increased by 8 per cent. The sales of the top food retailers, however, soared by more than 40 per cent.

While supermarkets account for a large share of retail sales in most developed and many developing countries, independent grocers continue to represent 85 per cent of retail sales in Vietnam and 77 per cent in India. The process of horizontal consolidation in the agricultural-input industry continues on a global scale. The three leading agrochemical companies, Bayer Crop Science, Syngenta, and BASF, account for roughly half of the total market. In contrast, the top five retailers do not capture more than a 13 per cent share of the market.

Global data, however, mask substantial differences between countries; while the top five retailers account for 57 per cent of grocery sales in Venezuela, they represent less than 4 per cent of sales in Indonesia. Vertical integration of the food supply chain increases the synergies between agricultural inputs, processing and retail, but overall competition within the different segments of the world food chain remains strong.

CHANGING SUPPLY-AND-DEMAND FRAMEWORK

The above-mentioned changes on the supply and demand side of the world food equation have led to imbalances and drastic price changes. Between 2000 and 2006,world demand for cereals increased by 8 per cent while cereal prices increased by about 50 per cent. Thereafter, prices more than doubled by early 2008 (compared to 2000). Supply is very inelastic, which means that it does not respond quickly to price changes. Typically, aggregate agriculture supply increases by 1 to 2 per cent when prices increase by 10 per cent. The supply response decreases further when farm prices are more volatile, but increases as the result of improved infrastructure and access to technology and rural finance. The consumption of cereals has been consistently higher than production in recent years and that has reduced stocks. A breakdown of cereal demand by type of use gives insights into the factors that have contributed to the greater increase in consumption.

While cereal use for food and feed increased by 4 and 7 per cent since 2000, respectively, the use of cereals for industrial purposes, such as biofuel production, increased by more than 25 per cent. In the United States alone, the use of corn for ethanol production increased two and a half times between 2000 and 2006.

Supply and demand changes do not fully explain the price increases. Financial investors are becoming increasingly interested in rising commodity prices and speculative transactions are adding to increased commodity-price volatility. In 2006, the volume of traded global agricultural futures and options rose by almost 30 per cent.

Commodity exchanges can help to make food markets more transparent and efficient. They are becoming more relevant in India and China and African countries are initiating commodity exchanges as well, as has occurred in Ethiopia, for example.

Due to government price policies, trade restrictions, and transportation costs, changes in world commodity prices do not automatically translate into changes in domestic prices. In the case of Mexico, the margin between domestic and world prices for maize has ranged between 0 and 35 per cent since the beginning of 2004, and a strong relationship between domestic and world prices is evident. In India, the differences between domestic and international rice prices were greater, averaging more than 100 per cent between 2000 and 2006.[4]

While domestic price stabilization policies diminish price volatility, they require fiscal resources and cause additional market imperfections. Government policies also change the relationship between consumer and producer prices. For instance, producer prices of wheat in Ethiopia increased more than consumer prices from 2000 to 2006.

Though international price changes do not fully translate into equivalent domestic farm and consumer price changes because of the different policies and trade positions adopted by each country, they are in fact transmitted to consumers and producers to a considerable extent. The prices of commodities used in biofuel production are becoming increasingly linked with energy prices.

In Brazil, which has been a pioneer in ethanol production since the 1970s, the price of sugar is very closely connected to the price of ethanol. A worrisome implication of the increasing link between energy and food prices is that high energy-price fluctuations are increasingly translated into high food-price fluctuations. In the past five years, price variations in oilseeds, wheat and corn have increased to about twice the levels of previous decades.

The increasing demand for high-value commodities has resulted in surging prices for meat and dairy products and this is driving feed prices upward, too. Since the beginning of 2000, butter and milk prices have tripled and poultry prices have almost doubled. The effects of price increase on consumption are different across different countries and consumer groups. Consumers in low-income countries are much more responsive to price changes than consumers in high-income countries (Table 4). Also, the demand for meat, dairy, fruits, and vegetables is much more sensitive to price, especially among the poor, than is the demand for bread and cereals.

TABLE 4
Consumption Spending Response (%) when Prices Change by 1% (Elasticity)

	Low-income Countries	High-income Countries
Food	–0.59	–0.27
Bread and cereals	–0.43	–0.14
Meat	–0.63	–0.29
Dairy	–0.70	–0.31
Fruit and vegetables	–0.51	–0.23

Source: Seale, Regmi and Bernstein, 2003.

THE EFFECT OF BIOFUELS

When oil prices range between US$ 60 and $ 70 a barrel, biofuels are competitive with petroleum in many countries, even with existing technologies. Efficiency benchmarks vary for different biofuels, however, and ultimately, production should be established and expanded where comparative advantages exist. With oil prices above US$ 90, the competitiveness is of course even stronger. Feedstock represents the principal share of total biofuel production costs. For ethanol and biodiesel, feedstock accounts for 50–70 per cent and 70–80 per cent of overall costs, respectively. Net production costs—which are all costs related to production, including investments—differ widely across countries. For instance, Brazil produces ethanol at about half the cost of Australia and one-third the cost of Germany.

Significant increases in feedstock costs (by at least 50 per cent) in the past few years impinge on comparative advantage and competitiveness.

The implication is that while the biofuel sector will contribute to feedstock price changes, it will also be a victim of these price changes. Food-price projections have not yet been able to fully take into account the impact of biofuels expansion. When assessing potential developments in the biofuels sector and their consequences, the OECD-FAO outlook makes assumptions for a number of countries, including the United States, the European Union, Canada, and China. New biofuel technologies and policies are viewed as uncertainties that could dramatically impact future food prices. The Food and Agricultural Policy Research Institute (FAPRI) conducts a detailed analysis of the potential impact of policy on biofuels and links between the ethanol and petrol markets, but its extensive modelling is limited to the United States. A new, more comprehensive global scenario analysis using IFPRI's International Model for Policy Analysis of Agricultural Commodities and Trade (IMPACT), examines current price effects and estimates future ones.

In view of the dynamic world food situation and the rapidly changing biofuels sector, IFPRI continuously updates and refines its related models, so the results presented here should be viewed as work in progress. Recently, the IMPACT model incorporated 2005-06 developments in supply and demand, and generated two future scenarios based on these developments:

- *Scenario 1* is based on the actual biofuel investment plans of many countries that have such plans and assumes biofuel expansions for identified high-potential countries that have not specified their plans.
- *Scenario 2* assumes a more drastic expansion of biofuels to double the levels used in Scenario 1. Under the planned biofuel expansion scenario (Scenario 1), international prices increase by 26 per cent for maize and by 18 per cent for oilseeds. Under the more drastic biofuel expansion scenario (Scenario 2), maize prices rise by 72 per cent and oilseeds by 44 per cent (Table 5). Under both scenarios, the increase in crop prices resulting from expanded biofuel production is also accompanied by a net decrease in the availability of and access to food, with calorie consumption estimated to decrease across all regions compared to baseline levels.

Food-calorie consumption decreases the most in Sub-Saharan Africa, where calorie availability is projected to fall by more than 8 per cent if biofuels expand drastically. One of the arguments in favour of biofuels is that they could positively affect net carbon emissions as an alternative to fossil fuels. That added social benefit might justify some level of subsidy and regulation, since these external benefits would not be internalized by

TABLE 5
Changes in World Prices of Feedstock Crops and Sugar by 2020 under Two Scenarios Compared with Baseline Levels (%)

Crop	Scenario 1 Biofuel Expansion[a]	Scenario 2 Drastic Biofuel Expansion[b]
Cassava	11.2	26.7
Maize	26.3	71.8
Oilseeds	18.1	44.4
Sugar	11.5	26.6
Wheat	8.3	20.0

a. Assumptions based on actual biofuel production plans and projections in relevant countries and regions.
b. Assumptions based on doubling actual biofuel production plans and projections in relevant countries and regions.
Source: IFPRI IMPACT projections (in constant prices).

markets. However, potential forest conversion for biofuel production and the impact of biofuel production on soil fertility are environmental concerns that require attention. As is the case with any form of agricultural production, biofuel feedstock production can be managed in sustainable or in damaging ways. Clear environment-related efficiency criteria and sound process standards need to be established, that internalize the positive and negative externalities of biofuels and ensure that the energy output from biofuel production is greater than the amount of energy used in the process. In general, subsidies for biofuels that use agricultural production resources are extremely anti-poor because they implicitly act as a tax on basic food, which represents a large share of poor people's consumption expenditures and becomes even more costly as prices increase, as shown above.

Great technological strides are expected in biofuel production in the coming decades. New technologies converting cellulosic biomass to liquid fuels would create added value by both utilizing waste biomass and by using less land resources. These second-generation technologies, however, are still being developed and third-generation technologies (such as hydrogene) are at an even earlier phase. Even though future technology development will very much determine the competitiveness of the sector, it will not solve the food–fuel competition problem. The trade-offs between food and fuel will actually be accelerated when biofuels become more competitive relative to food and when, consequently, more land, water and capital are diverted to biofuel production.

To soften the trade-offs and mitigate the growing price burden for the poor, it is necessary to accelerate investment in food and agricultural science and technologies. For many developing countries, it would be appropriate to wait for the emergence of second-generation technologies, and 'leapfrog' onto them later.

PREDICTING FUTURE FOOD PRICE CHANGES

How will food prices change in coming years? This is one of the central questions that policymakers, investors, speculators, farmers and millions of poor people ask. Though the research community does its best to answer this question, the many uncertainties created by supply, demand, market functioning and policies mean that no straightforward answer can be given. However, a number of studies have analyzed the forces driving the current increases in world food prices and have predicted future price developments.

The Economic Intelligence Unit predicts an 11 per cent increase in the price of grains in the next two years and only a 5 per cent rise in the price of oilseeds.The OECD-FAO outlook has higher price projections (it expects the prices of coarse grains, wheat, and oilseeds to increase by 34, 20, and 13 per cent, respectively, by 2016–17). The Food and Agricultural Policy Research Institute (FAPRI) expects increases in corn demand and prices to last until 2009–10 and thereafter expects corn production growth to be on par with consumption growth. FAPRI does not expect biofuels to have a large impact on wheat markets, and predicts that wheat prices will stay constant due to stable demand as population growth offsets declining per capita consumption.[5]

Only the price of palmoil—another biofuel feedstock—is projected to dramatically increase by 29 per cent. In cases where demand for agricultural feedstock is large and elastic, some experts expect petroleum prices to act as a price floor for agricultural commodity prices. In the resulting price corridor, agricultural commodity prices are determined by the product's energy equivalency and the energy price. In order to model recent price developments, changes in supply and demand from 2000 to 2005 as well as biofuel developments were introduced into the IFPRI IMPACT model (see *Scenario 1*). The results indicate that biofuel production is responsible for only part of the imbalances in the world food equation.

Other supply and demand shocks also play important roles. The price changes that resulted from actual supply and demand changes during 2000–05 capture a fair amount of the noted increase in real prices for grains in those years. For the period from 2006 to 2015, the scenario suggests further increases in cereal prices of about 10 to 20 per cent in current U.S. dollars. Continued depreciation of the U.S. dollar—which many expect—may further increase prices in U.S.-dollar terms. The results suggest that changes on the supply side (including droughts and other shortfalls and the diversion of food for fuel) are powerful forces affecting the price surge at a time when demand is strong due to high income growth in developing countries.

Under a scenario of continued high income growth (but no further supply shocks), the preliminary model results indicate that food prices would remain at current high livels. The usual supply response embedded in the model would not be strong enough to turn matters around in the near future. Who benefits and who loses from high prices? An increase in cereal prices will have uneven impacts across countries and population groups. Net cereal exporters will experience improved terms of trade, while net cereal importers will face increased costs in meeting domestic cereal demand.

TABLE 6
Net Cereal Exports and Imports for Selected Countries (Three-year Averages 2003–05)

Country	1000 tons
Japan	–24,986
Mexico	–12,576
Egypt	–10,767
Nigeria	–2,972
Brazil	–2,670
China	–1,331
Ethiopia	–789
Burkino Faso	29
India	3,637
Argentina	20,431
United States	76,653

Source: FAO 2007a.

There are about four times more net cereal-importing countries in the world than net exporters. Even though China is the largest producer of cereals, it is a net importer of cereals due to strong domestic consumption (Table 6). In contrast, India—also a major cereal producer—is a net exporter. Almost all countries in Africa are net importers of cereals. Price increases also affect the availability of food aid. Global food aid represents less than 7 per cent of global official development assistance and less than 0.4 per cent of total world food production. Food aid flows, however, have been declining and have reached their lowest level since 1973. In 2006, food aid was 40 per cent lower than in 2000.

Emergency aid continues to constitute the largest portion of food aid. Faced with shrinking resources, food aid is increasingly targeted to fewer countries—mainly in sub- Saharan Africa—and to specific beneficiary groups. At the microeconomic level, whether a household will benefit or lose from high food prices depends on whether the household is a net seller or buyer of food. Since food accounts for a large share of the poor population's total expenditures, a staple-crop price increase would translate into lower quantity and quality of food consumption. Household surveys provide insights into the potential impact of higher food prices on the poor.

Surveys show that poor net buyers in Bolivia, Ethiopia, Bangladesh, and Zambia purchase more staple foods than net sellers sell (Table 7). The impact of a price increase is country and crop specific. For instance, two-thirds of rural households in Java own between 0 and 0.25 hectares of land, and only 10 per cent of households would benefit from an increase in rice prices. In sum, in view of the changed farm-production and market situation that the poor face today, there is not much supporting evidence for the idea that higher farm prices would generally cause poor households to gain

TABLE 7
Purchases and Sales of Staple Foods by the Poor (1% of Total Expenditure of all Poor)

Staple Foods	Bolivia 2002	Ethiopia 2000	Bangladesh 2001	Zambia 1998
Purchases by all poor net buyers	11.3	10.2	22.0	10.3
Sales by all poor net sellers	1.4	2.8	4.0	2.3

Source: World Bank, 2007a.

more on the income side than they would lose on the consumption-expenditure side.

Adjustments in the farm and rural economy that might indirectly create new income opportunities due to the changed incentives will take time to reach the poor.

Many of those who are the poorest and hungriest today will still be poor and hungry in 2015, the target year of the Millennium Development Goals. Research has shown that 160 million people live in ultra poverty on less than 50 cents a day.The fact that large numbers of people continue to live in intransigent poverty and hunger in an increasingly wealthy global economy is the major ethical, economic and public health challenge of our time.

POVERTY AND THE FOOD/NUTRITION SITUATION

The number of undernourished in the developing world actually increased from 823 million in 1990 to 830 million in 2004. In the same period, the share of undernourished declined by only 3 percentage points—from 20 to 17 per cent. The share of the ultra poor—those who live on less than US$ 0.50 a day—decreased more slowly than the share of the poor who live on US$ 1 a day. In Sub-Saharan Africa and Latin America, the number of people living on less than US$0.50 a day has actually increased. Clearly, the poorest are being left behind.

Behind the global figures on undernourishment, there are also substantial regional differences. In East Asia, the number of food-insecure people has decreased by more than 18 per cent since the early 1990s and the prevalence of undernourishment decreased on average by 2.5 per cent per annum, mostly due to economic growth in China. In sub-Saharan Africa, however, the number of food-insecure people increased by more than 26 per cent and the prevalence of undernourishment increased by 0.3 per cent per year. South Asia remains the region with the largest number of hungry, accounting for 36 per cent of all undernourished in the developing world. Recent data show that in the developing world, one of every four children under the age of five is still underweight and one of every three is stunted.

Children living in rural areas are nearly twice as likely to be underweight as children in urban areas. An aggregate view on progress—or lack thereof—is given by the Global Hunger Index (GHI). It evaluates manifestations of hunger beyond dietary energy availability. The GHI is a combined measure of three equally weighted components: (i) the proportion of undernourished as a percentage of the population, (ii) the prevalence of underweight in children under the age of five, and (iii) the under-five mortality rate.

The Index ranks countries on a 100-point scale, with higher scores indicating greater hunger. Scores above 10 are considered serious and scores above 30 are considered extremely alarming. From 1990 to 2007, the GHI improved significantly in South and Southeast Asia, but progress was limited in the Middle East and North Africa and in sub-Saharan Africa. The causes and manifestations of hunger differ substantially between regions. Although Sub-Saharan Africa and South Asia currently have virtually the same scores, the prevalence of underweight children is much higher in South Asia, while the proportion of calorie-deficient people and child mortality is much more serious in Sub-Saharan Africa.

In recent years, countries' progress towards alleviating hunger has been mixed. For instance, progress slowed in China and India and accelerated in Brazil and Ghana. Many countries in Sub-Saharan Africa have considerably higher GHI values than countries with similar incomes per capita, largely due to political instability and war. Index scores for Ethiopia moved up and down, increasing during times of war and improving considerably between 1997 and 2003. Climate change will create new food insecurities in coming decades.[6] Low-income countries with limited adaptive capacities to climate variability and change are faced with significant threats to food security. In many African countries, for example, agricultural production as well as access to food will be negatively affected, thereby increasing food insecurity and malnutrition. When taking into account the effects of climate change, the number of undernourished people

TABLE 8

Expected Number of Undernourished in Millions Incorporating the Effects of Climate Change

Region	1990	2020	2050	2080	2080-90 Ratio
Developing countries	885	772	579	554	0.6
Asia, Developing	659	390	123	73	0.1
Sub-Saharan Africa	138	273	359	410	3.0
Latin America	54	53	40	23	0.4
Middle East and North Africa	33	55	56	48	1.5

Source: Tubiello and Fischer, 2007.

in sub-Saharan Africa may triple between 1990 and 2080 under these assumptions (Table 7).

CONCLUSIONS

The main findings of this update on the world food situation are:

- ⌘ Strong economic growth in developing countries is a main driver of a changing world food demand towards high-value agricultural products and processed foods.
- ⌘ Slow-growing supply, low stocks, and supply shocks at a time of surging demand for feed, food, and fuel have led to drastic price increases, and these high prices do not appear likely to fall soon.
- ⌘ Biofuel production has contributed to the changing world food equation and currently adversely affects the poor through price-level and price-volatility effects.
- ⌘ Many small farmers would like to take advantage of the new income-generating opportunities presented by high-value products (meat, milk, vegetables, fruits, flowers). There are, however, high barriers to market entry. Therefore, improved capacity is needed to address safety and quality standards as well as the large scales required by food processors and retailers.
- ⌘ Poor households that are net sellers of food benefit from higher prices, but these are few. Households that are net buyers lose, and they represent the large majority of the poor.
- ⌘ A number of countries, including countries in Africa, have made good progress in reducing hunger and child malnutrition. But many of the poorest and hungry are still being left behind despite policies that aim to cut poverty and hunger in half by 2015 under the Millennium Development Goals.
- ⌘ Higher food prices will cause the poor to shift to even less-balanced diets, with adverse impacts on health in the short and long run. Business as usual could mean increased misery, especially for the world's poorest populations. A mix of policy actions that avoids damage and fosters positive responses is required. While maintaining a focus on long-term challenges is vital, there are five actions that should be undertaken immediately:

    1. Developed countries should facilitate flexible responses to drastic price changes by eliminating trade barriers and programmes that

set aside agriculture resources, except in well-defined conservation areas. A world confronted with more scarcity of food needs to trade more, not less, to spread opportunities fairly.

2. Developing countries should rapidly increase investment in rural infrastructure and market institutions in order to reduce agricultural-input access constraints, since these are hindering a stronger production response.
3. The acute risks facing the poor, reduced food availability and limited access to income-generating opportunities, require expanded social-protection measures. Productive social safety nets should be tailored to country circumstances and should focus on early childhood nutrition.
4. Placing agricultural and food issues onto the national and international climate-change policy agendas is critical for ensuring an efficient and pro-poor response to the emerging risks.

NOTES

1. The most food-insecure countries include the 20 countries with the highest prevalence of undernourishment and the 20 countries with the highest number of undernourished people as reported in FAO 2006a. Six countries overlap across both categories.
2. The data on stocks are estimates that need to be interpreted with caution since not all countries make such data available.
3. Carbon fertilization refers to the influence of higher atmospheric concentrations of carbon dioxide on crop yields.
4. Calculation based on data from Government of India 2007 and FAO 2007b.
5. The coefficient of variation of oilseeds in the past five years was 0.20, compared to typical coefficients in the range of 0.08–0.12 in the past two decades. In the past decade, the coefficient of variation of corn increased from 0.09 to 0.22.
6. The weather variables are partly synthesized because complete data are not available, so turning points on prices will not be precise, but the trend captures significant change.

CHAPTER 22

WORLD POPULATION: ACTUALS AND ESTIMATES

THE world population is the total number of living humans on Earth at a given time. As of June 2008, the world's population is believed to be just under 6.7 billion. In line with population projections, this figure continues to grow at rates that were unprecedented before the 20th century, although the rate of increase has almost halved since its peak of 2.2 per cent per year, which was reached in 1963. The world's population, on its current growth trajectory, is expected to reach nearly 9 billion by the year 2042.

POPULATION FIGURES

Below is a table with historical and predicted population figures shown in millions. The availability of historical population figures varies by region (Tables 9 and 10).

RATE OF INCREASE

Different regions have different rates of population growth, but in the unusual case of the 20th century, the world saw the biggest increase in its population in human history due to medical advances and massive increase in agricultural productivity made by the Green Revolution.

In 2000, the United Nations estimated that the world's population was then growing at the rate of 1.14 per cent (or about 75 million people) per year, down from a peak of 86 million per year in 1987. In the last few centuries, the number of people living on Earth increased many times over. By the year 2000, there were 10 times as many people on Earth as there

TABLE 9
World Historical and Predicted Population (in millions)

Region	1750	1800	1850	1900	1950	1999	2050	2150
World	791	978	1262	1650	2521	5978	8909	9746
Africa	106	107	111	133	221	767	1766	2308
Asia	502	635	809	947	1402	3634	5268	5561
Europe	163	203	276	408	547	729	628	517
Latin America and the Caribbean	16	24	38	74	167	511	809	912
Northern America	2	7	26	82	172	307	392	398
Oceana	2	2	2	6	13	30	46	51

TABLE 10
World Historical and Predicted Populations by Percentage Distribution

Region	1750	1800	1850	1900	1950	1999	2050	2150
World	100	100	100	100	100	100	100	100
Africa	13.4	10.9	8.8	8.1	8.8	12.8	19.8	23.7
Asia	63.5	64.9	64.1	57.4	55.6	60.8	59.1	57.1
Europe	20.6	20.8	21.9	24.7	21.7	12.2	7.0	5.3
Latin America and the Caribbean	2.0	2.5	3.0	4.5	6.6	8.5	9.1	9.4
Northern America	0.3	0.7	2.1	5.0	6.8	5.1	4.4	4.1
Oceana	0.3	0.2	0.2	0.4	0.5	0.5	0.5	0.5

were 300 years ago. According to data from the CIA's 2005–06 World Factbooks, the world human population increased by 203,800 every day. The 2007 CIA factbook increased this to 211,090 people every day.

Globally, the population growth rate has been steadily declining from its peak of 2.19 per cent in 1963, but growth remains high in the Middle East and Sub-Saharan Africa.

TABLE 11
Estimated World Population at Various Dates (in thousands)

Year	World	Africa	Asia	Europe	Latin America*	Northern America*	Oceania
70,000 BCE	2						
10,000 BCE	1,000						
9,000 BCE	3,000						
8,000 BCE	5,000						
7,000 BCE	7,000						
6,000 BCE	10,000						
5,000 BCE	15,000						
4,000 BCE	20,000						
3,000 BCE	25,000						
2,000 BCE	35,000						
1,000 BCE	50,000						
500 BCE	100,000						
1	200,000						
1000	310,000						
1750	791,000	106,000	502,000	163,000	16,000	2,000	2,000
1800	978,000	107,000	635,000	203,000	24,000	7,000	2,000
1850	1,262,000	111,000	809,000	276,000	38.000	26,000	2,000
1900	1,650,000	133,000	947,000	408,000	74,000	82,000	6,000
1950	2,518,629	221,214	1,398,488	547,403	167,097	171,616	12,812
1955	2,755,823	246,746	1,541,947	575,184	190,797	186,884	14,265
1960	2,981,659	277,398	1,674,336	601,401	209,303	204,152	15,888
1965	3,334,874	313,744	1,899,424	634,026	250,452	219,570	17,657
1970	3,962,492	357,283	2,143,118	655,855	284,856	231,937	19,443
1975	4,068,109	408,160	2,397,512	675,542	321,906	243,425	21,564
1980	4,434,682	469,618	2,632,335	692,431	361,401	256,068	22,828
1985	4,830,979	541,814	2,887,552	706,009	401,469	269,456	24,678
1990	5,263,593	622.443	3,167,807	721,582	441,525	283,549	26,687
1995	5,674,380	707,462	3,430,052	727,405	481,099	299,438	28,924
2000	6,070,581	795,671	3,679,737	727,986	520,229	315,915	31,043
2005	6,453,628	887,964	3,917,508	724,722	558,281	332,156	32,998*

Note: 'Northern America' indicates the northern countries and territories of North America: Canada, the United States, Greenland, Bermuda and St. Pierre and Miquelon. This should not be confused with the term 'North America' which typically includes Mexico. The United Nations data includes Mexico as a part of Latin America.

* This figure is disputed.

In some countries there is negative population growth (that is, net decrease in population over time), especially in Central and Eastern Europe (mainly due to low fertility rates) and Southern Africa (due to the high number of HIV-related deaths). Within the next decade, Japan and some countries in Western Europe are also expected to encounter negative population growth due to sub-replacement fertility rates.

Population growth which exceeds the carrying capacity of an area or environment results in overpopulation. Conversely, such areas may be considered 'underpopulated' if the population is not large enough to maintain an economic system. However, many who do not view overpopulation as a serious problem, fail to consider the sustainability of economic systems, the environmental degradation caused and the ecological footprint of the existing population.

The United Nations states that population growth is rapidly declining due to the demographic transition. The world population is expected to peak at 9.2 billion in 2050.

Asia accounts for over 60 per cent of the world population with almost 3.8 billion people. People's Republic of China and India alone comprise 20 and 17 per cent, respectively. Africa follows with 840 million people. Europe's 710 million people make up 11 per cent of the world's population. North America is home to 514 million (8 per cent), South America to 371 million (5.3 per cent), and Australia 21 million.

THE 15 MOST POPULOUS NATIONS

Approximately 4.3 billion people live in these 15 countries, representing roughly two-thirds of the world's population. If added together, all nations in the European Union, with 494 million people—about 7.3 per cent of the world's population in 2006—would be third in the list below (Table 13).

ETHNICITY

The world is made up of hundreds of thousands of ethnic groups and due to mass migration across the planet over millennia, it is impossible to tell how many people belonging to a certain ethnic group inhabit the earth. The single largest ethnic group on the planet by far is the Han Chinese, which represents 19.73 per cent of the global population. For comparison, 6.06 per cent of the planet's population is of full or partial Spanish ancestry,

TABLE 12
The 15 Most Populous Nations

Country	Population (millions)	Percentage
China	1,320	19.84
India	1,130	16.96
United States	304	4.56
Indonesia	232	3.47
Brazil	187	2.80
Pakistan	163	2.44
Bangladesh	159	2.38
Nigeria	148	2.22
Russia	142	2.13
Japan	128	1.92
Mexico	107	1.60
Philippines	89	1.33
Vietnam	84	1.31
Germany	82	1.23
Egypt	81	1.13

and on a wider scale 14.2 per cent of the earth's population is of Sub-Saharan descent (those identifying as 'Black').

DEMOGRAPHICS OF YOUTH

According to the 2006 CIA World Factbook, around 27 per cent of the world's population is below 15 years of age.

Before adding mortality rates, the 1990s saw the greatest number of raw births worldwide, especially in the years after 1995, despite the fact that the birth rate was not as high as in the 1960s. In fact, because of the 160 million-per-year raw births after 1995, the time it took to reach the next billion reached its fastest pace (only 12 years), as world population rose to 6 billion people in 1999, when at the beginning of the decade, the figure was designated for the year 2000, by most demographers. People aged 7 through 17 make up these births today.

The years 1985–90 marked the period with the fastest yearly population change in world history. Even though the early 1960s had a greater growth rate than in the mid and late 1980s, the population change hovered around 83 million people in the five-year period, with an all-time growth change of nearly 88 million in 1990. The reason is because the world's population was greater in the mid and late 1980s (around 5 billion) than in the early 1960s (around 3 billion). People aged 17 to 22 make up these births today.

FORECAST OF WORLD POPULATION

In the long run, the future population growth of the world is difficult to predict. Birth rates are declining slightly on average, but vary greatly between developed countries (where birth rates are often at or below replacement levels), developing countries and different ethnicities. Death rates can change unexpectedly due to disease, wars and catastrophes, or advances in medicine. The UN itself has issued multiple projections of future world population, based on different assumptions. Over the last 10 years, the UN had consistently revised these projections downward, until the 2006 revision issued March 14, 2007, revised the 2050 mid range estimate upwards by 273 million.

TABLE 13
Population Projections

Year	Population (billions)
2010	6.8
2020	7.6
2030	8.3
2040	8.9
2050	9.4

Source: US Census Bureau.

Alternatively, the United States Census Bureau issued a revised forecast for world population that increased its projection for the year 2050 to above 9.4 billion people (which was the UN's 1996 projection for 2050), up from 9.1 billion people.

TABLE 14
Other Population Projections
(in millions)

Year	World	Africa	Asia	Europe	Latin America	USA and Canada	Oceana
2010	6.830	984	4,149	720	594	348	35
%		14.4	60.7	10.5	8.7	5.1	0.5
2020	7.540	1,188	4,570	705	659	380	38
%		15.7	60.6	9.4	8.7	5.0	0.5
2025	7.540	1,188	4,570	705	659	380	39
%		15.7	60.6	9.4	8.7	5.0	0.5
2030	8,130	1,398	4,887	685	711	408	41
%		17.2	60.1	8.4	8.7	5.0	0.5
2035	8,378	1,504	5,007	674	732	419	43
%		18.0	59.8	8.0	8.7	5.0	0.5
2040	8,594	1,608	5,103	661	748	430	44
%		18.7	59.4	8.0	8.7	5.0	0.5
2045	8,774	1,708	5,175	647	760	439	45
%		19.5	59.0	7.4	8.7	5.0	0.5
2050	8,919	1,803	5,217	653	767	448	46
%		20.2	58.5	7.3	8.6	5.0	0.5

Other projections of population growth predict that the world's population will eventually crest, though it is uncertain exactly when or how. In some scenarios, the population will crest as early as the mid-21st century at under 9 billion, due to gradually decreasing birth rates. In other scenarios, disasters triggered by the growing population's demand for scarce resources will eventually lead to a sudden population crash, or even a Malthusian catastrophe.

PREDICTIONS BASED ON OUR GROWING POPULATION

In 1798, Thomas Malthus incorrectly predicted that population growth would eventually outrun food supply in the middle of the 19th century, resulting in catastrophe. In 1968, Paul R. Ehrlich re-ignited this argument with his book *The Population Bomb*, which helped give the issue significant attention throughout the 1960s and 1970s. The dire predictions of Ehrlich and other neo-Malthusians were vigorously challenged by a number of economists, notably Julian Simon.

On the opposite end of the spectrum there are a number of people who argue that today's low fertility rates in Europe, North America, Japan and Australia, combined with mass immigration, will have severe negative consequences for these countries.

Child poverty has been linked to people having children before they have the means to care for them. More recently, some scholars have put forward the Doomsday argument applying Bayesian probability to world population to argue that the end of humanity will come sooner than we usually think.

It should be noted that between 1950 and 1984, as the Green Revolution transformed agriculture around the globe, world grain production increased by 250 per cent. The energy for the Green Revolution was provided by fossil fuels in the form of fertilizers (natural gas), pesticides (oil) and hydrocarbon fuelled irrigation. The peaking of world hydrocarbon production may test Malthus and Ehrlich critics. As of May 2008, increased farming for use in biofuels, world oil prices at over $ 120 a barrel, global population growth, climate change, loss of agricultural land to residential and industrial development, and growing consumer demand in China and India have pushed up the price of grain. Food riots have recently taken place in many countries across the world.

The world population has grown by about four billion since the beginning of the Green Revolution and most believe that, without the Revolution, there would be greater famine and malnutrition than the UN presently documents (approximately 850 million people suffering from chronic malnutrition in 2005).

TOTAL NUMBER OF HUMANS EVER ON EARTH

Estimates of the total number of people who have ever lived range approximately from 45 billion to 125 billion. Many of the more robust estimates fall into the range of 90 to 110 billion humans. It is impossible to make a precise count of the number of human beings who have ever lived for the following reasons:

- ⌘ The set of specific characteristics which define a human being and distinguish early *Homo sapiens* from earlier or related species continues to be a subject of intense research and debate. It is thus not possible to know when to begin the count, nor which hominids to include.

- ⌘ Even if the scientific community reached wide consensus regarding which characteristics distinguished human beings, it would be nearly impossible to pinpoint the time of their first appearance to even the nearest millennium because the fossil record is simply too sparse. Only a few thousand fossils of early humans have been found, most no bigger than a tooth or a knucklebone. These bone fragments are used to extrapolate the population distribution of millions of early human beings spread across the continents.

- ⌘ Robust statistical data only exists for the last two or three centuries. Until the late 18th century, few nations, kingdoms, or empires had ever performed an accurate census. In many early attempts, the focus was on counting merely a subset of the people for purposes of taxation or military service. Even with the advent of agencies such as the United States Bureau of the Census, reliable census methods and technologies continue to evolve. All estimates of population sizes preceding the 18th century are estimates, and thus the margin of error for the total number of humans who have ever lived should be in the billions, or even tens of billions of people.

'Guesstimating the number of people ever born....requires selecting population sizes for different points from antiquity to the present and applying assumed birth rates to each period..."

According to one set of calculations based on 2002 data:

- ⌘ The number who have ever been born is around 106,000,000,000.
- ⌘ The world population in mid-2002 was approximately 6.215,000,000.
- ⌘ The percentage of those ever born who were living in 2002 was approximately 5.8.

CHAPTER 23

ROUND UP: CAUSES, IMPACTS, SOLUTIONS

THE food crisis that threatens the world in 2008 comes after a longer-term crisis of agriculture and food that has already left billions hungry and malnourished. In order to understand the full, dire implications of what is happening today it is necessary to look at the interaction between these short-term and long-term crises. Both crises arise primarily from the for-profit production of food, fibre and now biofuels, and the rift between food and people that this inevitably generates.

BEFORE THE 2008 CRISIS

Of the more than 6 billion people living in the world today, the United Nations estimates that close to 1 billion suffer from chronic hunger. But this number, which is only a crude estimate, leaves out those suffering from vitamin and nutrient deficiencies and other forms of malnutrition. The total number of food insecure people who are malnourished or lacking critical nutrients is probably closer to 3 billion, about half of humanity. The severity of this situation is made clear by the United Nations estimate, over a year ago, that approximately 18,000 children die daily as a direct or indirect consequence of malnutrition.

Lack of production is rarely the reason that people are hungry. This can be seen most clearly in the United States, where despite the production of more food than the population needs, hunger remains a significant problem. According to the U.S. Department of Agriculture, in 2006 over 35 million people lived in food-insecure households, including 13 million children. Due to lack of food, adults living in over 12 million households could not eat balanced meals and in over 7 million families someone had smaller portions or skipped meals. In close to 5 million families, children did not get enough to eat at some point during the year.

In poor countries too, it is not unusual for large supplies of wasted and misallocated food to exist in the midst of widespread and persistent hunger. A few years ago a *New York Times* article had a story with the following headline "Poor in India Starve as Surplus Wheat Rots" (December 2, 2002). As a *Wall Street Journal* headline put it in 2004 "Want Amid Plenty, An Indian Paradox: Bumper Harvests and Rising Hunger" (June 25, 2004).

RIGHT TO FOOD

Hunger and malnutrition generally are symptoms of a larger underlying problem—poverty in an economic system that recognizes, as Rachel Carson put it, no other gods but those of profit and production. Food is treated in almost all of the world's countries as just another commodity, like clothes, automobiles, pencils, books, diamond jewellery, and so on. People are not considered to have a right to purchase any particular commodity and no distinction is made in this respect between necessities and luxuries. Those who are rich can afford to purchase anything they want while the poor are often not able to procure even their basic needs. Under capitalist relations people have no right to an adequate diet, shelter and medical attention. As with other commodities, people without what economists call 'effective demand' cannot buy sufficient nutritious food. Of course, lack of 'effective demand' in this case means that the poor don't have enough money to buy the food they need.

Humans have a 'biological demand' for food—we all need food, just as we need water and air, to continue to live. It is a systematic fact of capitalist society that many are excluded from fully meeting this biological need. It's true that some wealthy countries, especially those in Europe, do help feed the poor, but the very way capitalism functions inherently creates a lower strata of society that frequently lacks the basics for human existence. In the United States there are a variety of government initiatives, i.e. food stamps and school lunch programmes—aimed at feeding the poor. Yet, the funding for these programmes does not come close to meeting the needs of the poor, and various charities fight an uphill battle trying to make up the difference.

In this era relatively few people actually die from starvation, aside from the severe hunger induced by wars and dislocations. Most become chronically malnourished and then are plagued by a variety of diseases that shorten their lives or make them more miserable. The scourge of malnutrition impedes children's mental and physical development, harming them for the rest of their lives.

THE ACUTE AND GROWING CRISIS

At this moment in history there are, in addition to the 'routine' hunger discussed above, two separate global food crises occurring simultaneously. The severe and acute crisis, about two years old, is becoming worse day by day. The severity of the current crisis cannot be overstated. It has rapidly increased the number of people around the globe that are malnourished. Although statistics of increased hunger during the past year are not yet available, it is clear that many will die prematurely or be harmed in other ways. As usual, it will be the young, the old and the infirm that will suffer the worst effects of the Great Hunger of 2008. The rapid and simultaneous rise in the world prices for all the basic food crops, corn (maize), wheat, soybeans, rice, and cooking oils, along with many other crops is having a devastating effect on an increasing portion of humanity.

The increases in the world market prices over the past few years have been nothing short of astounding. The prices of the 60 agricultural commodities traded on the world market increased 37 per cent last year and 14 per cent in 2006 (*New York Times,* January 19, 2008). Corn prices began their rise in the early fall of 2006 and within months had soared by some 70 per cent. Wheat and soybean prices also skyrocketed during this time and are now at record levels. The prices for cooking oils (mainly made from soybeans and oil palm), an essential foodstuff in many poor countries, have rocketed up as well. Rice prices have also risen over 100 per cent in the last year.

The reasons for these soaring food prices are fairly clear. First, there are a number of issues related directly or indirectly to the increase in petroleum prices. In the United States, Europe, and many other countries this has brought a new emphasis on growing crops that can be used for fuel, called biofuels (or agrofuels). Thus, producing corn to make ethanol or soybean and palm oil to make diesel fuel is in direct competition with the use of these crops for food. Last year over 20 per cent of the entire corn crop in the United States was used to produce ethanol—a process that does not yield much additional energy over that which goes into producing it. (It is estimated that over the next decade about one-third of the U.S. corn crop will be devoted to ethanol production.) Additionally, many of the inputs for large-scale commercial agricultural production are based on petroleum and natural gas, from building and running tractors and harvesting equipment to producing fertilizers and pesticides and drying crops for storage. The price of nitrogen fertilizer, the most commonly used fertilizer worldwide, is directly tied to the price of energy because it takes so much energy to produce.

A second cause of the increase in prices of corn and soybeans and soy cooking oil is the increasing demand for meat among the middle class in Latin America and Asia, especially China. The use of maize and soy to feed cattle, pigs and poultry has risen sharply to satisfy this demand. The world's total meat supply was 71 million tons in 1961. In 2007, it was estimated to be 284 million tons. Per capita consumption has more than doubled over that period. In the developing world, it rose twice as fast, doubling in the last 20 years alone. Feeding grain to more and more animals is putting growing pressure on grain stores. Feeding grain to produce meat is a very inefficient way of providing people with either calories or protein. It is especially wasteful for animals such as cows—with digestive systems that can derive energy from cellulose—because they can obtain all of their nutrition from pastures and will grow well without grain, although more slowly. Cows are not efficient converters of corn or soy to meat—to yield a pound of meat, cows require eight pounds of corn; pigs, five; and chickens, three.

A third reason for the big jump in world food prices is that a few key countries that were self-sufficient, that is, did not import foods, although plenty of people suffered from hunger, are now importing large quantities of food. As a farm analyst in New Delhi says: "When countries like India start importing food, then the world prices zoom....If India and China are both turning into bigger importers, shifting from food self-sufficiency as recently we have seen in India, then the global prices are definitely going to rise still further, which will mean the era of cheaper food has now definitely gone away". Part of the reason for the pressure on rice prices is the loss of farmland to other uses such as various development projects—some 7 million acres in China and 700,000 acres in Vietnam. In addition, rice yields per acre in Asia have reached a plateau. There has been no per acre increase for 10 years and yield increases are not expected in the near future.

Some of the reasons for the recent price increases for wheat and rice are related to weather. The drought in Australia, a major wheat exporting country, and low yields in a few other exporters has greatly affected wheat prices. A 2007 cyclone in Bangladesh destroyed approximately 600 million dollars worth of its rice crop, leading to rice price increases of about 70 per cent. The drought last year in north Central China combined with the unusual cold and snow during the winter will probably lead the government to greater food purchases on the international markets, keeping the pressure on prices.

Speculation in the futures market and hoarding at the local level are certainly playing a part in this crisis situation to make food more expensive. As the U.S. financial crisis deepened and spread in the winter of 2007, speculators started putting more money into food and metals to take advantage of what is being called the 'commodities super cycle.' (The dollar's decline relative to other currencies stimulates 'investment' in tangible commodities.) While it would be a mistake to see these aspects, however despicable and inhumane, as the cause of the crisis, they certainly add to the misery by taking advantage of tight markets. It is certainly possible that the commodity bubble will burst, bringing down food prices a bit. However, speculation and local hoarding will continue to put an upward pressure on food prices. Transnational corporations that process agricultural products, manufacture various foods and sell food to the public are, of course, all doing exceptionally well. Corporate profits usually do well in a time of shortages and price increases.

Although not a cause for the increase in prices of other foods, the higher prices for ocean fish have created an added burden for the poor and near poor. Overfishing of many ocean species is removing this important protein source from the diet of a large percentage of the world's population.

The response to the crisis has come in the form of demonstrations and riots as well as changes in government policies. Over the past few months there have been protests and riots over the increasing cost of food in many countries, including Pakistan, Guinea, Mauritania, Morocco, Mexico, Senegal, Uzbekistan, and Yemen. China has instituted price controls for basic foods and Russia has frozen the price of milk, bread, eggs and cooking oil for six months. Egypt, India, and Vietnam have banned or placed strict control on the export of rice so that their own people will have sufficient food. Egypt, the world's largest wheat importer, has expanded the number of people eligible to receive food aid by over 10 million. Many countries have lowered protectionist tariffs to try to lessen the blow of dramatically higher prices of imported foods. Countries heavily dependent on food imports such as the Philippines, the world's largest importer of rice, are scrambling to make deals to obtain the needed imports. But these various stop-gap efforts have mainly marginal effects on the problem. Almost all people are forced into a lower standard of living as those in the middle class become increasingly careful about the foods they purchase, the near poor drop into poverty, and the formerly poor become truly destitute and suffer greatly. The effects have been felt around the world in all classes of society except the truly wealthy. As the head of the UN's World Food Programme, said in February: "This is the new face of hunger....There is food on shelves but people are priced out of the market. There is vulnerability in urban areas we have not seen before. There are food riots in countries where we have not seen them before."

Although Haiti has been a very poor country for years—80 per cent of the people try to subsist on less than what two dollars a day can purchase in the United States—the recent situation has brought it to new depths of desperation. Two cups of rice, which cost thirty cents a year ago, now cost sixty cents. The description in an Associated Press January 29, 2008 article is most poignant in its details:

> It was lunchtime in one of Haiti's worst slums, and Charlene Dumas was eating mud. With food prices rising, Haiti's poorest can't afford even a daily plate of rice, and some take desperate measures to fill their bellies. Charlene, 16 with a 1-month-old son, has come to rely on a traditional Haitian remedy for hunger pangs: cookies made of dried yellow dirt from the country's central plateau.

The 'cookies' also contain some vegetable shortening and salt. Towards the end of the article is the following:

> Marie Noel, 40, sells the cookies in a market to provide for her seven children. Her family also eats them. "I'm hoping one day I'll have enough food to eat, so I can stop eating these," she said. "I know it's not good for me."

Many countries in Africa and Asia have been severely impacted by the crisis with hunger spreading widely, but all nations are affected to one extent or another. In the United States, where over the past year the price of eggs increased 38 per cent, milk by 30 per cent, lettuce by 16 per cent, and whole wheat bread by 12 per cent, many people are starting to purchase less costly products.

It should be noted here that while wheat prices are at record levels and prices of wheat products in the United States will certainly go higher, the cost of the wheat in a loaf of bread is only a small part of the retail price. When wheat prices double, as they have, the price of a loaf of bread may increase by 10 per cent, perhaps from $ 3 to $ 3.30. However, the effect of a doubling of prices for corn, wheat, soybeans and rice is devastating for poor people in the Third World who primarily purchase raw commodities.

With food pantries and soup kitchens stretched to the breaking point, the U.S. poor are experiencing deepening suffering. In general, the poor in the United States tend to first pay their rent, heat, gas (for a car to get to work), and electricity bills. That leaves food as one of the few 'flexible' items in their budgets. In the central part of Vermont, over the last year the use of food shelves (that is, aid from local, charitable food assistance programmes that give groceries directly to the needy) has increased 133 per cent among all users and 180 per cent among the working poor!

The economic recession is beginning to be felt in many parts of the United States, adding to the rise in requests for help from the various government food assistance programmes. But, frequently people using the inadequately funded government programmes, tend to run out of food towards the end of the month, resulting in a huge increase in demand at food shelves and soup kitchens at that time. And as the need for food has increased, food donations have actually declined—with a large drop in federal donations (with high prices there are fewer 'surplus' commodities from farm programmes, so $ 58 million in food was given to food shelves last year versus $ 242 million five years before).

Supermarkets have found ways to make money from damaged or dated goods they previously donated to charities. In Connecticut, there has been a surge in demand for food while supply is not keeping up. A food pantry in Stanford is supplying food to 400 families, double the number of a year ago. According to the food pantry's director, "I have had to turn people away....There were times I went home and wanted to cry." A professor at Cornell University who studies food-assistance programmes in the United States has summarized the situation: "There is a nascent crisis building....Demand for food-bank assistance is climbing rapidly when the resources are falling in dramatic terms because the dollars just don't go as far."

THE LONG-TERM FOOD CRISIS

As critical as the short-term food crisis is, demanding immediate world notice as well as attention within every country, the long-term, structural crisis is even more important. The latter has existed for decades and contributes to, and is reinforced by, today's acute food crisis. Indeed, it is this underlying structural crisis of agriculture and food in Third World societies which constitutes the real reason that the immediate food crisis is so severe and so difficult to surmount within the system.

There has been a huge migration of people out of the countryside to the cities of the Third World. They leave the countryside because they lack access to land. Often their land has been stolen as a result of the inroads of agribusiness, while they are also forced from the land by low prices they have historically received for their products. They move to cities seeking a better life but what they find is a very hard existence, life in slums with extremely high unemployment and underemployment. Most will try to scrape by in the 'informal' economy by buying things and then selling them in small quantities. Of the half of humanity that lives in cities (3 billion), some 1 billion, or one-third of city dwellers, live in slums. The chairman of a district in Lagos, Nigeria, described it as follows: "We have a massive growth in population with a stagnant or shrinking economy. Picture this city ten, twenty years from now. This is not the urban poor – this is the new urban destitute." A long *New Yorker* article on Lagos ended on a note of extreme pessimism: "The really disturbing thing about Lagos' pickers and vendors is that their lives have essentially nothing to do with ours. They scavenge an existence beyond the margins of macroeconomics. They are, in the harsh terms of globalization, superfluous."

One of the major factors pushing this mass and continuing migration to the cities, in addition to being landless or forced off land, is the difficulty to make a living as a small farmer. This has been made especially difficult, as countries have implemented the 'neo-liberal' policies recommended or mandated by the IMF, the World Bank and even some of the Western NGOs working in the poor countries of the Third World. The neo-liberal ideology holds that the so-called free market should be allowed to work its magic. Through the benign sanctions of the 'invisible hand,' it is said, the economy will function most efficiently and will be highly productive. But in order for the market to be 'free', governments must stop interfering.

With regard to agriculture, governments should stop subsidizing farmers to purchase fertilizers, stop being involved in the storage and transportation of food and just let farmers and food alone. This approach also holds that governments should stop subsidizing food for poor people and then the newly unbridled market will take care of it all. This mentality was evident as the Haitian food crisis started to develop late in 2007. According to the Haitian Minister of Commerce and Industry: "We cannot intervene and fix prices because we have to comply with free market regulations." This was the same response that colonial Britain adopted in response to the Irish potato famine as well as to the famines in India in the late 1800s. But to a certain extent this way of thinking is now internalized in the thinking of many leaders in the 'independent' countries of the periphery.

This ideology, of course, has no basis in reality. The so-called free market is not necessarily efficient at all. It is also absolutely unable to act as a mechanism to end poverty and hunger. We should always keep in mind that this ideology represents the exact opposite of what the core capitalist countries have historically done and what they are actually doing today. For example, the U.S. national government has supported farmers in many ways for over a century. This has occurred through government programmes for research and extension, taking land from Indians and giving it to farmers of European origin, subsidizing farmers directly through a variety of programmes including low-cost loans and stimulating the export of crops. It should also be noted that the United States, Europe and Japan all developed their industrial economies under protectionist policies plus a variety of programmes of direct assistance to industry.

The effects of the governments of the Third World stopping their support of small farmers and consumers has meant that the life for the poor in those countries has become more difficult. As an independent report commissioned by the World Bank put it: "In most reforming countries, the private sector did not step in to fill the vacuum when the public sector withdrew." For example, many African governments under pressure from the neo-liberal economic policies promoted by the World Bank, the IMF and the rich countries of the centre of the system, stopped subsidizing the use of fertilizers on crops. Although it is true that imported fertilizers are very expensive, African soils are generally of very low fertility and crop yields are low when you use neither synthetic nor organic fertilizers. As yields fell after governments were no longer assisting the purchase of fertilizers and helping in other ways, more farmers found that they could not survive and migrated to the city slums. Jeffrey Sachs, a partially recovered free-trade shock doctor, has had some second thoughts. According to Sachs: "The whole thing was based on the idea that if you take away the government for the poorest of the poor that somehow these markets will solve the problems....But markets can't step in and won't step in when people have nothing. And if you take away help, you leave them to die."

Last year one country in Africa, Malawi, decided to reverse course and go against all the recommendations they had received. The government reintroduced subsidies for fertilizers and seeds. Farmers used more fertilizers, the yields increased, and the country's food situation improved greatly. In fact, they were able to export some food to Zimbabwe, although there are those in Malawi, who consider that to have lowered their own supplies too far.

Another problem occurs as capitalist farmers in some of the poor countries of the periphery enter into world markets. While subsistence farmers usually sell only a small portion of their crops, using most for family consumption, capitalist farmers are those that market all or a large portion of what they produce. They frequently expand production and take over the land of small farmers, with or without compensation, and use fewer people than previously to work a given piece of land because of mechanized production techniques. In Brazil, the 'Soybean King' controls well over a quarter of a million acres (100,000 hectares) and uses huge tractors and harvesting equipment for working the land. In China corrupt village and city officials frequently sell 'common land' to developers without adequate compensation to the farmers. Sometimes there is no compensation at all.

Thus, the harsh conditions for farmers caused by a number of factors, made worse by the implementing of free-market ideology, have created a continuing stream of people leaving the countryside and going to live in cities that do not have jobs for them. And those now living in slums and without access to land to grow their own food are at the mercy of the world price for food.

One of the reasons for the growing consolidation of land holdings and forcing out of subsistence farmers, is the penetration of multinational agricultural corporations into the countries of the periphery. From selling seeds, fertilizers and pesticides to processing raw agricultural products to exporting or selling them through new, large supermarkets, agribusiness multinationals are having a devastating effect on small farmers. With the collapse of extension systems for helping farmers save seeds and with the disbanding of government seed companies the way was paved for multinational seed companies to make major inroads.

The giant transnational corporations such as Cargill and Monsanto now reach into most of the Third World, selling seeds, fertilizers, pesticides and feeds while buying and processing raw agricultural products. In the process they assist larger farms to become 'more efficient', to grow over larger land areas. The main advantage of genetically modified organism (GMO) seeds is that they help to simplify the process of farming and allow large acreages to be under the management of a single entity, a large farmer or corporation, squeezing out small farmers.

The negative effects of the penetration of large supermarket chains are being felt as well. As a 2004 headline in the *New York Times* put it 'Supermarket Giants Crush Central American Farmers.' Large supermarkets would rather deal with a few farmers growing on a large scale than with many small farmers. And the opening of large supermarkets does away with the traditional markets used by small farmers.

THE PROLONGED CRISIS IS INTENSIFYING

It seems logical that with higher food prices, farmers should be better off and produce more to satisfy the 'demand' indicated by the market. To a certain extent that is true—especially for farmers that can take advantage of all the physical and monetary advantages of large-scale production. Yet, the input costs for just about everything used in agricultural production have also increased, thus profit gains for farmers are not as large as might be expected. This is a particularly difficult problem for farmers raising animals fed on increasingly expensive grains.

In addition, things are not necessarily going well for small and subsistence farmers. Many are stuck in debt so deep that it's hard for them to get back on their feet. An estimated 25,000 Indian farmers committed suicide in 2007 because they could see no other way out of their predicament. (The Indian government has proposed a budget that includes loan waivers for small farmers that have borrowed through banks. However, not all the millions that have borrowed from local usurers will benefit.) The consolidation of land holdings and the removal of small farmers and landless workers from the land has been exacerbated by the exceptional crop price increases over the last few years.

Rising crop prices cause the price of farmland to increase—especially of large fields that can be worked by large-scale machinery. This is happening in the United States and in certain countries of the periphery. For example, Global Ag Investments, a company based in Texas, owns and operates 34,000 acres of Brazilian farmland. At one of its farms, a single field of soybeans covers 1,600 acres—that's two and a half square miles! A New Zealand company has purchased approximately 100,000 acres in Uruguay and has hired managers to operate dairy farms established on their land.

Private equity firms are purchasing farmland in the United States as well as abroad. A U.S. company is cooperating with Brazilian and Japanese partners to purchase 385 square miles in Brazil, approximately a quarter of a million acres! This is also happening with South American capital taking the lead, a Brazilian investment fund, Investimento em Participacoe, is buying a minority stake in an Argentine soybean producer that owns close to 400,000 acres in Uruguay and Argentina.

Rising crop prices have also led to an acceleration of deforestation in the Amazon basin, 1,250 square miles (about the size of Rhode Island) in the last five months of 2007, as capitalist farmers hunger for more land. In addition, huge areas of farmland have been taken for development, some of dubious use, such as building suburban style housing and golf courses for the wealthy.

In China during 2000-05, there was an average *annual* loss of 2.6 million acres as farmland was used for development. The country is fast approaching the self-defined minimum amount of arable farmland that it should have—approximately 290 million acres (120 million hectares)—and the amount of farmland will most likely continue to fall. As part of an effort to gain access to foreign agricultural production, a Chinese company has made an agreement to lease close to 2.5 million acres of land in the Philippines to grow rice, corn, and sugar, setting off a huge protest in the Philippines that has temporarily stalled the project. As one farmer put it: "The [Philippine] government and the Chinese call it a partnership, but it only means the Chinese will be our landlords and we will be the slaves."

ENDING WORLD HUNGER

Ending world hunger is conceptually quite simple. However, actually putting it into practice is far from simple. First, the access to a healthy and varied diet needs to be recognized for the basic human right that it clearly is. Governments must commit to ending hunger among their people and they must take forceful action to carry out this commitment. In many countries, even at this time, there is sufficient food produced to feed the entire population at a high level of nutrition. This is, of course, most evident in the United States, where so much food is produced. It is nothing less than a crime that so many of the poor in the United States are hungry, malnourished or don't know where their next meal will come from (which itself takes a psychological toll) when there is actually plenty of food.

In the short run, the emergency situation of increasingly severe hunger and malnutrition needs to be addressed with all resources at a country's disposal. Although mass bulk distribution of grains or powdered milk can play a role, countries might consider the Venezuelan innovation of setting up feeding houses in all poor neighbourhoods. When the people believe that the government is really trying to help them, and they are empowered to find or assist in a solution to their own problems, a burst of enthusiasm and volunteerism results. For example, although the food in Venezuela's feeding programme is supplied by the government, the meals for poor children, the elderly, and the infirm are prepared in, and distributed from, peoples' homes using considerable amounts of volunteer labour. In addition, Venezuela has developed a network of stores that sell basic foodstuffs at significant discounts over prices charged in private markets.

Brazil started a programme in 2003 that is aimed at alleviating the conditions of the poorest people. Approximately one-quarter of Brazil's population receive direct payments from the national government under the *Bolsa Família* (Family Fund) antipoverty programme. Under this programme a family with a per capita daily income below approximately $ 2 per person per day receives a benefit of up to $ 53 per month per person. This infusion of cash is dependent on the family's children attending school and participating in the national vaccination programme. This programme is certainly having a positive effect on peoples' lives and nutrition. It is, however, a system that does not have the same effect as Venezuela's programmes, which mobilize people to work together for their own and their community's benefit.

Urban gardens have been used successfully in Cuba as well as other countries to supply city dwellers with food as well as sources of income. These should be strongly promoted, with creative use of available space in urban settings.

Agriculture must become one of the top priorities for the Third World. Even the World Bank is beginning to stress the importance of governments assisting agriculture in their countries. As Dr. Ngozi Okonjo-Iweala, managing director of the World Bank, has stated,

> Today the attention of the world's policy makers is focused on the sub-prime woes, and the financial crises. But the real crisis is that of hunger and malnutrition...this is the real problem that should grab the world's attention. We know that 75 per cent of the world's poor people are rural and most of them depend on agriculture for their livelihoods. Agriculture is today, more than ever, a fundamental instrument for fighting hunger, malnutrition, and for supporting sustainable development and poverty reduction.
>
> —All-Africa Global Media, February 19, 2008

Almost every country in the world has the soil, water, and climate resources to grow enough food so that all their people can eat a healthy diet. In addition, the knowledge and crop varieties already exist in most countries so that if farmers are given adequate assistance they will be able to grow reasonably high yields of crops.

Although enhanced agricultural production is essential, much of the emphasis in the past has been on production of export crops. While this may help a country's balance of payments, export oriented agriculture does not ensure sufficient food for everyone nor does it promote a healthy rural environment. In addition to basic commodities such as soybeans, export-oriented agriculture also leads naturally to the production of high-value luxury crops demanded by export markets (luxuries from the standpoint of the basic food needs of a poor Third World country), rather than the low-value subsistence crops needed to meet the needs of the domestic population. Production of sufficient amounts of the right kinds of food within each country's borders, by small farmers working in cooperatives or on their own and using sustainable techniques, is the best way to achieve the goal of 'food security.' In this way the population may be insulated, at least partially, from the price fluctuations on the world market. This, of course, also means not taking land out of food production to produce crops for the biofuel markets.

One of the ways to do this and at the same time help with the problem of so many people crowded into urban slums, the people most susceptible to food price increases, is to provide land through meaningful agrarian reforms. But land itself is not enough. Beginning or returning farmers need technical and financial support in order to produce food. Additionally, social support systems, such as cooperatives and community councils, need to be developed to help promote camaraderie and to solidify the new communities that are developed. Perhaps each community needs to be 'seeded' with a sprinkling of devoted activists. Also, housing, electricity, water, and wastewater need to be available to make it attractive for people living in the cities to move to the countryside. Another way to encourage people to move to the country to become farmers is to appeal to patriotism and instil the idea that they are real pioneers, establishing a new food system to help their countries gain food self-sufficiency, that is, independence from transnational agribusiness corporations and provision of healthy food for all the nation's people. These pioneering farmers need to be viewed by themselves, the rest of the society, and their government as critical to the future of their countries and the well-being of the population. They must be treated with the great respect that they deserve.

Food is a human right and governments have a responsibility to see that their people are well fed. In addition, there are known ways to end hunger—including emergency measures to combat the current critical situation, urban gardens, agrarian reforms that include a whole support system for farmers, and sustainable agriculture techniques that enhance the environment. The present availability of food to people reflects very unequal economic and political power relationships within and between countries. A sustainable and secure food system requires a different and much more equitable relationship among people. The more the poor and farmers themselves are included in all aspects of the effort to gain food security, and the more they are energized in the process, the greater will be the chance of attaining lasting food security. As President Hugo Chávez of Venezuela, a country that has done so much to deal with poverty and hunger, has put it,

"Yes, it is important to end poverty, to end misery, but the most important thing is to offer power to the poor so that they can fight for themselves."

APPENDIX I

MILLENNIUM DEVELOPMENT GOALS: AUDIT 2007

THIS latest available progress review of the Millennium Development Goals (2007) is extracted from 40 One World Country Guides. Now more than midway to the target date of 2015, the picture is not encouraging, with, of course, a few exceptions, confirming the conclusions of the UN Report published in July 2007.

The review reveals that recurring problems include the failure of conventional economic growth to relieve poverty, extreme regional disparities, inadequate spending on health and education, and insufficient aid. A drastic shift in political will, both domestically and internationally, is necessary to realise the ideals of the Millennium Declaration.

ANGOLA

Angola signed the UN Millennium Declaration in 2000 but the standard framework of the Millennium Development Goals (MDGs) presents logistical difficulties. The civil conflict that wrecked the country for almost three decades ended only in 2002, two years after the start of the MDG assessment period. Even now, human development data is considered to be unreliable and a full census is planned for 2010.

Uncertainties over data do not however mask the reality that poverty in Angola is severe nor that the country is unlikely to achieve any of the MDGs at the current rate of progress, regardless of the basis of assessment. Over 60 per cent of the population lives under the poverty line with over 25 per cent in the more serious category of extreme poverty. Barely 50 per cent of women are literate and measures of the Gini coefficient confirm that inequality is rising.

AZERBAIJAN

Azerbaijan's approach to the MDGs is encouraging. A State Commission, chaired by the prime minister, is responsible for preparing the 2006-15 State Programme for Poverty Reduction and Sustainable Development (SPPRSD), which will be aligned with both the targets and the timescale of the MDGs. In a progress report published in 2005, Azerbaijan claims to be the first developing country to combine reporting of its poverty reduction strategy with MDG progress.

Significantly, the oil revenue that Azerbaijan can expect over the next 15 years, if responsibly invested, should provide the resources required to meet most of the MDGs. As well as spending oil revenues prudently, there are other major challenges to overcome if the Goals are to be achieved, in particular improving governance, reforming public services and reducing corruption.

BANGLADESH

A combination of generous international aid since 1990, a dynamic civil society culture and sympathetic government policies have created a generally positive environment for development indicators, illustrated especially by the attainment of gender equality in school enrolment, a rare achievement in South Asia. The headline poverty benchmark for the Millennium Development Goals (MDGs) of $ 1 per day has fallen significantly from 59 per cent in the baseline year to 36 per cent, whilst child mortality has come down from 151 to 80 per 1000. In these areas, progress is more rapid than in neighbouring India or Pakistan. Government budgets (as a percentage of 2007-08 national income) for health (6.3 per cent) and education (14 per cent) are rising whilst food and cash safety net schemes are in place for the poorest families.

Unfortunately, beneath the surface of these promising trends lies a stubborn hardcore of extreme poverty in Bangladesh which is not responding to government or NGO programmes. Possibly as many as 35 million people are in this category, 25 per cent of the population, unable to provide themselves with sufficient food, creating widespread severe malnutrition and overwhelming social safety nets. With nearly 50 per cent of children underweight, the child mortality rate has not fallen in recent years. A 2007 independent civil society report describes maternal mortality as a 'major blot in progress towards the MDGs' with only 9 per cent of births attended by a qualified health-worker and rates failing to improve since 2000. Although most children take advantage of free primary education by entering schools, the combination of poor teaching quality and the pressures of poverty has rocketed the drop-out rate to an alarming 47 per cent. Wide divergence in poverty indicators between urban and rural areas and between regions adds to the complexity of analysis.

It is abundantly clear, therefore, that many of the MDGs will not be achieved in Bangladesh without specific policy intervention and increased funding. The Director of the Millennium Project, Professor Jeffrey Sachs, has suggested an MDG price tag for Bangladesh of $ 4 billion per annum, far more than current levels of aid. An alternative perspective is the suggestion that the Goals cannot be achieved without universal access to electricity. Current coverage is barely more than 20 per cent. The government's target of access for all by 2020, is a vision that has been priced at $ 16 billion.

BENIN

Benin has a very underdeveloped economy with about half of its people considered poor or extremely poor. Over a quarter of the population suffers from such extreme poverty that it cannot meet its own basic food requirements. In addition to the HIV/AIDS crisis, the country faces serious health problems particularly with malaria, poor nutrition, maternal and child health and tuberculosis. Life expectancy is estimated at under 55 years.

Increased development assistance and better governance through reduced corruption and transfer of resources from the centre to the newly created decentralized government structures are needed to help empower people and achieve MDG goals.

BRAZIL

Uneven income distribution combines with other inequalities to pose the main obstacle to meeting the Millennium Development Goals (MDGs) in Brazil. Less than 3 per cent of the population controls two thirds of the land available for production. 4.8 million rural families are landless and more than 80 per cent of Brazilians are now concentrated in urban areas, where many live in *favelas* (shanty towns) with inadequate water supply, health facilities and educational opportunities. The inequality is also regional, the north-east of the country is the poorest region while research by a Brazilian NGO, Imazon, records that most MDG indicators in Brazil's Amazon states are well below the national average.

However, there is some cause for celebration. A government report on the MDGs published in August 2007, showed that the country has already met the first MDG target, having achieved a reduction in the percentage of Brazilians living on less than one dollar a day from 9.5 per cent to 4.2 per cent between 1992 and 2005.

BURUNDI

The MDGs are most unlikely to be fulfilled in Burundi. The baseline year of 1990 coincided with the beginning of a decade of political turmoil and conflict in which GDP fell by 20 per cent and extreme poverty increased from 33 to 67 per cent. With almost 55 per cent of the population still living on less than US$ 1 per day and 41 per cent believed to be chronically malnourished, the outlook is pessimistic for the MDG related to extreme poverty and hunger.

Another legacy of the civil war is the weak capacity for reliable data collection which handicaps projections for a number of the Goals. Nevertheless, the decision to allow universal free access to primary education from 2005 boosts the potential to achieve targets for youth literacy which is still considerably below that of other countries in the region, despite improving from 51 to 73 per cent between 1990 and 2004. There are worries however as to whether the education system's capacity can be scaled up to cope with half a million extra pupils.

CAMBODIA

UNDP has placed Cambodia in the 32 top priority countries where urgent action must be taken in order to overcome slow progress towards the deadline of 2015 for the Millennium Development Goals (MDGs). The latest World Bank Poverty Assessment shows that 35 per cent of Cambodia's population lives below the national poverty line, down by only about 10 per cent over the last decade.

With nearly 80 per cent of the population surviving on less than $ 2 per day, whilst a small elite enjoys a business boom in the capital city, Cambodia has become one of Asia's most unequal countries, especially between its rural and urban communities.

Cambodia's health care system is struggling. Both maternal and child mortality rates are exceptionally high for the region, the latter having increased since the baseline year of 1990, quite the reverse of MDG intentions. Two thirds of the population do not have access to clean water.

In the past two decades, the country has received immense financial aid and technical assistance from various international financial institutions, governments and NGOs. The most recent pledge totalling $ 690m will cover half of Cambodia's national budget for 2008.

CAMEROON

The heart of the strategy for achieving the Millennium Development Goals (MDGs) in Cameroon, as articulated in the Poverty Reduction Strategy Paper (PRSP) approved by development partners in 2003, lies in the assertion that strong national economic growth will leverage better lives for the poor. As in so many countries, this presumption is failing; whilst Cameroon has indeed performed reasonably well in recent years by conventional measures of economic prosperity, poverty indicators are stagnant or moving in reverse, with the notable exception of HIV prevalence which has dropped significantly.

The main poverty benchmark for the purpose of the MDGs in Cameroon is the level of income deemed necessary to meet basic living needs. Forty per cent of the population fall below this poverty line, a figure unchanged nationally since 2001 which implies that poverty in rural areas is increasing. There are inevitable doubts about meeting the target of 25 per cent by 2015.

The core problem is not hard to identify; the World Food Programme describes Cameroon as a food insecure country and has further demonstrated that food intake is lower now than in the early 1980s. The result is that over 30 per cent of young children are classified as suffering from 'moderate chronic malnutrition' and the child mortality rate is rising rather than falling. Despite the improved picture for HIV/AIDS, the broader measure of life expectancy has fallen below 50 years from a high of 59 years.

CHINA

There has been spectacular achievement in human development in China over the last 30 years and the country claims to be on course to achieve most of the Millennium Development Goals (MDGs) by 2015. According to the 2005 China Human Development Report, only 26 million Chinese live in absolute poverty, a reduction of nearly 225 million over the preceding 26 years. However, these figures are based on China's own definition of the poverty line which is barely one quarter of the UN's figure of $ 1 per day purchasing power; by this latter benchmark there are almost 220 million Chinese living in extreme poverty. Furthermore, the broad progress in human development is offset by regional unevenness, gender, HIV/AIDS and environmental issues which lag behind in progress and priority.

For example, the large investment in production and infrastructure has been concentrated on the developed urban eastern regions of Shanghai, Tianjin, and Guangdong. The majority of poor Chinese live in the underdeveloped western regions of Shaanxi, Guangxi, Sichuan and Gansu. In Tibet, 50 per cent of the population is illiterate. These regional disparities are creating a new category of poverty through migration to the eastern cities where 150–200 million workers grapple with the constraints of the *hukou* system of household registrations which expose them to exploitation in the cities.

COLOMBIA

Colombia has reduced the proportion of people living below the poverty line from 53.8 in 1991 to 45 per cent in 2006, and extreme poverty from 20.4 to under 16 per cent. That over 20 million people should live in poverty and that the overall rate of progress has been so slow in a country generously endowed with natural resources is testimony to the inability of its government to give adequate priority to the MDGs.

The years of internal conflict have not only diverted resources—over 80 per cent of U.S. aid is channelled to the military—but also devastated the rural economy isolating it from progress made in the cities. For example, the capital city, Bogotá, has similar development indicators to the cities of former Eastern Europe while Choco, a district on the Pacific coast, has indicators comparable to sub-Saharan Africa. The conflict has also disproportionately affected people of Afro-Colombian and indigenous origin, accentuating inequality between these groups and wealthy families of Spanish descent.

ERITREA

Where armies are assembled on either side of a disputed border, the countries involved are unlikely to allocate high priority to pursuit of the MDGs. The Eritrean government concedes that resources diverted to 'national security' have acted as a brake on human development. Indeed poverty has increased over the period of the MDG programme, rising from 53 per cent in the baseline period of the early 1990s to 66 per cent at the most recent point of assessment in 2003.

During 2007, the government published a progress report for the MDGs which acknowledged that Goals for poverty, universal education and the environment are very unlikely to be achieved. Net enrolment for primary education is only 44 per cent. Schools are short of classrooms and materials with teacher retention compromised by inadequate pay levels. Poor standards of sanitation are no help. In a recent 'national rapid assessment', UNICEF judged that only 1.5 per cent of people in rural areas have access to safe sanitation and only 58 per cent to a source of clean water.

ETHIOPIA

Ethiopia is consistently positioned close to the bottom of the annual UNDP Human Development Index. An interesting feature of the government's progress report for the MDGs published in 2004 is its willingness to place an estimate on the public spending cost necessary to achieve the Goals. The figure quoted is a staggering $ 37 billion. The improbability of raising such a sum alone provides the telling answer to questions about the likelihood of achieving all of the Goals by 2015. Indeed one of Ethiopia's major bilateral donors, the U.K. government, has said in 2006 that the country is 'unlikely to meet any of the MDG targets by 2015.' The specialist U.K. charity WaterAid says that efforts to achieve the Goals for water and sanitation are 'way off track' with access in rural areas still below 20 per cent.

GEORGIA

The price of freedom has been high for many poor people across the countries of the former Soviet Union, nowhere more so than in Georgia where a combination of civil wars and economic liberalisation caused a collapse in the economy through the 1990s. Due to these exceptional circumstances, the baseline for the MDGs has been moved back from 1990 to 2000 at which point the measure of extreme poverty was 14.3 per cent whilst the proportion below the poverty line was 51.8 per cent. These figures became worse rather than better in the years immediately following the millennium but the basis for calculating the poverty line has changed and the latest figure is believed to be around 35 per cent. Of particular concern in the context of the MDGs is that the extent of extreme poverty may still be increasing, especially in rural areas where 40–50 per cent of the population is dependent on subsistence agriculture. The elderly form another particularly vulnerable group.

Georgia's ranking in the UNDP Human Development Index remains significantly below most of the transitional countries in the region and it is clear that the government has given greater priority to headline economic growth than poverty reduction strategies. Indeed, there is no formal long-term plan for achieving the MDGs. In his re-election speeches in early 2008, the President has promised immediate pro-poverty actions associated with the slogan 'Georgia Without Poverty.' There is reference to an accountable new commission, but none of these initiatives yet refers to quantifiable targets which might be recognised as consistent with the MDGs.

GHANA

Ghana is often praised for one of the fastest rates of poverty reduction in Africa, the figures claiming a fall in poverty from 52 per cent in 1991 to 28 per cent in 2005, almost sufficient to achieve the Millennium Development Goal (MDG) of halving poverty. The World Food Programme plans to exit Ghana in 2010, describing the country as one of few to have met the 1996 Food Summit commitment of halving its number of undernourished people. No fewer than 17 donor countries have scrambled to embrace a success story in Africa, signing up to a joint funding strategy. The normally reticent Millennium Challenge Corporation has lavished its largest grant on Ghana, $ 547 million over 5 years.

Closer analysis of the figures throws an element of doubt on these superlatives. The MDG Progress Report published in 2003, defines the poverty line as the 'proportion below national basic needs' without further elaboration. The statistics themselves are drawn from a periodic census known as the Ghana Living Standards Survey (GLSS), but it is difficult to ascertain the basis for threshold levels of income poverty or how they evolve. Even the 177-page *Growth and Poverty Reduction Strategy 2006–09 (GPRS II)* fails to provide an explanation of how poverty is calculated in Ghana. Most telling of all, the internationally recognised threshold for extreme poverty, $ 1 per day of purchasing power, is assessed by the 2007 UNDP Human Development Report to capture 44.8 per cent of Ghana's population, almost unchanged from the 45.5 per cent recorded in the baseline year of 1990. And the proportion of underweight children has reduced only to 22 per cent from the baseline 27.4 per cent.

GUATEMALA

The 36-year civil war in Guatemala ended just over a decade ago in 1996, its detrimental economic impact overlapping with the 1990 baseline for assessment of the Millennium Development Goals (MDGs). Restoring social indicators has proved a volatile process and the country remains one of the poorest in Latin America with over half the population living below the poverty line, currently valued as $ 2.30 per day. Extreme poverty was reduced from 20 per cent in 1990 only to about 15 per cent; achieving the 10 per cent target by 2015 will be a formidable task. There has been progress towards universal enrolment in primary education for both boys and girls but ingrained cultural gender roles lead to a high dropout rate of girls. 60 per cent of indigenous women are illiterate.

Rural and indigenous populations experience high infant and maternal mortality with less than convincing progress towards MDG targets. Nearly 48 per cent of children suffer chronic malnutrition, the highest incidence in Latin America. A significant share of the population lacks access to affordable health services, largely down to inequitable targeting of public money, with highly-subsidised public facilities almost exclusively used by the non-poor.

GUINEA-BISSAU

Despite recent improvement in a number of areas, the pace of post-conflict rehabilitation in Guinea-Bissau looks to fall short of achieving the MDGs by 2015. Indeed the country remains close to the very bottom of the UN Human Development Index. The civil war that ended in 1999 caused a 28 per cent drop in GDP in that year alone, and subsequent chronic political instability alongside a fracturing of civil society have severely limited the progress of successive governments in improving citizens' lives.

The MDGs 2 and 3 pose particularly difficult benchmarks for Guinea-Bissau, owing to a permanent crisis within the public sector. The state is rarely able to pay its public service employees, to achieve even a minimum functioning, meaning that schools are routinely disrupted or non-operational for months at a time. It is not surprising therefore that illiteracy rates in the country are estimated at 50 per cent of men and 83 per cent of women—significantly higher than the regional average.

INDIA

Beneath the veneer of the affluent Indian middle class, about 15 per cent of the world's population face a daily struggle for essentials, including the 300 million Indians who survive on less than $ 1 per day. The global challenge of the Millennium Development Goals (MDGs) therefore rests disproportionately on the fight against poverty in India.

Large socio-economic regional disparities greatly complicate the picture. Almost half of India's most severe poverty is concentrated in just five states: Bihar, Orissa, Uttar Pradesh, Madhya Pradesh and Rajasthan. These poorest states also have to contend with the largest and fastest growing populations. In some pockets of the country, reports suggest that poverty indicators are even moving in a negative direction; indeed in many areas, the reliability of human development data is itself questionable. No national MDG progress report was produced for the Millennium World Summit in September 2005. A report was eventually announced in February 2006 but it has not been lodged with the other 179 reports in the UN online library.

The government has given assurances that the resources necessary to achieve the Goals will be forthcoming and that the targets will be reached in advance of the 2015 deadline. More cautious civil society observers might however point out that water table levels throughout India have collapsed, that teacher absenteeism in primary schools is 25 per cent with pupil drop-out rates of 40 per cent and that the UN Special Rapporteur on the Right to Food reported in March 2006 that 'food insecurity is growing.'

INDONESIA

The Indonesian Government has formulated reasonable poverty frameworks to work towards the Millennium Development Goals (MDGs). But the latest progress report discloses that 16.6 per cent of the population lived below the national poverty line in 2007, more than in 1990, the MDG baseline year. Another indicator which is rising rather than falling is the 8.8 per cent of children under age 5 assessed to be severely underweight. In this context the impact of rising food prices is bound to be worrying, given that almost 35 per cent of the population have incomes which place them only marginally above the poverty line and therefore vulnerable to adverse change.

More positive progress features in education, for which the government is committed to allocating an increasing share of the national budget, currently 17 per cent. Net enrolment in primary education has reached 95 per cent with no significant bias against access for girls. However, nationally aggregated statistics for any of the MDGs fail to capture the degree of underdevelopment among 'pockets of poor.' For example, whilst only 4.6 per cent of people living in Jakarta fall below the poverty line, the comparable figure in Papua is 40.8 per cent. Although the Goal to reduce extreme poverty (inability to buy sufficient food) to 10 per cent has already been achieved at the national level, this is largely due to development gains in a few wealthier regions.

JORDAN

Jordan is classified as a middle-income country whose government conveys a sense of genuine concern for poverty issues, allocating financial resources for social development at a proportion of national income which its regional peers rarely match.

Levels of acute poverty in Jordan are therefore low with reasonable prospects of further reduction. However, large numbers of families find themselves just above the poverty line where they remain exposed to volatile regional politics which have caused sustainable damage to Jordan's development strategies in the past.

This is broadly the message of Jordan's first MDG Report published in October 2004, which expresses confidence in varying degrees that each of the Goals will be achieved, but warns of the dependence on economic stability in the region.

For the present, Jordan can boast of an impressive health system and almost full primary school enrolment for both boys and girls. Gender inequality is however apparent in employment opportunities where women are at a marked disadvantage. Despite Jordan being a frontrunner amongst Arab countries in supporting political participation of women, poor representation in parliament (under 10 per cent) is recognized as a problem which will be difficult to rectify by 2015. A recent poll conducted in Jordan revealed a clear majority in local government.

KENYA

The prognosis for Kenya to meet its MDGs is bleak. Measured by the Human Development Index (HDI), Kenyans are worse off today than in 1980.

Progress towards attaining universal primary education is the one bright spot on an otherwise disappointing record. Beginning in 2003, Kenya instituted free primary education which has had the effect of increasing school enrolment by two million children. There is a further proposal for free tuition for secondary education.

Recent enrolment gains at primary level have benefited girls, resulting in near gender parity. Despite these gains, regional inequalities are pronounced, particularly in the enrolment of girls in arid and semi-arid regions.

Poverty remains an enormous challenge for Kenya. Indeed current trends indicate significant growth rather than reduction in the number of people consigned to the margins of economic activity. The Kenyan government has defined the poverty line as $ 17 per month in rural areas and $ 36 per month in urban areas. In 1994, about 47 per cent of Kenyans fell below this line; today that figure has grown to 56 per cent. Presently, 22.8 per cent of the population lives on less than $ 1 a day and 58.3 per cent lives on less than $ 2 per day.

Sadly, child mortality levels have kept pace with the swelling numbers of destitute. Due to the increasing paucity of immunization against curable diseases, child mortality has climbed steadily from 90 per 1000 in 1990 to 115 per 1000 in 2003. Likewise, infant mortality shows a similar trajectory during this same period, increasing from 60 to 77 per 1000 in 2003.

LAOS

Laos is the poorest and least developed country in Southeast Asia. Almost three-quarters of the population live on less than US$ 2 a day and food security is an ongoing problem faced by subsistence farmers in the northern mountainous region. The majority of rural communities lack access to safe water and sanitation and development plans are challenged by projections that the population will double in less than 25 years.

Laos ranks as a low income, highly indebted poor country, centrally managed by a state that has demonstrated a weak capacity for public service delivery and infrastructure development. While the Lao government has ambitiously committed itself to shedding its 'least developed country' status by 2020, the country remains heavily dependent on assistance from multilateral agencies, with over 70 per cent of public investment sourced from aid.

MALAWI

Malawi's progress towards achieving the Millennium Development Goals (MDGs) has been limited by the spread of HIV/AIDS, and the failure of structural adjustment programmes implemented in the 1980s and 1990s. n 2006, 45 per cent of the population lived below the poverty line which or Malawi is assessed by reference to the household cost of basic food and essential non-food requirements. While this figure is down from 54 per cent in 1998, the government admits that it is unlikely that the poverty arget of 32.7 per cent will be achieved by 2015.

UNICEF estimates that 22 per cent of under-5 children are underweight and 53 per cent suffer from stunting. Up to 35 per cent of the otal population does not have an adequate calorific intake in their diet and the maternal mortality rate of 1,100 per 100,000 live births is one of the highest in the world and a massive increase over the MDG baseline 1992 igure of 620. The 2015 target is a 75 per cent reduction. However, the under- mortality rate has fallen in recent years and life expectancy has risen harply, reversing some of the declines brought by the AIDS pandemic. Another success is in the field of education, with substantial progress owards achieving universal access and removing gender imbalances, albeit t some cost to quality with class sizes approaching an average of 00 children.

MALAYSIA

Malaysia is one of the wealthiest and most developed countries in outheast Asia, outranked only by Singapore and oil-rich Brunei. Since 1970, ne percentage of the population living below the poverty line has fallen om 50 per cent to 5 per cent, extreme poverty is rare, infant mortality has ropped from 40.9 to 7.9 per 1,000 live births, and adult literacy has increased om 60 to 94 per cent. Assessed by UNDP as already having achieved 7 of e 8 Millennium Development Goals (MDGs), the Malaysian experience being presented as a model for the Asia-Pacific region. The government oints in particular to its focus on agricultural productivity, development labour-intensive exports and investment in health and education.

Encouraging as these statistics are, they fail to identify underlying equality and the Gini coefficient for Malaysia is the highest in the region. overty mainly occurs in rural areas amongst indigenous groups, especially the Eastern Malaysian states of Sabah and Sarawak—in Sabah 23 per nt of households live below the poverty line and 20 per cent of its population have never been to school. The 9th Malaysia Plan, covering th period 2006–10, does acknowledge that economic growth alone i insufficient and that pro-poor policies should be introduced. The Plan aim to further reduce the poverty rate to 2.8 per cent and to eliminate the mos extreme form of poverty by 2015.

MALI

A 2004 Government and UNDP report held little prospect of achievin the MDGs by 2015, though there was some hope for food self-sufficiency universal primary education and access to potable water. Despite what mos would declare a gloomy picture, there has been real progress since 199 This is due to better, though certainly not perfect, governance. Problems i this area remain—such as widespread corruption and political parties bein more concerned with personalities than policies. Decentralization an empowerment of local people holds out the best hope. Fairer terms of trad for Mali's export crops and more development assistance to help Malian address health, education, food and water problems, are necessar conditions for meaningful progress to be achieved.

MEXICO

Most assessments suggest that extreme poverty in Mexico is fallin although the World Bank reports that the figure remained as high as 18 p cent in 2005. The latest progress report for the MDGs dated April 20 expresses confidence that the Goals will be achieved, with doubts concede only in relation to some individual targets for health. There has been hig investment in education over the last 10 years, with spending now reachir over 6 per cent of GDP, and the number of children out of school has bee halved since 2000.

However, such analyses fail to convey a true picture of poverty Mexico where pressures of a population in excess of 100 million combi with the faultlines of a largely deregulated open market economy to crea extremes of inequality. Bottlenecks of poverty are particularly four amongst rural indigenous groups and in the overcrowded shanty towns the country's vast cities. In 2005, over 45 per cent of the population ha difficulty in providing for basic needs and there is increasing consens that the National Development Plan (2007–12) currently under considerati must include more pro-poor policies to counter the shortcomings of t economic model.

NEPAL

The official position articulated in the MDG progress report published in 2005 recognises the constraints of social and regional inequality but nevertheless insists that, apart from difficulties with the Goals for education and HIV/AIDS, prospects for success are reasonably good. For example, the key per cent poverty indicator for extreme poverty ($ 1 per day) has reduced from 33.5 in the baseline year of 1990 to 24.1 per cent in 2005, suggesting that the Goal of halving poverty by 2015 could be achieved.

A rather more sobering MDG Needs Assessment Report published towards the end of 2006 estimates that attainment of the MDGs requires development funds of $ 12.6 billion over the period to 2015, necessitating not only a doubling of the level of current aid but also pro-poor spending by the government, especially on education, which in 2006 attracted a budget of only 3.4 per cent of GDP.

Predictions of future progress should also draw attention to the underlying risks to human development. A 2007 report by the World Food Programme (WFP) and the UN Food and Agriculture Organisation describes Nepal as 'chronically food insecure,' its inefficient production further undermined by natural disasters and climate change. WFP is already targeting over one million people with food aid. Regions that are the focus of poverty alleviation programmes tend also to be those most affected by the Maoist conflict. Successful implementation of the peace agreement is critical to the MDG programme in Nepal.

NIGERIA

The Nigerian Ministry of Finance boasts of impressive 5 per cent economic growth in 2006; but this is growth without a human face, as it is not reflected in the life of the ordinary citizen. The world's 8th largest oil exporter continues to languish in the bottom quartile of the Human Development Index, with over 70 per cent of its population surviving on less than $ 1 a day.

The international agency, ActionAid, estimates that one third of the population is hungry, in spite of adequate food production. Given that the population of about 140 million is the largest in Africa, Nigeria's failure to make inroads into the Millennium Development Goals (MDGs) significantly influenced the conclusion reached in the 2007 UN mid-term progress report that the Goals are very unlikely to be achieved in Sub-Saharan Africa.

Health figures reveal the most serious problem with indicators for infant and child mortality worse than they were in the baseline year of 1990—one in five children is expected to die before age five. Maternal mortality is also extremely high.

A contributory factor is undoubtedly the corresponding failure to provide access to improved sources of drinking water, another statistic which at 48 per cent has moved in reverse since 1990. Although 7 million children remain out of school, enrolment is rising slowly and there is a slightly more positive outlook on the Goal for universal primary education.

Poor coordination of development plans within the Federal government together with incompetent delivery of services at State and local government levels have greatly hampered progress towards the MDGs. An unusual government post of Special Adviser to the President on Millennium Development Goals has been established to address these administrative bottlenecks and to be accountable for directing proceeds of debt relief to MDG sectors. It has estimated that the cost of achieving the Goals in Nigeria exceeds $ 5 billion annually, a figure far above the current resources.

PAKISTAN

Pakistan is home to a significant proportion of the world's poor. Over 30 per cent of the country's 150 million people survive beneath the poverty line. In rural areas, literacy of women is as low as 20 per cent. A history of high government spending on military and business interests has been at the expense of the domains of health and education.

Little more than 1.5 per cent of the national budget is allocated to education. The drop-out rate from primary schools is thought to be the highest in the world, leaving many runaway children on the streets in major cities, whilst others approach adulthood through the inappropriate experience of factory labour.

On a more positive note, there are signs of structural change in moves towards decentralisation of government powers—a shift which development agencies have recommended as a means for health services in particular to reach areas where they are most needed. The Poverty Reduction Strategy Paper (PRSP) and the Medium Term Development Framework 2005–10 have both been realigned with the MDGs and Pakistan continues to attract generous aid programmes.

PERU

Like many of its neighbours in South America, Peru is ranked in absolute terms as a 'middle income' country, a status which has led to the U.K. Department for International Development (DFID) withdrawing its aid operations from Peru. Yet even DFID concedes that it is unlikely that Peru will achieve some of the MDGs, especially those relating to poverty, such is the degree of socio-economic inequality.

Recent years of relatively high economic growth have failed to make significant inroads into poverty reduction. By the government's own criteria, 48 per cent of the population lives below the poverty line. In rural areas, this figure rises to over 60 per cent, illustrating how poverty particularly impacts indigenous people as opposed to those of Spanish descent who dominate the urban business economy.

The impact of poverty is most evident in health indicators—about one quarter of the population has no access to health services despite the apparent introduction of free healthcare in 2002. The rate of maternal mortality is one of the highest in the region. Malnutrition is another inevitable consequence with children caught in a poverty trap and unable to benefit from economic growth.

PHILIPPINES

The Philippines is classed as a middle income country, but suffers from major development problems. Commitment to the Millennium Development Goals (MDGs) has come under painful scrutiny with the publication of results of the 2006 Family Income and Expenditure Survey, which shows that poverty increased in the three years since the previous survey. This was a period in which the Philippines boasted success by conventional measures of economic growth and in which neighbouring countries in Southeast Asia took enormous strides in lifting people out of poverty. By contrast, extreme poverty (assessed by inability to buy sufficient food) in the Philippines increased from 13.5 per cent to 14.6 per cent between 2003 and 2006 whilst the broader measure of poverty (assessed by inability to buy food and other basic essentials) increased from 30.0 to 32.9 per cent. These reverses raise doubts as to whether the respective 2015 MDG targets (12 and 22.5 per cent) for these two measures of poverty can be met.

The government has integrated the MDGs into the Medium-Term Philippine Development Plan (MTPDP) 2004–10 but its underlying commitment is questioned in an unusually frank 2007 MDG Midterm

Progress Report which observes that 'expenditures for social and economic services as a percentage of the total budget had been declining for the past seven years.' The funding gap to achieve the Goals by 2015 is estimated at around $ 15 billion, a figure well beyond current resources.

SOUTH AFRICA

A symptom of the inhumanity of the apartheid era was the exclusion of the black majority from surveys of social and economic status. Measuring progress of the MDGs in the new South Africa is therefore a challenge because no data exists for the baseline year of 1990. The starting point for poverty indicators has been shifted forward to 2000 at which point the measure of extreme poverty (less than $ 1 per day) was 11.3 per cent, with a target of 5.7 per cent by 2015.

By UN classification South Africa is a middle-income country with ample resources and by far the most developed country in Africa. In its 'Vision 2014,' the government sets out a strategy for fighting poverty through high rates of economic growth in parallel with direct welfare payments to the poor and high investment in education. The Mid-Term MDG Progress Review published in 2007 offers no update of the extreme poverty indicator but claims that incomes of the poorest households have risen strongly in this period and that the Goal is likely to be achieved. However, the most recent UNDP Human Development Report presents a figure of 10.7 per cent for extreme poverty in 2005, almost unchanged from the baseline position. Over 43 per cent of the population remains under the poverty line which is assessed as Rand 3,000 per annum at 2000 values.

Nevertheless, the Goals for education are already close to being achieved and the country has made impressive strides in the area of gender equality with over 30 per cent women's representation in both parliament and in the cabinet. Considerable progress has also been made in the provision of safe water and sanitation and the government promises universal access to these services by 2008 and 2010, respectively, far beyond the MDG targets.

SYRIA

Syria does not experience extreme poverty by the standard $ 1 per day measure adopted for the Millennium Development Goals (MDGs)—fewer than 0.5 per cent of the population fall below this threshold. However, in a country where military spending exceeds the budgets for health and education combined, progress in human development is constrained. A UNDP report published in 2005 found that the percentage living below the poverty line defined as the cost of basic food and non-food needs dropped only from 14.3 to 11.4 per cent in the period 1997–2004, with unemployment rising throughout those years. Furthermore, a wider definition of poverty captured over 30 per cent of the population.

The problem is particularly acute in the rural north-eastern region which seems trapped in a spiral of poor or non-existent education, low enrolment for girls and absence of employment opportunities. University enrolment is falling countrywide and reform of the educations them is acknowledged to be a priority.

Statistics are more favourable in the health sector where both child and infant mortality rates fell by about 50 per cent in the 1997–2004 period. Nevertheless, the dual pressure of a high rate of population increase and lack of investment ensures that the majority of Syrians endure poor quality of health services, the middle classes often resorting to private prescriptions and treatment.

TANZANIA

Tanzania is one of the poorest countries in the world, with 58 per cent of the population living below the $ 1 per day threshold for extreme poverty adopted by the UN. Based on Tanzania's own assessment of the minimum income for basic needs, the percentage is less acute, just under 36 per cent in 2004. The equivalent figure for 1990 was 39 per cent implying a disappointing rate of progress. The same is true for the percentage surviving below the more extreme food poverty line. The latest position is awaited in results of a Household Budget Survey conducted in 2007 but it appears likely that, taking into account population growth which continues at about 3 per cent per annum, there are more people now living in poverty in Tanzania than in the baseline year for the Millennium Development Goals (MDGs).

This gloomy picture is greatly cheered by the phenomenal progress in getting children into school that has occurred since 2004, thanks to the lifting of fees and the construction of hundreds of new schools. Net primary school enrolment rocketed from 65 per cent in 2001 to 96 per cent in 2006; with girls benefiting as much as boys, key MDG targets are close to fulfilment. Given that the number of primary pupils has almost doubled to

8 million in this five year period, there are inevitable problems of teacher-pupil ratio and the government has conceded that over 5,000 additional teachers are needed.

In a country which offers only one doctor per 20,000 people, child mortality is not improving fast enough to meet the MDG targets and, in common with many African countries, maternal mortality appears to be worsening. Data is unreliable but maternal mortality in 2005 has been estimated at 578 per 100,000 births, higher than the rate in 1996. Only 27 per cent of births in rural areas were attended by a qualified health worker.

THAILAND

Thanks to the strong performance of its economy during much of the 1990s, Thailand has already achieved, or is on its way to achieving, most of the MDGs. The percentage of people living in poverty has been reduced from 38 per cent in 1990 to 11 per cent in 2004 and, with literacy rates at 96 per cent for men and 91 per cent for women and almost universal primary education enrolment, the country is now concentrating on improvement of secondary education. Whilst divisions of wealth between rich and poor and between rural and urban communities are deepening, overall health indicators for child and maternal mortality are progressing well and the threat of malaria is limited to endemic regions and is under control. Thailand has also done unexpectedly well to achieve near universal access to safe water and sanitation due to well-financed government programmes.

The country has therefore set itself new targets, dubbed 'MDG plus,' including the aim to further decrease its poverty level to 4 per cent by 2009. Thailand has also produced regional MDG Reports for two provinces, a rare examination of the potential of decentralised MDG policymaking. As the MDG 2004 progress report on Thailand notes, people in the hills of the north and in the three Muslim majority provinces in the south bordering Malaysia tend to be marginalised; poverty in one southern province is as high as 23 per cent. Further problems lie in MDG 7 (sustainable development) because of the damage the environment has suffered through the period of rapid economic growth over recent decades and in MDG 3 (gender equality) due to the exceptionally low number of women in politics and in government employment.

TURKEY

Turkey's progress towards achieving the MDGs is moderate. The latest government reports for 2005 disclose that extreme poverty is rare with under 1 per cent of the population living on less than US$ 1 a day. Yet, over 20 per cent of the population falls below a broader definition of poverty and is vulnerable to any economic instability.

This rate is even higher in rural areas due to a stagnating agricultural economy and slow labour transition to non-agricultural activities. Infant and child mortality rates are very high and life expectancy is low by European standards, in part due to difficulties in meeting the costs of medical attention.

As for education, the adult literacy rate is 85 per cent, with a significant gap between the literacy rates of men (94 per cent) and women (78 per cent). There are serious disparities at the regional level too. Literacy is as high as 98 per cent in the western and north-western parts of the country, while it goes down to as low as 40 per cent (for women) in the eastern part. Turkey also needs to improve in the area of women's empowerment and entrenched gender discrimination.

The level of female economic activity is also significantly lower than that of males. Only half of the female population over 15 years of age is economically active and out of these mostly work in the agricultural sector at low levels of productivity.

UGANDA

Uganda presents both successes and failures in its progress towards attainment of the Millennium Development Goals (MDGs). Most creditably the country can claim significant progress towards the target to halt and reverse the spread of HIV/AIDS. Also to its credit is the Universal Primary Education (UPE) programme, which started in 1997 and which has increased enrolment from 3.1 million to 7.6 million (92 per cent) in 2006 by allowing free attendance. The MDG target for gender equality in primary schools is regarded as already achieved. There are also moves to allow free secondary education for selected pupils.

By contrast, infant and maternal mortality rates give cause for much concern, the latter being amongst the highest in the world. Absolute poverty continues to be a nightmare, increasing by the day and unalleviated by the economic liberalization which has otherwise led to a remarkable economic recovery. Macro-economic indicators cannot hide the disturbing reality that the proportion of Ugandans living below the national poverty line has been static, at around 35 per cent throughout the period 2000–05, falling to 31 per cent in 2006.

UZBEKISTAN

Uzbekistan is one of the three poorest countries in the Commonwealth of Independent States (CIS), with 28 per cent of the population unable to meet its basic needs and 46 per cent living on less than the equivalent of 2 dollars a day. The majority of the poor live in rural areas and rely on a struggling welfare system. Over 23 per cent of under five-year-olds were estimated to be malnourished in 2006, and women of reproductive age have the highest anaemia rates in the region.

The Uzbekistan government has officially recognized that poverty is widespread and has committed itself to reaching the MDGs. Its Welfare Improvement Strategy for 2005–10 integrates the MDGs and envisages a reduction in poverty to 20 per cent by the end of that period. The sharp fall in living standards that followed independence from the Soviet Union in 1991 greatly adds to the challenge of achieving the MDGs in Uzbekistan, given that the baseline year for the Goals is 1990.

VENEZUELA

The government of Hugo Chávez made major efforts to tackle poverty and social exclusion, especially through programmes known as *misiones*. Financed by oil revenues, these programmes include healthcare and education for poor communities, employment creation, reforestation, energy saving and measures against social exclusion.

In spite of the country's abundance of natural resources, 37.9 per cent of Venezuelan households live below the poverty line, notably the rural poor and indigenous people. The Venezuelan government has declared that it will be able to accomplish some of the MDGs before 2015, particularly those related to the eradication of illiteracy. However, progress is slow in other areas and clear policies are necessary to accelerate the process.

VIETNAM

Vietnam has the remarkable record for a developing country of achieving the first of the MDGs—halving poverty over the period 1990-2015—more than a decade in advance. Although the collection of accurate data is often constrained by local conditions, there is no question that key social indicators show spectacular improvement over recent years. The percentage of poor households has fallen from 58 per cent in 1993 to less than 24 per cent in 2004, whilst extreme poverty has dropped from 18.5 per cent to below 7 per cent. Over this same period child and infant mortality rates have halved and access to safe water has trebled. School enrolment at primary level is almost universal. More demanding goals for reducing poverty have been set for the period to 2010—these are known as the Vietnam Development Goals.

This success is widely attributed to the *doi moi* (open door) policy introduced by the Vietnamese government in 1986 and which signalled a move away from central planning and collectivist agriculture towards the beginnings of a market economy and farm ownership. However, the characteristic weaknesses of a more modern economy inevitably lurk beneath these aggregate statistics, in particular the widening divisions between the Western-oriented, infrastructure-rich south and the more populated but impoverished northern regions.

Gaps in wealth are also emerging between the urban and rural areas. These divisions manifest themselves especially in the quality of education which tends to be linked to the ability to pay suitable fees and in the provision of safe water and sanitation. Despite major government spending to support people living under the poverty line, illiteracy in remote areas or among ethnic minority groups remains a thorny issue and many international organizations focus their activities in this field.

YEMEN

Over 40 per cent of the Yemeni population lives in poverty, the majority concentrated in rural areas. The country is presently in the midst of a food crisis where approximately one-third of its population remains undernourished (rising to 46 per cent of children under-five). Almost 18 per cent of Yemenis exist below the food poverty line and the World Food Programme is actively assisting about one million people. A financially starved health sector has severely jeopardized maternal and child health, particularly in remote areas of the countryside where underdeveloped infrastructure restricts access to basic services.

Yemen's adult literacy rate of only 49 per cent is indicative of the low average net enrolment in primary education which at 72 per cent is one of the lowest in the Middle East and North Africa (MENA) region. Furthermore, this average figure conceals the vastly lower enrolment rates for girls, which sinks to 30 per cent in rural areas. The 2005 Arab Human Development Report cites poverty and cultural attitudes to women, such as early marriage and segregation between the sexes, for the gender gap in education. In a recent effort to boost girls' primary enrolment and to meet the MDG goal of education for all by 2015, the Ministry of Education announced its decision to waive primary school tuition fees for female students. With approximately half the population under the age of 15 and a population growth rate ranking sixth in the world, education needs to be a top priority for development policy in Yemen. Increasing evidence that as many as 400,000 children under 14 are engaged in child labour adds fresh concern.

Inappropriate allocation of public funds is considered the primary reason for the lack of human development. In 2002, only 1.0 per cent of GDP was spent on the health sector compared with a massive 7.1 per cent on assorted military acquisitions. The government however proclaims a quite different interpretation, attributing poor progress to inadequate aid support from the donor community.

Official development assistance (ODA) was 8.4 per cent of GDP in 1990 falling to a low of 2.2 per cent in 2003. A recent donor conference has raised hopes that more aid will be forthcoming but not on the scale of the vast sum of $ 48 billion estimated as the cost of attaining the MDGs in the Needs Assessment report for Yemen published in 2005.

ZAMBIA

The Zambian government has committed itself to achieving the Millennium Development Goals (MDGs) and the Fifth National Development Plan for 2006–11 gives reassuring priority to poverty reduction. Determined multi-sectoral initiatives seek to raise public awareness of the importance of the Goals. The task will nevertheless be formidable as Zambia has so far failed to make significant progress on the eradication of poverty and hunger (MDG 1).

The majority of the population (64 per cent) lives on less than $ 1 a day, and 87 per cent have less than $ 2, figures that are worse than in the MDG baseline year of 1990. Although harvests have been good for the last three years, the World Food Programme describes food insecurity as widespread due to sensitivity to local rainfall patterns; food aid remains in place for 370,000 beneficiaries. There is a growing gap between the rich and the poor. The elite (in the cities) have adopted a Western standard of living and put great emphasis on material wealth.

Nevertheless, Zambia has the potential to achieve nearly all of the MDGs, according to the Progress Report published in 2005. One important exception is maternal mortality (MDG 5) which has been increasing in recent years. This worrying trend is also true of literacy rates (MDG2) which have declined since 1990. Today one third of the adult population is illiterate. However, free primary education was introduced in 2003 and 95 per cent of children are now going to primary school.

APPENDIX II

FOOD SECURITY AND HUMAN RIGHTS

By May 2008, global food security had deteriorated to such an extent that the UN Human Rights Council held a special Seventh Session to consider the impact of food insecurity caused by soaring food prices on the right of food for all.

The Council called upon States, individually and through international cooperation and assistance, and other relevant stakeholders, to take all necessary measures to ensure the realization of the right to food as an essential human rights objective, and consider reviewing any policy or measure which could have a negative impact on the realization of the right to food. The Council stressed that States had the primary obligation to make their best efforts to meet the vital food needs of their own population, especially of vulnerable groups and households, while the international community should provide, through a coordinated response and upon request, support to national and regional efforts in terms of providing the necessary assistance for increasing food production.

In an explanatory note provided by the countries requesting the Special Session, it was estimated that 854 million people are in a state of food insecurity in the world. Sixty per cent of these persons live in Sub-Saharan Africa or in South Asia. In addition, two billion persons suffer from malnutrition, due to micronutrient deficiencies in vitamins and minerals. The world can produce enough food to feed twice the entire global population. Therefore, in a world overflowing with riches, hunger is not inevitable. It is a violation of human rights.

The lack of purchasing power for those in need is at the heart of the problem of hunger and malnutrition. The current food crisis is a major event. Overall, the price of food commodities in the international markets rose by 83 per cent over the last 36 months. The realization of the right to food, like other human rights, requires that States pursue international cooperation.

The seriousness of the situation can be gauged by the fact that the Council called the special session on May 22 despite the next regular session being scheduled as early as June 2, 2008.

The Special Rapporteur in his presentation on the right to food in his concluding remarks said that the role of the Human Rights Council in this crisis was to ensure the right to food when addressing the situation. The second message delivered was the national obligation of each State towards their populations and the international obligation of all States towards all people of the world. A third message, often underestimated, was the role of large agricultural cooperatives. Transnational corporations had an immense power on the market and were dictating their prices to small farmers.

In the debate, many speakers expressed the great importance they attached to this first ever thematic Special Session. They emphasized the need to address not just the immediate needs of vulnerable populations, but the root causes of the crisis. Many felt that the crisis was due to the increased privatisation and liberalization of markets, forced by the Bretton Woods institutions, with an excessive focus on exports, which had weakened the right to food, and the role of small producers, in addition to placing barriers to the economic and social rights of populations.

Others stressed a larger combination of factors, including climate change, natural disasters and soaring energy prices. Many acknowledged that the primary responsibility for preventing such a crisis and dealing with it was a national one, while noting also an international responsibility and need for international cooperation to address the issue.

The fact that the crisis had disproportionately affected countries of the South, developing countries, and African countries, was noted. It was observed that the current crisis threatened the African continent's stability and the progress achieved in past years. Concerns were voiced that if rising prices of food were not controlled, riots witnessed over the past few months would spread to other parts of the world.

In the General Debate, among the many speakers were:

Rebecca Sagar (United Kingdom) who said that, while it was important that the Council made its views known on this global debate, it was essential that Special Sessions such as this one, focused exclusively on human rights aspects of the issue in question and were not tempted to stray into other areas where the Council had neither the authority nor the competence to make a meaningful contribution.

The United Kingdom firmly believed that individual human rights could not be realized in isolation. That was true of the right to adequate food as it was of every other right. In fulfilling its mandate, the Human Rights Council had to be prepared to identify situations and countries where governments were unable to realize their populations' right to adequate food. If States, such as 'Burma (Myanmar)', found that—for whatever reason—their populations were unable to access adequate food, then they were duty-bound to seek and accept the help available to them.

High food prices were a global problem that would require coordinated and sustained international efforts. The United Kingdom supported social protection programmes which ensured that the poor and vulnerable groups had sufficient means to meet their basic needs.

They all had to support efforts to give greater priority and long-term attention to the underlying problems of poverty and hunger facing some 850 million people. Those were important challenges where the Council had a valid interest. The draft resolution contained many good elements, but missed some opportunities. Nevertheless, the United Kingdom would join the consensus on it.

Blaise Godet (Switzerland) who said as they were speaking in the Council, the lives of millions were threatened by hunger. The crisis had become worse and the situation was beginning to be intolerable for children and was creating instability in several countries. In the different issues raised by the crisis, only a global and coherent approach would provide an effective response. The Office of the High Commissioner for Human Rights should participate in the Secretary-General's Task Force and the High Commissioner should attend the Rome summit.

The rise in food prices was affecting many poor families, which were spending the majority of their budget on food. The crisis was affecting the most vulnerable people. The causes were multiple and interconnected in a complex way. The international community had to overcome the crisis and bring relief to the affected populations. In the medium and long-term, national policies should be more coherent. Human rights had to be placed back at the centre of the challenge and a clear message had to be sent to the world by adopting the resolution by consensus.

Barbara Ekwall, of the Food and Agricultural Organization (FAO), noted that millions of poor households in developing countries faced the spectrum of a worsening food security situation due to soaring food costs. FAO analysis showed that poor rural women were particularly hard hit. The present crisis carried complex, technical questions related to food production, the environment, energy, the economy and development. However, the human dimension of the crisis also raised important human rights considerations.

Urgent international response was needed to help developing countries to deal with the impact of high food prices, and to increase investments in agriculture that benefited those who were, or who were at risk of becoming food insecure.

Hubertus Matheus Van Megen (Holy See) said that the primary tasks before the global community were to develop a coherent response within the context of multiple initiatives under way and to 'mainstream' the crisis within the framework of human rights. Moreover, the problem of adequate food production was more than a temporary emergency. It was structural in nature and should be addressed in the context of economic growth that was just and sustainable.

It also required measures dealing not only with agriculture and rural development, but also with health, education, good governance and human rights. A renewed commitment to agriculture, particularly in Africa, appeared necessary. Unfair subsidies had to be eliminated. To remedy problems faced by small farms, cooperative structures should be organized. Hoarding and price speculation were unacceptable.

In this complex and urgent debate, a new mentality was required. It should treat people as people first and not simply focus on economic profit. Due to a lack of food, too many poor people died each day, while immense resources were allocated for arms. The international community had to be galvanized into action. The right to food regarded the future of the human family as well as peace in the global community.

Babacar Ba, of the Organization of the Islamic Conference, said this serious crisis called on all of them to act and ensure the survival of millions throughout the world. The food crisis was global, but certainly it threatened peace and security at the local level and required global attention to deal with it. The Organization of the Islamic Conference supported initiatives to deal with this challenge, meeting in Turkey to discuss the crisis and launching a new economic tool in Kuwait recently. A special programme for the development of Africa launched in Dakar was another measure launched to protect their countries.

But this was not enough. They had to deal with the structural problems and underlying causes. International instruments for the promotion and protection of human rights recognized the right to food as a fundamental right. All of the specialized agencies, such as the World Food Programme and the International Fund for Agricultural Development and others, recognized that those rights had to be ensured throughout the world. The Organization of the Islamic Conference welcomed the initiative to hold this Special Session and expressed its full support for decisions to be taken at it and in their implementation.

Sihasak Phuangketkeow (Thailand) said that this meeting was timely and relevant as it addressed a serious challenge. The present world food crisis would inevitably have a profound impact on the lives of ordinary people around the world, denying them one of their basic human rights. It would impact the vulnerable and make them more 'vulnerable'.

The world food crisis was a complex issue which stemmed from a wide range of interrelated factors, including rising consumption, lower productivity, climate change and soaring energy prices. It required a comprehensive solution. Thailand, as the top rice exporting country, attached great importance to the issue of food security and recognized its responsibility to maintain the level of its rice exports in order not to further aggravate the problem.

Thailand believed that the Human Rights Council could contribute substantially and in a complimentary manner to the existing concerted efforts.

Usman Sarki, of the African Union, said that, since 2005, a sharp rise in prices had been seen for all basic foodstuffs such as bread, milk and meat. Conscious of the particular challenges to food security faced by Africa, the continent that had always been the most affected by famine, the African Union had used all its resources to overcome that problem or at least mitigate its effects.

In that context, the Abuja Summit on Food Security had been organized in December 2006, which had elaborated a detailed programme for the development of African agriculture whose 'pillar three' focused on improving food supply, reducing hunger and better management of food crises. That was a framework action plan to revitalize African agriculture and reduce famine. It was strengthened by a thematic working group on agriculture and food security and by the United Nations initiative for the achievement of the Millennium Development Goalsin Africa.

The international community was aware of the sources and causes of the problem, as it was aware of its obligations to other parts of the world, as seen in the International Covenant on Economic, Social and Cultural Rights and the Millennium Development Goals, which remained crucial to the attainment of the enjoyment of the right to food. To that end, the international community had to adopt a global approach, oriented towards long-term solutions, that would ensure human dignity and the enjoyment of the right to food.

Alain Lambert, of the United Nations Development Programme (UNDP), Bureau for Crisis Prevention and Recovery, said that UNDP and the Bureau for Crisis Prevention and Recovery were extremely concerned about the extent of the global food crisis. Not only did the crisis reduce poor people's vulnerability to disaster, it created the basic conditions for more violent conflicts.

While there was no doubt that in the present crisis emergency relief was essential, the root causes were structural. For this reason, the Bureau for Crisis Prevention and Recovery wanted to draw the attention of all stakeholders and partners to the importance of prevention work. This was a man-made crisis, therefore it was up to all of them to address it. UNDP would stand firmly behind all the poor and hungry men, women and children and would redouble its efforts to promote the Millennium Development Goals, with its traditional partners, and also with new ones.

Abdul Ghafoor Mohamed (Maldives) said that the Maldives was characterized by very small dispersed coral islands and was heavily reliant on food imports and vulnerable to the shortages of food supplies. There was no doubt that the price increases had significant implications for the Maldives and countries like it.

This increase would also hinder the achievement of the Millennium Development Goals. The reasons for the soaring prices were many and complex. The Human Rights Council alone could not solve this problem, but it had to play its role to raise awareness of the human rights dimension to the problem as a vital way of increasing the moral and ethical imperative for the world to act decisively. The Maldives strongly supported the draft resolution.

Obaid Salem Saeed Al Zaabi (United Arab Emirates) said that the current crisis had many reasons, but one was that this Council had been unable to secure the right to food on the ground for many years. The failure was linked to the fact that many countries had separated this right from other human rights. The right to food was one of the basic human rights, without it others were hollow. This crisis should not be allowed to impede the Millennium Development Goals. The United Arab Emirates hoped that all organizations would work towards addressing the situation. It hoped that the Council would be doing its utmost to confirm once again that poverty should be banned and to find a lasting solution for this scourge.

APPENDIX III

FOOD SUBSIDIES IN THE U.S.A.

THE U.S. trade distorting farm subsidies more than doubled a decade after it committed to bring them down by 20 per cent in the Uruguay Round agreement of the World Trade Organisation in 1995. The overall trade distorting subsidies (OTDS) which was about $ 10 billion in 1995 increased to $22.5 billion in 2005 and then fell slightly to 17.4 billion is the following year.

India and other developing countries could not do anything about it as the U.S.A. had all its numbers in order. The country managed to actually increase the subsidies instead of cutting them down as it had sneaked in a footnote in its schedule of commitment for the Uruguay Round, an asterisked point, changing the base year of calculation from 1995 to 1986-88. Since its trade distorting subsidy was at an all-time high of $ 58 billion in 1986-88, a 20 per cent reduction would mean that it was mandated to reduce its subsidies to just $ 46 billion.

India, according to officials is unwilling to be taken for a ride a second time. Once the negotiations of the ongoing Doha round nears completion, the commerce department is planning to recruit and train at least 80 economics graduates to go through the schedules of implementation submitted by individual members, based on comments made during the negotiations. The idea is to identify and weed out the clauses members might introduce to nullify liberalisation commitments made.

India and other developing countries have already raised their vigil against similar moves by the U.S.A. during the current Doha round. While all members have agreed to accept the base year average of 1995-2000 for further reduction of OTDs, the U.S.A. is insisting on a base year of 2000-04. Officials said that since the U.SA.'s OTDs is higher in the 2000-04 period, increasing the base year average by four years would lower its reduction commitments to around $ 4 billion. 'The G-20, the developing country grouping on agriculture, has strongly objected to the U.S. move,' the officials added.

The group of young scholars to be appointed by the government to cross-check claims will be given training to go through the voluminous schedules submitted by members, especially the developed countries. Wherever a discrepancy is identified, the Indian government will approach the member concerned and the WTO secretariat to remove them. 'We will sign the final WTO agreement only when we are satisfied that there is no slip between the cup and the lip,' the source said.

Officials pointed out that since the schedules run into thousands of pages, developing countries failed to read the fine print during the Uruguay Round as they did not have enough officials to go through the text. The appointment of trainees for six months will hopefully take care of the manpower crunch. Although it seems that it would take a while before the Round, which involves not just agriculture but also industrial goods, services and rules among other issues, is negotiated, India is putting its house in order as it does not want to be caught napping again.

Source: *The Economic Times,* New Delhi, May 19, 2008.

APPENDIX IV

NOMINAL AND REAL VALUES AND PRICES

IN economics, nominal value is the value of anything expressed in money of the day, versus real value which includes the effect of inflation. Examples include a bundle of commodities, such as gross domestic product, and income.

For a series of nominal values in successive years, different values could be because of differences in the price level, an index of prices. But nominal values do not specify how much of the difference is from changes in the price level. Real values remove this ambiguity. Real values convert the nominal values as if prices were constant in each year of the series.

Any differences in real values are then attributed to differences in quantities of the bundle or differences in the amount of goods that the money incomes could buy in each year. Thus, the real values index the *quantities* of the commodity bundle or the purchasing power of the money incomes for each year in the series. The nominal/real value distinction can apply not only to time-series data, as above, but to cross-section data varying by region or householder characteristics.

Nominal values are related to *prices and quantities* (P and Q) and to real values by the following definitions: nominal value = P•Q = P•real value.

Numerical Example

If for years 1 and 2 (say 20 years apart) the nominal wage and P are, respectively,

$ 10 and $ 16
1.00 and 1.333,
real wages are, respectively,
$ 10 (= 10/1.00) and $ 12 (= 16/1.333).

The real wage so constructed in each different year indexes the amount of commodities in that year that could be purchased relative to other years. Thus, in the example the price level increased by 33 per cent, but the real wage rate still increased by 20 per cent, permitting a 20 per cent increase in the quantity of commodities the nominal wage could purchase.

USES AND EXAMPLES OF NOMINAL AND REAL VALUES

Nominal values such as nominal wages or (nominal) gross domestic product refer to amounts that are paid or earned in money terms. In the illustration of the previous section, for a single good with a nominal value, the nominal value of the good was divided by its unit price to calculate its real value, namely the quantity of the good. The same general method applies for calculation of other real values, except that a price index is used instead of the price of a single commodity.

Real values (such as real wages or real gross domestic product) can be derived by dividing the relevant nominal value (money wages or nominal GDP) by the appropriate price index. For consumers, a relevant bundle of goods is that used to compute the Consumer Price Index. So, for wage earners as consumers a relevant real wage is the nominal wage (after-tax) divided by the CPI. A relevant divisor of nominal GDP is the GDP price index.

Real values represent the purchasing power of nominal values in a given period, including wages, interest, or total production. In particular, price indexes are typically calculated relative to some base year. If for example the base year is 1992, real values are expressed in constant 1992 dollars, referenced as 1992=100, since the published index is usually normalized to equal 100 in the base year. To use the price index as a divisor for converting a nominal value into a real value, as in the previous section, the published index is first divided by the base-year price-index value of 100. Nominal GDP is called *GDP in current dollars/pounds/euros*, etc. (that is, in prices current for each designated year), and real GDP is called *GDP in [base-year] dollars/pounds/euros, etc.* (that is, in dollars that can purchase the same quantity of commodities as in the base year). In effect, the price index of 100 for the base year is a numéraire for price-index values in other years.

The terminology of classical economics used by Adam Smith used a unit of labour as the purchasing power unit, so monetary quantities were deflated by wages to indicate the number of hours of labour required to produce or purchase a given quantity.

APPENDIX V

2008 ROME FOOD SUBSIDY SUMMIT DECLARATION: TEXT

FULL Text of DECLARATION of the High-Level Conference on World Food Security: The Challenges of Climate Change and Bioenergy

WE, the Heads of State and Government, Ministers and Representatives of 180 countries and the European Community, have met in Rome at this High-Level Conference convened by the Food and Agriculture Organization of the United Nations, together with the United Nations World Food Programme, the International Fund for Agricultural Development and Bioversity International on behalf of the CGIAR system, to seek ways of achieving world food security and, in this context, to address challenges of higher food prices, climate change and bioenergy.

1. We reaffirm the conclusions of the World Food Summit in 1996, which adopted the Rome Declaration on World Food Security and the World Food Summit Plan of Action, and the objective, confirmed by the World Food Summit: five years later, of achieving food security for all through an ongoing effort to eradicate hunger in all countries, with an immediate view to reducing by half the number of undernourished people by no later than 2015, as well as our commitment to achieving the Millennium Development Goals (MDGs). We reiterate that food should not be used as an instrument for political and economic pressure. We also recall the Voluntary Guidelines to Support the Progressive Realization of the Right to Adequate Food in the Context of National Food Security. We reiterate that it is unacceptable that 862 million people are still undernourished in the world today.

2. We are here to address the challenges of bioenergy and climate change, and the current situation of soaring food prices that is having adverse impacts on food security, particularly in developing countries and countries in transition, all the more because the indications are that food prices will remain high in the years to come.

3. We are convinced that the international community needs to take urgent and coordinated action to combat the negative impacts of soaring food prices on the world's most vulnerable countries and populations. We are further convinced that actions by national governments, with the support of the international community, are required in the short, medium- and long-term, to meet global and household food security needs. There is therefore an urgent need to help developing countries and countries in transition expand agriculture and food production, and to increase investment in agriculture, agribusiness and rural development, from both public and private sources.

In adopting this Declaration, we pledge to embrace food security as a matter of permanent national policy, renew our commitment to achieving the World Food Summit objectives and the Millennium Development Goals, and commit ourselves to the following measures.

IMMEDIATE AND SHORT-TERM MEASURES

4. The global food situation calls for a strong commitment from governments as well as from all other stakeholders. We call upon all donors and the United Nations System to increase their assistance for developing countries, in particular least developed countries and those that are most negatively affected by high food prices. In the immediate future it is essential to proceed along two main lines.

5. The first line of action is to respond urgently to requests for assistance from affected countries.

(a) The relevant United Nations agencies should be assured the resources to expand and enhance their food assistance and support safety net programmes to address hunger and malnutrition, when appropriate, through the use of local or regional purchase.

(b) The appropriate regional organizations which have emergency food security arrangements should enhance their cooperation with a view to effectively cope with soaring food prices.

(c) All efforts by governmental and non-governmental organizations to strengthen immediate humanitarian and development assistance should be synergized with those of the multilateral organizations, and made coherent, to deal with the continuum from urgent to longer term assistance.

(d) All national and international efforts should be made to ensure that international emergency food assistance is delivered as quickly and efficiently as possible to populations in distress.

(e) To facilitate adjustment to higher food prices, donors and international financial institutions, in accordance with their mandates and in consultation with recipient countries, should provide in a timely manner, balance of payments support and/or budget support to food-importing, low-income countries. Other measures should be considered as necessary to improve the financial situation of the countries in need, including reviewing debt servicing as necessary. We also call on the relevant international institutions to simplify the eligibility procedures of existing financial mechanisms to support agriculture and environment.

6. The second line of action is immediate support for agricultural production and trade.

(a) All relevant organizations and cooperating countries should be prepared to assist countries, on their request, to put in place the revised policies and measures to help farmers, particularly small-scale producers, increase production and integrate with local, regional, and international markets. South-South cooperation must be encouraged.

(b) Development partners are invited to participate in and contribute to international and regional initiatives on soaring food prices and, in particular, under the FAO initiative launched on 17 December 2007, in support of country-led measures to give farmers in low-income food-deficit and the most affected countries access to appropriate locally adapted seeds, fertilizers, animal feed and other inputs, as well as technical assistance, in order to increase agricultural production.

(c) Development partners are called upon to undertake initiatives to moderate unusual fluctuations in the food grain prices. In particular, we call on relevant institutions to assist countries in developing their food stock capacities and consider other measures to strengthen food security risk management for affected countries.

(d) Members of WTO reaffirm their commitment to the rapid and successful conclusion of the WTO Doha Development Agenda and reiterate their willingness to reach comprehensive and ambitious results that would be conducive to improving food security in developing countries. Implementing an aid for trade package should be a valuable complement to the Doha Development Agenda to build and improve the trading capacity of the developing countries.

(e) We will strive to ensure that food, agricultural trade and overall trade policies are conducive to fostering food security for all. For this purpose we reaffirm the need to minimise the use of restrictive measures that could increase volatility of international prices.

MEDIUM AND LONG-TERM MEASURES

7. The current crisis has highlighted the fragility of the world's food systems and their vulnerability to shocks. While there is an urgent need to address the consequences of soaring food prices, it is also vital to combine medium and long-term measures, such as the following:

(a) We urge national governments, all financial institutions, donors and the entire international community to fully embrace a people-centred policy framework supportive of the poor in rural, peri-urban and urban areas and people's livelihoods in developing countries, and to increase investment in agriculture.

(b) It is essential to address the fundamental question of how to increase the resilience of present food production systems to challenges posed by climate change. In this context, maintaining biodiversity is key to sustaining future production performance. We urge governments to assign appropriate priority to the agriculture, forestry and fisheries sectors, in order to create opportunities to enable the world's smallholder farmers and fishers, including indigenous people, in particular in vulnerable areas, to participate in, and benefit from financial mechanisms and investment flows to support climate change adaptation, mitigation and technology development, transfer and dissemination. We support the establishment of agriculture systems and the sustainable forest management practices that positively contribute to the mitigation of climate change and ecological balance.

(c) In addition, we reaffirm the Mauritius Strategy for the sustainable development of small island developing states and call for its implementation in the context of the challenges of climate change and food security.

(d) We urge the international community, including the private sector, to decisively step up investment in science and technology for food and agriculture. Increased efforts in international cooperation should be directed to researching, developing, applying, transferring and disseminating improved technologies and policy approaches. We urge member states, to establish in accordance with the Monterrey Consensus, governance and policy environments which will facilitate investment in improved agricultural technologies.

(e) We encourage the international community to continue its efforts in liberalizing international trade in agriculture by reducing trade barriers and market distorting policies. Addressing these measures will give farmers, particularly in developing countries, new opportunities to sell their products on world markets and support their efforts to increase productivity and production.

(f) It is essential to address the challenges and opportunities posed by biofuels, in view of the world's food security, energy and sustainable development needs. We are convinced that in-depth studies are necessary to ensure that production and use of biofuels is sustainable in accordance with the three pillars of sustainable development and takes into account the need to achieve and maintain global food security. We are further convinced of the desirability of exchanging experiences on biofuels technologies, norms and regulations. We call upon relevant intergovernmental organizations, including FAO, within their mandates and areas of expertise, with the involvement of national governments, partnerships, the private sector, and civil society, to foster a coherent, effective and results-oriented international dialogue on biofuels in the context of food security and sustainable development needs.

MONITORING AND REVIEW

8. We request the Food and Agriculture Organization of the United Nations, in close partnership with WFP and IFAD and other relevant international organizations, including those participating in the High-Level Task Force on the Global Food Crisis and in collaboration with governments, civil society and the private sector, to monitor and analyse world food security in all its dimensions—including those addressed by this Conference—and to develop strategies to improve it.

9. In realizing the contents of the measures above, we stress the importance of the effective and efficient use of the resources of the United Nations system, and other relevant international organizations.

* * *

We firmly resolve to use all means to alleviate the suffering caused by the current crisis, to stimulate food production and to increase investment in agriculture, to address obstacles to food access and to use the planet's resources sustainably, for present and future generations.

We commit to eliminating hunger and to securing food for all today and tomorrow.

ROME, 5 JUNE 2008

This Declaration was adopted by the High-Level Conference on World Food Security: the Challenges of Climate Change and Bioenergy, on 5 June 2008. On the adoption of the Declaration, statements were made by Argentina, Cuba and Venezuela, which will be included in the Report of the High-Level Conference.

Appendix VI

2007 World Hunger Index

ONE in seven people go to bed hungry every day. That's 854 million people worldwide. Hunger is one of the world's major problems and therefore one of its most important challenges. People who are forced to live from hand to mouth are denied a life of dignity. The 2007 Global Hunger Index illustrates that this problem has assumed an alarming scale in 36 countries: 25 of these countries are in Sub-Saharan Africa, nine in Asia, one in the Middle East and Latin America, respectively. There is some progress in the fight against hunger in specific regions throughout the world, and the Millennium Development Goal agreed upon by 189 heads of state in 2000 to halve worldwide hunger by 2015 could be achieved. In fact, if the current trend continues, there will still be around 580 million people going hungry in 2015 – a situation we cannot accept. Without public pressure little can be done to alleviate worldwide hunger. There is no shortage of know-how, but there is a lack of political will.

The Global Hunger Index (GHI), developed by IFPRI is an ideal tool to record hunger and support lobby work and advocacy on both national and international platforms. Hunger has many faces and its causes are diverse. War and armed conflict are significant contributors to undernourishment. Refugees are unable to provide for themselves, family structures break down, arable land is mined or lies fallow, and the economy stagnates. It usually takes years for reconstruction to bear fruit in post-conflict zones, and destabilised countries can only slowly begin providing for themselves in the aftermath.

However, health-related matters also contribute to hunger, the most dramatic form being HIV/Aids infections. Family networks, particularly in Africa, are no longer able to cope with the repercussions of the pandemic, largely because the young men and women crucial to the productivity of the agricultural sector are dying. Many of the 15 million AIDS orphans worldwide are hit hard by hunger. Weather-related disasters such as droughts and flooding also play a part in the numerous hunger crises. According to estimates made by international climatologists, these occurrences will intensify in the course of climate change and, above all in Africa, already existing problems will become more acute. The current water shortage in many regions throughout the world is set to increase and will lead to migration in the future. At present 1.1 billion people have no access to safe drinking water. Put simply, the main cause of hunger is poverty. The poor have no access to key resources and with this they are denied a chance to shape their lives proactively. Poverty in combination with hunger results in a day to day struggle for survival with no prospects for the future.

There has been no progress in countries with bad governance. Hunger and undernourishment form a vicious circle which is often 'passed on' from generation to generation: The children of impoverished parents are often born underweight and are less resistant to disease. They grow up under conditions which impair their intellectual capacity for the whole of their life. According to estimates made by the World Health Organisation, 150 million children worldwide are suffering from chronic malnutrition and its lifelong ramifications. Half a million children go blind each year as a result of iodine deficiency which often causes otherwise preventable damage to the brain. Adults who were undernourished as children are physically and intellectually less productive, attain a lower level education, ultimately earn less money, and are more frequently ill than adults who enjoy a normal dietary intake as children.

It is imperative that progress is made in the fight against hunger and poverty not only through direct support of undernourished people in hunger crisis zones, but also with specific measures. In the case of chronic malnutrition this involves both short and long-term action, where possible in association with local partner organisations. Lobbying on behalf of the poor and hungry in conjunction with NGOs from both the North and the South is also a key priority.

THE CONCEPT OF THE GLOBAL HUNGER INDEX (GHI)

Because hunger has many faces, it makes sense to choose a multidimensional approach for calculating the Global Hunger Index (GHI). Such an approach has the following advantages:

1. It simultaneously captures various aspects of hunger and undernutrition.

2. The combination of indicators measured independently of each other reduces the impact of random measurement errors.
3. The condensing of information facilitates a quicker overview for decision makers in the public and political arenas.

In general, indexes are useful tools for lobbying and advocacy. If used in international rankings, indexes can foster a sense of competition among countries and thus help promote good policies. Combining the proportion of undernourished in the population with the two indicators relating to children under five ensures that both the food-supply situation of the population as a whole and the effects of inadequate nutrition on a physiologically very vulnerable group are captured. Children's nutritional status deserves particular attention because a lack of nutrients puts them at high risk of physical and mental impairment and death.

The GHI is based on three equally weighted indicators:

1. The proportion of undernourished as a percentage of the population (reflecting the share of the population with insufficient dietary energy intake);
2. The prevalence of underweight in children under the age of five (indicating the proportion of children suffering from weight loss and/or reduced growth); and
3. The under-five mortality rate (partially reflecting the fatal synergy between inadequate dietary intake and unhealthy environments).

Children in developing countries die from infectious diseases, but frequently the indirect cause of death is a weakened immune system due to a lack of dietary energy, vitamins, and minerals. Since the first two indicators—the proportion of undernourished and the prevalence of underweight in children—do not reveal premature death as the most tragic consequence of hunger, the under-five mortality rate is also included. The Global Hunger Index has the advantage of going beyond dietary energy availability, which is the focus of the Food and Agriculture Organisation of the United Nations' (FAO's) measure of undernourishment. The GHI's broader conceptual basis better reflects the multidimensional causes and manifestations of hunger.

The index takes into consideration inequitable resource allocations both between households and within households, since the latter also affect the physical well-being of children. Sufficient food availability at the household level does not guarantee that all members benefit from it in equal measure. All three index components are expressed as percentages and are equally weighted.

1. The GHI score varies between the best possible score of 0 and the worst possible score of 100. Higher scores indicate greater hunger; the lower the score, the better the country's situation.

2. GHI scores above 10 are considered serious, scores greater than 20 are alarming, and scores exceeding 30 are extremely alarming. For this report, the Global Hunger Index 2007 was calculated on the basis of data from the period 2000–05.

3. The calculation of the GHI is limited to the 97 developing countries and 21 transitional countries where measuring hunger is considered most relevant. A few Eastern European countries and Western developed nations are not taken into consideration because hunger has been largely overcome in those countries, and over-nutrition and unbalanced diets are a greater problem than a lack of food.

GLOBAL TRENDS AS OF 2007

4. For a little less than three-quarters of the 115 countries for which both the GHI 2007 and the GHI 2006 were calculated, the index has improved slightly in comparison with the previous year.

5. In two countries, GHI scores remained exactly the same, and in around a quarter more, the scores deteriorated slightly. As in 2006, Libya, Argentina, Lithuania, Romania, Chile, Ukraine, and Cuba rank in the GHI top 10, which comprises countries with a relatively high level of economic and social development.

6. Uruguay, Latvia, and Estonia newly joined this group. Libya tops the list thanks to a decline in child malnutrition. Eritrea, the Democratic Republic of the Congo, and Burundi, three countries that ranked at the very bottom of the list in 2006, are still on the losing side. Armed conflict and the widespread poverty resulting from it are major causes for these countries' poor GHI scores. Although there were generally only a few changes in comparison with 2006, a positive development can be seen in Ethiopia, whose GHI score fell by 3 points. Ethiopia now has a better ranking than the post-conflict country Sierra Leone. The improvement is partly attributable to a very small decrease in the under-five mortality rate by 0.3 per cent (3 deaths fewer per 1,000 live births), but mostly to a noteworthy decline in the prevalence of underweight in children from 47.2 per cent in 2000 to 38.4 per cent in 2005.

7. This positive trend is related to greater investment in the education and health care sectors since the 1990s. The World Bank estimates that the proportion of people living on less than one dollar a day in Ethiopia declined from 31 per cent in 1995 to 23 per cent in 2003.

8. Primary gross enrolment rates more than tripled during the 1990s and the female literacy rate rose from 20 per cent in 1990 to 34 per cent in 2002. In addition, normal weather patterns helped agricultural and gross domestic product growth recover in 2004–06. This helped make up for the loss in production following the major drought of 2002.

9. Furthermore, the year 2000 marked the end of the two-year war with Eritrea, thus permitting an economic recovery that is reflected in the more recent data on child malnutrition. Other larger changes in the GHI 2007 compared with the GHI 2006 for individual countries such as Mauritania, Georgia, and Djibouti should be interpreted with caution since they are largely the result of retrospective revisions of the data released by FAO and UNICEF, on which the calculation of the GJ II is based.

   The causes and manifestations of hunger in the individual regions differ considerably—a fact illustrated by the varying values in the three GHI components in the regions. In South Asia, the prevalence of underweight in children is relatively high, whereas in Sub-Saharan Africa, child mortality and the proportion of people who cannot meet their calorie requirements play a major role. Although these two regions have virtually identical GHI scores, their determining factors vary: in South Asia women have a lower nutritional status and more often give birth to babies with low birth weight.

10. In addition, young children are not fed properly for their age and are therefore often underweight. This is the result of the insufficient education of many South Asian women and their low status in society. However, it is noteworthy that while in South Asia a considerably smaller proportion of the population are unable to meet their minimum dietary requirements (1,800 kilocalories per capita) than in Sub-Saharan Africa, a high percentage still have a calorie supply below the average requirement of around 2,100 kilocalories.

11. In India, where the large majority of South Asia's population lives, economic growth in the agricultural sector has lagged considerably behind growth in other sectors over recent years. This has had a negative effect on progress in alleviating poverty and hunger in rural areas. Furthermore, members of the lower castes and certain ethnic minorities continue to be discriminated against in society and are therefore disadvantaged with regard to educational opportunities and the labour market.

12. In Africa, however, droughts, wars, malaria, and HIV/AIDS play a far greater role than in Asia. Besides low agricultural productivity, these factors are primary causes of food shortage and the high child mortality rate. Together with malaria and AIDS, extreme poverty contributes to high child mortality in Sub-Saharan Africa: 40 per cent of the population live below the absolute poverty line of one dollar a day and around two-fifths of this group live on less than 50 cents a day. In South Asia just over 30 per cent have to survive on a dollar a day, but only 4 per cent of this group live on less than 50 cents a day.

    Taking stock at the halfway point: GHI progress indicator shows developments in the fight against hunger. In signing the United Nations Millennium Declaration, 189 heads of state committed themselves to achieving binding and verifiable goals. The time frame for fulfilling the Millennium Development Goals (MDGs) is the period 1990–2015. Measurable targets have been set for that period, such as, for example, reducing the under-five mortality rate by two-thirds. On this basis, each country can determine the values it must reach by 2015 to fulfil its international commitments. The Millennium Declaration sets measurable targets for all three GHI components—the proportion of people who are calorie deficient, the prevalence of underweight in children under five and the under-five mortality rate. Those particular targets are defined under the first and fourth Millennium Development Goals. We can use the GHI progress indicator (GHI-P) to evaluate trends in the fight against hunger in individual countries in the period 1990–2015 and to assess whether those countries are on track to reach the MDGs.

13. Taking stock at the halfway point illustrates current trends and enables countries to make adjustments before 2015. A negative score on the GHI-P means that a country is losing ground and is drifting away from achieving the targets. A positive score indicates that a country is making progress; however, a country needs a score of 0.5 or higher to show that, given the continuation of present trends, it is on track to achieve its GHI target score for 2015 (derived from the MDGs) by halving the proportion of calorie-deficient people and underweight children and cutting under-five mortality by two-thirds. Ideally a GHI-P score of 1 would demonstrate that a country has already achieved all three MDG targets incorporated in the GHI as of the halfway point of the time frame—mid-2003.

14. For scores between -0.1 and 0.1, the change is considered too small to indicate a meaningful trend, and the countries falling into this category are classified as 'stagnating'.

SUMMARY

Investment in education, health, and the economy has positive effects, Africa lags behind.

Libya, Argentina, Lithuania, Romania, and Chile occupy the top five positions in the GHI 2007; Latvia, Ukraine, Estonia, Cuba, and Uruguay follow closely behind.

All of these countries are economically developed and have relatively well-functioning education and health care systems. At the bottom of the list are Eritrea, Burundi, and the Democratic Republic of the Congo (formerly Zaire), followed by other sub-Saharan African countries. Under-development, wars, and bad governance are largely responsible for these countries' high GHI scores.

The already-difficult situation in some countries is exacerbated by repeated droughts and the rapid spread of AIDS. Poverty is the main cause of hunger and undernutrition: the poor cannot afford enough food and are unable to provide themselves with a balanced diet. Poor farmers are not in a position to produce food of sufficient quantity and quality for their subsistence.

HUNGER HOT SPOTS

Discrimination against women exacerbates malnutrition The hot spots of hunger remain sub-Saharan Africa, where extreme poverty is most pronounced, and South Asia. Countries such as India, Nepal, Bangladesh, and Pakistan have a higher proportion of the population meeting their calorie requirements and a lower child mortality rate than sub-Saharan Africa. Because of cultural practices and the low status women hold in society in the region, however, South Asia has the highest child malnutrition rate in the world. In some parts of India, for instance, male family members eat first and women make do with the leftovers.

Children of undernourished and anaemic mothers have a higher risk of being born underweight. More than half of all children with low birth weight are born in South Asia. Forty per cent of the world's underweight children under five live in India alone.

TAKING STOCK OF THE MDG MIDPOINT

The GHI progress indicator allows us to evaluate which countries and regions are on track in the fight against hunger, that is, with regard to meeting the hunger-related MDG targets by 2015. About one-third of the 91 countries whose GHI-P was calculated should be able to reach their GHI target scores by 2015 if present positive trends continue.

Cuba tops that list, followed by other Latin American countries, Middle Eastern states, and countries in North Africa. (The transition countries in Eastern Europe and Central Asia were not included here because of a lack of data for the MDG base year of 1990.)

More than another third of the countries have also experienced improvements, but their efforts until now are not sufficient. In nine countries, seven of which are in sub-Saharan Africa, the situation is stagnating. Nearly a fifth of the countries have seen setbacks—above all, the last two countries in the GHI ranking, Burundi and the Democratic Republic of the Congo, both countries with a very precarious security situation.

Liberia also continues to suffer the consequences of a long-standing civil war, and Swaziland is particularly hard hit by the AIDS epidemic. North Korea, an isolationist country with economic mismanagement and high military expenditures, also falls into this group.

Comparing regions, Africa predominantly shows insufficient rates of progress. Only a few countries are on track, such as Mozambique, which is engaging in successful reconstruction after decades of civil war, and Ghana, which has benefited from a stable political climate. Yet all four countries at the bottom of the GHI-P ranking (Liberia, Swaziland, Burundi, and the Democratic Republic of the Congo) are located in sub-Saharan Africa.

In Asia, even those countries in South Asia with high undernutrition are making progress. That progress, however, is not sufficient to be on track to reach the 2015 target. High economic growth in many countries—particularly China and India—is a driving force behind this positive development together with investments in basic social services.

However, improvements in certain Asian countries are not in proportion to the economic boom: the poorest social stratum benefits much less than the wealthier section of the population. Here specific measures to eradicate malnutrition—particularly among children—are called for.

TOOLS FOR HUNGER ALLEVIATION

Community-based Therapeutic Care and the Millennium Villages Project:

On the basis of their experience with food crises in South Sudan, Ethiopia and Malawi, scientists and international experts in the field of development cooperation—including the relief agency Concern—have developed a new method to treat severely malnourished people. This is an efficient and low cost method since treatment takes place within the community and not, as before, in special feeding centres. Whereas before, only 10 to 20 per cent of the affected population received treatment, CTC can reach 80 per cent of those in need because it can be carried out by local health services and patients no longer have to spend up to 30 days away from home. This new approach has been generally accepted by the World Health Organisation since 2005 and at all UN levels since 2007, and should be increasingly implemented in the future.

Chronic hunger is widespread in rural areas. Three in four poor people live in the countryside. From 2006 to 2010, Deutsche Welthungerhilfe is carrying out a pilot scheme known as the Millennium Villages Project. In 15 villages throughout the world, MDGs are defined in dialogue with the local population and concrete projects are implemented in order to achieve these goals. Annual monitoring is carried out to evaluate progress and make adjustments where necessary. In the three case studies in Angola, Ethiopia and Nicaragua 88 to 97 per cent of the population lives on less than 37 US cents a day; the child mortality rate and underweight amongst children are also high. Specific projects focus on income-generation in the agricultural sector—as well as boosting harvests, health consultation and the development of infrastructure. Self-help groups receive support and local partner organisations act as consulting bodies. Ultimately, local partner organisations should be in a position to use their know-how to call for accountability from their respective governments and act as an advocate on behalf of the hungry in their country.

APPENDIX VII

A HISTORY OF FAMINE

A famine is a widespread shortage of food that may apply to any faunal species, a phenomenon that is usually accompanied by regional malnutrition, starvation, epidemic, and increased mortality. Famine is not really a cause of food insecurity as, in the grading of intensity, famine is rated higher than food insecurity. However, famine is relevant in the broader context of food security because the causes are often man-made and could apply equally to a food security crisis.

Although most famines coincide with regional shortages of food, famine in some human populations has occurred amid plenty or on account of acts of economic or military policy that have deprived certain populations of sufficient food to ensure survival. Historically, famines have occurred because of drought, crop failure, pestilence, and man-made causes such as war or misguided economic policies. Bad harvests, overpopulation and epidemic diseases like the Black Death helped cause hundreds of famines in Europe during the Middle Ages, including 95 in the British Isles and 75 in France.

During the 20th century, an estimated 70 million people died from famines across the world, of whom an estimated 30 million died during the famine of 1958–61 in China. The other most notable famines of the century included the 1942–45 disaster in Bengal, famines in China in 1928 and 1942, and a sequence of famines in the Soviet Union, including the Holodomor, Stalin's famine inflicted on Ukraine in 1932–33. A few of the great famines of the late 20th century included the Biafran famine in the 1960s, the disaster in Cambodia in the 1970s, the Ethiopian famine of 1983–85 and the North Korean famine of the 1990s.

Famine is typically induced by a human population exceeding the regional carrying capacity to provide food resources. An alternate view of famine is a failure of the poor to command sufficient resources to acquire essential food (the 'entitlement theory' of Amartya Sen), analyses of famine that focused on the political-economic processes, an understanding of the reasons for mortality in famines, an appreciation of the extent to which famine-vulnerable communities have strategies for coping with the threat of famine, and the role of warfare and terrorism in creating famine. Modern relief agencies categorize various gradations of famine according to a famine scale.

Many areas that suffered famines in the past have protected themselves through technological and social development. The first area in Europe to eliminate famine was the Netherlands, which saw its last peacetime famines in the early 17th century as it became a major economic power and established a complex economic organization. Noting that many famines occur under dictatorship, colonial rule or during war, Amartya Sen has posited that no functioning democracy has suffered a famine in modern times.

CHARACTERISTICS OF FAMINE

Famine strikes Sub-Saharan African countries the hardest, but with exhaustion of food resources, overdrafting of groundwater, wars, internal struggles and economic failure, famine continues to be a worldwide problem with millions of individuals suffering.

These famines cause widespread malnutrition and impoverishment. The famine in Ethiopia in the 1980s had an immense death toll, although Asian famines of the 20th century have also produced extensive death tolls. Modern African famines are characterized by widespread destitution and malnutrition, with heightened mortality confined to young children.

Relief technologies including immunization, improved public health infrastructure, general food rations and supplementary feeding for vulnerable children, has blunted the mortality impacts of famines, while leaving their economic consequences unchanged. Humanitarian crises also arise from civil wars, refugee flows and episodes of extreme violence and state collapse, creating famine conditions among the affected populations.

Despite repeated stated intentions by the world's leaders to end hunger and famine, famine remains a chronic threat in much of Africa and Asia. In July 2005, the Famine Early Warning Systems Network labelled Niger with emergency status, as well as Chad, Ethiopia, South Sudan, Somalia and Zimbabwe. In January 2006, the United Nations Food and

Agriculture Organization warned that 11 million people in Somalia, Kenya, Djibouti and Ethiopia were in danger of starvation due to the combination of severe drought and military conflicts. In 2006, the most serious humanitarian crisis in Africa was in Sudan's region Darfur.

Some believe that the Green Revolution was an answer to famine in the 1970s and 1980s. The Green Revolution began in the 20th century with hybrid strains of high-yielding crops. Between 1950 and 1984, as they transformed agriculture around the globe, world grain production increased by 250 per cent. Some criticize the process, stating that these new high-yielding crops require more chemical fertilizers and pesticides which can harm the environment. However, it was an option for developing nations suffering from famine. These high-yielding crops made it technically possible to feed much of the world population. They can provide enhanced nutrition enabling a well-nourished, well-developed population to emerge.

Some say that the problems of famine and ill-nourishment are the results of ethical dilemmas over using the technologies we have, as well as cultural and class differences. Furthermore, there are indications that regional food production has peaked in many world sectors, due to certain strategies associated with intensive agriculture such as groundwater overdrafting and overuse of pesticides and other agricultural chemicals.

Frances Moore Lappé, later co-founder of the Institute for Food and Development Policy (Food First) argued in *Diet for a Small Planet* (1971) that vegetarian diets can provide food for larger populations, with the same resources, compared to omnivorous diets.

Noting that modern famines are sometimes the outcome of misguided economic policies, political design to impoverish or marginalize certain populations, or acts of war, political economists have investigated the political conditions under which famine is prevented. Amartya Sen states that the liberal institutions that exist in India, including competitive elections and a free press, have played a major role in preventing famine in that country since independence. Alex de Waal has developed this theory to focus on the 'political contract' between rulers and people that ensures famine prevention, noting the rarity of such political contracts in Africa, and the danger that international relief agencies will undermine such contracts through removing the locus of accountability for famines from national governments.

CAUSES OF FAMINE

Traditionally, famines are thought to be caused by a population outgrowing its regional carrying capacity. In this perception, the operative cause of famine is an imbalance of population with respect to food supply. Most famines however, are caused by a combination of political, economic, and biological factors. Famines can be exacerbated or even caused by poor governance or inadequate logistics for food distribution. In some modern cases, it is political strife, poverty, and violence that disrupt the agricultural and food distribution processes.

Modern famines have often occurred in nations that, as a whole, were not initially suffering a shortage of food. One of the largest historical famines (proportional to the affected population) was the Great Irish Famine, which began in 1845 and occurred as food was being shipped *from* Ireland to England because only the English could afford to pay higher prices. The largest famine ever (in absolute terms) was the Chinese famine of 1958–61 that occurred as a result of the Great Leap Forward. Here it was principally government policy that led first to a decrease in food production and, second, did not try anything to prevent the famine. In a similar manner, the 1973 famine in Ethiopia was concentrated in the Wollo region, although food was being shipped out of Wollo to the capital city of Addis Ababa where it could command higher prices.

In contrast, at the same time that the citizens of the dictatorships of Ethiopia and Sudan had massive famines in the late-1970s and early-1980s, the democracies of Botswana and Zimbabwe avoided them, despite having worse drops in national food production. This was possible through the simple step of creating short-term employment for the worst-affected groups, thus ensuring a minimal amount of income to buy food, for the duration of the localized food disruption and was taken under criticism from opposition political parties and intense media coverage.

The failure of a harvest or the change in conditions, such as drought, can create a situation whereby large numbers of people live where the carrying capacity of the land has dropped radically. Famine is often associated with subsistence agriculture, that is, where most farming is aimed at producing enough food energy to survive. The total absence of agriculture in an economically strong area does not cause famine; Arizona and other wealthy regions import the vast majority of their food, since such regions produce sufficient economic goods for trade.

Disasters, whether natural or man-made, have been associated with conditions of famine ever since humankind has been keeping written records. The Torah describes how 'seven lean years" consumed the seven fat years, and 'plagues of locusts' could eat all of the available food stuffs. War, in particular, was associated with famine, particularly in those times and places where warfare included attacks on land, by burning or salting fields, or on those who tilled the soil.

As observed by the economist Amartya Sen, famine is sometimes a problem of food distribution and poverty. In certain cases, such as the Great Leap Forward, North Korea in the mid-1990s, or Zimbabwe in the early 2000s, famine can be caused as an unintentional result of government policy. Famine is sometimes used as a tool of repressive governments as a means to eliminate opponents, as in the Ukrainian famine of the 1930s. In other cases, such as Somalia, famine is a consequence of civil disorder as food distribution systems break down. Most cases are not simply the result of exceeding the Earth's carrying capacity.

Approximately 40 per cent of the world's agricultural land is seriously degraded. In Africa, if current trends of soil degradation continue, the continent might be able to feed just 25 per cent of its population by 2025, according to the Ghana-based Institute for Natural Resources in Africa. As of late 2007, increased farming for use in biofuels, along with world oil prices at over $ 135 a barrel, has pushed up the price of grain used to feed poultry and dairy cows and other cattle, causing higher prices of wheat (up 58 per cent), soybean (up 32 per cent), and maize (up 11 per cent) over the year. Food riots have recently taken place in many countries across the world. An epidemic of stem rust on wheat caused by race, Ug99, spread across Africa and into Asia and is causing major concern.

There are a number of ongoing famines caused by over population, loss of arable land, war or political intervention. Beginning in the 20th century, nitrogen fertilizers, new pesticides, desert farming, and other agricultural technologies began to be used as weapons against famine. Between 1950 and 1984, as the Green Revolution transformed agriculture around the globe, world grain production increased by 250 per cent. These agricultural technologies temporarily increased crop yields, but there are signs as early as 1995 that not only are these technologies reaching their peak of assistance, but they may now be contributing to the decline of arable land, for example, persistence of pesticides leading to soil contamination and decline of area available for farming. Developed nations have shared these technologies with developing nations with a famine problem, but there are ethical limits to pushing such technologies on lesser developed countries. This is often attributed to an association of inorganic fertilizers and pesticides with a lack of sustainability. In any case, these technological advancement might not be influential in those famines which are the result of war. Similarly, increased yield may not be helpful with certain distribution problems, especially those arising from political intervention.

David Pimentel, professor of ecology and agriculture at Cornell University, and Mario Giampietro, senior researcher at the National Research Institute on Food and Nutrition (INRAN), place in their study *Food, Land, Population and the U.S. Economy* the maximum U.S. population for a sustainable economy at 200 million. To achieve a sustainable economy and avert disaster, the United States must reduce its population by at least one-third, and world population will have to be reduced by two-thirds, says the study.

The authors of this study believe that the agricultural crisis will only begin to impact us after 2020 and will not become critical until 2050. The oncoming peaking of global oil production (and subsequent decline of production), along with the peak of North American natural gas production will very likely precipitate this agricultural crisis much sooner than expected. Geologist Dale Allen Pfeiffer claims that coming decades could see spiralling food prices without relief and massive starvation on a global level such as never experienced before.

Water deficits, which are already spurring heavy grain imports in numerous smaller countries, may soon do the same in larger countries, such as China or India. The water tables are falling in scores of countries (including Northern China, the U.S.A. and India) due to widespread over-pumping using powerful diesel and electric pumps. Other countries affected including Pakistan, Iran and Mexico. This will eventually lead to water scarcity and cutbacks in grain harvest. Even with the over-pumping of its aquifers, China has developed a grain deficit, contributing to the upward pressure on grain prices. Most of the three billion people projected to be added worldwide by mid-century will be born in countries already experiencing water shortages. After China and India, there is a second tier of smaller countries with large water deficits—Algeria, Egypt, Iran, Mexico and Pakistan. Four of these already import a large share of their grain. Only Pakistan remains marginally self-sufficient. But with a population expanding by 4 million a year, it will also soon turn to the world market for grain.

According to a UN climate report, the Himalayan glaciers that are the principal dry-season water sources of Asia's biggest rivers—Ganges,

Indus, Brahmaputra, Yangtze, Mekong, Salween and Yellow—could disappear by 2035 as temperatures rise and human demand rises. Approximately 2.4 billion people live in the drainage basin of the Himalayan rivers. India, China, Pakistan, Afghanistan, Bangladesh, Nepal and Myanmar could experience floods followed by severe droughts in coming decades. In India alone, the Ganges provides water for drinking and farming for more than 500 million people.

EFFECTS OF FAMINE

The demographic impacts of famine are sharp. Mortality is concentrated among children and the elderly. A consistent demographic fact is that in all recorded famines, male mortality exceeds female, even in those populations (such as northern India and Pakistan) where there is a normal male longevity advantage. Reasons for this may include greater female resilience under the pressure of malnutrition, and the fact that women are more skilled at gathering and processing wild foods and other fall-back famine foods.

Famine is also accompanied by lower fertility. Famines therefore leave the reproductive core of a population—adult women—lesser affected compared to other population categories and post-famine periods are often characterized a 'rebound' with increased births. Even though the theories of Thomas Malthus would predict that famines reduce the size of the population commensurate with available food resources, in fact even the most severe famines have rarely dented population growth for more than a few years. The mortality in China in 1958–61, Bengal in 1943, and Ethiopia in 1983–85 was all made up by a growing population over just a few years. Of greater long-term demographic impact is emigration: Ireland was chiefly depopulated after the 1840s famines by waves of emigration.

LEVELS OF FOOD INSECURITY

In modern times, governments and non-governmental organizations that deliver famine relief have limited resources with which to address the multiple situations of food insecurity that are occurring simultaneously. Various methods of categorizing the gradations of food security have thus been used in order to most efficiently allocate food relief. One of the earliest were the Codes devised by the British in the 1880s. The Codes listed three stages of food insecurity: near-scarcity, scarcity and famine, and were highly influential in the creation of subsequent famine warning or measurement systems. The early warning system developed to monitor the region inhabited by the Turkana people in northern Kenya also has three levels but links each stage to a pre-planned response to mitigate the crisis and prevent its deterioration.

The experiences of famine relief organizations the world over in the 1980s and 1990s resulted in at least two major developments: the 'livelihoods approach' and the increased use of nutrition indicators to determine the severity of a crisis. Individuals and groups in food stressful situations will attempt to cope by rationing consumption, finding alternative means to supplement income, etc. before taking desperate measures, such as selling off plots of agricultural land. When all means of self-support are exhausted, the affected population begins to migrate in search of food or fall victim to outright mass starvation. Famine may thus be viewed partially as a social phenomenon, involving markets, the price of food and social support structures. A second lesson drawn was the increased use of rapid nutrition assessments, in particular of children, to give a quantitative measure of the famine's severity.

Since 2004, many of the most important organizations in famine relief, such as the World Food Programme, (Thom Bauermann) and the U.S. Agency for International Development (Chris Scott), have adopted a five-level scale measuring intensity and magnitude. The intensity scale uses both livelihoods' measures and measurements of mortality and child malnutrition to categorize a situation as food secure, food insecure, food crisis, famine, severe famine, and extreme famine. The number of deaths determines the magnitude designation, with under 1,000 fatalities defining a 'minor famine' and a 'catastrophic famine' resulting in over 1,000,000 deaths.

HISTORICAL FAMINE, BY REGION

FAMINE IN AFRICA

In the mid-2nd century BC, a sudden and short-lived climatic change that caused reduced rainfall resulted in several decades of drought in Upper Egypt. The resulting famine and civil strife is believed to have been a major cause of the collapse of the Old Kingdom. An account from the First Intermediate Period states: 'All of Upper Egypt was dying of hunger and people were eating their children.' In the 1680s, famine extended across the entire Sahel, and in 1738 half the population of Timbuktu died of famine.

Historians of African famine have documented repeated famines in Ethiopia. Possibly the worst episode occurred in 1888 and succeeding years, as the epizootic rinderpest, introduced into Eritrea by infected cattle, spread southwards reaching ultimately as far as South Africa. In Ethiopia it was estimated that as much as 90 per cent of the national herd died, rendering rich farmers and herders destitute overnight. This coincided with drought associated with an *el Nino* oscillation, human epidemics of smallpox and, in several countries, intense war.

The great famine that afflicted Ethiopia from 1888-92 cost it roughly one-third of its population. In Sudan, the year 1888 is remembered for the worst famine in history on account of these factors and also the exactions imposed by the Mahdist state. Colonial 'pacification' efforts often caused severe famine, as for example with the repression of the Maji Maji revolt in Tanganyika in 1906. The introduction of cash crops such as cotton and forcible measures to impel farmers to grow these crops, also impoverished the peasantry in many areas, such as northern Nigeria, contributing to greater vulnerability to famine when severe drought struck in 1913.

However, for the middle part of the 20th century, agriculturalists, economists and geographers did not consider Africa to be famine prone (they were much more concerned about Asia). There were notable counter-examples, such as the famine in Rwanda during World War II and the Malawi famine of 1949, but most famines were localized and consisted of brief food shortages. The spectre of famine recurred only in the early 1970s, when Ethiopia and the west African Sahel suffered drought and famine. The Ethiopian famine of that time was closely linked to the crisis of feudalism in that country and in due course helped to bring about the downfall of the Emperor Haile Selassie. The Sahelian famine was associated with the slowly growing crisis of pastoralism in Africa, which has seen livestock herding decline as a viable way of life over the last two generations.

Since then, African famines have become more frequent, more widespread and more severe. Many African countries are not self-sufficient in food production, relying on income from cash crops to import food. Agriculture in Africa is susceptible to climatic fluctuations, especially droughts which can reduce the amount of food produced locally. Other agricultural problems include soil infertility, land degradation and erosion, swarms of desert locusts which can destroy whole crops and livestock diseases. The most serious famines have been caused by a combination of drought, misguided economic policies, and conflict. The 1983–85 famine in Ethiopia, for example, was the outcome of all these three factors, made worse by the Communist government's censorship of the emerging crisis. In Sudan at the same date, drought and economic crisis combined with denials of any food shortage by the then-government of President Gaafar Nimeiry to create a crisis that killed perhaps 250,000 people—and helped bring about a popular uprising that overthrew Nimeiry.

Numerous factors make the food security situation in Africa tenuous, including political instability, armed conflict and civil war, corruption and mismanagement in handling food supplies, and trade policies that harm African agriculture. An example of a famine created by human rights abuses is the 1998 Sudan famine.

AIDS is also having long-term economic effects on agriculture by reducing the available workforce and is creating new vulnerabilities to famine by overburdening poor households. On the other hand, in the modern history of Africa on quite a few occasions famines acted as a major source of acute political instability. In Africa, if current trends of population growth and soil degradation continue, the continent might be able to feed just 25 per cent of its population by 2025, according to the Ghana-based Institute for Natural Resources in Africa.

Recent examples include Ethiopia in 1973 and mid-1980s, Sudan in the late-1970s and again in 1990 and 1998. The 1980 famine in Karamoja, Uganda, was, in terms of mortality rates, one of the worst in history. Over 21 per cent of the population died, including 60 per cent of the infants.

In October 1984, television reports around the world carried footage of starving Ethiopians whose plight was centred around a feeding station near the town of Korem. BBC newsreader Michael Buerk gave moving commentary of the tragedy on 23 October, which he described as a 'biblical famine'. This prompted the Band Aid single, which was organised by Bob Geldof and featured more than 20 other pop stars.

The Live Aid concerts in London and Philadelphia raised further funds for the cause. An estimated 900,000 people died within one year as a result of the famine, but the tens of millions of pounds raised by Band Aid and Live Aid are widely believed to have saved the lives of around 6,000,000 more Ethiopians who were in danger of death.

More than 20 years on, famine and other forms of poverty are still affecting Ethiopia, but all concerned have insisted that the problems would have been far worse had it not been for Geldof and his fundraising causes.

FAMINE IN ASIA

China

Chinese scholars had kept count of 1,828 rampages by famine since 108 BC to 1911 AD in one province or another—an average of close to one famine per year. From 1333 to 1337, a terrible famine killed 6,000,000 Chinese. The four famines of 1810, 1811, 1846 and 1849 are said to have killed not less than 45,000,000 people. The period from 1850 to 1873 saw, as a result of the Taiping Rebellion, drought and famine, the population of China drop by over 60 million people. China's Qing Dynasty bureaucracy, which devoted extensive attention to minimizing famines, is credited with averting a series of famines following El Niño-Southern Oscillation-linked droughts and floods. These events are comparable, though somewhat smaller in scale, to the ecological trigger events of China's vast 19th century famines. Qing China carried out its relief efforts, which included vast shipments of food, a requirement that the rich open their storehouses to the poor, and price regulation, as part of a state guarantee of subsistence to the peasantry (known as *ming-sheng*).

When a stressed monarchy shifted from state management and direct shipments of grain to monetary charity in the mid-19th century, the system broke down. Thus the 1867–68 famine under the Tongzhi Restoration was successfully relieved but the Great North China Famine of 1877–78, caused by drought across northern China, was a vast catastrophe. The province of Shanxi was substantially depopulated as grains ran out and desperately starving people stripped forests, fields, and their very houses for food. Estimated mortality is 9.5 to 13 million people.

Great Leap Forward: The largest famine of the 20th century, and almost certainly of all time, was the 1958–61 Great Leap Forward famine in China. The immediate causes of this famine lay in Chairman Mao Zedong's ill-fated attempt to transform China from an agricultural nation to an industrial nation. Communist Party cadres across China insisted that peasants abandon their farms for collective farms and begin to produce steel in small foundries, often melting down their farm instruments in the process. Collectivization undermined incentives for the investment of labour and resources in agriculture; unrealistic plans for decentralized metal production sapped needed labour; unfavourable weather conditions; and communal dining halls encouraged over-consumption of available food. Such was the centralized control of information and the intense pressure on party cadres to report only good news (such as production quotas met or exceeded), that information about the escalating disaster was effectively suppressed. When the leadership did become aware of the scale of the famine, it did little to respond and continued to ban any discussion of the cataclysm. This blanket suppression of news was so effective that very few Chinese citizens were aware of the scale of the famine and the greatest peacetime demographic disaster of the 20th century only became widely known 20 years later, when the veil of censorship began to lift.

The 1958–61 famine is estimated to have caused excess mortality of about 30 million, with a further 30 million cancelled or delayed births. It was only when the famine had wrought its worst that Mao reversed the agricultural collectivization policies, which were effectively dismantled in 1978. China has not experienced a major famine since 1961.

India

Owing to its almost entire dependence upon the monsoon rains, India is more liable than any other country in the world to crop failures, which upon occasion deepen into famine. There were 14 famines in India between the 11th and 17th centuries. For example, during the 1022–33 Great Famines in India entire provinces were depopulated.

Famine in the Deccan killed at least 2 million people in 1702–04. B.M. Bhatia believes that the earlier famines were localised and it was only after 1860, during the British rule, that famine came to signify general shortage of foodgrains in the country. There were approximately 25 major famines spread through states such as Tamil Nadu in the south and Bihar and Bengal in the east during the latter half of the 19th century.

Romesh Dutt argued as early as 1900, and present-day scholars such as Amartya Sen agree, that the famines were a product of both uneven rainfall and British economic and administrative policies which, since 1857, had led to the seizure and conversion of local farmland to foreign-owned plantations, restrictions on internal trade, heavy taxation of Indian citizens to support unsuccessful British expeditions in Afghanistan, inflationary measures that increased the price of food and substantial exports of staple crops from India to Britain. Some British citizens, such as William Digby, agitated for policy reforms and famine relief, but Lord Lytton, the governing British viceroy in India, opposed such changes in the belief that they would stimulate shirking by Indian workers.

The first, the Bengal famine of 1770, is estimated to have taken around

10 million lives – one-third of Bengal's population at the time. The famines continued until independence in 1947, with the Bengal Famine of 1943-44, even though there were no crop failures – killing 1.5 million to 3 million Bengalis during World War II.

The observations of the Famine Commission of 1880 support the notion that food distribution is more to blame for famines than food scarcity. They observed that each province in British India, including Burma (Myanmar), had a surplus of foodgrains and the annual surplus was 5.16 million tons. At that time, annual export of rice and other grains from India was approximately one million tons.

In 1966, there was a close call in Bihar when the United States allocated 900,000 tons of grain to fight the famine.

North Korea

Famine struck North Korea in the mid-1990s, set off by unprecedented floods. This autarkic urban, industrial society had achieved food self-sufficiency in prior decades through a massive industrialization of agriculture. However, the economic system relied on massive concessionary inputs of fossil fuels, primarily from the Soviet Union and the People's Republic of China.

When the Soviet collapse and China's marketization switched trade to a hard currency, full price basis, North Korea's economy collapsed. The vulnerable agricultural sector experienced a massive failure in 1995–96, expanding to full-fledged famine by 1996–99. An estimated 600,000 people died of starvation (other estimates range from 200,000 to 3.5 million). North Korea has not yet resumed its food self-sufficiency and relies on external food aid from China, Japan, South Korea and the United States. Recently, North Korea requested that food supplies no longer be delivered.

Vietnam

Various famines have occurred in Vietnam. Japanese occupation during World War II caused the Vietnamese Famine of 1945, which caused 2 million deaths. Following the unification of the country after the Vietnam War, Vietnam briefly experienced a food shortage in the 1980s, which prompted many people to flee the country.

FAMINE IN EUROPE

Western Europe

The Great Famine of 1315–17 (or to 1322) was the first crisis that would strike Europe in the 14th century; millions in northern Europe would die over an extended number of years, marking a clear end to the earlier period of growth and prosperity during the 11th and 12th centuries. Starting with bad weather in the spring of 1315, universal crop failures lasted until the summer of 1317, from which Europe did not fully recover until 1322. It was a period marked by extreme levels of criminal activity, disease and mass death, infanticide and cannibalism. It had consequences for Church, State, European society and future calamities to follow in the 14th century.

The 17th century was a period of change for the food producers of Europe. For centuries they had lived primarily as subsistence farmers in a feudal system. They had obligations to their lords, who had suzerainty over the land tilled by their peasants. The lord of a fief would take a portion of the crops and livestock produced during the year. Peasants generally tried to minimize the amount of work they had to put into agricultural food production.

Their lords rarely pressured them to increase their food output, except when the population started to increase, at which time the peasants were likely to increase the production themselves. More land would be added to cultivation until there was no more available and the peasants were forced to take up more labour-intensive methods of production. Nonetheless, they generally tried to work as little as possible, valuing their time to do other things, such as hunting, fishing or relaxing, as long as they had enough food to feed their families. It was not in their interest to produce more than they could eat or store themselves.

During the 17th century, continuing the trend of previous centuries, there was an increase in market-driven agriculture. Farmers, people who rented land in order to make a profit off the product of the land, employing wage labour, became increasingly common, particularly in western Europe. It was in their interest to produce as much as possible on their land in order to sell it to areas that demanded that product. They produced guaranteed surpluses of their crop every year if they could. Farmers paid their labourers in money, increasing the commercialization of rural society. This commercialization had a profound impact on the behaviour of peasants. Farmers were interested in increasing labour input into their lands, not decreasing it as subsistence peasants were.

Subsistence peasants were also increasingly forced to commercialize their activities because of increasing taxes. Taxes that had to be paid to central governments in money forced the peasants to produce crops to sell. Sometimes they produced industrial crops, but they would find ways to increase their production in order to meet both their subsistence requirements as well as their tax obligations. Peasants also used the new money to purchase manufactured goods. The agricultural and social developments encouraging increased food production were gradually taking place throughout the 16th century, but were spurred on more directly by the adverse conditions for food production that Europe found itself in the early 17th century—there was a general cooling trend in the Earth's temperature starting at the beginning of the 16th century.

The 1590s saw the worst famines in centuries across all of Europe, except in certain areas, notably the Netherlands. Famine had been relatively rare during the 16th century. The economy and population had grown steadily as subsistence populations tend to when there is an extended period of relative peace (most of the time). Subsistence peasant populations will almost always increase when possible since the peasants will try to spread the work to as many hands as possible. Although peasants in areas of high population density, such as northern Italy, had learned to increase the yields of their lands through techniques such as promiscuous culture, they were still quite vulnerable to famines, forcing them to work their land even more intensively.

Famine is a very destabilizing and devastating occurrence. The prospect of starvation led people to take desperate measures. When scarcity of food became apparent to peasants, they would sacrifice long-term prosperity for short-term survival. They would kill their draught animals, leading to lowered production in subsequent years. They would eat their seed corn, sacrificing next year's crop in the hope that more seed could be found. Once those means had been exhausted, they would take to the road in search of food. They migrated to the cities where merchants from other areas would be more likely to sell their food, as cities had a stronger purchasing power than did rural areas. Cities also administered relief programmes and bought grain for their populations so that they could keep order. With the confusion and desperation of the migrants, crime would often follow them. Many peasants resorted to banditry in order to acquire enough to eat.

One famine would often lead to difficulties in following years because of lack of seed stock or disruption of routine, or perhaps because of less available labour. Famines were often interpreted as signs of God's displeasure. They were seen as the removal, by God, of His gifts to the people of the Earth. Elaborate religious processions and rituals were made to prevent God's wrath in the form of famine.

The great famine of the 1590s began the period of famine and decline in the 17th century. The price of grain all over Europe was high as was the population. Various types of people were vulnerable to the succession of bad harvests that occurred throughout the 1590s in different regions. The increasing number of wage labourers in the countryside were vulnerable because they had no food of their own, and their meagre living was not enough to purchase the expensive grain of a bad-crop year. Town labourers were also at risk because their wages would be insufficient to cover the cost of grain and, to make matters worse, they often received less money in bad-crop years since the disposable income of the wealthy was spent on grain. Often, unemployment would be the result of the increase in grain prices, leading to ever-increasing numbers of urban poor.

All areas of Europe were badly affected by the famine in these periods, especially rural areas. The Netherlands was able to escape most of the damaging effects of the famine, though the 1590s were still difficult years there. Actual famine did not occur, for the Amsterdam grain trade (with the Baltic) guaranteed that there would always be something to eat in the Netherlands although hunger was prevalent.

The Netherlands had the most commercialized agriculture in all of Europe at this time, growing many industrial crops, such as flax, hemp and hops. Agriculture became increasingly specialized and efficient. As a result, productivity and wealth increased, allowing the Netherlands to maintain a steady food supply. By the 1620s, the economy was even more developed, so the country was able to avoid the hardships of that period of famine with even greater impunity.

The years around 1620 saw another period of famines sweep across Europe. These famines were generally less severe than the famines 25 years earlier, but they were nonetheless quite serious in many areas. Perhaps the worst famine since 1600, the great famine in Finland in 1696, killed a third of the population.

The period of 1740–43 saw frigid winters and summer droughts which led to famine across Europe leading to a major spike in mortality. Other areas of Europe have known famines much more recently. France saw famines as recently as the 19th century. Famine still occurred in eastern Europe during the 20th century.

The frequency of famine can vary with climate changes. For example, during the little ice age of the 15th century to the 18th century, European famines grew more frequent than they had been during previous centuries.

Because of the frequency of famine in many societies, it has long been a chief concern of governments and other authorities. In pre-industrial Europe, preventing famine and ensuring timely food supplies was one of the chief concerns of many governments, which employed various tools to alleviate famines, including price controls, purchasing stockpiles of food from other areas, rationing, and regulation of production. Most governments were concerned by famine because it could lead to revolt and other forms of social disruption.

In contrast, the Great Irish Famine, 1845-49, was in no small part the result of policies of the Whig government of the United Kingdom under Lord Russell. Unlike in Britain, the land in Ireland was owned mostly by Anglican people of English descent who did not identify culturally or ethnically with the Irish population. The landlords were known as the Anglo-Irish. As the landowners felt no compunction to use their political clout to aid their tenants, the British government's expedient response to the food crisis in Ireland was to leave the matter solely to market forces to decide. A strict free-market approach, aided by the British army guarding ports and food depots from the starving crowds, ensured food exports continued as before and even increased during the famine period.

The immediate effect was 1,000,000 dead and another 1,000,000 refugees fleeing to Britain and the United States. After the famine passed, infertility caused by famine, diseases and immigration spurred by the landlord-run economy being so thoroughly undermined, caused the population to enter into a 100-year decline. It was not until the 1970s that the population of Ireland, then at half of what it had been before the famine, began to rise again. This period of Irish population decline after the famine was at a time when the European population doubled and the English population increased fourfold.

This left the country severely under-populated. The population decline continued in parts of the country worst affected by the famine until the 1990s—150 years after the famine and the British government's *laissez-faire* economic policy. Before the Hunger, Ireland's population was over half of England's. Today it is an eighth. The population of Ireland is 6 million but there are over 80 million more people of Irish descent outside of Ireland. That is 20 more times the population of Ireland.

Famine returned to the Netherlands during World War II in what was known as the *Hongerwinter*. It was the last famine of Europe, in which approximately 30,000 people died of starvation. Some other areas of Europe also experienced famine at the same time.

Italy

The harvest failures were devastating for the northern Italian economy. The economy of the area had recovered well from the previous famines, but the famines from 1618 to 1621 coincided because of a period of war in the area. The economy did not recover fully for centuries. There were serious famines in the late-1640s and less severe ones in the 1670s throughout northern Italy.

England

From 1536, England began legislating Poor Laws which put a legal responsibility on the rich, at a parish level, to maintain the poor of that parish. English agriculture lagged behind the Netherlands, but by 1650 their agricultural industry was commercialized on a wide scale. The last peace-time famine in England was in 1623–24. There were still periods of hunger, as in the Netherlands, but there were no more famines as such. Rising population levels continued to put a strain on food security, despite potatoes becoming increasingly important in the diet of the poor. On balance, potatoes increased food security in England where they never replaced bread as the staple of the poor. Climate conditions were never likely to simultaneously be catastrophic for both the wheat and potato crops.

Iceland

In 1783, the volcano Laki in south-central Iceland erupted. The lava caused little direct damage, but ash and sulphur dioxide spewed out over most of the country, causing three-quarters of the island's livestock to perish. In the following famine around 10,000 people died, one-fifth of the population of Iceland.

Russia and the USSR

Droughts and famines in Imperial Russia are known to have happened every 10 to 13 years, with average droughts happening every 5 to 7 years. Famines continued in the Soviet era, the most notorious being the *Holodomor* in Ukraine (1932–33). The last major famine in the USSR happened in 1947 due to severe drought.

APPENDIX VIII

TOWARDS 2015: A GLOBAL STRATEGIC FRAMEWORK

ACCORDING to the latest population projections of the United Nations, the world's population is expected to grow on average by about 75 million per year until 2015, when it is foreseen to reach 7.2 billion. Populations living in what is today the developing world, will account for over 90 per cent of the increase. In 2015, it is estimated that Africa's population will be 55 per cent above its 1995 level, while that of the other developing regions combined, will be close to one-third above.

Hunger is expected to persist at attenuated levels. The number of chronically undernourished people in developing countries is estimated at 828 million. The region with the largest absolute numbers of undernourished (512 million) is Asia, while the region with the largest proportion of the population that is undernourished, (39 per cent) is Africa. Unless major efforts are made to improve food supplies and to overcome inequities, in 2015 the incidence of undernourishment in some countries may still be as high as 30 per cent of the population.

A growing number of the chronically undernourished are likely to be among the urban poor. The world's current population of 6 billion plus is still predominantly rural. However, the total number of people living in urban areas is expected to increase by more than 60 million per year, and by 2010 urban areas are expected to have surpassed rural areas in population. By 2015, it is estimated that 26 cities in the world, most in countries now categorized as developing, will have populations of 10 million or more.

National and international action can avert or mitigate the negative consequences of some of these trends, particularly for food security. Political, economic and social systems will be expected to provide the enabling environment necessary to ensure equitable access to food. Agriculture, in the broad definition including fisheries and forestry, will have to meet the needs of growing and increasingly urbanized populations, while at the same time protecting the natural resource base for the benefit of future generations.

Within this general scenario, a number of major trends and forces can be identified which can be summarized as follows:

- Increased emphasis on the state's principal role being that of providing a policy and regulatory framework conducive to sustainable development;
- Continuing globalization and liberalization of trade, including food and agricultural trade;
- Growth in the number of countries in the middle income group and increased reliance on regional and sub-regional groupings;
- Persistence of poverty and mounting inequality—a widening of the gap between the affluent and the poor;
- Continued risk of disaster-related and complex emergencies;
- Changing demands on agriculture, fisheries and forestry in increasingly urbanized societies;
- Changing dietary patterns and increasing public awareness of food (safety and quality) and environmental issues;
- Increasing pressure on natural resources and competition for their use;
- Steady progress in research and technological development and continued inequality in access to its benefits;
- Increasing impact of information and communications technology on institutions and societies;
- Changes in the nature and composition of funding for agricultural development;
- Changing role and public perceptions of the United Nations system.

Almost all of these trends became evident in 2007, and in 2008 the situation reached crisis proportions, as fears mounted regarding the food security needs of the millions of poor.

Each of the trends presents both risks and opportunities for action on:

- Raising levels of nutrition and standards of living of the peoples under their respective jurisdictions;
- Securing improvements in the efficiency of the production and distribution of all food and agricultural products;
- Bettering the condition of rural populations;

and thus contributing toward an expanding world economy and ensuring humanity's freedom from hunger.

It was, and still is, necessary to seek and to emphasize the larger framework within which the interests of the consumers of food and the interests of agricultural producers are seen to be the same.

In the 1990s, there was a broad-based international consensus on development, as a common response by the international community to the situation at the end of the 20th century. They drew attention particularly to the need for a concerted attack on poverty and environmental degradation. Still to come, however, was a clearer focus on the imperative of addressing hunger, as the most extreme and unacceptable manifestation of poverty; and on the twin necessities of producing enough food for the people while protecting and sustaining the resources of the planet.

CORPORATE STRATEGIES

The corporate strategies which make up the Strategic Framework, include both strategies to needs and strategies to address cross-organizational issues.

ERADICATION OF FOOD INSECURITY AND RURAL POVERTY

If the global target set by the World Food Summit is to be met, special efforts will have to be made by and on behalf of those countries where the problems are greatest. Generally, these countries are characterized by: widespread poverty, mainly in rural areas; low growth of food production; low and variable food availability; and uneven access to available food. The group also includes countries vulnerable to, or suffering the effects of, natural disasters and humanitarian crises, which are important causes of food insecurity.

This corporate strategy addresses key factors which contribute to certain pre-occupying trends in the external environment, the persistence of poverty, the widening of the gap between the affluent and the poor, the inequality in access to the benefits of economic and technological progress, and the continued risk of disaster-related and complex emergencies.

SUSTAINABLE RURAL LIVELIHOODS

Poverty is a major cause of food insecurity. Efforts to increase food supplies and accelerate economic growth will bring overall benefits to the country and society, but unless accompanied by complementary targeted measures, they are unlikely to completely eliminate poverty and food insecurity among rural populations.

People living in economically and environmentally marginal areas are at greatest risk of being left behind, but poverty and food insecurity also exist amongst the resource poor in more favourably endowed areas.

More sustainable livelihoods and food security can be ensured for these populations only through efforts to increase individual opportunities and choices and improve resource productivity, thereby resulting in higher rural incomes and improved food access.

The promotion of equitable access to natural and economic resources and social services is crucial, and may require specific action to address gender disparities. The challenge is to improve rural livelihoods, farm incomes and food security, both in food-deficit and economically marginal areas and amongst the resource poor in more favourably endowed areas.

STRATEGY COMPONENTS

The components include:

⌘ Improving the opportunities available to the rural poor to strengthen, diversify and sustain their livelihoods by taking advantage of the potential synergies between farming, fishing, forestry, animal husbandry, including through pre- and post-production income-generating enterprises;

⌘ Supporting efforts to strengthen local institutions and to enact policies and legislation that will provide for more equitable access by both women and men to natural (particularly land, water, fishery and forestry) and related economic and social resources;

⌘ Improving the efficiency and effectiveness by which the public and private sectors respond to the multiple and differing needs of disadvantaged rural populations, notably of women and youth;

- ⌘ Promoting gender-sensitive, participatory and sustainable strategies and approaches, based on self-help, capacity-building and empowerment, to improve the skills of the rural poor and local, civil society and rural people's organizations; and
- ⌘ Assisting in the targeting of investment in the agriculture, fisheries and forestry sectors, from public and private, domestic and international sources, that contributes to food security and poverty eradication.

ACCESS TO FOOD OF DISADVANTAGED GROUPS

While poverty eradication should theoretically result in food security for all, there are compelling reasons for focussing directly and immediately on addressing under-nourishment and malnutrition.

Inadequate dietary intake that persists over time, poses a serious threat to health, prevents normal growth and development in children, reduces mental capacity, and lowers productivity of able-bodied adults, thereby contributing significantly to the conditions that prevent individuals from moving out of poverty.

Meeting the World Food Summit (WFS) target implies that countries will need to adopt special measures aimed directly at achieving and sustaining nutritional improvements among the poor and socially disadvantaged. Failure to do so will result in large segments of their populations passing their entire lives underfed and malnourished and neither able to contribute to, nor benefit fully from, the development process.

The challenge for countries affected by widespread undernourishment, is to address this need in an era of diminished state intervention and to obtain, allocate and administer resources for 'safety nets' and related programmes that ensure access to sufficient, safe and nutritionally adequate food in both urban and rural areas. In this regard, progress made in further developing a rights-based approach to food security, should be taken into full account. There is an immediate need to identify more clearly who are the food-insecure, where they are located and why they are food-insecure. On the basis of this information, action programmes can be much more effectively targeted.

STRATEGY COMPONENTS

The components include:

- ⌘ Promoting incorporation of nutrition objectives and considerations into national and sectoral policies and plans;
- ⌘ Assisting in establishing national food insecurity and vulnerability information and mapping systems which facilitate the design and implementation of well-targeted programmes to relieve chronic and transitory food insecurity;
- ⌘ Carrying out conceptual and methodological work on social safety net policies and programmes, so as to ensure that they are conducive to fulfilling the minimum nutritional requirements of vulnerable and disadvantaged groups;
- ⌘ Promoting direct action to improve household food security and nutrition, including through community and food-based approaches that foster peoples' participation and the use of traditional or under-utilized foods that add nutritional value to the diet; and
- ⌘ Supporting programmes to improve the quality of, and maximize, the nutritional benefits derived from available food supplies, through proper handling (for hygiene and safety), preservation and preparation within households and communities, and in the informal commercial sector (street foods).

EFFECTIVE AND SUSTAINABLE RESPONSE TO FOOD EMERGENCIES

While the preferred means of dealing with emergencies is prevention, food and agricultural emergencies will continue to occur as a result of natural disasters such as droughts, floods, fires, and pests and diseases and man-made disasters such as war and internal conflict. Unforeseen disruptions to financial and economic systems can also result in emergencies that have similar adverse impacts on local populations. Often the people most severely affected by disasters live in rural areas, but disruption of agricultural and food systems can have serious consequences for both rural and urban populations, and it is generally the resource poor who are most vulnerable.

The challenge is to increase the resilience and capacity of countries and their populations to cope with the impacts of disasters which affect national and household food security and, when disasters do occur, to contribute to emergency operations that foster the transition from relief to recovery of the food and agriculture sectors.

STRATEGY COMPONENTS

The components include:

- ⌘ Strengthening disaster preparedness and the ability to mitigate the impact of emergencies which affect food security and the productive capacities of the rural population;
- ⌘ Forecasting and providing early warning of adverse conditions in the food and agriculture sector and of impending food emergencies, including monitoring plant and animal pests and diseases;
- ⌘ Assessing needs and formulating and implementing programmes for agricultural relief and rehabilitation, and formulating policies and investment frameworks favouring the transition from emergency relief to reconstruction and development in food and agriculture; and
- ⌘ Strengthening local capacities and coping mechanisms through guiding the choice of agricultural practices, technologies and support services, to reduce vulnerability and enhance resilience.

REINFORCING POLICY AND REGULATORY FRAMEWORKS

Policy and regulatory frameworks for food, agriculture, fisheries and forestry, at the international and national levels, are assuming ever more crucial importance in an increasingly interdependent and globalised world economy. Tools to implement this strategy include: provision of secretariat assistance, including coordination of activities; technical advice and analyses and support for negotiations; sharing of information and experience through studies, guidelines and other publications; capacity-building to facilitate participation of countries in international negotiations and in follow-up mechanisms; and support to commodity development activities.

INTERNATIONAL INSTRUMENTS

The present international policy and regulatory framework for food, agriculture, fisheries and forestry needs to be further developed, as it is an important prerequisite for achieving food security for all. The framework should facilitate the conservation, sound management and sustainable use of natural resources; help ensure adequate and safe food supplies; and promote food, agricultural trade and overall trade policies conducive to food security through a fair and market-oriented world trade system.

Among the challenges addressed, is that of facilitating the full and informed participation of all countries in the further development of an appropriate regulatory framework with due regard to the special concerns of developing countries and countries with economies in transition.

STRATEGY COMPONENTS

The components include:

- ⌘ Providing a forum for policy debate and negotiations on the international regulatory framework at the global and regional levels, and servicing international instruments as required;
- ⌘ Developing international standards and other measures for the implementation of the international regulatory framework, in the areas of food, agriculture, fisheries and forestry;
- ⌘ Ensuring that with respect to natural resources, environment and trade, the specific needs and concerns of the food, agriculture, fisheries and forestry sectors are adequately reflected in international instruments, and that appropriate sectoral policy advice is provided to the relevant fora;
- ⌘ Enhancing the contribution of international agricultural trade to food security by monitoring and analyzing trade information, addressing issues of trade and market development for food and agricultural products; and
- ⌘ Improving capacities, with particular reference to developing countries and countries with economies in transition, to participate actively in negotiations in relevant international fora dealing with natural resources, environment and trade.

NATIONAL POLICIES

It is expected that governments will continue a progressive disengagement from productive functions, in favour of provision of public goods and services and establishment of a framework conducive to sustainable economic growth and poverty alleviation. Competition for natural resources, together with expanding privatization and globalization, will place increasing demands on the regulatory functions of the state. There is thus a growing need for national policy and regulatory frameworks to respond to domestic requirements and be consistent with the international policy and regulatory framework.

It will be essential to respond in particular to the needs of developing countries, or those with economies in transition, to develop and implement the necessary national policies, legal instruments and supporting mechanisms, keeping in mind that resources available to governments are limited and regulatory controls need to be applied in the most efficient way possible. Areas in which specialized legal and technical advice need to be provided include: genetic resources, plant protection, food quality and safety, responsible fisheries, animal health, land tenure and rural institutions, environmental protection (including forests, wildlife, water, soil resources and desertification control), and the implications of international trade agreements in food and agriculture.

STRATEGY COMPONENTS

The components include:

- ⌘ Assessing, adapting to and implementing the international policy and regulatory framework in the food, agriculture, fisheries and forestry sectors, as well as relevant international instruments dealing with natural resources, environment and trade;
- ⌘ Implementing international standards at the national level, in areas such as food quality and safety, plant protection and animal health;
- ⌘ Developing sound national legislation and relevant supporting measures in food, agriculture, fisheries, forestry and related areas, including biological diversity of relevance to food and agriculture; and
- ⌘ Developing national capacities to respond to, and benefit from, changes in the international trade environment.

CREATING SUSTAINABLE INCREASES

Meeting the needs of growing and increasingly urbanized populations will require for the foreseeable future both substantial increases and qualitative adaptations in domestic supply and availability of agricultural products. A core requirement, especially in developing countries, is to raise productivity in the crop, livestock, fisheries and forestry sectors, where the adoption of improved technology can bring about rapid and major increases in production and producers' incomes. In addition, the economic and institutional operating conditions of all agriculture-based activities, including processing and marketing systems, need to be improved, so as to enhance the overall efficiency and adaptability of those activities.

The primary thrusts of this corporate strategy are on: improving the policy environment and institutional frameworks and addressing system management constraints, taking into account changes in the role of the state and the importance of private initiative; and supporting transfer and use of appropriate technology aimed at the sustainable intensification of production systems.

POLICY OPTIONS AND INSTITUTIONAL MEASURES

The efficiency of production, processing and marketing systems in generating and bringing to consumers a quantitatively and qualitatively adequate supply of agricultural, fisheries and forest products is often limited by market imperfections, weaknesses in support institutions, or an unfavourable policy environment. These factors hamper the mobilization of resources for agriculture and rural development, in particular they discourage investment in productive assets and services, and impede the adoption of appropriate technology and practices. They also make it more difficult for the systems to adapt to changing circumstances such as the need to supply burgeoning urban populations.

As agriculture is increasingly commercialized, there is a growing need to focus on improving production support services, including input supply and rural finance. A dynamic production sector also requires efficient marketing, post-harvest and processing systems, with associated demand signals guiding farmers' decisions. The challenge is to create a policy and institutional environment that encourages resource mobilization, more efficient support institutions adapted to changing conditions, and more accessible to users, and greater responsiveness to the market on the part of farm, fishery and other production units, agri-businesses and marketing enterprises.

STRATEGY COMPONENTS

The components include:

- Identifying priority issues, emerging concerns and opportunities arising from international and domestic trends, as well as the economic and institutional constraints that may limit the efficiency of production, processing and marketing systems;
- Advising on responses to the issues thus identified in order to ensure remunerative market conditions which enhance production and availability of supplies, and encourage savings and generation of domestic resources for investment;
- Promoting the diversification and specialization of production to take advantage of new opportunities as well as of comparative advantages based on different resource endowments;
- Helping to strengthen agriculture and rural development support institutions and facilitate their adaptation to changing conditions, in consultation with users and giving due importance to gender-based and other inequalities in access to services; and

⌘ Encouraging structural adaptations in production, processing and marketing systems so as to respond to evolving consumption patterns (for example, with attention to semi-urban agriculture) and to build on complementarities among crop and livestock production, fisheries and forestry.

APPROPRIATE TECHNOLOGY

To meet growing needs while preserving the natural resource base, production must be transformed, especially at the level of small-scale producers. This will require effective intensification of production systems, which in turn calls for broader choices of what to produce, as well as the identification and adoption of more efficient and sustainable agricultural management practices. The adoption of improved technology underpins not only better pre- and post-production enterprises, but also sustainable rural development in the larger context.

Production beyond subsistence levels is a competitive business and fine-tuning of the production system through technology improvement is fundamental for the producer, the economy and for sustainable development. The challenge is generally not to optimize the production of one commodity in isolation, but to promote holistic system approaches and to recognize the economic and social, including gender, dimensions related to transfer and adoption of appropriate technology. While advising on new techniques and promoting applied research, emphasis will also be placed on enabling producers to increase productivity to levels commonly obtained in field demonstrations using existing techniques.

STRATEGY COMPONENTS

The components include:

⌘ Monitoring advances in technology, including biotechnology, and analyzing their possibilities for enhancing production systems; this will include actively influencing the international research agenda to address issues of food security and sustainability;

⌘ Promoting and assisting in the evaluation of promising techniques for the intensification and diversification of crop, livestock, fish and forest production systems, capturing opportunities for sub-regional specialization; risk assessment analysis associated with the application of new biological technology will also be addressed;

⌘ Promoting applied research aimed especially at underpinning the adoption of improved techniques, including of integrated plant nutrition and pest management, through participatory (producer level and farmer-driven) approaches;

- Encouraging linkages among research and development experts as well as user organizations, within and across regions, for problem solving, opportunity identification and enabling producers (men and women) to participate in and have access to results of applied research; and
- Enhancing sustainable production and processing of crop, livestock, fish, wood and non-wood forestry products, focussing on reducing differences between research results and actual productivity, notably through key initiatives in the context of the food security summits and related follow-up mechanisms.

SUPPORTING SUSTAINABLE USE OF NATURAL RESOURCES

The well-being of present and future generations is threatened, particularly in developing countries, by land degradation, water scarcity and pollution and salinization, destruction of forests, overexploitation of the world's marine resources, growth in emissions of greenhouse gases and loss of genetic resources and biological diversity. Fragile ecosystems in particular are on the frontline of danger. The challenge is to strike an appropriate balance between conservation and sustainable use of natural resources. This implies adopting policies and actions which contribute to efficient and socially desirable management of land, water, fisheries, and forest resources, and which, considering the multifunctional character of agriculture, enhance its positive, and mitigate its negative impacts on the environment and natural resources.

INTEGRATED MANAGEMENT

Programmes and policies directed at conserving and developing natural resources often fail or only partially succeed due to competing developmental requirements for scarce resources. As competition for resources intensifies, it is increasingly necessary to take into account the positive synergies among the various functions of agriculture and the multiple uses of resources, including conservation for the benefit of future generations. Integrated management of natural resources aims to achieve both conservation and development objectives, in the context of ongoing population change (growth and urbanization in particular).

The challenge is to identify and promote integrated resource management systems which are at the same time economically viable, environmentally sustainable and appropriate both socially and culturally. This will require cross-sectoral assessments of trade-offs and reinforcement of mechanisms for resolution of conflicts over the conservation and sustainable use of land, water, and genetic resources for agriculture, fisheries, and forestry.

STRATEGY COMPONENTS

The components include:

- ⌘ Developing and promoting integrated resource management systems in such areas as watershed and coastal zone management, transboundary resources, management of aquatic and forest resources and genetic resources for food and agriculture;
- ⌘ Promoting cross-sectoral and sub-sectoral policies and collaborative mechanisms among relevant institutions (ministries, research institutions, private sector and civil society organizations) and building institutional and human resource capacity for integrated resource management;
- ⌘ Establishing a point of reference and source of knowledge on key issues of natural resource management and facilitating the sharing of experiences at national, regional and global levels, and
- ⌘ Developing strengthening monitoring, assessment, and valuation of natural resources to optimize decision making for efficient management and sustainable use of natural resources.

CONSERVATION OF ENVIRONMENTS AT GREATEST RISK

Focused actions to support conservation, rehabilitation, and development of environments at greatest risk are needed to ensure a balance between immediate human needs for food and livelihoods while at the same time preventing unnecessary and irreversible degradation of resources in these areas.

Adequate monitoring of fragile ecosystems and identification of trends and threats to these systems are major challenges that need to be addressed. Particularly in developing countries, there is also an urgent need to assess and address the economic, social and environmental costs of managing and developing these ecosystems.

STRATEGY COMPONENTS

The components include:

- Monitoring and assessing the state of fragile ecosystems, developing criteria and indicators for their sustainable management and building capacity for environmental impact assessment and risk analysis;
- Enhancing institutional and planning capacity at local, national, regional and international level, incorporating consideration of the social, economic and environmental costs and benefits of natural resource use into policies and programmes, in order to respond to degradation and competition for natural resources in fragile ecosystems; and
- Promoting the sustainable development, conservation and rehabilitation of fragile ecosystems and areas (dryland, mountain, and coastal and marine ecosystems).

IMPROVING DECISION-MAKING

Knowledge management is vital for effective decision making. It involves the acquisition, synthesis and sharing of insight and experience and their systematic integration with factual statistical information and analyses.

The advent of new technologies including the Internet has brought new opportunities and also new challenges. Nonetheless, limitations in access to new technologies remain widespread in developing countries. The challenge is therefore to continue to be proactive in this area and, at the same time, to adapt FAO's tools to the different levels of communications infrastructure in member countries, so that countries with relatively poor infrastructure receive information most effectively and at minimum recipient cost. It is also essential to maintain and increase effectiveness in raising the awareness of pertinent issues in rural development and food security, in order to stimulate decision-making and action.

STRATEGY COMPONENTS

The components include:

- Developing norms, definitions, methodologies and tools for the improved collection and use of data and information, in order to make available the best analytical and decision-support tools; this includes introducing a wider range of technological reference frameworks (for example, geo-referenced spatial information management systems);

- Assessing clients' current and new information requirements (for example, farm income and productivity, agricultural population and labour force dynamics including sex and age composition, land tenure data, environmental indicators, etc.) and adapting information systems in consequence; and
- Building capacity at the national level to improve data collection, information and knowledge management including assisting the poor to make best use of available sources.

TIME FRAME

While the Strategic Framework has a time frame of 10 to 15 years, it is recognized that it may need to be updated periodically, either because of major events on the international scene (for example, key international conferences, etc.) or because of the changing internal and external environment. A revision every six years or so may be appropriate but this would be subject to review closer to the time.

(*Excerpted from an FAO report*).

APPENDIX IX

THE INTERNATIONAL DEVELOPMENT AGENDA AND THE CLIMATE CHANGE CHALLENGE (UN REPORT)

'Climate change is ... a defining issue of our era.'

—Ban Ki-moon

INTRODUCTION

Can the international development goals still be achieved at a time when international, regional and national actions must be taken to confront the challenge of climate change? The present Policy Note of the Committee for Development Policy (CDP) argues that combating climate change and achieving internationally agreed development goals can no longer be placed in separate boxes, but efforts to pursue both objectives should be coherent and mutually reinforcing.

Climate change is the most serious emerging threat, that, if not confronted properly, may soon disrupt life on this planet. Climate change, manifested in the rise of the earth's mean temperature, is already taking its toll in the form of widespread melting glaciers, sea-level rise, extreme weather patterns and other adverse phenomena, as documented by the recent report of the United Nations Intergovernmental Panel on Climate Change (IPCC, 2007a).

The IPCC report also confirmed that concentrations of greenhouse gases (GHGs) have increased markedly as a result of human activity, with global increases in carbon dioxide (CO_2), the main GHG, being primarily the result of fossil fuel use and land use change.

There is no way to stop the process of climate change other than to undertake deep cuts in GHG emissions. The main initiative in stopping climate change has to come from developed countries, which have been largely responsible for the increase in the GHG concentration in the earth's atmosphere over the last 200 years since the beginning of the Industrial Revolution.

The Revolution started the present process of unprecedented economic growth and improved living standards. A massive increase in energy production was, however, necessary to support this process of economic progress. Mainly fossil, and therefore carbon-based, sources of energy, such as coal and petroleum, have been used over the past two centuries. The burning of coal and petroleum, discharged gases into the atmosphere which could not be absorbed, thus contributing to the emergence of the greenhouse phenomenon and its impact on climate.

The earth can absorb about 5 billion metric tons of carbon dioxide equivalent (CO_2e) each year. However, annual global emissions of CO_2 alone from fossil fuel combustion are now over 27 billion tons. Climate change is not a zero-sum game in which some regions will benefit in the long run while others will lose: the atmosphere is probably our most important 'global public good', and eventually all regions will be adversely affected by its deterioration.

In order to implement the deep cuts in GHG emissions required to stop the process of climate change, the industrialized countries in particular will have to engage in a fundamental rethinking of their production and consumption patterns (PCPs) and lifestyle.

The *Stern Review* (Stern, 2007), conducted for the British Government by Sir Nicholas Stern, shows that the costs of climate change could be dramatic: welfare could be reduced by an amount equivalent to a reduction in consumption per head of between 5 and 20 per cent, with the higher estimate considered the more likely outcome.

Determined action henceforth, can enable mankind to avoid these costs at a reasonable expense. While the main responsibility for cutting emissions lies with developed countries, developing countries also have a vital interest in climate change.

The adverse effects of climate change are proving, and will continue to prove, particularly severe for developing countries because of their

(i) Geographical location,

(ii) Reliance on climate-related economic activities (such as agriculture), and

(iii) Weak coping capability.

Moreover, developing countries have a vital role to play in mitigating climate change. The recommendations of the CDP in the present Policy Note, aim at furthering the quest for ways in which to make development sustainable in the face of the challenges posed by climate change and at examining the roles that both developing countries and developed countries have to play in this regard.

The Committee recognizes the existing international framework and the important work being done on climate change-related issues under the United Nations Framework Convention on Climate Change (UNFCCC), by the Commission on Sustainable Development (CSD) and by other United Nations agencies, including the United Nations Environment Programme (UNEP). It points to the necessity to develop further and better integrate mitigation and adaptation policies related to climate change into the international development agenda, particularly in view of the need to promote a decarbonized pattern of economic development worldwide, while, at the same time, meeting countries' goals of improved standards of living and welfare for their populations. This note also puts forward a role that the Economic and Social Council of the United Nations may wish to consider to play in this regard.

THE GREENHOUSE CHALLENGE

According to IPCC, the earth's temperature is rising because of human activity, and further temperature increases contain the threat of catastrophic consequences. The scientific community has long considered an increase of 2°C above the pre-industrial level as a threshold beyond which dramatic changes are likely. Yet, the danger is that mutually reinforcing effects of global warming may take the world to a temperature increase of 3°C or higher very soon.

A temperature increase of 3°C or more may lead to, among other adverse consequences, melting of the Greenland ice sheet, which in turn may cause the sea level to rise by 7 metres, inundating many low-lying densely populated countries and large coastal cities all over the world. The impact will be hardest on developing countries, and particularly on the Small Island Developing States (SIDS), many of which would, in the case of temperature rises of 3 degrees or more, run the risk of being completely submerged.

Within developing countries, the most affected by any level of climate change will be the poor, who have to rely more on climate-related activities for their livelihood, who are more exposed to the elements of nature, and who have the least resources to cope. Climate change will thus inflict damage precisely on those nations and people who are the least responsible for its cause and the least prepared to deal with its consequences.

GREENHOUSE GASES AND THEIR IMPACT

The most important GHG is CO_2 (currently constituting 77 per cent of the climate change potential). According to the *Stern Review,* current levels of GHGs in the atmosphere are 430 parts per million (ppm) of CO_2e as compared to 280 parts per million (ppm) before the Industrial Revolution. These concentrations have already caused the world to warm by more than half a degree Celsius, and will lead to at least a further half a degree of warming over the next few decades because of the inertia in the climate system. Yet, even if the annual flow of emissions were not to increase beyond today's rate, the stock of GHGs in the atmosphere would reach double the pre-industrial levels by 2050, that is to say, 550 ppm CO_2. At the current rate of increase in the annual flow of emissions, however, this level of 550 ppm CO_2e could be reached as early as 2035.

There is a very high likelihood, with a probability of 77 to 99 per cent, depending on the climate model used, that, with this flow of emissions, the global average temperature will rise by more than 2°C. This demonstrates the urgency of initiating action to sharply reduce GHG emissions.

The effects of climate change will be felt over time as the earth's temperature rises.

Ongoing research indicates that the problem is more serious and more urgent than previously thought. For instance, a study undertaken by the University of East Anglia, United Kingdom, and the Max Planck Institute for Biogeochemistry in Jena, Germany, found that the increase in winds over the Southern Ocean, caused by man-made climate change and ozone depletion, had led to the release of stored carbon dioxide in the ocean into the atmosphere, which in turn is preventing the further absorption of GHGs. Thus a carbon 'sink', a means of absorbing carbon dioxide from the atmosphere, such as a wooded area, will prove less effective than anticipated. In addition, the release of the carbon dioxide is itself contributing to the acidification of the Southern Ocean (Le Quéré and others, 2007).

THE CURRENT LEVEL OF GHG EMISSIONS

Despite the targets established by the Kyoto Protocol (see discussion below), GHG emissions have continued to increase. Global CO_2 emissions increased 17 per cent between 1990 and 2003 (from 22 to 26 $GtCO_2$).

All regions contributed to the increase in emissions, with the exception of the countries of the former Soviet Union and other Eastern European countries, where there had been a decline owing to their severe recession and the closing down of many of their worst polluting industries following the transition from centrally planned to market economies. Emissions in North America increased by 16 per cent (from 5.5 to 6.4 $GtCO_2$), in Western Europe by 4.5 per cent, in Asia and the Pacific by 53 per cent (from 6.3 to 9.7 $GtCO_2$), in Africa by 47 per cent (from 0.6 to 0.9 $GtCO_2$) and in Latin America and the Caribbean by 24 per cent (from 1.0 to 1.3 $GtCO_2$) (see Table 15).

Most of the increase in carbon concentration in the atmosphere is the result of emissions from the industrialized world. In 2003, North America and Europe contributed 55 per cent of total CO_2 (down from 62 per cent in 1990), while Asia and the Pacific contributed 37 per cent. Annual per capita emissions in North America and Western Europe were 19.8 and 9 $GtCO_2$, respectively, while they were 1.2 and 1 $GtCO_2$ in South Asia and Central and East Africa, respectively.

The absolute levels of emissions are thus moving the world away from the Kyoto targets, with respect to emission reductions by 2012. In order to move towards these targets (and especially those of UNFCCC), without jeopardizing the economic growth needed for achieving developmental goals, there will have to be a significant decoupling or delinking of GHG emissions from economic growth.

The main initiative in cutting carbon emissions will have to come from developed countries, because of both their historical responsibility and their continued high current volumes of emissions.

THE CHALLENGE OF STABILIZATION

The volume of carbon emissions depends on four factors: population size, per capita income, energy intensity (or total primary energy use, from whatever source, per unit of GDP) and carbon intensity (carbon emissions per unit of energy consumption).

TABLE 15
Global Cereal Supply and Demand Indicators

	Average 2004–2005	2000/01– 2003–2004	2004–2005	2005–2006	2006–2007	2007–2008
			(percentage)			
1. Ratio of world stocks to utilization						
Wheat	33.8	26.2	28.8	28.9	25.6	22.9
Coarse grains	19.0	15.1	19.1	18.3	15.2	14.5
Rice	30.1	25.5	23.7	24.5	24.0	23.4
Total cereals	25.9	20.6	23.0	22.7	20.0	18.8
2. Ratio of major grain exporters supplies to normal mkt requirements	121	117	137	133	115	117
3. Ratio of major exporters' stocks to their total disappearance						
Wheat	20.4	17.0	21.8	22.2	14.8	10.6
Coarse grains	15.1	10.8	18.7	17.9	12.6	11.7
Rice	19.2	15.9	13.2	15.8	15.9	16.0
Total cereals	18.2	14.5	17.9	18.6	14.4	12.8

	Annual trend growth rate 1997-2006	Change from previous year 2003	2004	2005	2006	2007
				(Percentage)		
4. Changes in world cereal production	0.6	3.3	9.3	–1.0	–2.0	4.7
5. Changes in cereal production in LIFDCs	1.4	2.7	3.4	5.2	3.3	0.9

Continued...

...Continued

	Annual trend growth rate 1997-2006	2003	Change from previous year 2004	2005	2006	2007
				(Percentage)		
6. Changes in cereal production in LIFDCs less China Mainland and India	3.5	7.9	–0.2	7.0	4.1	–1.5

	Average 2000-01–2004-05	2003-04	Change from previous year 2004-05	2005-06	2006-07	2007-08*
				(Percentage)		
7.Selected cereal price indices						
Wheat (July/June)	110.8	–1.1	–1.0	5.2	25.4	91.4
Maize (July/June)	100.2	7.1	–15.2	6.4	44.6	22.9
Rice (Jan./Dec.)	87.7	24.9	5.4	8.9	17.0	46.2

Notes:
Utilisation is defined as the sum of food use, feed and other uses.

Cereals refer to wheat, coarse grains and rice. **Grains** refer to wheat and coarse grains.

Major Grain Exporters are Argentina, Australia, Canada, the EU and the United States. Major rice exporters are India, Pakistan, Thailand, the United States and Vietnam.

Normal market requirements for major grain exporters are defined as the average of domestic utilisation plus exports in the three preceding seasons.

Disappearance is defined as domestic utilisation plus exports for any given reason.

Price indices: the **wheat** price index has been constructed based on the IGC wheat price index, rebased to July/June 1997/98–1999/00 = 100; for **maize** the U.S. maize No. 2 Yellow (delivered U.S. Gulf ports) with base July/June 1997/98–1999/00 = 100; for **rice,** the FAO Rice Price Index, 1998–2000 = 100, is based on 16 rice export quotations.
*For **wheat** and **coarse grains**, July/March; for **rice,** Jan/March.

Source: *FAO Statistics.*

Their effect can be summed up in the following identity

$$C = P \times (Y/P) \times (E/Y) \times (C/E)$$

where

C is carbon dioxide emissions,

E is energy use,

Y is GDP (gross domestic product), and

P is population. *E/Y* is called the 'energy intensity of GDP'. *C/E* is called the 'carbon intensity' of energy supply.

In 2005, out of the total emission of 36 $GtCO_2$, about three quarters, that is, 27.5 $GtCO_2$ (equivalent to 7.5 billion tons of carbon),were emitted by energy systems alone, with the following numerical breakdown in terms of the above equation:

$$C = 6.42 \times 10^9 \text{ persons} \times \$\,6{,}541 \text{ per person} \times 12.1 \text{ MJ/\$} \times 54.3 \text{ kgC/GJ} = 27.5 \times 10^{12} \text{ kg } CO_2$$

where

GJ is giga (billion) joules of primary energy,

MJ is mega (million) joules of primary energy,

$KgCO_2$ is kilograms of carbon emitted, with there being 1,000 kilograms in a metric ton.

The magnitude of the challenge facing mankind can be appreciated by looking at the projections for the year 2100 under the IPCC baseline scenario IS92a. According to this scenario, the world population will increase from 6.42 billion in 2005 to 11.3 billion by 2100; world GDP will increase eightfold; and energy use will triple from current levels, even though the fraction of energy supplied from fossil fuels will drop from over 80 per cent to under 60 per cent and the energy intensity of production will fall. Thus, notwithstanding improvements in energy efficiency and reduction in dependence on fossil fuels, CO_2 emissions would reach 75 $GtCO_2$ by 2100 (and atmospheric CO_2 concentration would amount to over 700 ppm).

The identity defined above shows that a reduction in carbon emissions requires a reduction in one or more of the following:

Population: A decline in population growth would bring about a proportional reduction in emissions, without any change in affluence, energy efficiency or carbon intensity.

Income: A slowdown in growth of per capita income (although not considered desirable by most analyses) would similarly reduce emissions proportionately.

Energy and Carbon Intensity: By investing in energy-efficient production, fuel switching, land-use changes, carbon storage and sequestration and by improving the efficiency of the conversion of fossil fuels into energy, the volume of emissions would be reduced for a given quantum of energy use and, ultimately, production. Where feasible and appropriate, less energy- and carbon-intensive PCPs would reconcile economic growth and GHG emissions.

As Table 16 illustrates, there is some scope for action with respect to each of these three factors that determine carbon emissions.

Regarding population growth, for example, efforts could be made to bring the global population more in line with the carrying capacity of the earth. Yet, population change can take place only gradually, especially as many people born at the present time can expect to live an average of 80 years. At the same time, fertility rates are falling in many countries, a factor which, together with increased longevity, is posing socio-economic challenges. In any case, changes in the overall size of the world's population cannot be expected to take place within the required time frame, the next three decades, on a sufficient scale to have a major effect on mitigating climate change.

Regarding GDP growth, developed countries would need to focus much more on the quality of growth rather than just the quantity. Alternative settlement and consumption patterns in these countries can probably lead to a more satisfying life even at current or somewhat reduced income levels. Changes in PCPs may be needed to help reduce the energy intensity of income. Progress is already being seen in this direction. For example, with the enactment of tighter emission standards for vehicles, charges for bringing vehicles into the most congested parts of major cities (thereby also reducing pollution and traffic jams, and encouraging the use of public transport), stricter building codes and the use of more fuel-efficient light bulbs. These can only be seen as modest and preliminary steps and no doubt additional measures will be needed to reduce energy consumption.

TABLE 16

World Cereal Stocks[1] (million tonnes)

	2003	2004	2005	2006	2007 estimate	2008 forecast
TOTAL CEREALS	**486.3**	**417.3**	**469.3**	**469.8**	**425.6**	**405.1**
Wheat	**204.4**	**162.2**	**178.6**	**179.5**	**159.1**	**144.4**
held by:						
main exporters[2]	39.1	38.6	55.1	56.3	36.5	26.1
others	165.3	123.6	123.5	123.2	122.5	118.3
Coarse grains	**162.9**	**149.8**	**191.2**	**185.6**	**162.1**	**157.1**
held by:						
main exporters[2]	55.3	48.5	92.7	90.7	62.5	66.9
others	107.6	101.3	98.5	95.0	99.6	90.2
Rice (milled basis)	**119.0**	**105.3**	**99.5**	**104.7**	**104.5**	**103.5**
held by:						
main exporters[2]	21.7	22.5	18.9	22.9	23.7	24.1
others	97.3	82.8	80.6	81.8	80.8	79.4
Developed countries	**145.3**	**123.2**	**188.5**	**189.8**	**135.6**	**120.5**
Australia	5.2	8.8	10.0	13.6	6.0	5.7
European Union[3]	33.7	21.5	47.6	45.1	33.0	30.0
Canada	8.9	10.3	14.5	16.2	10.5	8.5
Hungary[4]	1.4	0.8	–	–	–	–
Japan	5.4	4.9	4.7	4.8	4.4	4.3
Poland[4]	2.9	2.4	–	–	–	–
Romania[5]	2.0	1.2	5.0	5.6	3.8	–
Russian Federation	12.5	7.3	9.1	9.3	8.5	8.6
South Africa	3.8	3.5	4.1	4.1	2.7	1.5
Ukraine	5.1	2.8	4.2	4.8	4.3	4.2
United States	45.1	44.4	74.7	71.7	49.9	48.1
Developing countries	**341.0**	**294.2**	**280.8**	**280.0**	**290.0**	**284.5**
Asia	**307.5**	**253.5**	**236.7**	**237.2**	**243.3**	**244.8**
China	209.4	163.3	152.8	149.0	153.2	156.4
India	39.8	32.9	26.7	25.8	29.4	33.2
Indonesia	5.7	6.0	5.7	5.1	5.8	6.4
Iran,	4.4	3.5	3.2	3.6	3.6	2.8
Korea, Republic of	2.8	2.9	2.5	2.8	3.0	2.3
Pakistan	2.9	1.9	2.0	3.2	3.3	3.9
Philippines	2.2	1.9	2.2	2.7	2.6	3.0
Syrian Arab Republic	4.1	4.2	4.5	4.6	3.1	2.3
Turkey	8.0	7.2	6.5	5.5	6.4	3.8

Continued...

...Continued

	2003	2004	2005	2006	2007 estimate	2008 forecast
Africa	**19.1**	**20.8**	**23.3**	**26.3**	**31.7**	**25.0**
Algeria	2.5	2.6	3.6	4.4	4.7	4.6
Egypt	3.2	2.7	3.1	4.3	4.1	3.1
Ethiopia	0.7	0.1	0.1	0.8	1.8	1.8 Mo-
rocco	1.8	3.0	4.9	2.7	4.0	1.9 Ni-
geria	1.9	1.6	1.3	1.4	2.1	0.9 Tu-
nisia	0.6	1.0	1.2	1.4	1.4	1.3
Central America	**5.6**	**5.8**	**6.3**	**4.6**	**4.5**	**5.0**
Mexico	3.7	3.9	4.6	2.8	2.6	3.3
South America	**8.5**	**13.8**	**14.2**	**11.6**	**10.3**	**9.5** Ar-
gentina	3.3	3.8	3.2	2.6	1.6	2.2 Bra-
zil	1.6	5.8	6.3	4.1	3.1	2.2

1 Stock data are based on an aggregate of carryovers at the end of national crop years and do not represent world stock levels at any point in time.
2 The major **wheat** and **coarse grains** exporters are Argentina, Australia, Canada, the EU and the United States. The major **rice** exporters are India, Pakistan, Thailand, the United States and Vietnam.
3 Up to 2004, 15 member countries; from 2005 to 2007, 25 member countries; in 2008, 27 member countries.
4 From 2005 included in the EU.
5 In 2008 included in the EU.

Note: Based on official and unofficial estimates. Totals computed from unrounded data.
Source: *FAO Statistics.*

The most promising area of action relates to CO_2 intensity of energy, which, under the IS92 scenario, is expected to show only a modest decline from 54.3 to 49.2 $KgCO_2/GJ$ (kilograms of CO_2 per gigajoule of energy). Fortunately, many technologies for low- and non-carbon energy generation are already available in developed countries and further progress can be made through vigorous research (Pacala and Socolow, 2004; Stern, 2007; United Nations Foundation and Sigma XI Scientific Expert Group on Climate Change, 2007). Wind and solar power could provide sources of carbon-free energy in countries with the right conditions. Wave power is at an early stage of development. Nuclear and hydropower are also alternatives, but both are problematic: nuclear, because of both the dangers of a plant malfunctioning and problems with the disposal of the radioactive waste; and hydroelectricity, because of the effects of climate change in reducing the flow of water into glacier-fed rivers, as is occurring in the Andes (Vergana and others, 2007).

Biomass technology is also advancing, but there are considerable disputes as to whether the production of some fuels, such as ethanol, is really cost and energy efficient and whether a surge in the production of biofuels from corn, wheat and soybeans would push up food prices, as already appears to be happening (United Nations, 2007b). Moreover, if forested land were cleared to make way for biofuel production, this could have a negative effect on climate change by reducing the size of carbon sinks.

At present, subsidies are often used to encourage the construction of facilities for generating clean power, and these might be needed for some time to come. However, recent calculations for Denmark have indicated that wind power actually saves consumers money, as the benefits resulting from lower power prices outweigh the falling costs of the subsidy.

As evidence accumulates on the damaging effects of climate change and the impossibility, as illustrated above, of 'business as usual', it begs the question: have the steps taken so far been adequate, and, in particular, were the goals realistic and have they been actually attained. If the answer is negative, the need for even more drastic action than presently contemplated, is reinforced.

POLICY RESPONSES SO FAR

MITIGATION

Article 2 of the 1992 UNFCCC set the goal of stabilizing the GHG concentration at a level that would allow 'development to proceed in a sustainable manner'. Following up on this goal, the Kyoto Protocol of 1997 focused on reduction of GHG emissions by the developed countries. According to the Protocol, these countries were committed to reduce their emissions by 5.2 per cent (relative to the level in 1990) over the period from 1997 till 2012. The Protocol refrained from imposing emission limits on developing countries in view of their

(a) negligible historical role in the creation of the GHG concentration,

(b) current relatively low levels of total and (particularly) per capita emissions, and

(c) urgent need to grow rapidly in order to deal with the problems of poverty.

The Kyoto Protocol developed so-called flexible instruments for realizing GHG emissions reductions in efficient ways, including Carbon Trading and the Clean Development Mechanism (CDM). These instruments were also supposed to create some link between developed and developing countries' climate change-related efforts. The aim of the CDM is to help the Annex I countries meet their emission-reduction obligations by investing in cost-effective solutions in developing countries, a link that could also help the developing countries (Non Annex I Parties) achieve sustainable development goals.

Unfortunately, even the modest targets of the Kyoto Protocol are not being fulfilled. Instead of decreasing, global CO_2 emissions have actually increased between 1990 and 2003. Efforts by developed countries to reduce emissions domestically have proved inadequate. Carbon trading is not proving to be as effective and a suitable policy instrument as was expected. The CDM often seems to be used by developed countries to avoid deeper changes in their own PCPs. Overall, the Kyoto Protocol was a step in the right direction, though important parties have still to sign and ratify it. However, given the enormity and urgency of the challenge faced, it must be concluded that the Kyoto Protocol remains an inadequate and limited mitigation response. A post-Kyoto agreement is thus necessary, and it will have to include much more ambitious targets, with appropriate and effective mechanisms to achieve them. Experience acquired during the operation of the Kyoto Protocol can be very helpful in the forthcoming international discussions.

More recently, considerable momentum towards achieving a successful post-Kyoto agreement was provided by the Group of Eight (G8) Summit, held in Heiligendamm, Germany, in June 2007. In their Summit declaration, participants accepted the conclusions of the recent IPCC report (its Fourth Assessment Report, released earlier in 2007), namely, 'that global temperatures are rising, that this is caused largely by human activities and, in addition, with increase in global average temperature, there are projected to be major changes in ecosystem structure and function, with predominantly negative consequences for biodiversity and ecosystems, for example, water and food supply.'

Participants also agreed that improving energy efficiency worldwide is the 'fastest, the most sustainable and the cheapest way to reduce greenhouse gas emissions and enhance energy security'. Moreover, they noted the decisions made by the European Union, Canada and Japan, which include at least a halving of global emissions by 2050, and committed themselves to achieving these goals also inviting the major emerging economies to join them in this endeavour. (This represented a significant advance from the Kyoto Protocol, which excluded the developing countries from obligations to reduce GHG emissions.) The participants committed themselves to taking a leading role in international efforts to combat global warming and to supporting the work of the United Nations in this field.

The United Nations climate process was acknowledged as the 'appropriate forum for negotiating future global action on climate change'. Participants also acknowledged that further action should be based on the UNFCCC principle of common but differentiated responsibilities and respective capabilities. G8 representatives had also met with representatives from Brazil, China, India, Mexico and South Africa in Berlin in May 2007 and will continue to meet with representatives of these and other major energy-consuming and GHG-emitting countries to consider the necessary components for successfully combating climate change. The United States agreed to host such a meeting later in the year. The major emitters' process should include '*inter alia,* national, regional and international policies, targets and plans, in line with national circumstances, an ambitious work programme within the UNFCCC, and the development and deployment of climate-friendly technology.' This dialogue would support the UN climate process and report back to the UNFCCC.

As shall be argued in more detail below, it is of the utmost importance that in this dialogue the mutual links (both positive and negative) between climate change (and policies addressing it), on the one hand, and development, on the other, be duly considered and elaborated. Chapter 12 of the 2007 Fourth Assessment Report of the Working Group III of the IPCC entitled "Sustainable Development and Mitigation" has begun to address these issues but more work will be needed (See IPCC, 2007c).

No specific mechanisms have been elaborated as yet on how to achieve the goals, and much discussion await. However, the summary of the G-8 Chair stated that 'technology, energy efficiency and market mechanisms, including emission trading systems or tax incentives are key to mastering climate change as well as enhancing energy security.'

ADAPTATION

In addition to the *mitigation* efforts envisaged by the Kyoto Protocol (that is to say, efforts to reduce the emission of GHGs), there have been some efforts at *adaptation* (that is, adjusting to the consequences of climate change). In particular, efforts will be needed to assist those countries that will be most affected by the present and future effects of climate change to adjust to the inevitable difficulties that they will face and which, it should be added, are overwhelmingly not of their own making. Even if as is clearly impossible the emission of GHGs were to cease immediately, climate change and the adverse effects already noted can be expected to worsen.

Several funds have been set up to promote adaptation measures at the national level, particularly in developing countries. The Global Environment Facility (GEF) provides about US$ 50 million per year for building capacity for adaptation. The Special Climate Change Fund (Adaptation Programme), finances technology transfer and economic diversification. Funding is at the $ 50 million level, though part of it will come from regular Official Development Assistance (ODA) sources; this fund has a development focus. The Least Developed Countries (LDC) Fund finances the preparation and implementation of National Adaptation Programmes of Action (NAPAs) in LDCs. This development-focused fund has a volume of $ 115 million. A final example is the Adaptation Fund, set up under the Kyoto process to finance the implementation of adaptation projects. It is financed by a levy on CDM projects (2 per cent of Certified Emission Reduction (CER) revenues) and by other contributions, with a possible reach of $ 100 million towards 2012 (Stern, 2007).

As these examples show, although steps are being taken to address the matter of adaptation, the sums involved are, at this stage, fairly small, compared to the billions of dollars worth of damage that the most vulnerable countries can be expected to suffer, especially as the adverse effects of climate change can be anticipated to worsen in future. Altogether, the adaptation-oriented measures remain inadequate in comparison with the challenges faced, and a considerable ratcheting-up must be planned. Any new protocol or agreement will need not only to recognise this, but also to articulate an adequate approach towards the development and implementation (including measures ensuring the facilitation thereof) of options for adaptation, especially in LDCs and SIDS.

DEVELOPMENT AND CLIMATE CHANGE: RETHINKING AND CURRENT APPROACH

The Secretary-General of the United Nations, Ban Ki-moon, has called climate change a 'defining issue of our era,' stressing that

> there is likely to be no single path or solution to all our problems (related to climate change). New technologies, conservation and fuel efficiency programmes, carbon-trading, improving land use practices, national environmental regulation all are part of the solution. The important thing is....that these policies be complementary and mutually reinforcing. The many strands must be woven into one cloth.

Climate change should thus be coordinated with social and economic development in an integrated manner, with a view to avoid adverse impacts on the latter, taking into full account the legitimate priority needs of developing countries for the achievement of sustained economic growth and the eradication of poverty.

In the long run, mankind may want to go beyond the UNFCCC stabilization goal and strive to reverse the increase in mean temperature of the earth that has taken place since industrialization. The measures taken so far appear to be aimed at modifying behaviour only at the periphery, whereas the challenge requires much more fundamental change, with an entirely different level of motivation and effort in order to reduce drastically the carbon intensity of human activity on the planet. Even with present targets for reductions in global emissions, global climate change will continue as anticipated emissions are still far greater than the earth's absorptive capacity. The earth will simply be warming at a slower pace than if no action were taken.

As mentioned above, developed countries have to continue to take the initiative and play the major role in confronting the threat of climate change. Several lines along which future efforts in these countries may proceed are as follows:

- ⌘ Wider and deeper recognition that climate change threatens the sustainability of life and societies in all countries.
- ⌘ Greater awareness that human intervention in the form of carbon emissions is the main cause of climate change, and that deep reductions are necessary to arrest the process of climate change.
- ⌘ Recognizing that the current lifestyle and consumption pattern of

developed countries (as well as those of the rich in developing countries) are not sustainable, and that fundamental changes are required if carbon emissions are to be decreased to the desired level. An outline of such changes needs to be developed and a societal agreement reached about this outline. The suggested changes could involve a greater focus by the developed countries on the quality and long-run sustainability of life rather than on the further augmentation of material possessions without regard to the consequences for the climate. Already, initiatives have been taken to make individuals aware of their 'carbon imprint' with, for instance, the British Royal Society of Arts' initiation of a carbon calculator so that individuals can see the impact of changes in lifestyle (Acher, 2006).

⌘ Forging an extensive partnership between Governments and the private sector to implement the agreed outline and bring about the necessary changes in infrastructure and industrial production, as well as in the development and deployment of the necessary technologies. Developed countries may launch a massive effort at further development and deployment of these technologies.

⌘ Renewing commitment towards helping developing countries to develop quickly and to do so in a way that will ensure sustainability and help confront, by adaptation, the dangers of climate change.

It is therefore recommended that, in the context of the renewed debate and negotiations on an international approach to climate change beyond the Kyoto Protocol, developed countries should immediately start working on post-Kyoto steps. These should aim at deep cuts in carbon emissions through appropriate regulatory measures and not overly rely on flexible mechanisms that have not proven particularly effective so far. Furthermore, the post-Kyoto arrangements need to bring development and climate change together and accord a more central place to the twin challenges of a faster and decarbonized growth faced by developing countries. Developed countries therefore also have a role to play in supporting (technologically and financially) developing countries in engaging in mitigative activities beyond those that would have immediate relevance for development.

At the same time, developing countries need to realize that it is also in their interest to engage in mitigation on developmental grounds and (in the case of new and emerging large-scale emitters among them) for reasons directly related to climate change. They can do so by decarbonizing their growth as much as possible. In recent years, GHG emissions by some developing countries have increased at a faster rate than the world average, as shown by the figures for Asia and the Pacific in Table 15. Developing countries aspire to improve the welfare of their populations and reach those standards currently prevailing in developed countries; however, the danger is that attempts by developing countries to achieve such parity will accelerate the growth of GHG emissions, unless the current development trajectory is significantly decarbonized.

In this regard, it is encouraging that many developing countries are drawing up plans that involve measures directed not only at adaptation but also at mitigation. Examples of such action at the regional and national level are given below:

India: India's Conservation Strategy highlights the need for coping mechanisms, especially in coastal areas. Some CDM projects have been initiated, and substantial research is under way on emissions reduction through the development of energy from sea waves and biomass, or through sustainable transport. India has recently established an Integrated Energy Policy providing the poor with access to clean energy and also increasing energy efficiency. The policy is to lead to an estimated reduction in GHG-intensity by one third.

Indonesia has developed a national climate strategy. The Government has prioritized adaptation measures over mitigation and is working to enhance coping capabilities, for instance, for sea-level rise.

Kenya has an emerging climate policy with associated institutions such as a National Committee on Climate Change.

Brazil has established inter-ministerial coordination for sustainable development and actively follows (and contributes to) international climate negotiations. Brazil plans for its share of renewable energy to be 10 per cent in 2030.

China aims at reducing its energy intensity (energy/GDP) by 20 per cent between 2005 and 2010 and at meeting 15 per cent of its energy needs from renewable sources within 10 years.

Africa: Almost all African countries have ratified the UNFCCC and many support the Kyoto Protocol. They are potential beneficiaries of its mechanisms. Detailed inventories of emissions and sinks have been provided by many countries. Options for exploitation of alternative energy sources (for example, solar, wind, biomass and hydro) are being explored. Mitigation and adaptation options must be found to cope with the impacts of changes in weather regimes, droughts and floods.

Asia: The Asia Least Cost Greenhouse Gas Abatement Strategies (ALGAS) project has identified a range of options to reduce GHG emissions.

Latin America and the Caribbean: Mitigation and adaption activities include energy saving methods in such sectors as transportation, agriculture and waste management. The region is actively involved in developing renewable energy and carbon sinks (forests), as well as wind energy.

The efforts of developing countries often also include afforestation, an area in which grass-roots organizations often play an important role. Overall, however, the adaptation measures taken by developing countries are still inadequate.

The challenge for developing countries is to achieve fast economic growth while adding the least possible amount of GHGs to the atmosphere. At the same time, the most vulnerable countries are faced with the costs of adaptation to the inevitable adverse consequences of climate change. Their multi-pronged effort, pursuing adaptive and mitigative efforts at the same time as achieving faster economic growth, will require the full support of the international community.

Meeting these challenges calls for a vast endeavour that includes:

- More in-depth research to formulate an appropriate development strategy.
- Formation of national consensus on the strategy adopted.
- Mobilization of necessary domestic and external resources.
- Actual implementation of the strategy.

Such a development strategy has to focus on the interlinkages between growth, poverty and climate change, and will have to give an important role to the poor as actors and not treat them just as a target group recipient of action by others. The policy instruments to be used by the strategy may include direct investment (in research and extension), large-scale public works, conventional regulation, subsidy and taxation, redistribution mechanisms, differential taxation, subsidy schemes favouring the poor, non-trading market mechanisms, community development, credit and microcredit programmes, development of climate-friendly institutions and legal action, ideally all backed and monitored by citizens and evaluated against short- and long-term targets. The desired development strategy will need to consider policies that pertain to population and reproductive health, land use and energy (including deployment of renewable energy, energy security, energy conservation and energy efficiency).

Further analysis of the linkage between poverty and climate change may have implications for concepts and indicators of vulnerability, especially those pertaining to least developed countries.

NEW PARTNERSHIPS TOWARDS SUSTAINABLE DEVELOPMENT

Efforts by developing and developed countries at the national and regional levels to reduce GHGs and to adapt to the inevitable future changes in climate are essential and should be prosecuted with ever-increased vigour. However, confronting climate change and sustaining development requires not only national and regional actions, but something much broader: a new partnership between developed and developing countries. The developed countries cannot avoid disruptions caused by climate change that will result if the developing countries run full steam towards industrialized country levels of per capita carbon emissions. The developing countries, on the other hand, cannot engage in a decarbonized or less carbonized growth process without adequate technological and financial support from the developed countries.

In devising climate-friendly technologies, the developed countries have to be attentive to their applicability in developing countries as well. In addition to contributing to mitigation worldwide, taking developing countries' needs into account also makes sense business wise, since the potential that developing countries offer in terms of markets will also improve the commercial viability of such technologies. However, short-run profitability should not stand in the way of the development and deployment of climate-friendly technologies. Similarly, intellectual property rights (IPRs) should not act as a hindrance to the dissemination, transfer, adaptation and actual deployment of climate-friendly technologies in developing countries.

Developed countries also need to provide the necessary technical support to enable developing countries to adapt and put these technologies into use. Developing countries themselves also need to upgrade their national technological capability both to adapt the climate-friendly technologies available in the developed countries and to develop their own climate-friendly technologies suitable to their unique conditions.

Given that developing countries often lack resources to address their urgent investment needs, they require additional resources to implement the less-carbonized or decarbonized development measures. Thus, mechanisms need to be identified enabling developing countries to follow more climate-friendly development trajectories. These may include financial assistance in addition to ODA and innovative international financing schemes such as carbon (or GHG) taxation.

The partnership between developed and developing countries in confronting climate change must be viewed neither as a matter of just 'giving and receiving aid' nor as a matter of intergovernmental transactions. The scope of necessary action is so vast that many different dimensions and channels may be envisaged that involve a role for Governments, private companies, individual entrepreneurs, civic and non-governmental organizations, professional bodies, etc.

What is clear is that major changes, likely to involve institutional changes, in the relationship between developed and developing countries are required and that the world is only at the beginning of a process which is essential to safeguard life on the planet and the continued growth of the poorest countries.

CONCLUSIONS AND RECOMMENDATIONS

The above analysis has led the CDP to make the following conclusions and recommendations for action at the international level by the appropriate United Nations bodies:

- The response to the climate change threat so far has been inadequate and there is an urgent need for:
- Raising the mitigation and adaptation efforts to an entirely different level. Any post-Kyoto arrangement has to go far beyond the present Protocol, in order to reflect properly the enormity and the urgency of the problem. This includes the articulation of an adequate approach towards the development and implementation (including measures ensuring the facilitation thereof) of options for adaptation, especially in LDCs and SIDS.
- While the Kyoto Protocol followed a one-track approach focusing on (marginal) reduction of emissions by developed countries and treating developing countries largely as onlookers, post-Kyoto arrangements have to adopt a simultaneous two-track approach. The first track would aim at very deep cuts in emissions by developed countries; the

second would provide a more central role to developing countries by enabling them to both grow faster and make their growth as less-carbonized and decarbonized as possible through the successful adoption and implementation of appropriate climate-friendly development strategies with the necessary technological and financial cooperation from developed countries.

⌘ The United Nations should further contribute to the post-Kyoto process, and the Economic and Social Council could provide a platform for an overarching and sustained policy dialogue about the relationship between climate and development. This policy dialogue should also lead to a process of future revision of the Millennium Development Goals so that the danger of climate change and its overshadowing impact on all other development issues find appropriate reflection. In this regard, there is need to consider the links and feedbacks between climate change (and also the policies adopted to address it) and development in a thorough and integrated way. On the one hand, development paths vary in the ways in which they have an impact on the climate; on the other, different climate policies will have different impacts on development trajectories and rates of economic growth. Even though these feedbacks within the climate-development nexus are not, as yet, fully understood, they should be explored in order to arrive at an appropriate strategy involving all parties concerned. The strategy would comprise those mitigation and adaptation measures (as well as the actions needed to facilitate their implementation) required to address effectively the challenge climate change poses to development.

Further work by the CSD will be of invaluable importance. The CDP, building on IPCC results, is also ready to assist in achieving a deeper understanding of the linkages between development and climate change and to contribute to the formulation of a conceptual framework in which the goals of advancing development, while arresting climate change, are integrated.

SUMMARY

The extent of the climate change challenge is such that it makes it impossible for the world to continue along a path of 'business as usual'. The present mechanisms in place are grossly inadequate. Focusing international cooperation on climate change solely on the establishment of emission targets is far from adequate. Such an approach will not properly address development challenges or help achieve internationally agreed goals. The current international development agenda needs to set forth the actions and approaches required to ensure that economic behaviour is compatible with environmental constraints in a way in which aggregate costs are minimised, the vulnerable are protected and economic growth is maximised. The integration of climate change and development goals will require a fundamental reorientation in the current developmental trajectory so that the carbon intensity of production is reduced while economic grown is maintained. It will also require a renewed and more effective partnership between the developed and developing countries as well as between the public and private sectors.

APPENDIX X

FOOD SOVEREIGNTY AS AN ALTERNATIVE FRAMEWORK

FOOD sovereignty is increasingly being promoted as an alternative framework to the narrower concept of food security, which mostly focuses on the technical problem of providing adequate nutrition. For instance, a food security agenda that simply provides surplus grain to hungry people would probably be strongly criticised by food sovereignty advocates as just another form of commodity dumping, facilitating corporate penetration of foreign markets, undermining local food production, and possibly leading to irreversible biotech contamination of indigenous crops with patented varieties. U.S. taxpayer subsidized exports of Bt corn to Mexico since the passage of NAFTA is a case in point.

HISTORY

At the Forum for Food Sovereignty in Sélingué, Mali, 27 February 2007, about 500 delegates from more than 80 countries adopted the **Declaration of Nyéléni,** which says in part:

> Food sovereignty is the right of peoples to healthy and culturally appropriate food produced through ecologically sound and sustainable methods, and their right to define their own food and agriculture systems. It puts those who produce, distribute and consume food at the heart of food systems and policies rather than the demands of markets and corporations. It defends the interests and inclusion of the next generation. It offers a strategy to resist and dismantle the current corporate trade and food regime and directions for food, farming, pastoral and fisheries systems determined by local producers. Food sovereignty prioritises local and national economies and markets and empowers peasant and family farmer-driven agriculture, artisanal fishing, pastoralist-led grazing and food production, distribution and consumption based on environmental,

> social and economic sustainability. Food sovereignty promotes transparent trade that guarantees a just income to all peoples and the rights of consumers to control their food and nutrition. It ensures that the rights to use and manage our lands, territories, waters, seeds, livestock and biodiversity are in the hands of those of us who produce food. Food sovereignty implies new social relations free of oppression and inequality between men and women, peoples, racial groups, social classes and generations.

Writing in Food First's *Backgrounder,* autumn 2003, Peter Rosset argues that 'Food sovereignty goes beyond the concept of *food security*... [Food security] means that... [everyone] must have the certainty of having enough to eat each day[,] ... but says nothing about where that food comes from or how it is produced.' Food sovereignty includes support for smallholders and for collectively owned farms, fisheries, etc., rather than industrializing these sectors in a minimally regulated global economy. In another publication, Food First describes 'food sovereignty' as 'a platform for rural revitalization at a global level based on equitable distribution of farmland and water, farmer control over seeds and productive small-scale farms supplying consumers with healthy, locally grown food.'

The preface to the ITDG publishing/FIAN paper on food sovereignty says:

> 'The Food Sovereignty policy framework starts by placing the perspective and needs of the majority at the heart of the global food policy agenda and embraces not only the control of production and markets, but also the Right to Food, people's access to and control over land, water and genetic resources and the use of environmentally sustainable approaches to production. What emerges is a persuasive and highly political argument for refocusing the control of food production and consumption within democratic processes rooted in localized food systems.'

'Food sovereignty' is a term originally coined by members of Via Campesina in 1996 to refer to a policy framework advocated by a number of farmers', peasants', pastoralists', fisherfolk, Indigenous Peoples', womens', rural youth and environmental organizations, namely the claimed 'right of peoples to define their own food, agriculture, livestock and fisheries systems,' in contrast to having food largely subject to international market forces.

PRINCIPLES

Via Campesina's seven principles of food sovereignty include:

1. **Food: A Basic Human Right.** Everyone must have access to safe, nutritious and culturally appropriate food in sufficient quantity and quality to sustain a healthy life with full human dignity. Each nation should declare that access to food is a constitutional right and guarantee the development of the primary sector to ensure the concrete realization of this fundamental right.

2. **Agrarian Reform.** A genuine agrarian reform is necessary which gives landless and farming people—especially women—ownership and control of the land they work and returns territories to indigenous peoples. The right to land must be free of discriminationon on the basis of gender, religion, race, social class or ideology; the land belongs to those who work it.

3. **Protecting Natural Resources.** Food Sovereignty entails the sustainable care and use of natural resources, especially land, water and seeds and livestock breeds. The people who work the land must have the right to practise sustainable management of natural resources and to conserve biodiversity free of restrictive intellectual property rights. This can only be done from a sound economic basis with security of tenure, healthy soils and reduced use of agro-chemicals.

4. **Reorganizing Food Trade.** Food is first and foremost a source of nutrition and only secondarily an item of trade. National agricultural policies must prioritize production for domestic consumption and food self-sufficiency. Food imports must not displace local production nor depress prices.

5. **Ending the Globalization of Hunger.** Food Sovereignty is undermined by multilateral institutions and by speculative capital. The growing control of multinational corporations over agricultural policies has been facilitated by the economic policies of multilateral organizations such as the WTO, World Bank and the IMF. Regulation and taxation of speculative capital and a strictly enforced Code of Conduct for TNCs is therefore needed.

6. **Social Peace.** Everyone has the right to be free from violence. Food must not be used as a weapon. Increasing levels of poverty and marginalization in the countryside, along with the growing oppression of ethnic minorities and indigenous populations, aggravate situations of injustice and hopelessness. The ongoing displacement, forced urbanization, repression and increasing incidence of racism of smallholder farmers cannot be tolerated.

7. **Democratic control.** Smallholder farmers must have direct input into formulating agricultural policies at all levels. The United Nations and related organizations will have to undergo a process of democratization to enable this to become a reality. Everyone has the right to honest, accurate information and open and democratic decision-making. These rights form the basis of good governance, accountability and equal participation in economic, political and social life, free from all forms of discrimination. Rural women, in particular, must be granted direct and active decisionmaking on food and rural issues.

TABLE 17

Cereal Import Requirements of Low-Income Food-Deficit Countries[1]— 2007-08 or 2008 Estimates (in '000 tonnes)

		2006-07 or 2007			2007-08 or 2008			
		Actual Imports				Import Position[2]		
	Marketing Year	Commercial Purchases	Food Aid	Total Commercial and Aid	Total Import Requirements (excluding re-exports)	Total Commercial and Aid	Food Aid Allocated Committed or Shipped	Commercial Purchases
AFRICA		**33,772.2**	**240.1**	**36,012.3**	**38,524.9**	**19,823.8**	**1.324.1**	**18.499.7**
North Africa		**15,743.5**	**24.5**	**15,768.0**	**38,351.0**	**13,804.9**	**0.0**	**13,804.9**
Egypt	July-June	11,895.5	24.5	11,920.0	12,330.0	9,200.5	0.0	9,200.5
Morocco	July-June	3,848.0	0.0	3,848.0	6,021.0	4,604.4	0.0	4,604.4
Eastern Africa		**4,039.5**	**317.9**	**5,374.4**	**4,917.0**	**1,924.5**	**648.5**	**1,276.0**
Burundi	Jan-Dec	80.9	45.1	126.0	139.0	3.2	3.2	0.0
Comoros	Jan-Dec	41.7	0.0	41.7	41.0	25.0	0.0	25.0
Djibouti	Jan-Dec	67.7	5.8	73.5	72.0	2.3	0.0	2.3
Eritrea	Jan-Dec	216.0	0.0	216.0	326.0	7.0	7.0	0.0
Ethiopia	Jan-Dec	27.2	472.2	499.4	258.0	95.0	94.5	0.5
Kenya	Oct-Sep	999.9	180.4	1,180.3	1,022.0	392.3	130.3	262.2
Rwanda	Jan-Dec	176.0	16.0	192.0	206.0	8.7	8.7	0.0
Somalia	Aug-July	323.2	116.8	440.0	480.0	84.1	81.6	2.5
Sudan	Nov-Oct	1,284.1	351.8	1,599.9	1,442.0	650.2	231.4	418.8
Uganda	Jan-Dec	165.5	89.3	254.8	181.0	51.7	50.3	1.4
Tanzania	June-May	693.3	40.5	733.8	750.0	605.0	41.5	563.5

Continued...

...Continued

		2006-07 or 2007			2007-08 or 2008			
		Actual Imports				Import Position[2]		
	Marketing Year	Commercial Purchases	Food Aid	Total Commercial and Aid	Total Import Requirements (excluding re-exports)	Total Commercial and Aid	Food Aid Allocated Committed or Shipped	Commercial Purchases
Southern Africa		**2,503.9**	**363.7**	**2,867.6**	**3,413.0**	**2,779.9**	**481.8**	**2,298.1**
Angola	April/March	649.3	20.7	670.0	698.0	479.6	5.8	473.8
Lesotho	April/March	181.3	10.1	191.4	219.0	209.2	19.5	189.7
Madagascar	April/March	227.4	34.3	261.7	310.0	285.7	60.0	225.7
Malawi	April/March	161.4	63.0	224.4	176.0	168.2	56.7	111.5
Mozambique	April/March	779.5	103.5	883.0	771.0	600.1	58.8	541.3
Swaziland	May/April	122.2	5.8	128.0	138.0	119.8	12.1	107.7
Zambia	May/April	55.8	28.1	83.9	69.0	53.7	18.9	34.8
Zimbabwe	April/March	327.0	98.2	425.2	1 032.0	863.6	250.0	613.6
Western Africa		**9,912.9**	**432.7**	**10,345.6**	**10,142.4**	**1,203.6**	**153.8**	**1,049.8**
Coastal Countries		**7,589.6**	**132.0**	**7,721.6**	**7,768.0**	**733.7**	**48.1**	**685.6**
Benin	Jan./Dec.	102.5	0.3	102.8	97.0	50.0	0.0	50.0
Côte d'Ivoire	Jan./Dec.	1,151.1	17.4	1,168.5	1,240.0	289.4	1.3	288.1
Ghana	Jan./Dec.	686.5	35.0	721.5	735.0	86.3	13.8	72.5
Guinea	Jan./Dec.	510.4	12.1	522.5	502.0	37.2	4.4	32.8
Liberia	Jan./Dec.	205.1	37.6	242.7	240.0	27.6	27.6	0.0
Nigeria	Jan./Dec.	4,580.0	0.0	4,580.0	4,580.0	208.8	0.0	208.8
Sierra Leone	Jan./Dec.	270.1	28.9	299.0	289.0	13.4	0.0	13.4
Togo	Jan./Dec.	83.9	0.7	84.6	85.0	21.0	1.0	20.0

Continued...

...Continued

		2006-07 or 2007			2007-08 or 2008			
		Actual Imports				Import Position[2]		
	Marketing Year	Commercial Purchases	Food Aid	Total Commercial and Aid	Total Import Requirements (excluding re-exports)	Total Commercial and Aid	Food Aid Allocated Committed or Shipped	Commercial Purchases
Sahelian Countries		**2 323.3**	**300.7**	**2 624.0**	**2 374.4**	**469.9**	**105.7**	**364.2**
Burkina Faso	Nov./Oct.	248.4	25.9	274.3	279.0	12.2	7.5	4.7
Cape Verde	Nov./Oct.	65.1	8.7	73.8	73.6	6.4	3.0	3.4
Chad	Nov./Oct.	65.5	72.0	137.5	126.2	51.5	47.7	3.8
Gambia	Nov./Oct.	92.8	9.6	102.4	100.5	32.6	1.2	31.4
Guinea-Bissau	Nov./Oct.	95.4	8.4	103.8	86.9	3.7	3.7	0.0
Mali	Nov./Oct.	326.9	46.5	373.4	308.7	14.9	4.1	10.8
Mauritania	Nov./Oct.	318.4	33.2	351.6	296.0	76.2	14.0	62.2
Niger	Nov./Oct.	204.1	83.1	287.2	236.7	29.0	19.5	9.5
Senegal	Nov./Oct.	906.7	13.3	920.0	866.8	243.4	5.0	238.4
Central Africa		**1 572.4**	**101.3**	**1 673.7**	**1 701.5**	**110.9**	**40.0**	**70.9**
Cameroon	Jan./Dec.	628.4	1.6	630.0	630.0	51.5	0.5	51.0
Cent.Afr.Rep.	Jan./Dec.	42.6	19.7	62.3	43.5	8.9	8.9	0.0
Congo	Jan./Dec.	310.9	6.1	317.0	317.0	14.2	1.1	13.1
Congo, Dem. Rep.	Jan./Dec.	554.6	72.4	627.0	675.0	33.0	29.5	3.5
Equatorial Guinea	Jan./Dec.	24.0	0.0	24.0	24.0	0.0	0.0	0.0
Sao Tome and Principe	Jan./Dec.	11.9	1.5	13.4	12.0	3.3	0.0	3.3

Continued...

...Continued

	Marketing Year	2006-07 or 2007 Actual Imports Commercial Purchases	Food Aid	Total Commercial and Aid	2007-08 or 2008 Total Import Requirements (excluding re-exports)	Import Position[2] Total Commercial and Aid	Food Aid Allocated Committed or Shipped	Commercial Purchases
ASIA		**40,977.4**	**550.0**	**42,527.4**	**39,862.4**	**23,659.3**	**852.1**	**22,807.2**
CIS in Asia		**3,253.0**	**452.0**	**3,705.0**	**3,774.0**	**2,765.3**	**31.1**	**2,734.2**
Armenia	July/June	216.0	86.0	302.0	343.0	213.3	4.2	209.1
Azerbaijan	July/June	1,265.0	119.0	1,384.0	1,052.0	1,039.0	2.8	1,036.2
Georgia	July/June	890.0	95.0	985.0	862.0	589.2	6.9	582.3
Kyrgyzstan	July/June	263.0	58.0	321.0	310.0	275.7	0.0	275.7
Tajikistan	July/June	277.0	94.0	371.0	506.0	288.8	17.2	271.6
Turkmenistan	July/June	4.0	0.0	4.0	271.0	253.6	0.0	253.6
Uzbekistan	July/June	338.0	0.0	338.0	430.0	105.7	0.0	105.7
Far East		**27,787.4**	**897.0**	**28,684.4**	**24,943.4**	**15,154.6**	**690.5**	**14,464.1**
Bangladesh	July/June	2,835.5	172.4	3,007.9	3,750.0	2,332.2	368.2	1,964.0
Bhutan	July/June	70.6	0.4	71.0	71.0	0.0	0.0	0.0
Cambodia	Jan./Dec.	31.3	8.7	40.0	40.0	1.5	1.5	0.0
China Mainland	July/June	2,366.0	0.0	2,366.0	2,377.0	791.8	0.0	791.8
D.P.R. of Korea	Nov./Oct.	254.8	401.4	656.2	1,660.0	332.1	231.4	100.7
India	April/March	6,730.0	35.3	6,765.3	1,900.0	1,804.9	30.7	1,774.2
Indonesia	April/March	8,159.9	32.9	8,192.8	7,242.0	4,984.4	17.2	4,967.2
Lao, P.D.R.	Jan./Dec.	16.4	11.4	27.8	27.4	1.5	1.5	0.0
Mongolia	Oct./Sept.	216.4	42.6	259.0	279.0	85.7	5.0	80.7
Nepal	July/June	232.4	7.6	240.0	160.0	10.5	10.5	0.0

Continued...

...Continued

		2006-07 or 2007			2007-08 or 2008			
		Actual Imports				Import Position[2]		
	Marketing Year	Commercial Purchases	Food Aid	Total Commercial and Aid	Total Import Requirements (excluding re-exports)	Total Commercial and Aid	Food Aid Allocated, Committed or Shipped	Commercial Purchases
Pakistan	May/April	357.7	65.9	423.6	1 521.0	1 117.6	2.1	1 115.5
Philippines	July/June	5,271.8	83.0	5,354.8	4,676.0	3,576.0	14.0	3,562.0
Sri Lanka	Jan./Dec.	1,184.6	35.4	1,220.0	1,180.0	110.8	8.4	102.4
Timor-Leste	July/June	60.0	0.0	60.0	60.0	5.6	0.0	5.6
Near East		**9 937.0**	**201.0**	**10,138.0**	**11,145.0**	**5,739.4**	**130.5**	**5,608.9**
Afghanistan	July/June	631.4	151.1	782.5	690.0	421.9	116.1	305.8
Iraq	July/June	4,022.6	7.4	4,030.0	4,230.0	3,855.6	6.5	3,849.1
Syrian Arab Republic	July/June	2,441.7	8.3	2,450.0	2,950.0	1,353.9	4.3	1,349.6
Yemen	Jan./Dec.	2,841.3	34.2	2,875.5	3,275.0	108.0	3.6	104.4
CENTRAL AMERICA		**1,497.1**	**155.5**	**1,652.6**	**1,533.0**	**864.6**	**145.2**	**719.4**
Haiti	July/June	487.5	95.5	583.0	593.0	234.0	57.0	177.0
Honduras	July/June	671.7	33.1	704.8	580.0	379.5	41.2	338.3
Nicaragua	July/June	337.9	26.9	364.8	360.0	251.1	47.0	204.1
SOUTH AMERICA		**921.2**	**30.0**	**951.2**	**1,010.0**	**749.2**	**0.0**	**749.2**
Ecuador	July/June	921.2	30.0	951.2	1,010.0	749.2	0.0	749.2
OCEANIA		**415.7**	**0.0**	**415.7**	**415.7**	**87.6**	**0.0**	**87.6**
Kiribati	Jan./Dec.	8.7	0.0	8.7	8.7	0.0	0.0	0.0

Continued...

...Continued

	Marketing Year	2006-07 or 2007: Actual Imports: Commercial Purchases	Food Aid	Total Commercial and Aid	2007-08 or 2008: Total Import Requirements (excluding re-exports)	Import Position[2]: Total Commercial and Aid	Food Aid Allocated, Committed or Shipped	Commercial Purchases
Papua New Guinea	Jan./Dec.	358.0	0.0	358.0	358.0	87.6	0.0	87.6
Solomon Is.	Jan./Dec.	29.5	0.0	29.5	29.5	0.0	0.0	0.0
Tonga	Jan./Dec.	6.4	0.0	6.4	6.4	0.0	0.0	0.0
Tuvalu	Jan./Dec.	1.1	0.0	1.1	1.1	0.0	0.0	0.0
Vanuatu	Jan./Dec.	12.0	0.0	12.0	12.0	0.0	0.0	0.0
EUROPE		**1,569.0**	**0.0**	**1,569.0**	**1,070.0**	**389.7**	**0.0**	**389.7**
Albania	July/June	440.0	0.0	440.0	480.0	205.9	0.0	205.9
Belarus	July/June	599.0	0.0	599.0	120.0	6.7	0.0	6.7
Bosnia and Herzegovina	July/June	530.0	0.0	530.0	470.0	177.1	0.0	177.1
TOTAL		**79,152.6**	**975.6**	**83,128.2**	**82,416.0**	**45,574.2**	**2,321.4**	**43,252.8**

[1] Includes food deficit countries with per capita income below the level used by the World Bank to determine eligibility for IDA assistance (i.e. USD 1575 in 2004). which is in accordance with guidelines and criteria agreed to by the CFA that they should be given priority allocation of food aid.

[2] Estimates based on information available as of late March 2008.

Source: *FAO Statistics.*

BIBLIOGRAPHY

Adesina, A.A. and Zinnah, M.E. 'Technology Characteristics, Farmers Perceptions, and Adoption Decisions: A Tobit Model Application in Sierra Leone'. *Agricultural Economics* 9: 297-311, 1993.

Batz, F.-J., Peters, K. J. and Janssen, W. 'The Influence of Technology Characteristics on the Rate and Speed of Adoption'. *Agricultural Economics* 21: 121–130, 1999.

Block; Steven and Timmer, C. Peter. 'Agriculture and Economic Growth: Conceptual Issues and the Kenyan Experience.' CAER Discussion Paper No. 26, Harvard Institute of International Development, September 1994.

Boserup, E. *The Conditions of Agricultural Growth.* London, U.K.: Earthscan, 1965.

Cleaver, K., and Scherieber, G.A. 'Reversing the Spiral. The Population, Agriculture and Environment Nexus in Sub-Saharan Africa. Directions in Development'. The World Bank, Washington, U.S.A., 1994.

de Waal, A. 'Emergency Food Security in Western Sudan: What is it for?' in S. Maxwell (Ed.). *To Cure all Hunger: Food Policy and Food Security in Sudan.* London, U.K.: Intermediate Technology, 1991.

Deichmann, U. *Population Density for Africa in 1960, 70, 80 and 90.* Third edition. Santa Barbara, U.S.A.: University of California, 1997.

Food and Agricultural Organization. *The State of World Food Insecurity 2000.* http://www.fao.org/sof/sofi/indexen.htm

Gabbert, S. and Weikard, H. 'How Widespread is Under nourishment? A Critique of Measurement Methods and New Empirical Results'. *Food Policy* 26: 209–228, 2001.

Gallagher, P.W. 'Some Productivity-Increasing and Quality-Changing Technology for the Soybean Complex: Market and Welfare Effects'. *Amer. J. Agr. Econ.* 80: 165–174. February 1998.

Maxwell, D. G. 'Measuring Food Insecurity: the Frequency and Severity of "Coping Strategies."' *Food Policy* 21(3):291–303, 1996.

Maxwell, D. G. 'The Evolution of Thinking about Food Security'. In: *Food Security in Sub-Saharan Africa.* (Eds.). S. Devereux and S. Maxwell. Institute of Development Studies. TDG Publishing, London, U.K., 2000.

Olsson, L. 'Desertification and Land Degradation in Perspective'. Invited paper at the Sahel Conference in Dryland Degradation—Causes and Consequences. (Eds.). Poulsen and Lawesson. Aarhus University Press, 1991.

Rosegrant, Mark W., Agcaoili-Sombilla, M. and Perez, N.D. Global Food Projections of 2020, Implications for Investment, Food, Agriculture and the Environment. Discussion Paper, No. 5. IFPRI, Washington D.C., U.S.A., October 1995.

Scherr, J. S. 'A Downward Spiral? Research Evidence on the Relationship between Poverty and Natural Resource Degradation'. *Food Policy* 25: 479–498, 2000.

Sen, A. '*Poverty and Famines*. Oxford, U.K.: Clarendon Press, 1981.

Smith, L. C. 'Can FAO's Measure of Chronic Under-nourishment be Strengthened?' *Food Policy* 23: 425–445, 1999.

Smith, Lisa, and Haddad, Lawrence. 'Explaining Child Nutrition in Developing Countries: A Cross Country Analysis,' IFPRI, Washington. D.C., U.S.A. Draft, April 1998.

Spencer, Dunstan. 'Infrastructure and Technology Constraints to Agricultural Development in the Humid and Sub-humid Tropics of Africa.' EFPRI/ EPTD Discussion Paper No. 3, August 1994.

Strauss, J. and Thomas, D. *Human Resources: Empirical Modeling of Household and Family Decisions, Handbook of Development Economics*, Vol. 3.A (Ch. 34), pp. 1894-1895. Amsterdam: North Holland, 1995.

Stryker, J. Dirck and Selina Pandolfi. 'Impact of Outward Looking, Market-Oriented Policy Reform on Economic Growth and Poverty. CAER II Discussion Paper No. 7, June 1997.

Svedberg, P. '841 Million Undernourished?' *World Development* 27 (12): 2081–98, 1999.

Timmer, C. Peter. 'How Well do the Poor Connect to the Growth Process?' CAER II Discussion Paper No. 17, Harvard Institute of International Development. World Development Report, 1994, Infrastructure for Development, World Bank, 1994.

Williams, J. R., Jones, C. A., Kiniry, J. R. and Spaniel, D. A. 1989. 'The EPIC Crop Growth Model'. *Transactions of the American Society of Agricultural Engineers* 32: 497–511, 1989.

INDEX

D

E

F

G

H

I

R

S

T

U